THE FIRST URBAN CHURCHES 2
ROMAN CORINTH

WRITINGS FROM THE GRECO-ROMAN WORLD SUPPLEMENT SERIES

Clare K. Rothschild, General Editor

Number 8

THE FIRST URBAN CHURCHES 2
ROMAN CORINTH

Edited by
James R. Harrison and L. L. Welborn

 PRESS

Atlanta

Copyright © 2016 by SBL Press

All rights reserved. No part of this work may be reproduced or transmitted in any form or by any means, electronic or mechanical, including photocopying and recording, or by means of any information storage or retrieval system, except as may be expressly permitted by the 1976 Copyright Act or in writing from the publisher. Requests for permission should be addressed in writing to the Rights and Permissions Office, SBL Press, 825 Houston Mill Road, Atlanta, GA 30329 USA.

Library of Congress Cataloging-in-Publication Data

First urban churches / edited by James R. Harrison and L. L. Welborn.
    volumes cm. — (Society of Biblical Literature. Writings from the Greco-Roman world Supplement series ; Number 7)
    Includes bibliographical references.
    Contents: 1. Methodological foundations.

    ISBN 978-1-62837-102-4 (v. 1 : pbk. : alk. paper) — ISBN 978-1-62837-104-8 (v. 1 : ebook) — ISBN 978-1-62837-103-1 (v. 1 : hardcover : alk. paper)
    ISBN 978-0-88414-111-2 (v. 2 : pbk. : alk. paper) — ISBN 978-0-88414-112-9 (v. 2 : ebook) — ISBN 978-0-88414-113-6 (v. 2 : hardcover : alk. paper)
    1. City churches. 2. Church history—Primitive and early church, ca. 30–600. 3. Cities and towns—Religious aspects—Christianity. I. Harrison, James R., 1952- editor.
    BV637.F57 2015
    270.109173'2—dc23
                                                            2015021858

Printed on acid-free paper.

Contents

Abbreviations vii

Introduction: Excavating the Urban Life of Roman Corinth
    James R. Harrison 1

Inequality in Roman Corinth: Evidence from Diverse Sources
Evaluated by a Neo-Ricardian Model
    L. L. Welborn 47

Negotiating Multiple Modes of Religion and Identity in Roman
Corinth
    Cavan Concannon 85

Between Polis, Oikos, and Ekklesia: The Challenge of Negotiating
the Spirit World (1 Cor 12:1–11)
    Kathy Ehrensperger 105

Brother against Brother: *Controversiae* about Inheritance
Disputes and 1 Corinthians 6:1–11
    Michael Peppard 133

The Changing Rural Horizons of Corinth's First Urban Christians
    David K. Pettegrew 153

Mixed-Language Inscribing at Roman Corinth
    Bradley J. Bitner 185

"The God of This Age" (2 Cor 4:4) and Paul's Empire-Resisting
Gospel at Corinth
    Fredrick J. Long 219

Paul and the *Agōnothetai* at Corinth: Engaging the Civic Values
of Antiquity
    James R. Harrison 271

Contributors...327
Primary Sources Index 329
Modern Authors Index..347

Abbreviations

Primary Sources

Ab urbe cond.	Livy, *Ab urbe condita*
Ach.	Aristophanes, *Acharnenses*
Ad Nic.	Isocrates, *Ad Nicoclem*
Aeg.	Manetho, *Aegyptiaca*
Aen.	Vergil, *Aeneid*
And.	Lysias, *Contra Andocides*
Ann.	Tacitus, *Annales*
Ant.	Josephus, *Antiquitates judaicae*
Apol.	Plato, *Apologia*; Tertullian, *Apologeticus*
Apos. Con.	Apostolic Constitutions and Canons
Arat.	Plutarch, *Aratus*
Arch.	Vitruvius, *De architectura*
Ascen. Isa.	Ascension of Isaiah [Mart. Ascen. Isa. 6–11]
Bell. civ.	Appian, *Bella civilia*
Bib. hist.	Diodorus Siculus, *Bibliotheca historica*
B.J.	Josephus, *Bellum judaicum*
C. Ap.	Josephus, *Contra Apionem*
Caes.	Aurelius Victor, *De Caesaribus*; Plutarch, *Caesar*
Cal.	Suetonius, *Gaius Caligula*
Cat.	Cicero, *In Catalinam*
Char.	Theophrastus, *Characteres*
Cher.	Philo, *De cherubim*
Claud.	Suetonius, *Divus Claudius*
Clem.	Seneca the Younger, *De clementia*
Cleom.	Plutarch, *Cleomenes*
Cod. justin.	Codex justinianus
Conc. Apam.	Dio Chrysostom, *De concordia cum Apamensibus* (*Or.* 40)

Conf.	Philo, *De confusione linguarum*
Cont.	Dio Chrysostom, *Contio* (*Or.* 47)
Contr.	Elder Seneca, *Controversiae*
[*Cor.*]	Dio Chrysostom, *Corinthiaca* (*Or.* 37)
Cyr.	Xenephon, *Cyropaedia*
De or.	Cicero, *De oratore*
Decal.	Philo, *De decalogo*
Def. orac.	Cicero, *De defectu oraculorum*
Deip.	Athenaeus, *Deipnosophistae*
Demon.	Lucian, *Demonax*
Descr.	Pausanias, *Graeciae descriptio*
Dial.	Seneca the Younger, *Dialogi*
Dial. d.	Lucian, *Dialogi deorum*
Din.	Dionysius of Halicarnassus, *De Dinarcho*
Div.	Cicero, *De divinatione*
Eccl.	Aristophanes, *Ecclesiazusae*
Ecl.	*Eclogae*
Ep.	*Epistulae*; Seneca the Younger, *Epistulae morales*
Epit.	Justin, *Epitoma historiarum Philippicarum*
Epitr.	Menander, *Epitrepontes*
Eq.	Aristophanes, *Equites*
Eth. nic.	Aristotle, *Ethica nicomachea*
Euthyd.	Plato, *Euthydemus*
Fact.	Valerius Maximus, *Facta et dicta memorabilia*
Flac.	Cicero, *Pro Flacco*
Flam.	Plutarch, *Titus Flamininus*
Frat. amor.	Plutarch, *De fraterno amore*
Geogr.	Strabo, *Geographica*
Hel. Syn. Pr.	Hellenistic Synagogal Prayers
Hell.	Xenophon, *Hellenica*
Hist.	*Histories*
Hist. rom.	Dio Cassius, *Historia romana*
Il.	Homer, *Iliad*
Inst.	Quintilian, *Institutio oratoria*
Leg.	Cicero, *De legibus*
Legat.	Philo, *Legatio ad Gaium*
Leoc.	Lycurgus, *Contra Leocrates*
Lex.	Valerius Harpocration, *Lexicon in decem oratores Atticos*

ABBREVIATIONS

Ling.	Varro, *De lingua latina*
Marc.	Plutarch, *Marcellus*
Mem.	Xenophon, *Memorabilia*
Metam.	Apuleius, *Metamorphoses*
Mor.	Plutarch, *Moralia*
Nat.	Pliny the Elder, *Naturalis historia*
Nat. d.	Cicero, *De natura deorum*
Nic.	Lysias, *Contra Nicomachus*
Od.	Homer, *Odyssey*
Pelop.	Thucydides, *History of the Peloponnesian War*
Per.	Plutarch, *Pericles*
Phars.	Lucan, *Pharsalia*
Pol.	Aristotle, *Politica*; Plato, *Politicus*
Praec. ger. rei publ.	Plutarch, *Praecepta gerendae rei publicae*
Prot.	Plato, *Protagoras*
Quaest. conv.	Plutarch, *Quaestionum convivialum libri IX*
Ran.	Aristophanes, *Ranae*
[*Reg. imp. apophth.*]	Plutarch, *Regum et imperatorum apophthegmata*
Rep.	Cicero, *De republica*
Resp.	Plato, *Respublica*
Rhod.	Dio Chrysostom, *Rhodiaca* (*Or.* 31)
Rom.	Plutarch, *Romulus*
Rust.	Columella, *Res rustica*
Sacr.	Philo, *De sacrificiis Abelis et Caini*
Sat.	Juvenal, *Satirae*
Sib. Or.	Sibylline Oracles
Somn.	Philo, *De somniis*
Spec.	Philo, *De specialibus legibus*
Strat.	Frontinus, *Strategemata*
Theog.	Hesiod, *Theogonia*
Thesm.	Aristophanes, *Thesmophoriazusae*
Tib.	Suetonius, *Tiberius*
Tim.	Aeschines, *In Timarchum*; Plutarch, *Timoleon*
Trapez.	Isocrates, *Trapeziticus*
Tusc.	Cicero, *Tusculanae disputations*
Vat.	Cicero, *In Vatinium*
Vesp.	Aristophanes, *Vespae*; Suetonius, *Vespasianus*
Virt.	Dio Chrysostom, *De virtute* (*Or.* 8)
Vit. aere al.	Cicero, *De vitando aere alieno*

Vit. Apoll.	Philostratus, *Vita Apollonii*
Vit. soph.	Philostratus, *Vitae sophistarum*
Vit. Thuc.	Marcellinus, *Vita Thucydidis*

Secondary Sources

ABD	*Anchor Bible Dictionary.* Edited by David Noel Freedman. 6 vols. New York: Doubleday, 1992.
ABR	*Australian Biblical Review*
ABSA	*Annual of the British School at Athens*
AE	*L'Année épigraphique*
AGJU	Arbeiten zur Geschichte des antiken Judentums und des Urchristentums
AJA	*American Journal of Archaeology*
AJP	*American Journal of Philology*
ANF	*The Ante-Nicene Fathers: Translations of the Writings of the Fathers Down to A.D. 325.* Edited by Alexander Roberts and James Donaldson. 10 vols. 1885–87.
ANRW	*Aufstieg und Niedergang der römischen Welt: Geschichte und Kultur Roms im Spiegel der neueren Forschung.* Part 2, *Principat.* Edited by Hildegard Temporini and Wolfgang Haase. Berlin: de Gruyter, 1972–.
ANTC	Abingdon New Testament Commentaries
Arch	*Archaeology*
AYB	Anchor Yale Bible
BA	*Biblical Archaeologist*
BASP	*Bulletin of the American Society of Papyrologists*
BBR	*Bulletin for Biblical Research*
BCH	*Bulletin de correspondance hellénique*
BCHSup	Supplement to Bulletin de correspondance hellénique
BCHSup	Bulletin de correspondance hellénique Supplements
BDAG	Danker, Frederick W., Walter Bauer, William F. Arndt, and F. Wilbur Gingrich. *Greek-English Lexicon of the New Testament and Other Early Christian Literature.* 3rd ed. Chicago: University of Chicago Press, 2000 (Danker-Bauer-Arndt-Gingrich).

BE	*Bulletin épigraphique*
BGU	*Aegyptische Urkunden aus den Königlichen Staatlichen Museen zu Berlin, Griechische Urkunden.* Berlin: Weidmann, 1895–.
BICSSup	Bulletin Supplement (University of London Institute of Classical Studies)
BiH	Biblische Handbibliothek
BNP	*Brill's New Pauly: Encyclopaedia of the Ancient World.* Edited by Hubert Cancik. 22 vols. Leiden: Brill, 2002–2011.
BNTC	Black's New Testament Commentaries
BSGRT	Bibliotheca Scriptorum Graecorum et Romanorum Teubneriana
BTB	*Biblical Theology Bulletin*
BurH	*Buried History: Quarterly Journal of the Australian Institute of Archaeology*
BZNW	Beihefte zur Zeitschrift für die neutestamentliche Wissenschaft
CBQ	*Catholic Biblical Quarterly*
CHL	Commentationes humanarum litterarum
CIG	*Corpus Inscriptionum Graecarum.* Edited by August Boeckh. 4 vols. Berlin, 1828–1877.
CIJ	*Corpus Inscriptionum Judaicarum.* Edited by Jean-Baptiste Frey. 2 vols. Rome: Pontifical Biblical Institute, 1936–1952.
CIL	*Corpus Inscriptionum Latinarum.* Berlin, 1862–.
CP	*Classical Philology*
CQ	*Classical Quarterly*
CR	*Classical Review*
CurTM	*Currents in Theology and Mission*
ECL	Early Christianity and Its Literature
EKKNT	Evangelisch-katholischer Kommentar zum Neuen Testament
FGrHist	*Die Fragmente der griechischen Historiker.* Edited by Felix Jacoby. Leiden: Brill, 1954–1964
FRLANT	Forschungen zur Religion und Literatur des Alten und Neuen Testaments
GR	*Greece and Rome*
GRBS	*Greek, Roman, and Byzantine Studies*

Hell	Hellenica: Recueil d'épigraphie, de numismatique et d'antiquités grecques
Hesperia	Hesperia: Journal of the American School of Classical Studies at Athens
HTR	Harvard Theological Review
HTS	Harvard Theological Studies
IBC	Interpretation: A Bible Commentary for Teaching and Preaching
ICC	International Critical Commentary
IDelos	Dürrbach, Félix, et al., eds. 7 vols. *Inscriptions de Délos*. Paris: Champion; de Boccard, 1926–1972.
IEph	Wankel, Hermann, et al., eds. *Die Inschriften von Ephesos*. 8 vols. Bonn: Habelt, 1979–1984.
IG	*Inscriptiones Graecae*. Editio Minor. Berlin: de Gruyter, 1924–
IGBulg	Mihailov, Georgi, ed. *Inscriptiones graecae in Bulgaria repertae*. 5 vols. Sofia: Academiae litterarum bulgaricae, 1958-1970, 1997.
IGRR	*Inscriptiones graecae ad res romanas pertinentes*. Edited by René Cagnat et al. 3 vols. Paris: Leroux, 1906–1927.
IGSK	Inschriften griechischer Städte aus Kleinasien
IKorinthKent	Kent, John Harvey, ed. *The Inscriptions, 1926–1950*. Vol. 8.3 of *Corinth: Results of Excavations Conducted by the American School of Classical Studies at Athens*. Princeton: American School of Classical Studies at Athens, 1966.
IKorinthMeritt	Meritt, Benjamin Dean, ed. *Greek Inscriptions, 1896–1927*. Vol. 8.1 of *Corinth: Results of Excavations Conducted by the American School of Classical Studies at Athens*. Cambridge: American School of Classical Studies at Athens, 1931.
IKorinthStroud	Stroud, Ronald S. *The Sanctuary of Demeter and Kore: The Inscriptions*. Vol. 18.6 of *Corinth: Results of Excavations Conducted by the American School of Classical Studies at Athens*. Princeton: American School of Classical Studies at Athens, 2013.
IKorinthWest	West, Allen Brown, ed. *Latin Inscriptions, 1896–1926*. Vol. 8.2 of *Corinth: Results of Excavations*

ABBREVIATIONS xiii

	Conducted by the American School of Classical Studies at Athens. Cambridge: American School of Classical Studies at Athens, 1931.
ILS	Dessau, Hermann. *Inscriptiones latinae selectae*. 3 vols. in 5 parts. Berlin: Weidman, 1892–1916.
JBL	*Journal of Biblical Literature*
JECS	*Journal of Early Christian History*
JEH	*Journal of Ecclesiastical History*
JHS	*Journal of Hellenic Studies*
JRA	*Journal of Roman Archaeology*
JRASup	Journal of Roman Archaeology Supplements
JRS	*Journal of Roman Studies*
JSNT	*Journal for the Study of the New Testament*
JSNTSup	Journal for the Study of the New Testament Supplement Series
JTS	*Journal of Theological Studies*
KEK	Kritisch-exegetischer Kommentar über das Neue Testament (Meyer-Kommentar)
LCL	Loeb Classical Library
LGS	*Leges Graecorum Sacrae e Titulis Collectae*. Edited by Johannes von Prott and Ludwig Ziehen. 2 vols. 1896-1906. Repr., Chicago: Ares, 1988.
LNTS	Library of New Testament Studies
LS	*Louvain Studies*
LSAM	Sokolowski, Franciszek. *Lois sacrées de l'Asie Mineure*. Paris: de Boccard, 1955.
LSCG	Sokolowski, Franciszek. *Lois sacrée des Cités grecques*. École Française d'Athènes 18. Paris: de Boccard, 1969.
LSJ	Liddell, Henry George, Robert Scott, Henry Stuart Jones. *A Greek-English Lexicon*. 9th ed. with revised supplement. Oxford: Clarendon, 1996.
MAMA	*Monumenta Asiae Minoris Antiqua*. Edited by W. M. Calder et al. London: Manchester University Press; Longmans, Green, 1928–.
MEFRA	*Mélanges de l'École française de Rome. Antiquité*
NASB	New American Standard Bible
NAWG	*Nachrichten der Akademie der Wissenschaften in Göttingen*

Neot	*Neotestamentica*
NewDocs	*New Documents Illustrating Early Christianity.* Edited by G. H. R. Horsley et al. North Ryde, NSW: The Ancient History Documentary Research Centre, Macquarie University, 1981–.
NGSL	Lupu, Eran. *Greek Sacred Law: A Collection of New Documents (NGSL).* RGRW 152. Leiden: Brill, 2005.
NIBCNT	New International Biblical Commentary on the New Testament
NICNT	New International Commentary on the New Testament
NIGTC	New International Greek Testament Commentary
NovT	*Novum Testamentum*
NTAbh	Neutestamentliche Abhandlungen
NTM	New Testament Monographs
NTS	*New Testament Studies*
OGI	*Orientis Graeci Inscriptiones Selectae.* Edited by Wilhelm Dittenberger. 2 vols. Leipzig: Hirzel, 1903–1905.
OJA	*Oxford Journal of Achaeology*
OLD	*Oxford Latin Dictionary.* Edited by P. G. W. Glare. 2 vols. Oxford: Clarendon, 1982.
PTMS	Princeton Theological Monograph Series
PW	*Paulys Real-Encyclopädie der classischen Altertumswissenschaft.* New edition by Georg Wissowa and Wilhelm Kroll. 50 vols. in 84 parts. Stuttgart: Metzler and Druckenmüller, 1894–1980.
QD	Quaestiones Disputatae
RAC	*Reallexikon für Antike und Christentum.* Edited by Theodor Klauser et al. Stuttgart: Hiersemann, 1950–.
RB	*Revue biblique*
RdA	*Rivista di archeologia*
RE	*Realenzyklopädie für protestantische Theologie und Kirche*
REG	*Revue des études grecques*
RevPhil	*Revue de Philologie*
RGG	*Religion in Geschichte und Gegenwart.* Edited by

	Kurt Galling. 3rd ed. 7 vols. Tübingen: Mohr Siebeck, 1957–1965.
RGRW	Religions in the Graeco-Roman World
RPC	*Roman Provincial Coinage.* Edited by Andrew Burnett et al. London: British Museum Press; Paris: Bibliothèque Nationale, 1992–.
RTR	*Reformed Theological Review*
SB	*Sammelbuch griechischer Urkunden aus Aegypten.* Edited by Friedrich Preisigke et al. Wiesbaden: Harrassowitz, 1915–.
SBLDS	Society of Biblical Literature Dissertation Series
SBLSymS	Society of Biblical Literature Symposium Series
SCHNT	Studia ad Corpus Hellenisticum Novi Testamenti
SEG	*Supplementum epigraphicum graecum*
SIG	*Sylloge inscriptionum graecarum.* Edited by Wilhelm Dittenberger. 4 vols. 3rd ed. Leipzig: Hirzel, 1915–1924.
SMSR	*Studi e materiali di storia delle religioni*
SNTSMS	Society for New Testament Studies Monograph Series
SNTW	Studies of the New Testament and Its World
SP	Sacra Pagina
Spengel	Leonhard von Spengel, *Rhetores graeci.* 2 vols. Leipzig: Teubner, 1853–1856.
SVF	*Stoicorum Veterum Fragmenta.* Hans Friedrich August von Arnim. 4 vols. Leipzig: Teubner, 1903–1924.
TAM	*Tituli Asiae Minoris.* Edited by Ernst Kalinka et al. Vienna: Hoelder, 1901–.
TAPA	*Transactions of the American Philological Association*
TDNT	*Theological Dictionary of the New Testament.* Edited by Gerhard Kittel and Gerhard Friedrich. Translated by Geoffrey W. Bromiley. 10 vols. Grand Rapids: Eerdmans, 1964–1976.
TENTS	Texts and Editions for New Testament Study
TG	*Tijdschrift voor Geschiedenis*
TK	Texte und Kommentare

TynBul	*Tyndale Bulletin*
TZ	*Theologische Zeitschrift*
VC	*Vigiliae Christianae*
VT	*Vetus Testamentum*
WBC	Word Biblical Commentary
WGRWSup	Writings from the Greco-Roman World Supplement Series
ZAC	*Zeitschrift für antikes Christentum*
ZNW	*Zeitschrift für die neutestamentliche Wissenschaft und die Kunde der älteren Kirche*
ZPE	*Zeitschrift für Papyrologie und Epigraphik*
ZTK	*Zeitschrift für Theologie und Kirche*

Other Abbreviations

l(l).	line(s)
pl(s).	plate(s)

Introduction:
Excavating the Urban Life of Roman Corinth

James R. Harrison

1. The Development of Corinth as a Greek and Roman City-State

1.1. Pre-Roman Greek Corinth

Modern scholarship on the archaeological, social, and political history of ancient Corinth has had to grapple with the extensive period of settlement at the site. Corinth's development was characterized by a dramatic rise to power as a polis, a spectacular fall to the all-conquering Rome, and an unexpected restoration to political significance and renewed wealth under Julius Caesar. Originally established as a settlement in the Neolithic period (ca. 6500/5000 BCE),[1] the site of Corinth, along with the coastal settlement of Ayios Gerasmos at Lechaion and Korakou near the later Lechaion Harbor, experienced Mycenaean occupation during the Bronze Age.[2] Robert John Hopper has suggested that it was an important settlement, perhaps even controlling the land route from Mycenaean sites in central Greece to Mycenae itself.[3] This conclusion, however, is somewhat overstated, given the "unprepossessing and poorly preserved" nature of the Mycenaean remains found in the sanctuary of Demeter and Kore.[4] We are

---

1. Walter Leaf, "Corinth in Prehistoric Times, " *AJA* 27 (1923): 151–56; Saul S. Weinberg, "Remains from Prehistoric Corinth," *Hesperia* 6 (1937): 487–524; John C. Lavezzi, "Prehistoric Investigations at Corinth." *Hesperia* 47 (1978): 402–51.
2. A. Shewan, "Mycenaean Corinth," *CR* 38 (1924): 65–68; Jeremy Rutter, "The Last Mycenaeans at Corinth," *Hesperia* 48 (1979): 348–92.
3. Robert John Hopper, "Ancient Corinth," *GR* 2 (1955): 4.
4. Rutter, "The Last Mycenaeans," 389. Rutter concludes that the only surviving Mycenaean remains of a building found in the sanctuary of Demeter and Kore

not dealing with a large Mycenaean fortress city in this stage of the site's development but rather with a fairly rudimentary agricultural hamlet.[5]

However Corinth's rise from a backwater in the Bronze and Dark Ages to a prominent, wealthy, and luxurious city-state in archaic Greece first occurred under the clan of the Dorian Bacchiadae.[6] Our highly fragmentary literary tradition regarding the migration of the Dorians to Corinth attributes its origins to Hippotes, the commander of the Dorian host at Naupactus. Having been banished from the city, Hippotes sailed from the Malian gulf and took Corinth by surprise (ca. 900 BCE), establishing the dynasty from which the Bacchiadae kings emerged.[7] The royal family belonged to the Dorian clan until the clan eventually abolished kingship (ca. 747 BCE), electing instead a prytanis (or yearly president) from among their members (Diodorus Siculus, *Bib. hist.* fr. 7.9.2–6), marrying among themselves (Herodotus, *Hist.* 5.92), and ruling as an oligarchy until 657

---

at Corinth—including a terrace wall just to the north of it—represent "part of a small cluster of buildings, possibly a farming hamlet" (ibid., 392).

5. As Nicos Papahatzis states (*Ancient Corinth: The Museums of Corinth, Isthmia and Sicyon* [Athens: Ekdotike Athenon, 1994], 17), "the settlement of Korakou (on the coastal stretch between Nea Corinthos and Lechaion) ... was more important than Corinth in Mycenaean times." Papahatzis (ibid., 18) subsequently adds that during Mycenaean times, in Homeric perspective (*Il.* 2.570–576), "Corinth was simply a province of Agamemnon's kingdom, like Sicyon, Cleonae, and other Corinthian towns." It is true that Corinth's beginnings go back to the Neolithic period. But whether the Homeric portrait of Corinth's wealth in the Mycenaean age ("wealthy Corinth": Homer, *Il.* 2.570; cf. 13.664), exceeding that of Mycenae, so Papahatzis posits (ibid., 18), is questionable in light of the site's sparse Mycenaean archaeological remains. By contrast, Richard R. Losch (*The Uttermost Part of the Earth: A Guide to Places in the Bible* [Grand Rapids: Eerdmans, 2005], 73) asserts that Homer's "wealthy Corinth" is the prosperous trading city of Korakou, whereas I would argue that Homer (fl. ca. 750–650 BCE), with poetic license, has retrospectively backdated the proverbial wealth of Bacchiadic Corinth to the time of the Mycenaean city, knowing little about the Mycenaean age other than what oral tradition had passed down.

6. Two eighth-century BCE inscriptions found in the Potter's Quarter in Corinth demonstrate that writing was a permanent feature of Greek civilization under the rule of the Bacchiadae by 775–750 BCE. On one of the inscribed sherds was a list of names, possibly accompanying "the gift of the vase to a certain person or its dedication in his honour to some god" (Agnes N. Stillwell, "Eighth Century BC Inscriptions from Corinth," *AJA* 37 [1933]: 606).

7. Noel Robertson, "The Dorian Migration and Corinthian Ritual," *CP* 75 (1980): 1–22, esp. 4–10. We should not forget, however, the Homeric myth (*Il.* 6.152–153; cf. *Od.* 11.734) that Sisyphus was the founder and first king of Ephyra (Corinth).

BCE.⁸ The achievements of the Bacchiadae at Corinth were impressive. The archaic temple of Apollo at Corinth was one of the prominent monuments erected during their reign (Pausanias, *Descr.* 2.3.6; cf. 2.3.3, 2.3.8; Plutarch, *Arat.* 40; Herodotus, *Hist.* 3.52).⁹ Further, during the Bacchiadic period, Corinth established the western colonies at Corcyra (Strabo, *Geogr.* 6.2.4; Timaeus, *FGrHist* 566 F 80) and Syracuse (Thucydides, *Pelop.* 6.3.2) in 733 BCE. Significantly, this process of colonization continued under the tyrants, with Cypselus and his son Gorgus establishing northwest colonies at Leucas, Ambracia, and Anactorium (Strabo, *Geogr.* 10.2.8). Epidamnus was founded under the reign of Periander (Thucydides, *Pelop.* 1.24.2), and Apollonia was founded with the help of the Corcyreans at approximately the same time (Strabo, *Geogr.* 7.5.8: ca. 588 BCE). Like other Greek cities involved in the colonization movement (800–500 BCE), Corinth also established the colony of Potideia in the northeast (Thucydides, *Pelop.* 1.56.2; Nicolaus of Damascus, *FGrHist* 90 F 59).¹⁰ In sum, as Raphael Sealey notes,¹¹ the colonization movement had begun at Corinth under the aristocratic Bacchiadae, but their policies continued and were intensified under the tyrant rulers.

---

8. On pre-Hellenistic Corinth, see J. B. Salmon, *Wealthy Corinth: A History of the City to 338 BC* (Oxford: Clarendon, 1984); Timo Stickler, *Korinth und seine Kolonien: Die Stadt am Isthmus im Mächtegefüge des klassischen Griechenland* (Berlin: Akademie, 2010). See also Edouard Will, *Korinthiaka. Recherches sur l'histoire et la civilisation de Corinthe des origines aux guerres médiques* (Paris: de Boccard, 1955). Stewart Irvin Oost, "Cypselus the Bacchiad," *CP* 67 [1972]: 10–30, esp. 10–11) suggests that the title of "king" (βασιλεύς) may nevertheless have been retained as a "sacerdotal" honorific among the aristocratic Bacchiadae because of the king's unique position as intercessor before the gods.

9. N. G. L. Hammond, "The Peloponnese," in *The Expansion of the Greek World, Eighth to the Sixth Centuries BC*, ed. J. Boardman and N. G. L. Hammond, vol. 3.3 of *The Cambridge Ancient History*, 2nd ed. (Cambridge: Cambridge University Press, 1982), 336. See Nancy Bookidis and Robert S. Stroud, "Apollo and the Archaic Temple at Corinth," *Hesperia* 73 (2003): 401–26.

10. Raphael Sealey (*A History of the Greek States, 700–338 BC* [Berkeley: University of California Press, 1976], 51–52) argues that the choice of the sites of Epidamnus, Apollonia, and Potideia was determined by that fact that these cities "held the western ends of the sole natural route leading eastwards across the Balkans into Macedon, the route taken in Roman times by the Via Egnata." Undoubtedly, by the time of Periander, "the Corinthians were interested in opening up the interior of Macedon to trade" (ibid.), among other motives.

11. Ibid., 52.

Corinth continued to expand as a polis under the anti-Dorian tyrannies of Cypselus and Periander (657–583 BCE; cf. Herodotus, *Hist.* 5.92, 3.48–53; Aristotle, *Pol.* 3.1284A26–33).[12] The city began to mint its own coinage around 587 BCE, alluding to its mythological origins in its iconography.[13] Corinth established far-flung trade networks throughout the west of Greece by means of its colonies and strategic position at the Isthmus. Thus it manufactured its celebrated bronzeware,[14] produced special garments colored with blue purple,[15] and exported its innovatively decorated pottery and painted terracotta slabs, until its pottery was eventually eclipsed by Attic black-figured vases as the dominant style.[16] It was also

---

12. On the Cypselid tyrants at Corinth, see ibid., 48–55. On tyrannies in Greece more generally, see Antony Andrews, *The Greek Tyrants* (London: Hutchinson, 1974); James F. McGlew, *Tyranny and Political Culture in Ancient Greece* (Ithaca, NY: Cornell University Press, 1993).

13. From the sixth to the fourth century BCE many issues of silver *pegasi* were minted at Corinth. See Colin M. Kraay, *Archaic and Classical Greek Coins* (London: Methuen, 1976), 78–88. The Corinthian numismatic iconography alludes to the story about the mythical founder of the city, King Sisyphus—doomed to roll a large boulder uphill in Hades—and the dynasty that he founded though his son Glaucus and his grandson Bellerophon (Homer, *Il.* 6.152–170). Pegasus, the winged horse of Sisyphus's grandson, became the symbol of Corinth on its coinage.

14. Jerome Murphy-O'Connor, "Corinthian Bronze," *RB* 90 (1982): 23–26.

15. Democritus of Ephesus (*FGrHist* 267 F 1 [= Athenaeus, *Deip.* 12.29.525c (Gulick)]) writes: "The garment of the Ionians are violet-dyed, and purple, and saffron, woven with a lozenge pattern: but the top borders are marked at equal intervals with animal designs. Then there are the sarapeis, quince-yellow, purple and white, others again of sea-purple. And Corinthian-made kalasireis; some of these are purple, some violet-dyed, some hyacinth; one might also buy these in flame-colour, or the colour of the sea. There are also Persian kalasireis, which are the finest of all." See also Chrysoula Kardara, "Dyeing and Weaving Works at Isthmia," *AJA* 65 (1961): 261–66.

16. See Hopper, "Ancient Corinth," 9–11. See also Martha K. Risser, *Corinthian Conventionalizing Pottery* (Athens: American School of Classical Studies at Athens, 2001); Risser, "Corinthian Archaic and Classical Pottery: The Local Style," in *Corinth, the Centenary 1896–1996*, ed. Charles K. Williams II and Nancy Bookidis, vol. 20 of *Corinth: Results of Excavations Conducted by the American School of Classical Studies at Athens* (Athens: American School of Classical Studies at Athens, 2003), 157–65; E. G. Pemberton, "Vase Painting in Ancient Corinth," *Arch* 31.6 (1978): 27–33; Pemberton, "Classical and Hellenistic Pottery from Corinth and Its Athenian Connections," in Williams and Bookidis, *Corinth, the Centenary*, 167–79; Mary Campbell Roebuck, "Archaic Architectural Terracottas from Corinth," *Hesperia* 59 (1972): 47–63; Roebuck, "Architectural Terracottas from Classical and Hellenistic Corinth," *Hesperia Supplement* 27 (1994): 39–52.

in the early sixth century BCE that Corinth became the administrator of the Panhellenic games,[17] held every two years at the Isthmus of Corinth in honor of Poseidon.[18] Last, datable to the time of Periander, is the construction of the δίολχος—a stone track with grooves for the transport of wheeled wagons from Kenchreai to Lechaion—providing, scholars have alleged, a conduit of trade from the Saronic to the Corinthian gulf. However, David K. Pettegrew has convincingly challenged this consensus, as his essay in this volume demonstrates,[19] arguing that the δίολχος was not the traditionally proposed commercial thoroughfare but rather was a means for the communication, transport, travel, and strategic operations of Corinth and her allies.[20]

In the classical age (500–336 BCE) Corinth was ruled by an expanded Doric aristocracy, rivaling Athens and Thebes as an economic power because of its control of the Isthmian trade routes. Its maritime dominance, so Thucydides claims (*Pelop.* 1.13.2–5), could also be attributed to the fact that Corinth was the first city-state in Greece to construct war vessels (triremes) in 700 BCE or, alternatively, in the third quarter of the sixth century BCE.[21] However, Corinth suffered considerably during the first

---

17. Sarah B. Pomeroy (*Ancient Greece: A Political, Social, and Cultural History* [Oxford: Oxford University Press, 2011], 127) dates the commencement of the Isthmian games to 581 BCE.

18. See Oscar Broneer, "The Isthmian Victory Crown," *AJA* 66 (1962): 259–63; Broneer, "The Apostle Paul and the Isthmian Games," *BA* 25 (1962): 2–31; Elizabeth R. Gebhard, "The Sanctuary of Poseidon on the Isthmus of Corinth and the Isthmian Games," in *Mind and Body: Athletic Contests in Ancient Greece*, ed. Olga Tzachou-Alexandri (Athens: Ministry of Culture, National Hellenic Committee ICOM, 1989), 82–88; Gebhard, "The Isthmian Games and the Sanctuary of Poseidon in the Early Empire," in *The Corinthia in the Roman Period*, ed. Timothy E. Gregory, JRASup 8 (Ann Arbor: Journal of Roman Archaeology, 1993), 78–94.

19. See also David K. Pettegrew, "The *Diolkos* of Corinth," *AJA* 115 (2011): 549–74.

20. See the five Latin elegiac couplets (Allen Brown West, *Latin Inscriptions, 1896–1926*, vol. 8.2 of *Corinth: Results of Excavations Conducted by the American School of Classical Studies at Athens* [Cambridge: American School of Classical Studies at Athens, 1931 = IKorinthWest], §1) commemorating the hauling of the Roman fleet of the praetor Marcus Antonius across the Isthmus in 102 BCE (translated in Elizabeth R. Gebhard and Matthew W. Dickie, "The View from the Isthmus, ca. 200 BC–44 BC," in Williams and Bookidis, *Corinth, The Centenary*, 261–78, at 272.

21. Evelyn S. Shuckburgh, *A Short History of the Greeks from the Earliest Times to BC 146* (Cambridge: Cambridge University Press, 1901), 33. Other scholars are

(460–446 BCE) and second (431–404 BCE) Peloponnesian Wars, precipitating the first war by attacking Megara, while, in the case of the second war, forging alliances with other Greek city-states in order to fight Sparta in a protracted and unsuccessful conflict.

With the emergence of the διάδοχοι (successor) kingdoms in the early Hellenistic age, Corinth had to negotiate its political place with the Macedonian rulers. If Michael D. Dixon is correct,[22] this was accomplished by means of the reciprocal cultivation of εὔνοια (goodwill) on the part of Corinth and Macedon. Nevertheless, caution is required here. We must not forget that Corinthian political alliances shifted several times during the period of 243–146 BCE. This was because of Corinth's choice to become a member of the newly reformed Achaian League (243 BCE), as well as the Macedonian loss of its garrison on the Acrocorinth during the Achaian interlude (243–224 BCE).[23] Additionally, with the Roman defeat of the Macedonians at Cynocephalae in 197 BCE, Corinth was free again to resume her membership of the Achaian League without external interference until 147 BCE. The proclamation of *libertas* to the Greeks by the Roman general Flaminius at the stadium in Isthmia in 197 BCE had seemingly secured Corinthian independence.

But such shifts in political alliance would have affected loyalties within Corinth. One expects that there would have been groups and individuals within the polis who adopted an anti-Macedonian posture, overtly or covertly, as circumstances changed in the Greek East. In other words, εὔνοια toward the Macedonians was not a diplomatic "given" or an axiomatic policy adopted by Corinth in this period: its implementation depended on the exigencies of the military and political situation facing the city and the advantages it spawned for the aristocratic rulers. The situation was probably more ambiguous than Dixon suggests, though we do not have source

---

more skeptical regarding the status of Thucydides's evidence regarding the Corinthian development of the trireme (e.g. Philippe de Souza, "War at Sea," in *The Oxford Book of Warfare in the Classical World*, ed. Brian Campbell and Lawrence A. Tritle [Oxford: Oxford University Press, 2013], 372–73; Fik Meijer, *The History of Seafaring in the Classical World* [1986; repr., New York: Routledge, 2014], 34–36).

22. For discussion, see Michael D. Dixon, *Late Classical and Early Hellenistic Corinth* (New York: Routledge, 2014). On the centrality of εὔνοια, see ibid., 2–4.

23. On the shifting Corinthian alliances during 243–147 BCE, see Donald W. Engels, *Roman Corinth: An Alternative Model for the Classical City* (Chicago: University of Chicago Press, 1990), 14.

evidence to confirm this.[24] We turn now to Roman Corinth, the city that the apostle Paul visited and in which he ministered for a year and a half (Acts 18:11). In what follows, I will concentrate on the development of the Roman colony of Corinth up to the end of the first century CE, the period of the initial growth of the Corinthian church.

1.2. Roman Corinth

1.2.1. The Destruction of the Greek City of Corinth (146 BCE)

The gradual emergence of Rome as a "superpower" in the Western Mediterranean basin occurred from the fifth century BCE onward, whereas intense rivalries and dissensions had regularly erupted among the city-states of the Greek East, converging in various alliances and protracted wars during the classical and early Hellenistic periods. By the time Rome had established total dominance in the Latin West by, its defeat of Carthage under Scipio Aemilianus in the third Punic War (149–146 BCE)—systematically burning the city for seventeen days and enslaving its inhabitants (Polybius, *Hist.* 8.3–11, 39.7–17; Strabo, *Geogr.* 8.6.23)[25]—Rome's relationship with Corinth and the Achaian League in the Greek East was already at flashpoint. This came to a culmination in the years of 147–146 BCE. Initially the Romans tried to resolve diplomatically the tensions of the Achaian League with Sparta by intervening in the dispute and threatening the dissolution of the league if the issues of contention with Sparta were not resolved. After the Achaian League rejected two Roman diplomatic embassies in 147 BCE, Corinth, fatally for her, rejected a third Roman embassy in 146 BCE and declared war on Sparta.

Rome acted decisively in the face of Achaian provocation. The Roman general Lucius Mummius was victorious over the Achaian League at the Isthmus of Corinth in 146 BCE (Pausanias, *Descr.* 2.1.2). Pausanias states that all the male citizens were executed and the women, children, and *liberti* (freed slaves) were sold into slavery (*Descr.* 7.16.8; cf. Plutarch, *Quaest.*

---

24. I am indebted to Bill Caraher's incisive comments about Dixon's book (*Late Classical and Early Hellenistic Corinth*) in his online review, "Hellenistic Corinth," *The Archaeology of the Mediterranean World* (blog), October 1, 2014, http://tinyurl.com/SBL4208a.

25. See Robin Waterfield, *Taken at the Flood: The Roman Conquest* (Oxford: Oxford University Press, 2014), 214–36.

conv. 9.2 [737A]). However, the scholarly construct of Mummius's troops indiscriminatingly setting fire to all the city's buildings (Pausanias, *Descr.* 2.1.2; Diodorus Siculus, *Bib hist.* 27.1, 32.4.5) is questionable: the evidence points to a more selective and partial destruction as opposed to a wholesale conflagration.[26]

Notwithstanding, the impact of Corinth's destruction sent psychic reverberations throughout the Greek East regarding the rise of Rome. The poet Crinagoras of Mytilene (b. 70 BCE), who was in Rome in 45 BCE when plans were being made to resettle Corinth, highlights the (imagined) shock of the original aristocratic Bacchiadae over the prospective new settlers of the deserted city (*Anthologia Graeca* 9.284).

> What inhabitants, O luckless city, have you received, and in place of whom? Alas for the great calamity to Greece! Would, Corinth, that you be lower than the ground and more desert than the Libyan sands, rather than wholly abandoned to such a crowd of scoundrelly slaves, you should vex the bones of the ancient Bacchiadae.[27]

Although Crinagoras presents "more a Greek's lament for glories past than an accurate report" of Corinth's destruction,[28] his poetry registers well the Greek shame and horror over their loss of independence, illustrated now by the reconstruction of Corinth as a Julian colony.

But other contemporary observers of the disaster and its aftermath made telling observations. Polystratus (*Anthologia Graeca* 7.297), while grieving that "Lucius has smitten the great Achaian Acrocorinth, the Star of Hellas and the twin parallel shores of the Isthmus," nevertheless admits that the Roman destruction of Corinth brought retribution for the Greek destruction of Troy.[29] A fictitious funerary inscription of Antipater of

---

26. See James Wiseman, "Corinth and Rome, I: 228 BC–AD 267," *ANRW* 7.1:491–96. See also Irene B. Romano, "A Hellenistic Deposit from Corinth: Evidence for Interim Period Activity (146–44 B.C.)," *Hesperia* 63 (1994): 57–104.

27. Jerome Murphy-O'Connor, *St. Paul's Corinth: Texts and Archaeology* (1983; repr., Collegeville, MN: Liturgical Press, 2002), 49.

28. Ibid.

29. Polystratus writes (*Anthologia Graeca* 7.297; ca. 100 BCE): "One heap of stones covers the bones of those slain in the rout; and the sons of Aeneas left unwept and unhallowed by the funeral rites the Achaeans who burnt the house of Priam" (Murphy-O'Connor, *St. Paul's Corinth*, 41). Donald Walter Baranowski (*Polybius and Roman Imperialism* [London: Bloomsbury, 2011], 39–40) reflects: "Although Polystra-

INTRODUCTION: THE URBAN LIFE OF ROMAN CORINTH

Sidon recounts the decision of a mother and daughter to commit suicide in freedom at the end of the Achaian war rather than submit to slavery to Rome (*Anthologia Graeca* 7.493: "but ourselves, when dreadful Ares burnt the city of Corinth our country, chose a brave death"). In another epigram Antipater registers his outrage over the savage destruction of Corinth and its people (*Anthologia Graeca* 9.151), stating with hyperbole that "not even a trace is left" of the city.[30] Last, Cicero, who visited Corinth around 79–77 BCE, says that in his youthful days he saw among the ruins "some natives of Corinth who were slaves," but "the sudden sight of the ruins had more effect upon [him]" than upon the inhabitants who were long since hardened to the city's destitute condition (*Tusc.* 3.53). In conclusion, although old Corinth was not totally erased from existence, in the Greek consciousness it was popularly deemed so for a long time afterward.[31]

---

tus represents the catastrophe as a penalty for the destruction of Troy by the Homeric Achaeans, it might be felt that the interval of a thousand years separating the crime and the punishment suggests in the fate of Corinth the gratuitous savagery of Rome more than the inexorable execution of impartial justice."

30. Antipater (*Anthologia Graeca* 9.151) laments: "Where is thy celebrated beauty, Doric Corinth? Where are the battlements of your towers and your ancient wealth? Where are the temples of your immortals, the houses of the matrons of the town of Sisyphus, and her myriads of people?" (Murphy-O'Connor, *St. Paul's Corinth*, 40).

31. The "miserable huts" often cited as archaeological evidence for the inhabitation of Corinth in the interim period (146 BCE–46 CE) should be excluded from scholarly consideration, Benjamin W. Millis has recently claimed ("'Miserable Huts' in Post-146 BC Corinth," *Hesperia* 75 [2006]: 387–404), because they cannot be securely dated. For discussion of contemporary reactions to the destruction, see K. W. Arafat, *Pausanias' Greece: Ancient Artists and Roman Rulers* (Cambridge: Cambridge University Press, 1996), 89–97. However, Gebhard and Dickie ("View from the Isthmus") argue that the fragmentary inscription regulating the affairs of the Isthmian-Nemean guild of the Dionysiac Artists (John Harvey Kent, *The Inscriptions, 1926–1950*, vol. 8.3 of *Corinth: Results of Excavations Conducted by the American School of Classical Studies at Athens* [Princeton: American School of Classical Studies at Athens, 1966 = IKorinthKent], §40) was erected at Corinth, contra to Kent (ibid.), *after* the 146 BCE destruction. Gebhard and Dickie conclude regarding the erection of this inscription after 146 BCE ("View from the Isthmus," 272): "Whoever was responsible must have believed that there was some point in such a gesture. This must mean that there were still people in Corinth or who passed through Corinth to whom the dispute between the rival guilds meant something."

1.2.2. Roman Corinth: Interpreting the Material Evidence

1.2.2.1. From Julian to Flavian Colony and Back Again: Late First-Century BCE and First-Century CE Corinth

In 44 BCE Julius Caesar founded the *Colonia Laus Iulia Corinthiensis* at the site, organizing the agricultural land into plots (*centuriation*) for distribution to Roman settlers (Strabo, *Geogr.* 8.6.23), including the freedmen and urban plebs drawn from Rome, as well as his own veterans (Plutarch, *Caes.* 57.5; Appian, *Bell. civ.* 136.4–6).[32] J. Brian Tucker, drawing on the evidence of Cicero (*Tusc.* 3.22), sums up the surviving remnants of the pre-146 BCE city thus: "All that remains of the Greek city are sections of the *agora*, pillars of a central temple, and a fountain."[33] In 27 BCE Corinth became the capital of the Roman senatorial province of Achaia. After complaints about the steep taxation imposed by the Romans, Tiberius revoked the senatorial status of the province in 15 CE, converting both Achaia and Macedonia into imperial provinces and attaching them to Moesia (Suetonius, *Claud.* 25; Dio Cassius, *Hist. rom.* 60.24). However, under the reign of Claudius, Achaia regained its senatorial status (Tacitus, *Ann.* 1.76.4, 1.80.1; Suetonius, *Claud.* 25.3). This meant that the honor of Corinth being the capital of the province, temporarily lost under Tiberius's reorganization of the Greek provinces, was restored, a fact underscored by the proconsul Gallio's arraignment of the apostle Paul in Corinth at the Bema (Acts 18:12–17).

Nero's grant of freedom from Roman rule to Achaia and, additionally, freedom from taxation in 67 CE was short-lived,[34] with Vespasian subsequently withdrawing Nero's act of grace toward the province (Suetonius, *Vesp.* 8.4; Pausanias, *Descr.* 7.17.4; cf. *SIG* 814). Once again, Achaia resumed its senatorial status, but we know from inscriptional evidence that the Julian name of Corinth was changed to *Colonia Iulia Flavia*

---

32. For a brief history of the colony, see Engels, *Roman Corinth*, 16–21. See also Mary E. Hoskins Walbank, "The Foundation and Planning of Early Roman Corinth," *JRA* 10 (1997): 95–130.

33. J. Brian Tucker, *You Belong to Christ: Paul and the Formation of Social Identity in 1 Corinthians 1–4* (Eugene, OR: Pickwick, 2010), 94.

34. *SIG* 814; cf. Suetonius, *Nero* 24.2; Plutarch, *Flam.* 12.13; Pliny the Elder, *Nat.* 4.6.22; Dio Cassius, *Hist. rom.* 63.11.1; Pausanias, *Descr.* 7.17.2.

Augusta Corinthiensis.[35] The Flavian name for the colony was still found in the legends of the Corinthian coins issued under Domitian (COL IVL FLAV AVG CORINT).[36] But the legend on the reverse of several Corinthian coins in the age of Domitian reverts to COL IVG AVG COR,[37] with the accompanying iconography of the genius of the colony sacrificing to (presumably) Domitian or Roma on one coin.[38] Correspondingly, the obverse shows the radiate bust of Domitian along with his name (IMP CAES DOMIT AVG GERM). There is no doubt that, as the reign of Domitian gradually unfolded, the colonial identity of Corinth reverted to its Julian nomenclature. What should we conclude about the colonial identity of Corinth in the first century CE?

Tucker had argued that the various transitions in colonial status and identity, which had been the experience of first-century Roman Corinth, would have had an impact on the psyche of its inhabitants, including the members of the house churches.[39] As we have seen, there was vacillation between senatorial and imperial provincial status, a brief emancipation from Roman rule and a return to subjugation to Rome again, and fluctuating attachments to the imperial house (Julian or Flavian?) from which the colony derived its name. Moreover, the resumption of Corinth's former status as the Peloponnesian city hosting the Isthmian games and its further acquisition of the honor of hosting the Caesarian games would also have represented a significant reversal of the dishonor experienced when Sicyon had taken over the control of the Isthmian games after Corinth's destruction of 146 BCE.

In all of this, we must reckon with the continuous impact of the imperial rulers, Julio-Claudian and Flavian, in determining the status of colonial Corinth and that of its inhabitants in the city's various transitions of identity and power. Thus Paul's critical attitude toward the imperial rulers of the age (1 Cor 2:6, 8) and his rejection of their quasi-divine status (1 Cor

---

35. IKorinthKent §82.

36. Andrew Burnett, Michel Amandry, and Ian Carradice, *From Vespasian to Domitian (AD 69–96)*, vol. 2 of *Roman Provincial Coinage* (London: British Museum Press; Paris: Bibliothèque Nationale, 1999 = *RPC* 2), e.g., §§105, 107, 113, 119, 126, 129, 131, 133–35, 137–38, 139–45, 147–52, 154–57. On Flavian Corinth, see Mary E. Hoskins Walbank, "What's in a Name? Corinth under the Flavians," *ZPE* 139 (2002): 251–64.

37. *RPC* 2, §§108–9.

38. *RPC* 2, §109.

39. Tucker, *You Belong to Christ*, 101.

8:5–6: λεγόμενοι θεοὶ εἴτε ἐν οὐρανῷ εἴτε ἐπὶ γῆς) are all the more remarkable in their Corinthian context.[40] The current age was passing away (1 Cor 7:31b) and, in sharp contrast to the Julio-Claudian propaganda, the fulfillment of the ages had come upon the weak and foolish believers (10:11b; cf. 1:27) and not upon the wise and powerful Julio-Claudian house and its provincial clients.[41] Therefore the socially influential in the body of Christ were commanded to flee the temptations of the games of the federal imperial cult at the Isthmus (1 Cor 10:14–22), as well as involvement in the meals and rituals in honor of the ruler and the Roman gods in the local temples at Corinth (1 Cor 8:10).[42] By contrast, those who are in Christ Jesus possess the divine righteousness, holiness, and redemption (1 Cor 1:30b). In this vast social and soteriological reordering accomplished by God in Christ, "the things that are" have been nullified by "the things that are not" (1 Cor 1:29b).

Furthermore, Paul redefines the Isthmian and Caesarian athletic ideal for the Corinthian believers.[43] Rather than the athletic ideal being directed toward the personal glory of the athlete, his family and city, and the imperial ruler in whose honor the games were held, the self-discipline of the believer as a "spiritual athlete" (1 Cor 9:24–27) is directed toward denying the self-centered desires of the body (9:27). These desires, if unchecked, inevitably lead to selfish and insensitive behavior among believers in the body of Christ (8:1b, 7–13; 10:23, 28–29a, 32). Instead, Paul, with a view to

---

40. Joseph D. Fantin, *The Lord of the Entire World: Lord Jesus, a Challenge to Lord Caesar?* NTM 31 (Sheffield: Sheffield Phoenix, 2011), 225–30.

41. For the eschatology of the Julio-Claudian rulers, see James R. Harrison, *Paul and the Imperial Authorities at Thessalonica and Rome: A Study in the Conflict of Ideology*, WUNT 273 (Tübingen: Mohr Siebeck, 2011), 97–144, 170–77.

42. Bruce W. Winter (*After Paul Left Corinth: The Influence of Secular Ethics and Social Change* [Grand Rapids: Eerdmans, 2001], 269–86) argues that some of the Corinthian elite in the house churches were seduced by the idolatry associated with games of the federal imperial cult at the Isthmus in the early 50s. See also John Fotopoulos, *Food Offered to Idols in Roman Corinth: A Social-Rhetorical Reconstruction of 1 Corinthians 8:1–11:1*, WUNT 2/151 (Tübingen: Mohr Siebeck, 2003). On the imperial cult in Greece generally, see Maria Kantiréa, *Les Dieux et les Dieux Auguste: Le culte impérial en Grèce sous les Julio-claudiens et les Flaviens. Études épigraphiques et archéologiques*, Meletemata 50 (Athens: Centre de recherche de l'Antiquité grecque et romaine, 2007).

43. See James R. Harrison, "Paul and the Athletic Ideal in Antiquity: A Case Study in Wrestling with Word and Image," in *Paul's World*, ed. Stanley E. Porter, Pauline Studies 4 (Leiden: Brill, 2007), 81–109.

winning over the polarized groups within the Corinthian house churches (1 Cor 9:19b, 20a, 20b, 21b, 22a), advocates a lifestyle of other-centered service (9:19; 10:24, 33) by identifying with and accepting the ethnically and culturally diverse believers within the body of Christ (9:20, 20b, 21a, 21b). The principle of accommodation enunciated here—becoming "all things to all people" (1 Cor 9:22b)—finds it origin in the cross of Christ. Because of his atoning identification with fallen humanity (2 Cor 5:21), Christ had become all things to all people by reconciling them to God and to each other. Thus the imitation of Christ advocated by Paul (1 Cor 11:1) is cruciform. Although the believer's crown—contrasted implicitly by Paul with the Isthmian prize of the celery crown (1 Cor 9:25b: φθαρτὸν στέφανον)—is eschatologically postponed, it is nevertheless accorded imperishable honor (9:25b: ἄφθαρτον). In sum, Paul's eschatology and soteriology provides the impetus for a radical redefinition of Corinth's athletic ideal, whether traditionally conceived within an Isthmian context, or imperially reconfigured under the Julio-Claudian rulers.

Despite these fluctuations in Corinth's colonial identity, the administration and building program of Roman Corinth continued to prosper in the first century CE. The administration of the colony that emerged from 44 BCE onward is still a worthwhile inscriptional study to be pursued in Corinthian scholarship. Its profit would be enhanced if it were brought into dialogue with the Corinthian numismatic evidence and the Julian colonial charter of Spanish Urso, our paradigm for reconstructing the lost colonial charter of Corinth.[44] The election of the city magistrates (the two chief *duoviri iure dicundo*; the two aediles; the ἀγωνοθέται; the *curator annonae*, etc.) through the *comitia tributa* and the administration of the colony by the *decuriones* in the local "senate" (*decurio*; Greek, βουλή, "council") are well represented in the Corinthian inscriptions. Readers are advised to consult John Harvey Kent's volume for a proper understanding of their role and activities at Corinth and also my own study of the figure of the ἀγωνοθέτης in this volume.[45]

A valuable but patchy portrait of the various building activities undertaken at Corinth by the funding of (primarily local) benefactors in the

---

44. See Michel Amandry, *Le Monnayage des duovirs Corinthiens*, BCHSup 15 (Athens: École française d'Athènes; Paris: de Boccard, 1988). On the Julian charter of Urso, see n. 73 below.

45. See IKorinthKent: *duoviri*, §§149–51; *agōnothetai*, §§208–30; *aediles* and *curator annonae*, §§231–38; *decurio* and *decuriones*, §§137, 150, 150, 224, 233, 276.

Julio-Claudian and Flavian periods can be reconstructed from the honorific inscriptions.[46] Needless to say, the portrait has to be supplemented by the Corinthian archaeological evidence,[47] but the inscriptions nevertheless provide us insight into the city's expansion and benefactors. At the outset, little is said in the Corinthian inscriptions about the council supervision of building activities in the city. Only two examples are available. A certain P. Licinius Priscus Juventianus, who lived outside our period (ca. 160–170 CE), bought a portion of *ager publicus* in order to build fifty dwelling units near the Isthmian sanctuary, which, by council decree, could be made available to the athletes free of charge at the time of the games.[48] There is mention of a market (*macellum*)—initially thought by West to be a *macellum piscarium* (fish market) but now considered by Ned Nabers to be a reference to a "meat market"[49]—"with [- - -] and facilities for fish [- - - - -]." Built in the time of Augustus, the meat market, with its supplementary storage area (?) for fish,[50] was underwritten by wealthy members of the social elite, who gave the market, by council decree,[51] as a gift to the city in the Lechaion Road area early in the history of the colony.

But, in addition to the meat market, there was an explosion in building activity during the reign of Augustus funded by various civic benefactors, if the inscriptions are sufficiently representative: the rehabilitation of

---

46. For a helpful commentary, see IKorinthKent, 20–22. On honor and the Corinthian community, see Harry A. Stansbury, "Corinthian Honor, Corinthian Conflict: A Social History of Early Roman Corinth and Its Pauline Community" (PhD diss., University of California Irvine, 1991).

47. On the website of the American School of Classical Studies at Athens, the vast range of ASCSA archaeological publications on Corinth, spanning 1932–2013, may be accessed. See "Corinth," http://tinyurl.com/SBL4208b. For a handy summary, see Tucker, *You Belong to Christ*, 95–96. For the archaeological evidence, spanning the period from Augustus to Claudian, see the essay of L. L. Welborn in this volume.

48. See IKorinthKent §306.

49. IKorinthWest §§124–25; IKorinthKent §321; Ned Nabers, "A Note on Corinth VIII, 2, 125," *AJA* 73 (1975): 73–74; D. W. J. Gill, "The Meat-Market at Corinth (1 Corinthians 10:25)," *TynBul* 43.2 (1992): 389–93.

50. The phrases "et pi[scario ---]" (IKorinthKent §321) and "[cum pi]scario et bilac ---" (IKorinthWest §125) have been variously translated by both epigraphers: respectively, "fish market" and "with fish market and having two cisterns or tanks." Translation certainty is unachievable.

51. IKorinthWest §125.

the Asclepeion;[52] the building of a stoa at the Isthmian sanctuary;[53] the construction of two baths at different sites;[54] the establishment of a temple and statue of Apollo Augustus, along with ten shops;[55] and, last, the erection of various honorific dedications and monuments in several unidentified buildings.[56] In the reign of Tiberius, the famous Babbius monument was erected.[57] Revetments were added to the Julian Basilica, the Bema, the Southeast building, and the Peirene in the reigns of Caligula, Claudius, Nero, and Hadrian respectively.[58] The Southeast building, in particular, already had its portico built by Cn. Babbius Philinus in the reign of Tiberius,[59] with (probably) his son contributing to further construction by adding the revetments, noted above.[60] The elaborately decorated background of the theater stage (*scaena frons*) in the Odeion was constructed in the reign of Domitian,[61] as was the white marble epistyle of Temple E.[62] However, the famous pavement built by the aedile Erastus—formerly assigned by Kent to the reign of Nero, located east of the Theater, and iden-

---

52. IKorinthKent §311.
53. IKorinthKent §153.
54. IKorinthKent §§130, 314.
55. IKorinthWest §120. Regarding the cult of "Apollo Augustus" at Corinth, Latin inscriptions mention the existence of the cult elsewhere. See Johann Kaspar von Orelli, *Inscriptionum Latinarum Selectarum* (Turici: Orelli, Fuessli, 1828), §§404, 1436, 2548, 2628. The temple of Apollo Augustus and its precise location cannot be identified. Potential candidates for an Augustan temple of Apollo or Apollo Augustus are rare. Building K in Corinth has been posited, on the basis of the evidence of Pausanias (*Descr.* 2.3.6), to be the temple of Apollo, but it is not even certain that the building was a temple (Wiseman, "Corinth and Rome, I," 529). Alternatively, Charles K. Williams II ("A Re-evaluation of Temple E and the West End of the Forum of Corinth," in *The Greek Renaissance in the Roman Empire: Papers from the Tenth British Museum Classical Colloquium*, ed. Susan Walker and Averil Cameron [London: University of London, Institute of Classical Studies, 1989], 156–62, at 158) has argued that Temple G, erected at the side of the temple of Venus in the Corinthian Forum, was the temple of Clarian Apollo, honoring the patron deity of Augustus and his house. Was this perhaps the Augustan temple that L. Hermidius Celsus and L. Retilius [------], both possibly priests of Apollo, actually built? Unfortunately definitive proof is lacking.
56. E.g. IKorinthKent §156, among others.
57. See below, n. 87; cf. IKorinthKent §323.
58. IKorinthWest §130; IKorinthKent §§322, 327, 170.
59. IKorinthWest §122.
60. I.e., IKorinthKent §327.
61. IKorinthKent §334.
62. IKorinthKent §333. On Temple E not being a temple dedicated to the imperial

tified with the Erastus of Rom 16:23b[63]—is now under serious scholarly challenge, and its traditional dating, location, and identification can no longer be assumed, at least not without strong countervailing argument.[64] The proconsular construction and maintenance of roads was an expression of Flavian beneficence: Lucius Calpurnius Proclus is said to be the curator of the Trajanic roads,[65] but whether this extended to the Corinthian roads in Trajan's reign is unknown. Last, although the evidence is not epigraphic, mention should be made of Nero's failed attempt to build a canal across the Isthmus.[66]

In conclusion, the inscriptional evidence gives us keen insight into the honorific culture that elicited civic beneficence from the powerful elites of Corinth for a range of building projects. Of course, it only affords insight into constructions designed for the praise of the wealthy aristocratic families, who cultivated the favor of the gods, Roman and indigenous, in a *do ut des* contract ("I give in order that you may give"), ingratiated themselves with the Julio-Claudian/Flavian rulers and their local representatives by means of their beneficence, and competed for social precedence among each other. But we gain no real insight from the inscriptions where the poor lived, from whom were drawn many of the early Christians (1 Cor

---

worship of Octavia and Jupiter Capitolinus at Corinth, see Mary E. Hoskins Walbank, "Pausanias, Octavia and Temple E at Corinth," *ABSA* 84 (1989): 369–84.

63. IKorinthKent §232.

64. For recent summaries of the scholarship, see L. L. Welborn, *An End to Enmity: Paul and the "Wrongdoer" of Second Corinthians*, BZNW 185 (Berlin: de Gruyter, 2011), 260–83; Paul Trebilco, "Epigraphy and the Study of Polis and Ekklēsia in the Greco-Roman World," in *Methodological Foundations*, ed. James R. Harrison and L. L. Welborn, WGRWSup 7, vol. 1 of *The First Urban Churches* (Atlanta: SBL Press, 2015), 89–109, esp. 96–98. On the issue of representatives from the social elites among the early Christian house churches, see now Alexander Weiss, *Soziale Elite und Christentum: Studien zu ordo-Angehörigen unter den frühen Christen* (Berlin: de Gruyter, 2015).

65. IKorinthKent §125.

66. For discussion, with literary sources, see David Gilman Romano, "City Planning, Centuriation, and Land Division in Roman Corinth: Colonia Laus Iulia Corinthiensis and Colonia Iulia Flavia Augusta Corinthiensis," in Williams and Bookidis, *Corinth, The Centenary*, 297–98. See David Pettegrew's discussion, in his essay in this volume, of the first-century archaeological evidence. Pettegrew highlights the heavy resources and detailed strategy required for the canal's excavation by Nero, thereby underscoring the Roman ruler's intentionality and forward planning, in Pettegrew's view, to ensure the safe passage of grain to Rome.

4:11; 11:22; 2 Cor 6:10b; 8:1–5, 9; 11:27), and how they eked out their meager existence on the margins of the city. In this regard, the essay of L. L. Welborn in this volume is a meticulous source examination of social inequality in Corinth.

There is little doubt that city council endorsed the plethora of statues and private monuments, reciprocating the benefactor's beneficence, inscribing their bases with "by decree of the city council,"[67] thereby ensuring that the city's reputation for gratitude before their own citizens and the other Peloponnesian city-states was upheld, and publicly obligating the city council itself to maintain and protect the monuments in perpetuity. The "endless chatter" of the honorific inscriptions, which dominated the urban landscape by virtue of their size and ubiquity, reduced the socially marginalized to ciphers in the vast city in which they lived.[68] It was a problem with which Paul was intimately familiar in reconstructing Christian identity corporately as God's "building" and the Holy Spirit's "temple" (1 Cor 1:26–30; 3:9; 6:19).[69] Paradoxically, for Paul, it was precisely in the charismatic noise of teaching, prophecy, tongues, and worship in the Christian house churches—not in the reverend cultic silence of the Corinthian temples—that God was to be found (1 Cor 14:24–25). Nor should we forget in this regard how the assemblies (ἐκκλησίαι) of the Corinthian church (see IKorinthKent §728; cf. §724: "[The - - -] church of [Saint] Paul": ninth–tenth century CE) would have been perceived, both by insiders and outsiders, against the backdrop of the political assemblies of the eastern Mediterranean cities.

1.2.2.2. Corinth's Roman Colonial Identity and Its Greek Antecedents

Scholars have discussed extensively the Roman character of the colony of Corinth,[70] highlighting the following features:

---

67. IKorinthKent, 22: Ψ(ηφίσματι) Β(ουλῆς); D(ecreto) D(ecurionum).

68. I am indebted to Assistant Professor Christine Thomas, Department of Religious Studies, UC Santa Barbara, for this insight.

69. On Paul's constitutional and building language in 1 Cor 3:5–4:5 against the background of the Julian colonial charters of Urso and Greek building contracts, see Bradley J. Bitner, *Paul's Political Strategy in 1 Corinthians 1–4: Constitution and Covenant*, SNTSMS 163 (Cambridge: Cambridge University Press, 2015), 197–301.

70. For general discussion, see Robert M. Grant, *Paul in the Roman World: The Conflict at Corinth* (Louisville: Westminster John Knox, 2001); David G. Horrell and Edward Adams, "The Scholarly Quest for Paul's Church at Corinth: A Critical Survey,"

1. The dominance of Latin inscriptions over Greek inscriptions at Corinth, as well as the production of locally minted coins in Latin, each pointing to the official use of Latin in the city.[71]
2. The elements of *Romanitas*, including hunting shows and gladiatorial contests in the amphitheater, as well as a circus for chariot races.[72]

---

in *Christianity at Corinth: The Quest for the Pauline Church*, ed. David G. Horrell and Edward Adams (Louisville: Westminster John Knox, 2004), 6–7; Anthony C. Thiselton, *The First Epistle to the Corinthians: A Commentary on the Greek Text*, NIGTC (Grand Rapids: Eerdmans, 2000), 3–8; Tucker, *You Belong to Christ*, 93–97.

71. On the dominance of Latin in the official inscriptions, see IKorinthKent, 19. Note the connection between the use of Latin and Corinth's reestablishment as a military veteran's colony: Marjeta Šašel Kos, "A Latin Epitaph of a Roman Legionary from Corinth," *JRS* 68 (1978): 22–25. On Latin and the Corinthian coinage, see Amandry, *Le Monnayage*; Mary E. Hoskins Walbank, "Image and Cult: The Coinage of Roman Corinth," in *Corinth in Context: Comparative Studies on Religion and* Society, ed. Steven J. Friesen, Daniel N. Schowalter, and James C. Walters (Leiden: Brill, 2011), 151–98.

72. On the Corinthian amphitheater, see Katherine E. Welch, "Negotiating Roman Spectacle Architecture in the Greek World: Athens and Corinth," in *The Art of Ancient Spectacle*, ed. Bettina Ann Bergmann and Christine Kondoleon (New Haven: Yale University Press, 1999), 125–45; Welch, *The Roman Amphitheatre: From Its Origins to the Colosseum* (Cambridge: Cambridge University Press, 2007), 163–85, 255–59. On gladiator reliefs at the Corinthian theater, see Theodore Leslie Shear, "Excavations at Corinth in 1925," *AJA* 29 (1925): 381–97, esp. 383–85; Shear, "Excavations in the Theatre District of Corinth in 1926," *AJA* 30 (1926): 444–63, esp. 451–52. On gladiatorial imagery in the Corinthian epistles, see James R. Unwin, "'Thrown Down but Not Destroyed': Paul's Use of a Spectacle Metaphor in 2 Corinthians 4:7–15," *NovT*, forthcoming. On Corinthian pottery lamps showing gladiators, see Oscar Broneer, *Terracotta Lamps*, vol. 4.2 of *Corinth: Results of Excavations Conducted by the American School of Classical Studies at Athens* (Cambridge: Harvard University Press, 1930), §§427, 460–61, 492, 534, 634–53, 1192–97. See also Philippe Bruneau, "Lampes corinthiennes," *BCH* 95 (1971): 437–501. On Corinthian gladiator inscriptions, see Louis Robert, *Les gladiateurs dans l'orient grec* (Amsterdam: Hakkert, 1971), §§60–61; Michael Carter, "A *Doctor Secutorum* and the *Retiarius Draukos* from Corinth" *ZPE* 12 (1999): 262–68. On the Corinthian circus, see David Gilman Romano, "A Roman Circus in Corinth," *Hesperia* 74 (2005): 585–611. See also the first-century Argive petition regarding the financing of wild beast shows (τὰ κυνηγέσια) at Corinth (Pseudo-Julian, *Letters* 198) and, arising from this, the debate regarding the interface of Greek and Roman identity. On the Argive petition, see Antony J. S. Spawforth, "Corinth, Argos and the Imperial Cult: Pseudo-Julian, Letters 198," *Hesperia* 63 (1994): 211–32; Tucker, *You Belong to Christ*, 94–95; Cavan W. Concannon, *"When You Were Gentiles": Specters of Ethnicity in Roman Corinth and Paul's Corinthian Correspondence*, Syn-

3. The rebuilding of Corinth in the Roman manner: that is, according to the *centuriation* pattern where the land is marked out in squares and rectangles, as well as the colonial charter of the city's overall design as far as it can be reconstructed from the extant Spanish colonial charters.[73]
4. The colonial pattern and ethos of Corinthian civic administration, again according to what can be gleaned from the Spanish colonial charters and also from the Corinthian inscriptions.[74]
5. The Roman architectural elements incorporated in the rebuilding program.[75]
6. The presence of Roman dining customs based on the architecture of the *triclinium* and the atrium in the houses of the wealthy (1 Cor 11:17–34),[76] though some elements of this construct have been recently challenged,[77] as well as Roman patronal influences

---

krisis: Comparative Approaches to Early Christianity in Greco-Roman Culture (New Haven: Yale University Press, 2014), 137–41.

73. Romano, "City Planning," 279–302. Although the original colonial charter of Corinth is no longer extant, it was undoubtedly identical to the Julian charter found in the Spanish Roman colony of Urso (Allan Chester Johnson, Paul Robinson Coleman-Norton, and Frank Card Bourne, *Ancient Roman Statutes* [Austin: University of Texas Press, 1961], §114). On the Spanish colonial charter in relation to Corinth's constitution, cultural ethos, and city design and its exegetical consequences for 1 Corinthians, see Bitner, *Paul's Political Strategy*.

74. On the Spanish colonial charter of Urso and its relation to Corinth's (now lost) charter, see n. 73 above. For the Corinthian inscriptions, see Benjamin Dean Meritt, *Greek Inscriptions, 1896–1927*, vol. 8.1 of *Corinth: Results of Excavations Conducted by the American School of Classical Studies at Athens* (Cambridge: American School of Classical Studies at Athens, 1931); IKorinthWest; IKorinthKent; Ronald S. Stroud, *The Sanctuary of Demeter and Kore: The Inscriptions*, vol. 18.6 of *Corinth: Results of Excavations Conducted by the American School of Classical Studies at Athens* (Princeton: American School of Classical Studies at Athens, 2013 = IKorinthStroud).

75. See Tucker, *You Belong to Christ*, 95–96. See also the immensely helpful Corinthian archaeological updates of David K. Pettegrew's blog *Corinthian Matters: A Resource for the Study of the Corinthia, Greece*, http://www.corinthianmatters.com/.

76. On the triclinium and atrium in relation to 1 Cor 11:17–24, see Murphy-O'Connor, *St. Paul's Corinth*, 178–85.

77. For discussion and evaluation of recent challenges to Murphy-O'Connor's construct, see Edward Adams, "Placing the Corinthian Common Meal," in *Text, Image, and Christians in the Graeco-Roman World: A Festschrift in Honor of David Lee Balch*, ed. Aliou Cissé Niang and Carolyn Oseik, PTMS 176 (Eugene, OR: Wipf & Stock, 2012), 22–37.

explaining some of the problems that the Corinthian church faced.[78]
7. The nature of Roman civil law and its impact on litigation within the house churches (1 Cor 6:1-8), a subject ably discussed in Michael Peppard's essay in this volume.[79]
8. The presence of the imperial cult in the city (1 Cor 8:5-6; cf. Pausanias, *Descr.* 2.3.1),[80] including its operation in the Julian Basilica and in Temple E (temple of Octavia or Jupiter Capitolinus?).[80]

---

78. John K. Chow, *Patronage and Power: A Study of Social Networks in Corinth*, JSNTSup 75 (Sheffield: JSOT Press, 1992); Andrew D. Clarke, *Secular and Christian Leadership in Corinth: A Socio-historical and Exegetical Study of 1 Corinthians 1-6* (Leiden: Brill, 1993), 75-88; Winter, *After Paul Left* Corinth, 186-205; Joshua Rice, *Paul and Patronage: The Dynamics of Power in 1 Corinthians* (Eugene, OR; Pickwick, 2013).

79. Michael Peppard's essay in this volume, presented in the "Polis and Ekklesia: Investigations of Urban Christianity" session at the Society of Biblical Literature Annual Meeting in 2012 (Chicago), was subsequently published in *JBL* 133 (2014): 179-92, and is reproduced here with permission. See also Chow, *Patronage and Power*, 123-30; Clarke, *Secular and Christian Leadership*, 59-71; Winter, *After Paul Left Corinth*, 58-75; Alan C. Mitchell, "Rich and Poor in the Courts of Corinth: Litigiousness and Status in 1 Corinthians 6:1-11," *NTS* 39 (1993): 562-86; David G. Horrell, *The Social Ethos of the Corinthian Correspondence: Interests and Ideology from 1 Corinthians to 1 Clement* (Edinburgh; T&T Clark, 1996), 109-12.

80. E. H. Swift, "A Group of Roman Imperial Portraits at Corinth," *AJA* 25 (1921): 142-59; Swift, "A Group of Roman Imperial Portraits at Corinth. II. Tiberius," *AJA* 25 (1921): 248-65; Swift, "A Group of Roman Imperial Portraits at Corinth. III. Gaius and Lucius Caesar, " *AJA* 25 (1921): 337-63; Swift, "A Group of Roman Imperial Portraits at Corinth. IV. The Four Torsos," *AJA* 26 (1922): 131-47; F. P. Johnson, "The Imperial Portraits at Corinth," *AJA* 30 (1926): 158-76; Oscar Broneer, "An Official Rescript from Corinth," *Hesperia* 8 (1939): 181-90; Henry S. Robinson, "A Monument of Roma at Corinth," *Hesperia* 43 (1974): 470-84; Mary E. Hoskins Walbank, "Evidence for the Imperial Cult in Julio-Claudian Corinth," in *Subject and Ruler: The Cult of the Ruling Power in Classical Antiquity*, ed. Alastair Small, JRASup 17 (Ann Arbor: Journal of Roman Archaeology, 1993), 201-14; Winter, *After Paul Left Corinth*, 269-96; Paul D. Scotton, "A New Fragment of an Inscription from the Julian Basilica at Roman Corinth," *Hesperia* 74 (2005): 95-100; David Gilman Romano, "Urban and Rural Planning in Roman Corinth," in *Urban Religion in Roman Corinth: Interdisciplinary Approaches*, ed. Daniel N. Schowalter and Steven J. Friesen (Cambridge: Harvard University Press, 2005), 25-59; F. Camia and M. Kantiréa, "The Imperial Cult in the Peloponnese," in *Society, Economy and Culture under the Roman Empire: Continuity and Innovation*, vol. 3 of *Roman Peloponnese*, ed. A. D. Rizakis and C. E. Lepenioti (Athens: National Hellenic Research Foundation, 2010), 375-406; Tucker, *You Belong*

9. The reestablishment of the Isthmian games under the control of Corinth as opposed to Sicyon (40 BCE) and, concomitantly, the inauguration of the Caesarian games in Corinth and their reestablishment at the sanctuary of Poseidon at Isthmia (40–50 CE).[82]
10. Corinth as the capital of the Roman senatorial province of Achaia (27 BCE) and the place of residence of its governor Gallio upon Achaia's reestablishment as a senatorial province under Claudius' reign (Acts 18:12–17).[83]
11. The importance of Roman social institutions such as the baths in the daily life of Corinth.[84]
12. Domestic Roman material remains found in the city.[85]

However, it would be naive to assume that aspects of the Greek culture and traditional mythology associated with the pre-146 BCE city were not revived in the new Roman colony. It would be equally naive to assume that Roman and Greek identities in the colony did not somehow intersect to create elements of (what some scholars, drawing on Homi K. Bhabha's sociological research, have called) "hybrid" identity for its inhabitants.[86]

---

to Christ, 97–99; Bruce W. Winter, "The Enigma of Imperial Cultic Activities and Paul in Corinth," in *Graeco-Roman Culture and the New Testament*, ed. David E. Aune and F. E. Brenk (Leiden: Brill, 2012), 49–72.

81. Contra Walbank, "Pausanias, Octavia and Temple E."
82. Gebhard, "Isthmian Games." Note IKorinthKent §153: "[To Lucius Castricius Regulus, son of ---, of the tribe ---, aedile, prefect *iure dicundo*], duovir, quinquennial duovir, agonothete of the Isthmian and the Caesarean games, who was [the first] to preside over the Isthmian games at the Isthmus under the sponsorship of Colonia Laus Julia Corinthiensis." See also Mika Kajava, "When Did the Isthmian Games Return to the Isthmus? Rereading Corinth 8.3.153," *CP* 97 (2002): 168–78.
83. For the Gallio inscription and discussion, see Murphy-O'Connor, *St. Paul's Corinth*, 161–62. On Gallio, see Joshua Yoder, *Representatives of Roman Rule: Roman Provincial Governors in Luke-Acts* (Berlin: de Gruyter, 2014), 254–76.
84. Jane C. Biers, "*Lavari est vivere*: Baths in Roman Context," in Friesen, Schowalter, and Walters, *Corinth in Context*, 305–19.
85. E.g., Doreen C. Spitzer, "Roman Relief Bowls from Corinth," *Hesperia* 11 (1942): 162–92; Aileen Ajootian, "A Roman Table Support at Ancient Corinth," *Hesperia* 69 (2000): 487–507.
86. For sociological discussion, see Homi K. Bhabha, *The Location of Culture* (New York: Routledge, 2004). In the case of Concannon (*When You Were Gentiles*, 16–17; cf. 51, 186–87 n. 55), he employs the concept of hybridity "to refer to the ways in which Paul and others in and around Corinth adapted, appropriated, and adopted

But the essay of Brad Bitner on bilingual inscriptions at Corinth in this volume adeptly demonstrates both the complexities and the need for clearly articulated and sound methodologies in determining the extent of "hybridity." Whatever cultural intersections there may have been, the Roman colonial ethos was the determinative factor in this confluence of cultures. Even in Nero's much-vaunted but short-lived liberation of the province of Achaia (67 CE), in reciprocation of the Greek gods' providential care of himself (*SIG* 814 ll. 23–24, 35–37), Nero underscores the present cultural and political inferiority of Greece in the Roman world in comparison to his total superiority as the world benefactor: "Would that Greece were still at its peak as I grant you this gift, in order that more people might enjoy this favor of mine" (*SIG* 814 ll. 18–19). The local aristocratic elites and the nouveau riche of Achaia,[87] therefore, created new pathways of upward mobility for themselves within the Roman provincial *cursus honorum* (course of honors), integrating the city's original foundation myths and deities with the new realities of Roman rule and cult in the Peloponnese.[88] Two examples of this integration of Greek culture within the Roman hegemony are adduced below.

---

identities as a means of resisting, negotiating, and participating in the production of Roman provincial society." For an argument for the "hellenization" of Corinth, see Marcin L. Pawlak, "Corinth after 44 BC: Ethnical and Cultural Changes," *Electrum* 20 (2013): 143–62. See also B. M. Millis, "The Social and Ethnic Origins of the Colonists in Early Roman Corinth," in Friesen, Schowalter, and Walters, *Corinth in Context*, 13–35.

87. A good example of the advancement of the nouveau riche at Corinth is the career of Cn. Babbius Philinus. For the podium inscription of the Babbius monument, see IKorinthKent §155. The same text is found on the epistyle: see IKorinthKent §241. For artist images of the reconstructed Babbius monument and photos of its remains at Corinth, see "Corinth Monument: Babbius Monument," ASCSA Digital Collections, http://tinyurl.com/SBL4208c. For other Babbius inscriptions, see IKorinthWest §§2–3, 98–99, 100–101, 131; SEG 55.386.

88. On the Corinthian elite, see Antony J. S. Spawforth, "Roman Corinth: The Formation of a Colonial Elite," in *Roman Onomastic in the Greek East: Social and Political Aspects. Proceedings of the International Colloquium on Roman Onomastics, Athens, 7–9 September 1993*, ed. A. D. Rizakis, Meletemata 21 (Athens: Institouton Hellenikes kai Romaikes Archaiotetos Ethnikon Hidryma Ereunon, 1996), 167–82; Spawforth, *Greece and the Augustan Cultural Revolution* (Cambridge: Cambridge University Press, 2011), 45, 48, 53, 54, 227. More generally, see Jesper Majbom Madsen, "The Romanization of the Greek Elite in Achaia, Asia and Bithynia: Greek Resistance or Regional Discrepancies?" *Orbis Terrarum* 8 (2006): 87–113.

First, in Room C of the South Stoa of Corinth—the (presumed) office of the city's president of the Isthmian games—there is a Severan mosaic portraying a nude male athlete after his triumph. Betsey A. Robinson has convincingly argued that the mosaic represents a fusion of the Roman civic gods with the traditional indigenous Greek deities of the city.[89] Second, Corinthian coins with Latin legends have reverse types showing various Greek deities (e.g., Poseidon, Athena, Dionysius), while the anonymous bronze coins are minted with the iconography of myths, deities, and agonistic motifs of Greece (e.g., the Bellepheron/Pegasos founding myth of the city; the local deities Melicertes and Ino; Isthmos, athletes, etc.).[90] The heavy numismatic emphasis on Poseidon and Aphrodite may be attributed to the fact that, as Donald Engels argues,[91] the colonists felt the need

---

89. Betsey A. Robinson, "'Good Luck' from Corinth: A Mosaic of Allegory, Athletics, and City Identity," *AJA* 116 (2012): 105–32.

90. For discussion, see Mary E. Hoskins Walbank, "Aspects of Corinthian Coinage in the Late First and Early Second Centuries AD," in Williams and Bookidis, *Corinth, the Centenary*, 337–50; Walbank, "Image and Cult." I will limit my citation of the Corinthian coin evidence bearing Greek deities and athletic motifs to the period of 44 BCE–96 CE. For late republican and Julio-Claudian coins bearing the image of Poseidon, see Andrew Burnett, Michel Amandry, and Pere Pau Ripollés, *From the Death of Caesar to the Death of Vitellius (44 BC–AD 69)*, vol. 1 of *Roman Provincial Coinage* (London: British Museum Press; Paris: Bibliothèque Nationale, 1992; rev. 2006 = *RPC* 1), §§1117, 1125, 1137, 1185, 1192, 1212, 1225, 1234; Athena: *RPC* 1, §1118; Dionysos: *RPC* 1, §1122; Pegasos: *RPC* 1, §§1117, 1121, 1127–28, 1133, 1145, 1147, 1162, 1201, 1223, 1225, 1234, 1235–36; Melicertes: *RPC* 1, §§1162, 1172, 1186–88; Isthmos: *RPC* 1, §§1164, 1168, 1222; athletes: *RPC* 1, §1135. For Domitianic coins bearing the image of Poseidon, see *RPC* 2, §§101, 141–43, 148–50, 183–93, 207–19; Melicertes: *RPC* 2, §§101, 114–16; Ino (*RPC* 2, §114); Pegasos: *RPC* 2, §§113, 137–39, 178–81; Isthmos: *RPC* 2, §§101, 133–35, 174–77; Athena: *RPC* 2, §156; athletes: *RPC* 2, §§126, 208–17. For other Greek deities spanning the Julio-Claudian and Domitianic periods, see Zeus (*RPC* 2, §207), Herakles (*RPC* 2, §§173, 218), Triptolemos (*RPC* 2, §§200–203), Helios (*RPC* 1, §§1195, 1227; *RPC* 2, §§170–72), Aphrodite (*RPC* 1, §§1127–28, 1197, 1200; *RPC* 2, §§125, 153–54), Nike (*RPC* 1, §1119) and Tyche (*RPC* 1, §1207, 1213). On the Greek deities at Corinth, see Engels, *Roman Corinth*, 93–101. On Melicertes, see Elizabeth R. Gebhard, "Rites for Melikertes-Palaimon in the Early Roman Corinthia," in Schowalter and Friesen, *Urban Religion in Roman Corinth*, 165–203. More generally, see Mary E. Hoskins Walbank, "The Cults of Roman Corinth: Public Rituals and Personal Belief," in Rizakis and Lepenioti, *Society, Economy and Culture*, 357–74.

91. Engels, *Roman Corinth*, 94. Engels (ibid., 96) makes the intriguing observation that the same deities, Poseidon and Aphrodite, hardly appear in the Latin inscriptions at all, with Roman imperial and state gods and their priesthoods dominating. We

to worship the two gods who dwelled in and had protected the Corinthia from time immemorial. Admittedly, this diversity of Greek gods is even more prominent in the second-century CE Corinthian coinage,[92] but it is sufficiently represented in the first-century CE coinage for the Greek influence to be clearly seen. Mary E. Hoskins Walbank makes the significant observation that whereas other Roman colonies employ stereotyped foundation types on their coinage (e.g., the legionary eagle between two standards, the furrowing of the *pomerium* before settlement, etc.), Corinth recognized the city's antecedents by emphasizing its Greek cults.[93] The essay of Cavan Concannon in this volume gives us further insight into the negotiated nature of Corinthian religion and identity.

But we must resist the temptation to overstate Greek influence in the first-century Roman colony. Engels notes in regard to the Latin dedications in Corinth that "fully twenty-five of the Latin dedications are to uniquely Roman gods or abstractions."[94] Furthermore, the honorific inscriptions recording civic priesthoods highlight the "Corinthian aristocracy's devotion to (or even obsession with) the imperial cult."[95] The

---

must conclude that these "contradictory perspectives from different types of sources" (ibid.) reveal the versatility of the Corinthian elites as the moneyers and epigraphers of the city—their productions endorsed by the city council and the annually elected chief officials, the duovirs—rendered honor to their recent Roman colonial founders and their Julio-Claudian heirs and, more fundamentally, paid homage to the founding myths and deities associated from time immemorial within the Corinthia region in the Peloponnese.

92. For discussion, see Robert S. Dutch, *The Educated Elite in 1 Corinthians: Education and Community Conflict in Graeco-Roman Context* (London: T&T Clark, 2005), 50–51; Walbank, "Image and Cult," 152–56. Engels (*Roman Corinth*, 71–74) agues for an increasing change in ethnicity at Corinth from Roman colonists to Greek immigrants from mid-first century CE onward. Interestingly, Pliny the Younger (*Ep.* 8.26), writing in the early second century CE, considered the province of Achaia to be "pure and genuine Greece."

93. Walbank, "Image and Cult," 152–53.

94. Engels, *Roman Corinth*, 102; cf. 101.

95. Ibid., 102. Engels sums up the statistics arising from the Corinthian priesthood inscriptions thus: "Of the thirty-one extant references, twenty-eight are in Latin, and of these twenty are to priests of imperial cults. Five are to uniquely Roman gods: Jupiter Capitolinus (4), and Janus (1), and the remainder are to Victoria (1), Saturn (1), and the Genius of the Colony (1). The three Greek references to priesthoods are to Asklepios, Demeter and Kore, and Cronos, and date to the late second or third century."

Julio-Claudian coins of Corinth, in spite of their heavy preponderance of Greek motifs, nonetheless highlight the colonial status of the city and various traditional gods and abstractions of Rome,[96] while paying scrupulous attention to the numismatic portraits and legends in honor of the Julio-Claudian rulers and their family members. To be sure, Greek and Roman deities could be joined together (e.g., the turreted head of Tyche with Roma: *RPC* 1, §1213); alternatively, a Greek deity could be associated with the triumphant Roman ruler himself (e.g., the turreted Tyche crowning Nero: *RPC* 1, §1207). But in these two cases we are witnessing how in the imperial provinces the Greek goddess Tyche was increasingly absorbed or appropriated as a potent iconographic symbol for the Roman goddess Fortuna, underscoring thereby Rome's world domination and the ruler's divine right to rule. In conclusion, as Tucker states, "The Romans in Corinth and throughout the empire, as the process of Romanization continued, adopted various components of Greek culture and provided it with a new Roman context ... for their own civic purposes."[97] Indeed, the total familiarity of Paul's auditors at Corinth with the Roman world and its allurements allowed the apostle Paul, Fred Long exegetically argues in this volume, to critique the inflated claims of the Julio-Claudian rulers to power, honor, and prestige in 2 Corinthians.

1.2.3. Five Methodological Challenges

We are in a very strong position, therefore, as far as the availability of substantial archaeological, inscriptional, numismatic, and iconographic evidence for the reconstruction of a reliable portrait of Roman Corinth. Many New Testament scholars and commentators, to their great credit, have astutely employed this material in recent decades in their discussion of the Corinthian epistles. But there remain methodological and concep-

---

96. Note the following Roman motifs (sometimes linked to imperial family members): the genius of the Roman colony sacrificing (*RPC* 1, §§1189; *RPC* 2, §§109, 124); Victoria standing/standing on globe (*RPC* 1, §§1146, 1148, 1214; *RPC* 2, §110, 122, 145–46, 152, 204); Livia/Pietas (*RPC* 1, §§1155–56, 1160–61); Livia/Salus (*RPC* 1, §§1153, 1159). On the Roman deities at Corinth, see Engels, *Roman Corinth*, 101–2.

97. Tucker, *You Belong to Christ*, 101–2. For a scholar arguing for "hybrid" identity of Corinth in a sophisticated manner, see Concannon, *When You Were Gentiles*, 69–73.

tual challenges in using these diverse genres of evidence. Several examples will suffice.

First, there needs to be a closer study of Corinth in relation to its two well-known harbor ports (Lechaion, Kenchreai), including their related countryside, considering that some of the leaders of the congregation lived and ministered in nearby Kenchreai (Rom 16:1–2).[98] Extensive archaeological excavation of Kenchreai has been undertaken,[99] with several archaeological studies of Lechaion also having been published.[100] The historical and interpretative dividends of this type of study are easily demonstrated. First, the ideological importance of the Lechaion Road as an entry point to and exit from Roman Corinth is emphasized by the imperial iconography of conquest adorning the arch on the route. The fragments of a low relief carving from the area of the arch over the Lechaion Road at the

---

98. David Pettegrew, in his contribution to this volume, draws attention to the third less well-known and smaller port of Corinth, Schoenus. He also notes the importance of study the accompanying countryside of these cities, traditionally overlooked in Corinthian studies.

99. Robert Scranton, Joseph W. Shaw, and Leila Ibrahim, eds., *Topography and Architecture*, vol. 1 of *Kenchreai, Eastern Port of Corinth* (Leiden: Brill, 1978); Leila Ibrahim, *The Panels of Opus Sectile in Glass*, vol. 2 of *Kenchreai, Eastern Port of Corinth* (Leiden: Brill, 1976); Robert L. Hohlfelder, *The Coins*, vol. 3 of *Kenchreai, Eastern Port of Corinth* (Leiden: Brill, 1978); Beverley Adamsheck, *The Pottery*, vol. 4 of *Kenchreai, Eastern Port of Corinth* (Leiden: Brill, 1979); Hector Williams, *The Lamps*, vol. 5 of *Kenchreai, Eastern Port of Corinth* (Leiden: Brill, 1981); Wilma Olch Stern, *Ivory, Bone, and Related Wood Finds*, vol. 6 of *Kenchreai, Eastern Port of Corinth* (Leiden: Brill, 2007). See also John G. Hawthorne, "Cenchreae, Port of Corinth," *Arch* 18.3 (1965): 191–200; Robert Scranton and Edwin S. Ramage, "Investigations at Corinthian Kenchreai," *Hesperia* 36 (1987): 124–86; Christopher A. Faraone and Joseph L. Rife, "A Greek Curse against a Thief from the Koutsongila Cemetery at Roman Kenchreai," *ZPE* 160 (2007): 141–57.

100. Joshua M. Sears Jr., "The Lechaeum Road and the Propylaea at Corinth," *AJA* 6 (1902): 439–54; C. W. J. Eliot and Mary Eliot, "The Lechaion Cemetery Near Corinth," *Hesperia* 37 (1968): 345–67; Charles M. Edwards, "Programmatic Sculpture in Roman Corinth: The Lechaion Road Arch," *AJA* 91 (1987): 485–86; Edwards, "The Arch over the Lechaion Road at Corinth and Its Sculpture," *Hesperia* 63 (1994): 263–308; Richard M. Rothaus, "Lechaion, Western Port of Corinth: A Preliminary Archaeology and History," *OJA* 14.3 (1995): 293–306; Aileen Ajootian, "Simulacra Civitatum at Roman Corinth," *Hesperia* 83 (2014): 315–77. Note, too, the fragmentary inscription of imperial Lechaion (*SEG* 23.170), which, importantly for ancient "association" studies, refers to a possible thiasos of Aphrodite: θιάσου [Ἀφροδίτης(?) - - - - - - - θία]σος Ἀφ[ροδίτης(?) - - - - - - - - Ἀφρο]δίτῃ Ἐπ[ακτίᾳ - - - - - - - - - - - - -].

forum entrance (ca. 117 CE) depicts arms and armor, a trophy tree with a bound barbarian at the base, and human figures involved in the sacrifice of a bull (*immolation boum*).[101] Not only does this demonstrate continuity with the imperial iconography on the earlier first-century arches of Pisidian Antioch and Gaul, but also it illuminates by sharp contrast the countercultural nature of Paul's indebtedness to the "barbarians,"[102] the surprise of God's election of the despised "nothings" of the world, and the multicultural and ethnically diverse composition of body of Christ (Rom 1:14; 13:8–19; Col 3:11; 1 Cor 1:28; 12:13).

Second, the same may be said about the sculpture program adorning the Lechaion Road Basilica, which was an unusual amalgam of heroes, gods, and personifications of the member cities of the Peloponnesian Achaian League.[103] Built in the early 120s CE and likely representing the itinerary of Hadrian's first visit to Greece (124 CE), the sculpture program illustrates the reciprocal engagement of the Roman rulers with their colonies in the eastern Mediterranean basin, along with their aristocratic elites. In the case of the Roman ruler, the traditional Greek heroes and gods are diplomatically endorsed in an urban setting. As far as the colony and the Greek cities, the unreserved and continuing submission of the Peloponnesian Achaian League members to Rome is strongly reaffirmed in the sculpture program. The interplay of between traditional Corinthian identity and colonial allegiance to Rome is therefore spotlighted.

---

101. See Edwards, "Programmatic Sculpture," 486; cf. James R. Harrison, "'More Than Conquerors' (Rom 8:37): Paul's Gospel and the Augustan Triumphal Arches of the Greek East and Latin West," *BurH* 47 (2011): 3–21; Harrison, "Paul's 'Indebtedness' to the Barbarian (Rom 1:14) in Latin West Perspective," *NovT* 55 (2013): 311–48. Gilded statues of Phaethon and Helios topped the Lechaion Road arch (Pausanias, *Descr.* 2.3.2).

102. For a plate of the bound barbarian captive on the relief carving of the Lechaion Road arch, see Edwards, "Arch over the Lechaion Road," 68 pl. 28. The Roman arch at Isthmia, however, did not have any iconography at all. See Timothy E. Gregory and Harrianne Mills, "The Roman Arch at Isthmus," *Hesperia* 53 (1984): 407–55. In the Corinth Museum there are two colossal statues of barbarians, each postdating the New Testament era, as well as a much smaller (first-century CE?) statue of a bound barbarian captive. Respectively, see Papahatzis, *Ancient Corinth*, 92 fig. 22, 93 fig. 25; Harrison, "More Than Conquerors," 4 fig. 2. See, too, the essay of James R. Harrison in this volume devoted to the iconographic perceptions of barbarians in urban centers and Paul's challenge to Roman imperialism in this regard.

103. See Ajootian, "Simulacra Civitatum."

A lead curse tablet found in the Koutsongila cemetery at Roman Kenchreai (*SEG* 57.332: mid-first century CE, or late third century CE) is revealing for Corinthian studies. The tablet is a prayer against a thief who had stolen an item of clothing. The author of the curse summons the chthonic deities for assistance, invoking the supernatural power of Lord Abrasax: "take revenge and completely mow down the son of Caecil(i)us, O Lord Chan Sêreira Abrasax!"[104] Materials such as this throw light on the conceptual background to Paul's warning to the Corinthians and Cenchraeans about being led astray by idols, as they had been in their pre-conversion days (1 Cor 12:2; cf. 10:7, 14–22). Believers who are led by the Spirit of God, Paul avers, can never say "Let Jesus be cursed!": rather they will always confess "Jesus is Lord" (1 Cor 12:3).[105] The fine exegetical essay of Kathy Ehrensperger in this volume provides further insight into Paul's engagement with the spirit world in 1 Corinthians.

Second, the nearby city of Isthmia, some thirteen kilometers east of Roman Corinth, throws light on Corinth's newly restored role as the administrator of the Isthmian games in 43 CE. In view of Isthmia's proximity to Corinth and Paul's use of athletic imagery in 1 Cor 9:24–27,[106] the material culture of Isthmia (archaeology, inscriptions, iconography) must be taken into account when discussing the athletic ideal in Corinth and the competitive nature of its society more generally. Admittedly, we are uncertain whether the games had returned to the sanctuary of Isthmia or were still being held at Corinth at the time of Paul's visit in 51 CE. Nevertheless, Isthmia has been extensively excavated,[107] though the inscriptions remain to be published as a collection.[108] While the connection between

---

104. See Faraone and Rife, "A Greek Curse against a Thief."
105. For a similar text at Corinth, see IKorinthStroud §127.
106. Harrison, "Paul and the Athletic Ideal in Antiquity."
107. On the website of the American School of Classical Studies at Athens, nine ASCSA publications on Isthmia, spanning 1973–2012, may be accessed. See "Isthmia," http://tinyurl.com/SBL4208d. On the excavations of Isthmia undertaken by the University of Chicago, see http://www.lucian.uchicago.edu/blogs/isthmia/. For the Ohio State University excavations at Isthmia, see http://www.isthmia.osu.edu/.
108. See, however, Louis Robert, "Un edifice du sanctuaire de l'Isthme dans une inscription de Corinth," *Hellenica* 1 (1940): 43–53; William R. Biers and Daniel J. Geagan, "A New List of Victors in the Caesarea at Isthmia," *Hesperia* 39 (1970): 79–93; D. J. Geagan, "A Letter of Trajan to a Synod at Isthmia," *Hesperia* 44 (1975): 397–401; Geagan, "The Isthmian Dossier of P. Licinius Priscus Juventianus," *Hesperia* 58 (1989): 349–60; M. Šašel-Kos, "The Latin Inscriptions from Isthmia," *Vestnik (Ljubljana)* 29

the Isthmian games and the agonistic imagery in Paul's letters has been well traversed by commentators, scholars have overlooked the important inscription honoring the orator and ἀγωνοθέτης Nikias of Isthmia, and the light that it throws on the Corinthian absorption with rhetoric in assessing the competence of their leaders. This background is important, because, as I argue later in this volume, the Isthmian games had become a celebrated venue for visiting orators and philosophers, compounding the Corinthian fascination with the ancient rhetorical celebrity circuit, both at an elite and plebeian level.[109] Last, the terracotta lamps of Isthmia, like their Corinthian counterparts, show gladiatorial scenes,[110] confirming their ubiquity in the Peloponnese (above n. 34), along with other Roman motifs such as chariot races at the circus.[111] In sum, the interconnectedness of Corinth's history with the city of Isthmia means that New Testament scholars need to bring its civic, religious, and agonistic ethos into dialogue with the urban culture of Roman Corinth for a fuller understanding of the Corinthian house churches.

Third, as Bitner has recently demonstrated,[112] there needs to be greater sophistication in the use of Corinthian numismatic evidence by New Testament scholars in discussing the Roman ethos of Corinth. Bitner's

---

(1978): 346–53; David R. Jordan and Antony J. S. Spawforth, "A New Document from the Isthmian Games," *Hesperia* 51 (1982): 65–68; David R. Jordan, "Inscribed Lead Tablets from the Games in the Sanctuary of Poseidon on the Isthmus of Corinth," *Hesperia* 63 (1994): 111–26. Professor Matthew Trundle, University of Auckland, is currently collecting the Latin inscriptions of Isthmia in the Roman period for an epigraphic publication. In private correspondence, he said that he hopes to have made completion of the collection by 2015 or thereafter, with a view to its publication.

109. At the museum of Isthmia, there are two ivory plaques from Kenchreai depicting seated men who are probably philosophers: Papahatzis, *Ancient Corinth*, 102–3 figs. 38–39.

110. Oscar Broneer, *Terracotta Lamps*, vol. 2 of *Isthmia: Excavations of the University of Chicago under the Auspices of the American School of Classical Studies at Athens* (Princeton: American School of Classical Studies at Athens, 1977), §§2529–30, 2532–33.

111. Ibid., §§2735–85.

112. Bradley J. Bitner, "Coinage and Colonial Identity: Corinthian Numismatics and the Corinthian Correspondence," in Harrison and Welborn, *Methodological Considerations*, 151–87. More generally, Harikleia Papageorgiadou-Bani, *The Numismatic Iconography of the Roman Colonies in Greece: Local Spirit and the Expression of Imperial Policy*, Meletemata 39 (Athens: Institouton Hellenikes kai Romaikes Archaiotetos Ethnikon Hidryma Ereunon, 2004).

insightful essay is exemplary in its nuanced articulation of the more careful methodology required for the responsible use of numismatic evidence. He interacts with Andrew Clarke, Jorunn Økland, and Robert Dutch in this regard,[113] appreciating their substantial contributions to Corinthian studies through their use of the Roman provincial numismatic evidence, yet urging greater caution, sophistication, and nuance on the part of each New Testament researcher.

Bitner's comments regarding the handling of the numismatic evidence by Clarke and Økland will be adequate for our purposes. In discussing Roman patterns of leadership over against Paul's alternative construct in 1 Cor 1–4, Clarke did not take into account the patterns of magistracy acquisition reflected in the coinage of the Corinthian elites and the understanding of colonial identity promoted therein. This additional interpretative dimension, arising from the numismatic evidence, would have strengthened Clarke's discussion.[114] Again, Økland missed out on the subtlety of architectural elements in the iconography of the coinage pertinent to her discussion of Corinthian women, sacred space, and Paul's construction of gender roles in the Corinthian epistles. Is the architecture depicted on the coin an actual representation of the monument, which, therefore, can be legitimately invoked as "photographic" evidence for the period under discussion? Or is the image more ideological in function, representing in idealized form either an anniversary or an important event associated with or symbolized by the monument?[115] In this case, we are not necessarily dealing with an accurate iconographic representation on the coin. In other words, in light of Bitner's masterly analysis of the scholarly use of numismatic evidence in Corinthian studies, New Testament researchers have to spend time learning the methodological subtleties of the genres of evidence they are dealing with or at the very least draw on sophisticated classical scholarship that does.

Fourth, surprisingly, there is still insufficient attention paid to the inscriptional evidence of Corinth by some New Testament scholars. The scarcity of inscriptions in Jerome Murphy-O'Connor's extensive collection of literary texts on St. Paul's Corinth testifies to the continuing schol-

---

113. Clarke, *Secular and Christian Leadership*; Jorunn Økland, *Women in Their Place: Paul and the Corinthian Discourse of Gender and Sanctuary Space* (London: T&T Clark, 2004); Dutch, *Educated Elite in 1 Corinthians*.

114. Bitner, "Coinage and Colonial Identity," 157, 176–82.

115. Ibid., 157–58, 182–83.

arly blind spot in this regard.[116] Gratifyingly, the archaeological evidence is included in the collection,[117] but the evidential base of the collection is overwhelmingly literary. The "mirror" of the Greek and Latin inscriptions, which reflects the ethos of Corinth in miniature, politically, socially, and religiously, is inexplicably bypassed. However, a renewed study of the inscriptions always produces worthwhile dividends. An intriguing and important sample of the light that can be thrown on the social composition of the Corinthian church and the internal conflicts that it inevitably generated can be found in L. L. Welborn's discussion of the Corinthian inscriptions in relation to his (hypothetical) identification of the "wrongdoer" in 2 Corinthians.[118]

Fifth, there is always a danger in overstating the contribution that inscriptions make in uncovering the urban life of antiquity. Inscriptions are often (1) fragmentary, (2) heavily restored by their editors due to damage to the text,[119] (3) relocated from what was their original position in antiquity (or, worse, their initial location not recorded at the time of their discovery), (4) deliberately erased by invidious rivals in antiquity, and (5) often without precise chronological markers, other than the dates assigned by epigraphists on stylistic grounds.[120] Moreover, their accompanying iconography is sometimes removed, badly weathered, or broken. Furthermore, the inscriptions mostly provide an elitist perspective regarding the urban life of the city, bypassing, as I have noted, the concerns of the marginalized and the poor. This may pose unresolved interpretative problems for scholars. It can also prompt unwise exegetical decisions if New Testament interpreters are not sufficiently cautious.

A recently published bilingual inscription from Corinth on a stela, comprising four fragmentary Latin lines and two in Greek, illustrates the point I am making.[121] Unfortunately, the name of the dedicant is not preserved, and although the inscription was found in Corinth, there is no

---

116. See n. 68 above.

117. For the archaeological evidence employed, see Murphy-O'Connor, *St. Paul's Corinth*, part 3.

118. Welborn, *An End to Enmity*, 301–34.

119. Ernst Badian, "History from 'Square Brackets,'" *ZPE* 79 (1989): 59–70.

120. See the erasure in the inscription of the orator Nikias of Isthmia, discussed in my essay ("Paul and the *Agōnothetai* at Corinth: Engaging the Civic Values of Antiquity") in this volume.

121. Michael D. Dixon, "A New Latin and Greek Inscription from Corinth," *Hesperia* 69 (2000): 335–42.

guarantee that this was the stela's initial location: it may have been moved there subsequently.[122] The fragmentary nature of the inscription does not allow us to assert that this is a "true bilingual inscription," where the Greek provides a literal translation of the Latin: we cannot even conclude that the inscribing of the Greek text was contemporaneous with the Latin.[123] The date of the inscription, given that there are no chronological markers in the text, is assigned a Hadrianic or post-Hadrianic date in the second century CE on stylistic grounds.[124] But this is too early to be associated with the extensive building programs of the later second-century Corinthian and Isthmian benefactor P. Licinius Priscus Iuventianus.[125]

In terms of the text itself, a [SAC]ERDOS [P]ROSPERINAE (priest of Prosperina) is mentioned, as well as "a stoa and temple of Pluto" ([στο] ὰν καὶ ναὸν Πλου[τῶνος - -]), although the text is restored to some extent in each case. There are references made to MARMOREA (architectural elements or decorations, such as revetments),[126] as well as to [- - τὰ] προσκοσμήματα (adornments in buildings).[127] But whether the original monument was located at Corinth or at the Isthmian sanctuary of Poseidon is impossible to determine. Dixon lays out the alternatives: "The monuments mentioned on this new inscription ... raise various other possibilities: 1) that the stone refers to monuments at Isthmia and was originally set up there; 2) that the stone refers to monuments at Isthmia, but was originally set up at Corinth; or 3) the stone refers to buildings at Corinth and was originally set up there."[128]

Dixon's conclusion is frustrating for the historian and the Corinthian exegete. Here we have our first reference, so far as we can tell, to the worship of Pluto at its temple and stoa in the Corinthiaka,[129] but we cannot tell whether it was located at Isthmia or at Corinth. It might be possible to posit on the basis of this text that the cultic worship of Pluto (the earlier god Hades) and Prosperina (the Roman equivalent of Persephone) existed in first-century CE Roman Corinth. Were the god and goddess

---

122. Ibid., 341.
123. Ibid., 338.
124. Ibid., 339.
125. Ibid., 339–41; Geagan, "Isthmian Dossier."
126. Dixon, "New Latin and Greek Inscription," 337.
127. Ibid., 339.
128. Ibid., 341.
129. Ibid., 341.

INTRODUCTION: THE URBAN LIFE OF ROMAN CORINTH

of the underworld shaping first-century Corinthian attitudes to death and burial rituals, with Prosperina, as a life-death-rebirth deity, offering annual renewal to the city and its inhabitants?

Richard E. DeMaris has argued that evidence for the worship of Demeter and Kore at Roman Isthmia—along with their worship at the Acrocorinth in the same period—also underscores the increasing importance of Pluto and Persephone in the Roman Corinthiaka.[130] At the sanctuary of Demeter and Kore at the Acrocorinth, the representation of Persephone on a Corinthian vase painting (475–450 BCE)[131] and, purportedly, an inscriptional reference to a priestess of Kore/Persephone on a second-century CE mosaic[132] have been found. In another inscription, P. Licinius Priscus Iuventianus, mentioned above, is later said to have established a sanctuary to Pluto, a rarity in the ancient world, in a glen at Isthmia, although no supporting archaeological evidence has been unearthed to ratify this.[133] In this culture of meticulous attention to the underworld and its deities, DeMaris postulates that we perhaps see here the origin of the practice of some Corinthian believers being vicariously baptized on behalf of the dead (1 Cor 15:29: ὑπὲρ τῶν νεκρῶν), a custom mentioned but not endorsed by Paul.[134]

While this conclusion is possible, we should be careful not to argue "hypothesis by hypothesis" in terms of the inscriptions. As we have seen, our epigraphic evidence regarding Persephone at the sanctuary of Kore and Demeter at the Acrocorinth comes from the second century CE and not from first-century Corinth. Even the identification of the "priestess of Neotera" (below, n. 131) with Kore/Perspehone is disputable, with Egyptologists considering it to be a reference to Nephthys, the younger sister of Isis.[135] In terms of Corinth itself, this leaves us with the Corinthian vase-painting evidence from the classical period and a hero relief from

---

130. Richard E. DeMaris, "Demeter in Roman Corinth," *Numen* 42 (1995): 105–17.

131. IKorinthStroud §28.

132. IKorinthStroud §14. The inscription states: "Octavius Agathopous, neokoros, had the mosaic installed when Chara was priestess of Neotera [Νεωτέρας]." Stroud (IKorinthStroud, 15), on the basis of epigraphic and literary parallels from Athens and Eleusis, proposes that the epithet νεωτέρα refers to Kore/Persephone.

133. Geagan, "Isthmian Dossier," 350, 353; cf. Broneer, "Official Rescript."

134. DeMaris, "Demeter in Roman Corinth," 114.

135. IKorinthStroud, 15.

the Hellenistic age,[136] but this is hardly decisive proof for Corinth's preoccupation with underworld deities in the first century CE. The two inscriptional references to sanctuaries to Pluto, one definitely from Isthmia and the other possibly from Isthmia or Corinth, are impressive, but they range in date from the early to late second century CE. At best, we can say that interest in funerary and chthonic worship rituals increased in the Roman Corinthiaka from the second century CE onward, but it remains a moot point whether this preoccupation with the underworld began in the first century CE. In dealing with the inscriptions, therefore, clear chronological and location markers place our arguments on a firm basis: but without such markers we are vulnerable to greater subjectivity of judgment. That does not automatically rule out our judgments: but we have to qualify our conclusions with appropriate caveats and embrace an attitude of cautious skepticism in handling the epigraphic evidence.

2. Conclusion

This essay has attempted to cover the rise, fall, and rise again of Corinth through to the early Flavian period in the first century CE. The sweep of evidence and its diverse genres is enormous, demanding sophisticated skills on the part of the New Testament exegete. Thankfully, in contrast to many other areas of New Testament exegesis, commentators and historians are bringing this evidence into dialogue with the Corinthian epistles with richness of insight in terms of the exegetical dividends achieved and increasingly contributing to our understanding of an important site for the expansion of early Christianity. The essays in this volume are further evidence of this rewarding engagement.

Bibliography

Adams, Edward. "Placing the Corinthian Common Meal." Pages 22–37 in *Text, Image, and Christians in the Graeco-Roman World: A Festschrift in Honor of David Lee Balch*. Edited by Aliou Cissé Niang and Carolyn Osiek. PTMS 176. Eugene: Wipf & Stock, 2012.

---

136. An early third-century BCE relief, found in the Corinthian agora, shows an underworld male deity reclining and wearing the *polos* of Hades/Pluto. See Oscar Broneer, "Hero Cults in the Corinthian Agora," *Hesperia* 11 (1942): 131 (fig. 1), 133.

Adamsheck, Beverley. *The Pottery*. Vol. 4 of *Kenchreai, Eastern Port of Corinth*. Leiden: Brill, 1979.

Ajootian, Aileen. "A Roman Table Support at Ancient Corinth." *Hesperia* 69 (2000): 487–507.

———. "Simulacra Civitatum at Roman Corinth," *Hesperia* 83 (2014): 315–77.

Amandry, Michel. *Le Monnayage des duovirs Corinthiens*. BCHSup 15. Athens: École française d'Athènes; Paris: de Boccard, 1988.

Andrews, Antony. *The Greek Tyrants*. London: Hutchinson, 1974.

Arafat, K. W. *Pausanias' Greece: Ancient Artists and Roman Rulers*. Cambridge: Cambridge University Press, 1996.

Athenaeus. *The Deipnosophists*. Translated by Charles Burton Gulick. 7 vols. LCL. London: Heinemann, 1927–1941.

Badian, Ernst. "History from 'Square Brackets.'" *ZPE* 79 (1989): 59–70.

Baranowski, Donald Walter. *Polybius and Roman Imperialism*. London: Bloomsbury, 2011.

Bhabha, Homi K. *The Location of Culture*. New York: Routledge, 2004.

Biers, Jane C. "*Lavari est vivere*: Baths in Roman Corinth." Pages 303–19 in *Corinth, the Centenary 1896–1996*. Edited by Charles K. Williams II and Nancy Bookidis. Vol. 20 of *Corinth: Results of Excavations Conducted by the American School of Classical Studies at Athens*. Athens: American School of Classical Studies at Athens, 2003.

Biers, William R., and Daniel J. Geagan. "A New List of Victors in the Caesarea at Isthmia." *Hesperia* 39 (1970): 79–93.

Bitner, Bradley J. "Coinage and Colonial Identity: Corinthian Numismatics and the Corinthian Correspondence." Pages 151–87 in *Methodological Foundations*. Edited by James R. Harrison and L. L. Welborn. WGRWSup 7. Vol. 1 of *The First Urban Churches*. Atlanta: SBL Press, 2015.

———. *Paul's Political Strategy in 1 Corinthians 1–4: Constitution and Covenant*. SNTSMS 163; Cambridge: Cambridge University Press, 2015.

Bookidis, Nancy, and Ronald S. Stroud. "Apollo and the Archaic Temple at Corinth." *Hesperia* 73 (2003): 401–26.

Broneer, Oscar. "The Apostle Paul and the Isthmian Games." *BA* 25 (1962): 2–31.

———. "Hero Cults in the Corinthian Agora." *Hesperia* 11 (1942): 128–61.

———. "The Isthmian Victory Crown." *AJA* 66 (1962): 259–63.

———. "An Official Rescript from Corinth." *Hesperia* 8 (1939): 181–90.

———. *Terracotta Lamps*. Vol. 2 of *Isthmia: Excavations of the University of*

Chicago under the Auspices of the American School of Classical Studies at Athens. Princeton: American School of Classical Studies at Athens, 1977.

———. *Terracotta Lamps*. Vol. 4.2 of *Corinth: Results of Excavations Conducted by the American School of Classical Studies at Athens*. Cambridge: Harvard University Press, 1930.

Bruneau, Philippe. "Lampes corinthiennes." *BCH* 95 (1971): 437–501.

Burnett, Andrew, Michel Amandry, and Ian Carradice. *From Vespasian to Domitian (AD 69–96)*. Vol. 2 of *Roman Provincial Coinage*. London: British Museum Press; Paris: Bibliothèque Nationale, 1999.

Burnett, Andrew, Michel Amandry, and Pere Pau Ripollés. *From the Death of Caesar to the Death of Vitellius (44 BC–AD 69)*. Vol. 1 of *Roman Provincial Coinage*. London: British Museum Press; Paris: Bibliothèque Nationale, 1992. Revised 2006.

Camia, F., and Maria Kantiréa. "The Imperial Cult in the Peloponnese." Pages 375–406 in *Society, Economy and Culture under the Roman Empire: Continuity and Innovation*. Vol. 3 of *Roman Peloponnese*. Edited by A. D. Rizakis and C. E. Lepenioti. Athens: National Hellenic Research Foundation, 2010.

Carter, Michael. "A *Doctor Secutorum* and the *Retiarius Draukos* from Corinth." *ZPE* 12 (1999): 262–68.

Chow, John K. *Patronage and Power: A Study of Social Networks in Corinth*. JSNTSup 75; Sheffield: JSOT, 1992.

Clarke, Andrew D. *Secular and Christian Leadership in Corinth: A Socio-historical and Exegetical Study of 1 Corinthians 1–6*. Leiden: Brill, 1993.

Concannon, Cavan W. *"When You Were Gentiles": Specters of Ethnicity in Roman Corinth and Paul's Corinthian Correspondence*. Synkrisis: Comparative Approaches to Early Christianity in Greco-Roman Culture. New Haven: Yale University Press, 2014.

DeMaris, Richard E. "Demeter in Roman Corinth." *Numen* 42 (1995): 105–17.

Dixon, Michael D. *Late Classical and Early Hellenistic Corinth*. New York: Routledge, 2014.

———. "A New Latin and Greek Inscription from Corinth." *Hesperia* 69 (2000): 335–42.

Dutch, Robert S. *The Educated Elite in 1 Corinthians: Education and Community Conflict in Graeco-Roman Context*. London: T&T Clark, 2005.

Edwards, Charles M. "The Arch over the Lechaion Road at Corinth and Its Sculpture." *Hesperia* 63 (1994): 263–308.

———. "Programmatic Sculpture in Roman Corinth: The Lechaion Road Arch." *AJA* 91 (1987): 485–86.

Eliot, C. W. J., and Mary Eliot. "The Lechaion Cemetery Near Corinth." *Hesperia* 37 (1968): 345–67.

Engels, Donald W. *Roman Corinth: An Alternative Model for the Classical City.* Chicago: University of Chicago Press, 1990.

Fantin, Joseph D. *The Lord of the Entire World: Lord Jesus, a Challenge to Lord Caesar?* NTM 31. Sheffield: Sheffield Phoenix, 2011.

Faraone, Christopher A., and Joseph L. Rife. "A Greek Curse against a Thief from the Koutsongila Cemetery at Roman Kenchreai." *ZPE* 160 (2007): 141–57.

Fotopoulos, John. *Food Offered to Idols in Roman Corinth: A Social-Rhetorical Reconstruction of 1 Corinthians 8:1–11:1.* WUNT 2/151. Tübingen: Mohr Siebeck, 2003.

Geagan, Daniel J. "The Isthmian Dossier of P. Licinius Priscus Juventianus." *Hesperia* 58 (1989): 349–60.

———. "A Letter of Trajan to a Synod at Isthmia." *Hesperia* 44 (1975): 397–401.

Gebhard, Elizabeth R. "The Isthmian Games and the Sanctuary of Poseidon in the Early Empire." Pages 78–94 in *The Corinthia in the Roman Period.* Edited by Timothy E. Gregory. JRASup 8. Ann Arbor: Journal of Roman Archaeology, 1993.

———. "Rites for Melikertes-Palaimon in the Early Roman Corinthia." Pages 165–203 in *Urban Religion in Roman Corinth: Interdisciplinary Approaches.* Edited by Daniel N. Schowalter and Steven J. Friesen. Cambridge: Harvard University Press, 2005.

———. "The Sanctuary of Poseidon on the Isthmus of Corinth and the Isthmian Games." Pages 82–88 in *Mind and Body: Athletic Contests in Ancient Greece.* Edited by Olga Tzachou-Alexandri. Athens: Ministry of Culture, National Hellenic Committee ICOM, 1989.

Gebhard, Elizabeth R., and Matthew W. Dickie. "The View from the Isthmus, ca. 200 BC–44 BC." Pages 261–78 in *Corinth, the Centenary 1896–1996.* Edited by Charles K. Williams II and Nancy Bookidis. Vol. 20 of *Corinth: Results of Excavations Conducted by the American School of Classical Studies at Athens.* Athens: American School of Classical Studies at Athens, 2003.

Gill, D. W. J. "The Meat-Market at Corinth (1 Corinthians 10:25)." *TynBul* 43.2 (1992): 389–93.
Grant, Robert M. *Paul in the Roman World: The Conflict at Corinth*. Louisville: Westminster John Knox, 2001.
Gregory, Timothy E. and Harrianne Mills. "The Roman Arch at Isthmia." *Hesperia* 53 (1984): 407–55.
Hammond, N. G. L. "The Peloponnese." Pages 696–744 in *The Expansion of the Greek World, Eighth to the Sixth Centuries BC*. Vol. 3.3 of *The Cambridge Ancient History*. Edited by John Boardman and N. G. L. Hammond. 2nd ed. Cambridge: Cambridge University Press, 1982.
Harrison, James R. "'More Than Conquerors' (Rom 8:37): Paul's Gospel and the Augustan Triumphal Arches of the Greek East and Latin West." *BurH* 47 (2011): 3–21.
———. "Paul and the Athletic Ideal in Antiquity: A Case Study in Wrestling with Word and Image." Pages 81–109 in *Paul's World*. Edited by Stanley E. Porter. Pauline Studies 4. Leiden: Brill, 2007.
———. *Paul and the Imperial Authorities at Thessalonica and Rome: A Study in the Conflict of Ideology*. WUNT 273. Tübingen: Mohr Siebeck, 2011.
———. "Paul's 'Indebtedness' to the Barbarian (Rom 1:14) in Latin West Perspective." *NovT* 55 (2013): 311–48.
Hawthorne, John G. "Cenchreae, Port of Corinth." *Arch* 18.3 (1965): 191–200.
Hohlfelder, Robert L. *The Coins*. Vol. 3 of *Kenchreai, Eastern Port of Corinth*. Leiden: Brill, 1978.
Hopper, Robert John. "Ancient Corinth." *GR* 2.1 (1955): 2–15.
Horrell, David G. *The Social Ethos of the Corinthian Correspondence: Interests and Ideology from 1 Corinthians to 1 Clement*. Edinburgh: T&T Clark, 1996.
Horrell David G., and Edward Adams. "The Scholarly Quest for Paul's Church at Corinth: A Critical Survey." Pages 1–49 in *Christianity at Corinth: The Quest for the Pauline Church*. Edited by David G. Horrell and Edward Adams. Louisville: Westminster John Knox, 2004.
Ibrahim, Leila. *The Panels of Opus Sectile in Glass*. Vol. 2 of *Kenchreai, Eastern Port of Corinth*. Leiden: Brill, 1976.
Johnson, Allan Chester, Paul Robinson Coleman-Norton, and Frank Card Bourne. *Ancient Roman Statutes*. Austin: University of Texas Press, 1961.
Johnson, F. P. "The Imperial Portraits at Corinth." *AJA* 30 (1926): 158–76.

Jordan, David R. "Inscribed Lead Tablets from the Games in the Sanctuary of Poseidon." *Hesperia* 63 (1994): 111–26.
Jordan, David R., and Antony J. S. Spawforth. "A New Document from the Isthmian Games." *Hesperia* 51 (1982): 65–68.
Kajava, Mika. "When Did the Isthmian Games Return to the Isthmus? Rereading 'Corinth' 8.3.153." *Classical Philology* 97 (2002): 168–78.
Kantiréa, Maria. *Les Dieux et les Dieux Auguste. Le culte imperial en Grèce sous les Julio-claudiens et les Flaviens. Études épigraphiques et archéologiques.* Meletemata 50. Athens: Centre de recherche de l'Antiquité grecque et romaine, 2007.
Kardara, Chrysoula. "Dyeing and Weaving Works at Isthmia." *AJA* 65 (1961): 261–66.
Kent, John Harvey. *The Inscriptions, 1926–1950*. Vol. 8.3 of *Corinth: Results of Excavations Conducted by the American School of Classical Studies at Athens*. Princeton: American School of Classical Studies at Athens, 1966.
Kraay, Colin M. *Archaic and Classical Greek Coins*. London: Methuen, 1976.
Lavezzi, John C. "Prehistoric Investigations at Corinth." *Hesperia* 47 (1978): 402–51.
Leaf, Walter. "Corinth in Prehistoric Times." *AJA* 27 (1923): 151–56.
Losch, Richard R. *The Uttermost Part of the Earth: A Guide to Places in the Bible*. Grand Rapids: Eerdmans, 2005.
Madsen, Jesper Majbom. "The Romanization of the Greek Elite in Achaia, Asia and Bithynia: Greek Resistance or Regional Discrepancies?" *Orbis Terrarum* 8 (2006): 87–113.
McGlew, James F. *Tyranny and Political Culture in Ancient Greece*. Ithaca, NY: Cornell University Press, 1993.
Meijer, Fik. *The History of Seafaring in the Classical World*. 1986. Repr., New York: Routledge, 2014.
Meritt, Benjamin Dean. *Greek Inscriptions, 1896–1927*. Vol. 8.1 of *Corinth: Results of Excavations Conducted by the American School of Classical Studies at Athens*. Cambridge: American School of Classical Studies at Athens, 1931.
Millis, Benjamin W. "'Miserable Huts' in Post-146 BC Corinth." *Hesperia* 75 (2006): 387–404.
———. "The Social and Ethnic Origins of the Colonists in Early Roman Corinth." Pages 13–35 in *Corinth in Context: Comparative Studies on*

Religion and Society. Edited by Steven J. Friesen, Daniel N. Schowalter, and James C. Walters. Leiden: Brill, 2010.

Mitchell, Alan C. "Rich and Poor in the Courts of Corinth: Litigiousness and Status in 1 Corinthians 6:1–11." *NTS* 39 (1993): 562–86.

Murphy-O'Connor, Jerome. "Corinthian Bronze." *RB* 90 (1982): 23–26.

———. *St. Paul's Corinth: Texts and Archaeology*. 1983. Repr., Collegeville, MN: Liturgical Press, 2002.

Nabers, Ned. "A Note on Corinth VIII, 2, 125." *AJA* 73 (1975): 73–74.

Økland, Jorunn. *Women in Their Place: Paul and the Corinthian Discourse of Gender and Sanctuary Space*. London: T&T Clark, 2004.

Oost, Stewart Irvin. "Cypselus the Bacchiad." *CP* 67 (1972): 10–30.

Orelli, Johann Kaspar von. *Inscriptionum Latinarum Selectarum*. 2 vols. Turici: Orelli, Fuessli, 1828.

Papageorgiadou-Bani, Harikleia. *The Numismatic Iconography of the Roman Colonies in Greece: Local Spirit and the Expression of Imperial Policy*. Meletemata 39. Athens: Institouton Hellenikes kai Romaikes Archaiotetos Ethnikon Hidryma Ereunon, 2004.

Papahatzis, Nicos. *Ancient Corinth: The Museums of Corinth, Isthmia and Sicyon*. Athens: Ekdotike Athenon, 1994.

Pawlak, Marcin L. "Corinth after 44 BC: Ethnical and Cultural Changes," *Electrum* 20 (2013): 143–62.

Pemberton, Elizabeth G. "Classical and Hellenistic Pottery from Corinth and Its Athenian Connections." Pages 167–79 in *Corinth, the Centenary 1896–1996*. Edited by Charles K. Williams II and Nancy Bookidis. Vol. 20 of *Corinth: Results of Excavations Conducted by the American School of Classical Studies at Athens*. Athens: American School of Classical Studies at Athens, 2003.

———. "Vase Painting in Ancient Corinth." *Arch* 31.6 (1978): 27–33.

Pettegrew, David K. "The *Diolkos* of Corinth." *AJA* 115 (2011): 549–74.

Pomeroy, Sarah B. *Ancient Greece: A Political, Social, and Cultural History*. Oxford: Oxford University Press, 2011.

Rice, Joshua. *Paul and Patronage: The Dynamics of Power in 1 Corinthians*. Eugene, OR: Pickwick, 2013.

Risser, Martha K. "Corinthian Archaic and Classical Pottery: The Local Style." Pages 157–65 in *Corinth, the Centenary 1896–1996*. Edited by Charles K. Williams II and Nancy Bookidis. Vol. 20 of *Corinth: Results of Excavations Conducted by the American School of Classical Studies at Athens*. Athens: American School of Classical Studies at Athens, 2003.

———. *Corinthian Conventionalizing Pottery*. Athens: American School of Classical Studies at Athens, 2001.

Robert, Louis. "Un edifice du sanctuaire de l'Isthme dans une inscription de Corinth." *Hell* 1 (1940): 43–53.

———. *Les gladiateurs dans l'orient grec*. Amsterdam: Hakkert, 1971.

Robertson, Noel. "The Dorian Migration and Corinthian Ritual." *CP* 75 (1980): 1–22.

Robinson, Betsey A. "'Good Luck' from Corinth: A Mosaic of Allegory, Athletics, and City Identity." *AJA* 116 (2012): 105–32.

Robinson, Henry S. "A Monument of Roma at Corinth." *Hesperia* 43 (1974): 470–84.

Roebuck, Mary Campbell. "Archaic Architectural Terracottas from Corinth." *Hesperia* 59 (1972): 47–63.

———. "Architectural Terracottas from Classical and Hellenistic Corinth." *Hesperia Supplement* 27 (1994): 39–52.

Romano, David Gilman. "City Planning, Centuriation, and Land Division in Roman Corinth: Colonia Laus Iulia Corinthiensis and Colonia Iulia Flavia Augusta Corinthiensis." Pages 279–302 in *Corinth, the Centenary 1896–1996*. Edited by Charles K. Williams II and Nancy Bookidis. Vol. 20 of *Corinth: Results of Excavations Conducted by the American School of Classical Studies at Athens*. Athens: American School of Classical Studies at Athens, 2003.

———. "A Roman Circus in Corinth." *Hesperia* 74 (2005): 585–611.

———. "Urban and Rural Planning in Roman Corinth." Pages 25–59 in *Urban Religion in Roman Corinth: Interdisciplinary Approaches*. Edited by Daniel N. Schowalter and Steven J. Friesen. Cambridge: Harvard University Press, 2005.

Romano, Irene B. "A Hellenistic Deposit from Corinth: Evidence for Interim Period Activity (146–44 B.C.)." *Hesperia* 63 (1994): 57–104.

Rothaus, Richard M. "Lechaion, Western Port of Corinth: A Preliminary Archaeology and History." *OJA* 14.3 (1995): 293–306.

Rutter, Jeremy. "The Last Mycenaeans at Corinth." *Hesperia* 48 (1979): 348–92.

Salmon, J. B. *Wealthy Corinth: A History of the City to 338 BC*. Oxford: Clarendon, 1984.

Šašel Kos, Marjeta. "A Latin Epitaph of a Roman Legionary from Corinth." *JRS* 68 (1978): 22–25.

———. "The Latin Inscriptions from Isthmia." *Vestnik (Ljubljana)* 29 (1978): 346–53.

Scotton, Paul D. "A New Fragment of an Inscription from the Julian Basilica at Roman Corinth." *Hesperia* 74 (2005): 95–100.

Scranton, Robert, and Edwin S. Ramage. "Investigations at Corinthian Kenchreai." *Hesperia* 36 (1987): 124–86.

Scranton, Robert, Joseph W. Shaw, and Leila Ibrahim. *Topography and Architecture*. Vol. 1 of *Kenchreai, Eastern Port of Corinth*. Leiden: Brill, 1978.

Sealey, Raphael. *A History of the Greek States, 700–338 BC*. Berkeley: University of California Press, 1976.

Sears, Joshua M., Jr. "The Lechaeum Road and the Propylaea at Corinth." *AJA* 6 (1902): 439–54.

Shear, Theodore Leslie. "Excavations at Corinth in 1925." *AJA* 29 (1925): 381–97.

———. "Excavations in the Theatre District of Corinth in 1926." *AJA* 30 (1926): 444–63.

Shewan, A. "Mycenaean Corinth." *CR* 38 (1924): 65–68.

Shuckburgh, Evelyn S. *A Short History of the Greeks from the Earliest Times to BC 146*. Cambridge: Cambridge University Press, 1901.

Souza, Philip de. "War at Sea." Pages 369–94 in *The Oxford Book of Warfare in the Classical World*. Edited by Brian Campbell and Lawrence A. Tritle. Oxford: Oxford University Press, 2013.

Spawforth, Antony J. S. "Corinth, Argos and the Imperial Cult: Pseudo-Julian, Letters 198." *Hesperia* 63 (1994): 211–32.

———. *Greece and the Augustan Cultural Revolution*. Cambridge: Cambridge University Press, 2011.

———. "Roman Corinth: The Formation of a Colonial Elite." Pages 167–82 in *Roman Onomastic in the Greek East: Social and Political Aspects. Proceedings of the International Colloquium on Roman Onomastics, Athens, 7–9 September 1993*. Edited by A. D. Rizakis. Meletemata 21. Athens: Institouton Hellenikes kai Romaikes Archaiotetos Ethnikon Hidryma Ereunon, 1996.

Spitzer, Doreen C. "Roman Relief Bowls from Corinth." *Hesperia* 11 (1942): 162–92.

Stansbury, Harry A. "Corinthian Honor, Corinthian Conflict: A Social History of Early Roman Corinth and Its Pauline Community." PhD diss., University of California Irvine, 1991.

Stern, Wilma Olch. *Ivory, Bone, and Related Wood Finds*. Vol. 6 of *Kenchreai, Eastern Port of Corinth*. Leiden: Brill, 2007.

Stickler, Timo. *Korinth und seine Kolonien: Die Stadt am Isthmus im Mächtegefüge des klassischen Griechenland*. Berlin: Akademie, 2010.
Stillwell, Agnes N. "Eighth Century BC Inscriptions from Corinth." *AJA* 37 (1933): 605–10.
Stroud, Ronald S. *The Sanctuary of Demeter and Kore: The Inscriptions*. Vol. 18.6 of *Corinth: Results of Excavations Conducted by the American School of Classical Studies at Athens*. Princeton: American School of Classical Studies at Athens, 2013.
Swift, Emerson Howland. "A Group of Roman Imperial Portraits at Corinth." *AJA* 25 (1921): 142–59.
———. "A Group of Roman Imperial Portraits at Corinth. II. Tiberius." *AJA* 25 (1921): 248–65.
———. "A Group of Roman Imperial Portraits at Corinth. III. Gaius and Lucius Caesar." *AJA* 25 (1921): 337–63.
———. "A Group of Roman Imperial Portraits at Corinth. IV. The Four Torsos." *AJA* 26 (1922): 131–47.
Thiselton, Anthony C. *The First Epistle to the Corinthians: A Commentary on the Greek Text*. NIGTC. Grand Rapids: Eerdmans, 2000.
Trebilco, Paul. "Epigraphy and the Study of Polis and Ekklēsia in the Greco-Roman World." Pages 89–109 in *Methodological Foundations*. Edited by James R. Harrison and L. L. Welborn. Vol. 1 of *The First Urban Churches*. Atlanta: SBL Press, 2015.
Tucker, J. Brian. *You Belong to Christ: Paul and the Formation of Social Identity in 1 Corinthians 1–4*. Eugene, OR: Pickwick, 2010.
Unwin, James R. "'Thrown Down but Not Destroyed': Paul's Use of a Spectacle Metaphor in 2 Corinthians 4:7–15." *NovT*, forthcoming.
Walbank, Mary E. Hoskins. "Aspects of Corinthian Coinage in the Late First and Early Second Centuries AD." Pages 337–50 in *Corinth, the Centenary 1896–1996*. Edited by Charles K. Williams II and Nancy Bookidis. Vol. 20 of *Corinth: Results of Excavations Conducted by the American School of Classical Studies at Athens*. Athens: American School of Classical Studies at Athens, 2003.
———. "The Cults of Roman Corinth: Public Rituals and Personal Belief." Pages 357–74 in *Society, Economy and Culture under the Roman Empire: Continuity and Innovation*. Vol. 3 of *Roman Peloponnese*. Edited by A. D. Rizakis and C. E. Lepenioti. Athens: National Hellenic Research Foundation, 2010.
———. "Evidence for the Imperial Cult in Julio-Claudian Corinth." Pages

201–14 in *Subject and Ruler: The Cult of the Ruling Power in Classical Antiquity*. Edited by Alastair Small. JRASup 17. Ann Arbor: Journal of Roman Archaeology, 1993.

———. "The Foundation and Planning of Early Roman Corinth." *JRA* 10 (1997): 95–130.

———. "Image and Cult: The Coinage of Roman Corinth." Pages 151–98 in *Corinth in Context: Comparative Studies on Religion and Society*. Edited by Steven J. Friesen, Daniel N. Schowalter, and James C. Walters. Leiden: Brill, 2011.

———. "Pausanias, Octavia and Temple E at Corinth." *ABSA* 84 (1989): 369–84.

———. "What's in a Name? Corinth under the Flavians." *ZPE* 139 (2002): 251–64.

Waterfield, Robin. *Taken at the Flood: The Roman Conquest*. Oxford: Oxford University Press, 2014.

Weinberg, Saul S. "Remains from Prehistoric Corinth." *Hesperia* 6 (1937): 487–524.

Weiss, Alexander. *Soziale Elite und Christentum: Studien zu ordo-Angehörigen unter den frühen Christen*. Berlin: de Gruyter, 2015.

Welborn, L. L. *An End to Enmity: Paul and the "Wrongdoer" of Second Corinthians*. BZNW 185. Berlin: de Gruyter, 2011.

Welch, Katherine E. "Negotiating Roman Spectacle Architecture in the Greek World: Athens and Corinth." Pages 125–45 in *The Art of Ancient Spectacle*. Edited by Bettina Ann Bergmann and Christine Kondoleon. New Haven: Yale University Press, 1999.

———. *The Roman Amphitheatre: From Its Origins to the Colosseum*. Cambridge: Cambridge University Press, 2007.

West, Allen Brown. *Latin Inscriptions, 1896–1926*. Vol. 8.2 of *Corinth: Results of Excavations Conducted by the American School of Classical Studies at Athens*. Cambridge: American School of Classical Studies at Athens, 1931.

Will, Edouard. *Korinthiaka. Recherches sur l'histoire et la civilisation de Corinthe des origines aux guerres médiques*. Paris: de Boccard, 1955.

Williams, Charles K., II. "A Re-evaluation of Temple E and the West End of the Forum of Corinth." Pages 156–62 in *The Greek Renaissance in the Roman Empire: Papers from the Tenth British Museum Classical Colloquium*. Edited by Susan Walker and Averil Cameron. London: University of London, Institute of Classical Studies, 1989.

Williams, Hector. *The Lamps.* Vol. 5 of *Kenchreai, Eastern Port of Corinth.* Leiden: Brill, 1981.

Winter, Bruce W. *After Paul Left Corinth: The Influence of Secular Ethics and Social Change.* Grand Rapids: Eerdmans, 2001.

———. "The Enigma of Imperial Cultic Activities and Paul in Corinth." Pages 49–72 in *Graeco-Roman Culture and the New Testament.* Edited by David E. Aune and Frederick E. Brenk. Leiden: Brill, 2012.

Wiseman, James. "Corinth and Rome, I: 228 BC–AD 267." *ANRW* 7.1:491–96.

Yoder, Joshua. *Representatives of Roman Rule: Roman Provincial Governors in Luke-Acts.* Berlin: de Gruyter, 2014.

Inequality in Roman Corinth: Evidence from Diverse Sources Evaluated by a Neo-Ricardian Model

L. L. Welborn

Scholarship on the Pauline Epistles represents Roman Corinth as a city in which sharp contrasts between rich and poor were especially apparent. In his classic commentary on 1 Corinthians, Johannes Weiss asserted: "Dass in einer solchen Stadt ungeheure Vermögens-unterschiede und eine gewaltige Kluft zwischen Arm und Reich sich bildeten, liegt an der Sache."[1] When Gerd Theissen undertook his pioneering exploration of the social stratification of early Christian groups, it was to Paul's Corinthian correspondence that he turned, concluding that the internal stratification of the Corinthian church was rooted in the social structure of the city of Corinth itself, a city where, to quote Theissen, "the social strata were more clearly differentiated from one another than in other places."[2] Justin Meggitt based his argument for the poverty of the Pauline Christians on the evidence of the Corinthian epistles, insisting that the pattern of unequal distribution that characterized Greco-Roman cities generally existed at Corinth as well.[3] Finally, a recent collection of essays on contrasts in the

---

1. Johannes Weiss, *Der erste Korintherbrief* (Göttingen: Vandenhoeck & Ruprecht, 1910), x.

2. Gerd Theissen, "Social Stratification in the Corinthian Community: A Contribution to the Sociology of Early Hellenistic Christianity," in *The Social Setting of Pauline Christianity: Essays on Corinth* (Philadelphia: Fortress, 1982), 69–119; originally published as "Soziale Schichtung in der korinthischen Gemeinde: Ein Beitrag zur Soziologie des hellenistischen Urchristentums," ZNW 65 (1974): 232–72.

3. Justin J. Meggitt, *Paul, Poverty and Survival* (Edinburgh: T&T Clark, 1998), 97–153, and esp. the concluding remarks on 153 n. 417.

texture of social life at Corinth bears the characteristic subtitle "Studies in Inequality."[4]

How far is the perception of a great gulf between rich and poor at Corinth justified by the evidence? Indeed, what sort of evidence bears on this question? How, for example, is one to assess the reputation for lavish wealth and grinding poverty that attaches to Corinth in ancient literature? How, particularly, should one evaluate the evidence of fictitious epistles and novels? What evidence of inequality has been disclosed by archaeology at Corinth, including the analysis of skeletal remains? What data are furnished by documentary sources, such as inscriptions? For the most part, the surviving inscriptions of Roman Corinth celebrate the benefactions of the elite to the life of the city. Scholars rightly lament the limited access that public documents provide to the lives of the poor at Corinth and elsewhere.[5] But might one elaborate a theoretical framework capable of disclosing a meaningful correlation between the munificence of the elite and the poverty of the masses? Finally, what value should one ascribe to the evidence of inequality in Paul's Corinthian epistles? How does the data of this epistolary archive relate to data from other sources?

As is well known, Strabo devotes a paragraph of his priceless *Geographica*[6] to a discussion of Corinth's traditional epithet ἀφνειός, "wealthy."[7] Strabo identifies three sources of Corinth's wealth: first, the "commerce" (τὸ ἐμπόριον) generated by the passage of goods across the isthmus, both

---

4. Steven J. Friesen, Sarah A. James, and Daniel N. Schowalter, eds., *Corinth in Contrast: Studies in Inequality* (Leiden: Brill, 2014).

5. Harry A. Stansbury, "Corinthian Honor, Corinthian Conflict: A Social History of Early Roman Corinth and Its Pauline Community" (PhD diss., University of California Irvine, 1990), 24, 151; Steven J. Friesen, "Inequality in Corinth," in Friesen, James, and Schowalter, *Corinth in Contrast*, 2.

6. Completed in 7 BCE, the *Geographica* was revised under Tiberius in 18 CE; see Ettore Pais, "The Time and Place in Which Strabo Composed His Historical Geography," in *Ancient Italy*, trans. C. Densmore Curtis (Chicago: University of Chicago Press, 1908), 379–430; J. G. C. Anderson, "Some Questions Bearing on the Date and Place of Composition of Strabo's *Geography*," in *Anatolian Studies Presented to Sir W. M. Ramsay*, ed. W. H. Buckler and W. M. Calder (Manchester: University of Manchester Press, 1923), 1–13.

7. Strabo, *Geogr.* 8.6.20; the adjective ἀφνειός is taken from Homer, *Il.* 2.570. Cf. Theissen, *Social Setting*, 101; Jerome Murphy-O'Connor, *St. Paul's Corinth: Texts and Archaeology* (Collegeville, MN: Glazier, 1983), 55; Stansbury, "Corinthian Honor," 64–65.

from sea to sea and in and out of the Peloponnesus; second, the crowds of people drawn to the biennial Isthmian games; and third, the scale of prostitution in Aphrodite's city.[8] The illustrations of wealth that Strabo provides are drawn from the pre-146 BCE city (Strabo, *Geogr.* 8.6.20).[9] Yet, with respect to revenues derived from trade, Strabo insists that "to later times this remained ever so, and to the Corinthians of later times still greater profits were added" (διέμεινε δὲ τοῦτο καὶ εἰς ὕστερον μέχρι παντός, τοῖς δ' ὕστερον καὶ πλείω προσεγίνετο πλεονεκτήματα) (Strabo, *Geogr.* 8.6.20).[10] In a subsequent paragraph Strabo names two other sources of Corinth's wealth: "the arts of the craftsmen" (αἱ τέχναι αἱ δημιουργικαί), especially the bronze work, and "the affairs of state" (τὰ πολιτικά) (Strabo, *Geogr.* 8.6.23). Strabo summarizes his description of Corinth: "The city of the Corinthians, then, was always great and wealthy" (Strabo, *Geogr.* 8.6.23).

Strabo's account of Corinth's wealth and its sources is confirmed in essentials by later writers. In an oration attributed to Dio Chrysostom (*Cor.* 37, the *Corinthian*; Cohoon and Crosby, LCL),[11] but probably written by his pupil Favorinus,[12] the speaker mentions "the many who each year put in at Cenchreae [Kenchreai, Corinth's eastern port], whether as merchant or spectator or ambassador or passing traveler" (*Cor.* 8). Notice that the merchant-trader (ἔμπορος) heads the list of visitors to Corinth.[13] The spectator (θεωρός) is probably bound for the Isthmian games,[14] but perhaps

---

8. In respect to the last named source of wealth, Strabo elaborates: "It was on account of these prostitutes that the city was crowded with people and became rich; for ship-captains freely squandered their money, and hence the proverb, 'Not for every man is the voyage to Corinth.'"

9. The wealth of the Bachiadae, of the tyrant Cypselus, and of Demaratus; the wealth of the temple of Aphrodite, with its thousand temple prostitutes. On the dubious historical value of the latter tradition, see Hans Conzelmann, "Korinth und die Mädchen der Aphrodite: Zur Religionsgeschichte der Stadt Korinth," *NAWG* 8 (1967–1968): 247–61; Charles K. Williams II, "Corinth and the Cult of Aphrodite," in *Corinthiaca: Studies in Honor of Darrell A. Amyx*, ed. Mario Aldo Del Chiaro and William R. Biers (Columbia: University of Missouri Press, 1986), 12–24.

10. Translations of Strabo are my own.

11. Further translations of Dio Chrysostom are from Cohoon and Crosby, LCL.

12. Adelmo Barigazzi, *Favorino di Arelate, Opere: Introduzione, Testo Critica e comment* (Firenze: Felice le Monnier, 1966).

13. See Theissen, *Social Setting*, 101; Murphy-O'Connor, *St. Paul's Corinth*, 100.

14. Translating the term θεωρός as "spectator" rather than "pilgrim"; see LSJ, 797 s.v. θεωρός III.

also for the theater or the Roman-style amphitheater.[15] The ambassador (πρεσβευτής) attests the importance of Corinth as the seat of the Roman proconsul of Achaia (Tacitus, *Ann.* 1.76.4).[16] Finally, the passing traveler (διερχομενός) evokes the position of Corinth as the crossroads of the Mediterranean. Later in the same oration, Favorinus emphasizes the prosperity of Corinth as the cause of envy by other cities: "For you [Corinthians] are now, as the saying goes, both prow and stern of Hellas, having been called prosperous [ὄλβιοι] and wealthy [ἀφνειοί] and other such names by poets ... from ancient times, times when some of the other cities also had wealth and power; but now, since wealth has deserted both Orchomenos and Delphi, though they may surpass you in exciting pity, none can do so in exciting envy" (Dio Chrysostom, *Cor.* 36).

Plutarch, who was in Corinth on more than one occasion (*Praec. ger. rei publ.* 20 [816D]),[17] mentions another source of Corinthian wealth related to commerce, namely, money lending. In an essay of advice against borrowing (*De vitando aere alieno* [827D–832A]), Plutarch puts Corinth at the head of the list of the banking centers of Roman Greece (*Vit. aere al.* 7 [831A]). The context of Plutarch's reference to Corinth is important for assessing the scope of the loans involved. The audience of Plutarch's warnings is wealthy provincial Greeks, men of his own social class, who feel pressured to contract debts in order to pay court to their Roman friends and to compete successfully for local honors. "Thus, becoming debtors, we flatter men who ruin houses, we accompany them as attendants, give them dinners, make them presents, and pay them tribute, not because of our poverty, but because of our extravagance" (*Vit. aere al.* 7 [830D]). "Luxury produced

---

15. The theater at Corinth held upwards of 15,000 spectators; see Richard Stillwell, *The Theatre*, vol. 2 of *Corinth: Results of Excavations Conducted by the American School of Classical Studies at Athens* (Princeton: American School of Classical Studies at Athens, 1952), 135–41. On the amphitheater, see Katherine E. Welch, "Negotiating Roman Spectacle Architecture in the Greek World: Athens and Corinth," in *The Art of Ancient Spectacle*, ed. Bettina Ann Bergmann and Christine Kondoleon (New Haven: Yale University Press, 1999), 125–45, esp. 133–40.

16. Returned to senatorial control by Claudius in 44 CE, according to Suetonius, *Claud.* 25.3; Acts 18:12. For discussion of the evidence for the date at which Corinth began to serve as the proconsul's primary residence, see James Wiseman, "Corinth and Rome, I: 228 BC–AD 267," *ANRW* 7.1:501–2; Stansbury, "Corinthian Honor," 166–70.

17. See Konrat Ziegler, "Plutarchos," *RE* 22.1 (1964): 656–57. Translations of Plutarch are my own. Plutarch mentions an embassy upon which he was sent as a young man to the proconsul of Achaia. I assume the proconsul had his seat in Corinth.

money-lenders," Plutarch explains, "for our debts are incurred, not to pay for bread or wine, but for country estates, slaves, banquet-halls, and tables, and because we give shows to the cities with unrestrained expenditure, contending in fruitless and thankless rivalries." Plutarch concludes, "Once a man has become entangled, he remains a debtor all his life, exchanging, like a horse that has once been bridled, one rider for another" (*Vit. aere al.* 7 [830E]). At this point, then, Plutarch mentions Corinth, the importance of the reference enhanced by its incidental character:[18] "And so, one after another takes over the borrower, first a money-lender [τοκιστής] or broker [πραγματευτής] of Corinth, then one of Patrae, then an Athenian, until, attacked on all sides by all of them, he is dissolved and chopped up into the small change of interest payments ... ; so in their transfers and changes of loans, by assuming additional interest payments ... they weigh themselves down more and more" (*Vit. aere al.* 7 [831A–B]).

In the sections of the *Metamorphoses* located at Corinth (Apuleius, *Metam.* 10.18–35), Apuleius repeatedly emphasizes the sordid love of gain, the base covetousness, for which the city had a reputation.[19] Upon arrival at Corinth, Lucius's owner devises a plan for making money by charging admission to those who wish to see the performing animal (Apuleius, *Metam.* 10.19). Lucius's keeper is only too happy to arrange for sexual intercourse with a wealthy Corinthian matron, because "he cared for nothing but for gain of money" (*lucro suo tantum contentus*) (Apuleius, *Metam.* 10.19). In pursuit of greater profits, Lucius's master seeks a volunteer to have intercourse with the ass in the theater *grandi praemio* (Apuleius, *Metam.* 10.23). In the story of the woman who poisons her husband, a Corinthian doctor supplies the drug for fifty pieces of gold (Apuleius, *Metam.* 10.25). The wicked woman then murders the doctor and his wife in order to avoid paying the promised money (Apuleius, *Metam.* 10.25–27), and eventually kills her own daughter, "lusting after the child's inheritance" (Apuleius, *Metam.* 10.28). Apuleius's story of the woman condemned to have intercourse with the ass is interrupted by a diatribe against judicial corruption, in which Apuleius complains that "all our judges nowadays sell their judgments for money" (Apuleius, *Metam.* 10.33). Apuleius chose Corinth as the venue for his tale of greed,[20] on the

---

18. Rightly, Murphy-O'Connor, *St. Paul's Corinth*, 108.

19. See esp. Hugh J. Mason, "Lucius at Corinth," *Phoenix* 25 (1971): 160–65.

20. In the version of the ass tale ascribed to Lucian (*Onos*), the action is set in Thessaly; Apuleius makes Lucius a native of Corinth (*Metam.* 1.22, 2.12), and sub-

assumption that his readers would be familiar with the reputation of the city as a place where love of gain engendered a willingness to make money by any means, however violent and sordid.[21]

It should come as no surprise that elite authors such as Strabo and Favorinus have nothing to say about the poor of Corinth, even as they expand on the city's wealth. For a glimpse of poverty, one must turn to Alciphron, whose fictitious epistles draw on comedy and satire to portray low-class character types—fishermen, farmers, parasites, and courtesans.[22] In one of Alciphron's *Letters of Parasites*, he speaks of the glaring contrast between the rich and the poor at Corinth: "I did not go further into Corinth," one parasite explains to another, "having learned in a short time the sordidness [βδελυρία] of the rich there and the misery [ἀθλιότης] of the poor" (Alciphron, *Letters of Parasites* 24 [3.60.1] [Benner, LCL]). The Greek word βδελυρία denotes behavior that is arrogant and abusive, the contempt of the rich for the poor.[23] By contrast, ἀθλιότης describes wretchedness and degradation, the suffering to which poverty gives rise.[24] Alciphron's parasite proceeds to relate a scene of starvation-level poverty that he witnessed in one of the suburbs of Corinth (Alciphron, *Letters of Parasites* 24 [3.60.2] [Benner, LCL, slightly modified]):

> At midday, after most people had bathed, I saw some talkative and clever young men creeping about, not near the residences but near the Craneium and especially where the women who sell bread and fruit are accustomed to do their business. There the young men would stoop to the ground, and one would pick up lupine pods, another would examine the nutshells to make sure that none of the edible part was left anywhere and had escaped notice, while another would scrape with his fingernails the pomegranate rinds ... to see whether he could extract any of the seeds anywhere, while others would actually gather up and devour the

---

stitutes Corinth for Thessalonica in book 10. See Paul Veyne, "Apulée a Cenchrées," *RevPhil* 39 (1965): 241–51.

21. Mason, "Lucius at Corinth," 160, 164–65.

22. See Francis H. Fobes, introduction to *The Letters of Alciphron*, trans. A. R. Benner, LCL (Cambridge: Harvard University Press, 1962), 3–18. Little is known about Alciphron; on the basis of his similarity to Lucian, a date in the second or third century CE has been suggested.

23. LSJ, 312 s.v. βδελυρία; see esp. Theophrastus, *Char.* 11.

24. LSJ, 32 s.v. ἀθλιότης.

pieces that fell from the loaves of bread—pieces that had already been trodden under many feet.

Alciphron's parasite reflects bitterly: "Such is the gateway to the Peloponnesus, the city that lies between two seas, a city charming indeed to look upon and taking in luxuries abundantly on both sides, but possessing inhabitants who are ungracious and entirely without love" (Alciphron, *Letters of Parasites* 24 [3.60.3] [Benner, LCL, slightly modified]). The parasite concludes with an ironic epilogue to the myth of Aphrodite's blessing of Corinth: "If perhaps to the women Aphrodite is consecrated as guardian of the city, to the men only Famine" (Alciphron, *Letters of Parasites* 24 [3.60.3] [Benner, LCL, slightly modified]). How seriously should one take Alciphron's portrait of economic disparity between the inhabitants of Corinth? Is Alciphron's account of lesser worth because it is couched in a fictitious epistle, or of greater value because it builds on an already existing reputation?[25]

So much, then, for literary sources relevant to the question of inequality at Corinth. One may next query what evidence of inequality archaeology has disclosed. Here one confronts a major obstacle, for despite the fact that archaeological excavations have been diligently pursued at Corinth for more than a century,[26] most of the Roman city remains underground, and what has been exposed reveals little about the lower classes.[27] Excavations have concentrated on the area around the forum, in the theater district, and on the sanctuaries of Demeter and Kore, and of Asclepius. Nevertheless, several features of the archaeological remains permit inferences about the scale of Corinthian wealth and allow a glimpse of one segment of the population of poor—namely, slaves.

First, the size and magnificence of the forum. The forum of Corinth was over 160 meters, longer than the Forum Romanum, and among the largest known anywhere.[28] The temples, basilica, stoa, fountains, monu-

---

25. See Mason, "Lucius at Corinth," 164; Murphy-O'Connor, *St. Paul's Corinth*, 126–27.

26. Results of the excavations of the American School of Classical Studies at Corinth are published in vols. 1–20 of *Corinth: Results of Excavations Conducted by the American School of Classical Studies at Athens*; see further excavation reports in *Hesperia*.

27. Stansbury, "Corinthian Honor," 22–24, 151; Friesen, James, and Schowalter, "Inequality in Corinth," 2.

28. Robert L. Scranton, *Monuments in the Lower Agora and North of the Archaic*

ments, and shops that crowded the central area mostly date from the late Augustan period to the end of the reign of Claudius.[29] The surviving dedications of these impressive structures suggest that many were the benefactions of local elites.[30] For example, an architrave block of white

---

Temple, vol. 1.3 of *Corinth: Results of Excavations Conducted by the American School of Classical Studies at Athens* (Princeton: American School of Classical Studies at Athens, 1951), 133.

29. The North Basilica was constructed in ca. 10-5 BCE, according to ibid., 150. A *peribolos* of Apollo was constructed on the Lechaion Road just north of the Peirene fountain sometime in the reign of Augustus; Richard Stillwell, Robert L. Scranton, and Sarah Elizabeth Freeman, *Architecture*, vol. 1.2 of *Corinth: Results of Excavations Conducted by the American School of Classical Studies at Athens* (Cambridge: Harvard University Press, 1941), 32-38; cf. Wiseman, "Corinth and Rome I," 520. Temple C was constructed in the late Augustan or early Tiberian period; Scranton in Stillwell, Scranton, and Freeman, *Architecture*, 146-47. The construction of the fountain house of Glauke probably dates to the early first century CE, according to Charles K. Williams II, "Corinth, 1983: The Route to Sicyon," *Hesperia* 53 (1984): 97-100. The shops that run along the central terrace of the forum were probably constructed late in the reign of Tiberius; Scranton, *Monuments in the Lower Agora*, 126-27. Three monuments on the forum's western terrace have been dated to the reign of Tiberius: the Babbius monument, a fountain dedicated to Poseidon, and Temple F; ibid., 17-32. The Julian Basilica at the east end of the forum has been dated to the reign of Claudius: Saul S. Weinberg, "Roman Twins: Basilicas at Corinth," *Arch* 13 (1960): 139, 142; cf. Brunilde Sismonde Ridgway, "Sculpture from Corinth," *Hesperia* 50 (1981): 432-33. The new Southeast Building, which probably functioned as a *tabularium*, has been dated to the reign of Claudius: Saul S. Weinberg, *The Southeast Building, the Twin Basilicas, the Mosaic House*, vol. 1.5 of *Corinth: Results of Excavations Conducted by the American School of Classical Studies at Athens* (Princeton: American School of Classical Studies at Athens, 1960), 12-13; cf. Michel Amandry, *Le Monnayage des duovirs Corinthiens*, BCHSup 15 (Athens: École Francaise D'Athènes; Paris: de Boccard, 1988), 59-66, 76. The elliptical Bouleterion in the South Stoa was probably built during the reign of Claudius; Oscar Broneer, *The South Stoa and Its Roman Successors*, vol. 1.4 of *Corinth: Results of Excavations Conducted by the American School of Classical Studies at Athens* (Princeton: American School of Classical Studies at Athens, 1954), 129-32. The poros predecessor of Temple E should probably be dated to the reign of Claudius: Freeman in Stillwell, Scranton, and Freeman, *Architecture*, 179, 187-89; cf. Wiseman, "Corinth and Rome I," 518-19; Mary E. Hoskins Walbank, "Pausanias, Octavia and Temple E at Corinth," *ABSA* 84 (1989): 361-94.

30. Allen Brown West, *Latin Inscriptions, 1896-1926*, vol. 8.2 of *Corinth: Results of Excavations Conducted by the American School of Classical Studies at Athens* (Cambridge: Harvard University Press, 1931 = IKorinthWest), 94-111, "Inscriptions on Buildings."

marble from a complex of buildings not yet located names L. Hermidius Celsus and L. Rutilius, along with two other Hermidii, as donors of "the temple and statue of Apollo Augustus and ten shops" (*aedem et statuam Apollinis Augusti et tabernas decem*).[31] While the Hermidii are otherwise unknown, the Rutilii were a prominent Corinthian family distinguished by occupancy of the highest civic offices.[32] This extensive set of constructions demonstrates the wealth of the donors.[33]

A second relevant archaeological feature is the amphitheater.[34] Located about one kilometer east of the city center, the Corinthian amphitheater was quarried out of the surrounding bedrock; a relatively small *cavea* (78 meters by 52 meters) was divided into twelve wedges (*cunei*), surmounted, evidently, by a superstructure of wood.[35] A recent survey has demonstrated that the amphitheater was placed at the northeastern corner of the centuriated grid-plan of the colony,[36] a location which suggests that "the amphitheater was built, or at least planned, at the time of the colo-

---

31. IKorinthWest §120, pp. 94–95.

32. Rutilius Plancus was *duovir* between 12/13 and 15/16 CE; Rutilius Fuscus was *isagogeus* of the games during the reign of Claudius in 51 CE; Rutilius Piso was *duovir* in 67 CE; see IKorinthWest §§82, 84, 120; Amandry, *Le Monnayage*, 12–14, 19–22, 24–26, 67–69; John Harvey Kent, *The Inscriptions, 1926–1950*, vol. 8.3 of *Corinth: Results of Excavations Conducted by the American School of Classical Studies at Athens* (Princeton: American School of Classical Studies at Athens, 1966 = IKorinthKent), §251, p. 104; Antony J. S. Spawforth, "Roman Corinth: The Formation of a Colonial Elite," in *Roman Onomastics in the Greek East: Social and Political Aspects*, ed. Athanasios D. Rizakis (Athens: Research Center for Greek and Roman Antiquity, 1996), 181.

33. Cf. Stansbury, "Corinthian Honor," 227.

34. Ferdinand J. de Waele, *Theater en Amphitheater te oud Korinthe* (Utrecht: Dekker, 1928); Harold N. Fowler and Richard Stillwell, *Introduction, Topography, Architecture*, vol. 1.1 of *Corinth: Results of Excavations Conducted by the American School of Classical Studies at Athens* (Cambridge: Harvard University Press, 1932), 89–91, figs. 54–56, with plan, 79.

35. Fowler and Stillwell, *Introduction, Topography, Architecture*, 90; Welch, "Negotiating Roman Spectacle Architecture," 133–34.

36. David Gilman Romano, "Post-145 B.C. Land Use in Corinth, and Planning of the Roman Colony of 44 B.C.," in *Corinthia in the Roman Period*, ed. Timothy E. Gregory (Ann Arbor: University of Michigan Press, 1993), 9–30; Romano, "Urban and Rural Planning in Roman Corinth," in *Urban Religion in Roman Corinth: Interdisciplinary Approaches*, ed. Daniel N. Schowalter and Steven J. Friesen (Cambridge: Harvard University Press, 2005), 40–42; cf. Welch, "Negotiating Roman Spectacle Architecture," 134–35, 137.

nization of Corinth."[37] Although gladiatorial games were held for only a limited number of days per year during the imperial cult festivals,[38] the expense of these spectacles would have been considerable.[39] One recalls that the owner of the ass-Lucius in Apuleius's *Metamorphoses* had traveled to Thessaly in order to purchase gladiators for the Corinthian arena, in discharge of his obligations as the newly elected *duovir quinquennalis* of the colony (Apuleius, *Metam.* 10.18).[40] Like the resumption of Corinthian control of the Isthmian games (sometime between 7 BCE and 3 CE),[41] the amphitheater, with its gladiatorial shows, provides unmistakable evidence of extraordinary wealth at the top of Corinthian society.[42]

A third archaeological feature relevant to the question of inequality at Corinth is the Roman market north of the Archaic temple.[43] A large rectangular plaza, paved with mosaics, is bordered on three sides by a series of shops.[44] Here archaeologists place the Corinthian slave market.[45] How extensive was the slave trade that flowed through this market? On the basis of the frequency of Corinthus as a slave name,[46] it has been suggested that Roman Corinth replaced the island of Delos as "the eastern 'clearing house' for the slave trade."[47] Whether this inference from nomenclature is

---

37. Welch, "Negotiating Roman Spectacle Architecture," 137: the Corinthian amphitheater was evidently the first of its kind in Roman Greece.

38. Georges Ville, *La gladiature en Occident des origins à la mort de Domitien* (Rome: École française de Rome, 1981), 389–95; Thomas E. J. Wiedemann, *Emperors and Gladiators* (London: Routledge, 1992), 11–12, 47, 56; Patrizia Sabbatini Tumolesi, *Gladiatorum parie: Annunci di spettacoli gladiatorii a Pompeii* (Rome: Edizion da storia e letteratura, 1980), 133–38.

39. On prices of *munera*, see Donald G. Kyle, *Spectacles of Death in Ancient Rome* (New York: Routledge, 1998), 84, 86, 94–95, 160, 250.

40. Cf. Mason, "Lucius at Corinth," 162.

41. IKorinthKent §152, p. 70; cf. Stansbury, "Corinthian Honor," 228–30.

42. For this inference, see already Weiss, *Der erste Korintherbrief*, x; see also Stansbury, "Corinthian Honor," 233.

43. Ferdinand J. de Waele, "The Roman Market North of the Temple at Corinth," *AJA* 34 (1930): 432–54; Scranton, *Monuments in the Lower Agora*, 180–94.

44. The arrangement of the Corinthian market resembles that found in Priene and Pompeii; see de Waele, "Roman Market," 435.

45. Ibid., 453–54; Scranton, *Monuments in the Lower Agora*, 192–94.

46. For example, *CIL* 5.1305, 6.11541, 6.3956, 6.4454; see also P. M. Fraser and E. Matthews, *The Aegean Islands, Cyprus, Cyrenaica*, vol. 1 of *A Lexicon of Greek Personal Names* (Oxford: Clarendon, 1987), 269.

47. S. Scott Bartchy, ΜΑΛΛΟΝ ΧΡΗΣΑΙ: *First-Century Slavery and the Inter-*

justified, the number of slaves in the Corinthia may have been significant, given Corinth's location on the isthmus; the profits from slave trading, with the gains extracted from slave labor, may have been considerable.[48]

The analysis of skeletal remains from Corinth provides a fourth glimpse of economic conditions. A group of ninety-four individuals dating to the Roman period has been analyzed by Sherry Cox and the results compared with skeletons from Paphos.[49] Although the general state of preservation of the skeletons is not good,[50] some conclusions can be drawn. The average age of adults is greater at Corinth than at Paphos, although more individuals survived childhood at Paphos.[51] Corinthians exhibit relatively more enamel hypoplasias when compared to Paphians, suggesting that more people at Corinth suffered from nutritional deficiencies.[52] Cox summarizes: "Greater infant mortality, relatively shorter statures and greater evidence of stress characterize the Corinthians when compared to the Paphians during Roman times."[53] The impression that emerges from analysis of Corinthian skeletal remains is of a population with a high proportion of persons who show signs of malnourishment and stressful, hard work.

Although the inscriptions of Corinth are mutilated and broken,[54] enough survives so that, together with the evidence of coins, a rather complete list of the holders of the various magistracies can be drawn up, from

---

pretation of 1 Corinthians 7:21 (Atlanta: Scholars Press, 1985), 58 n. 185, following Mary L. Gordon, "The Nationality of Slaves under the Early Roman Empire," in *Slavery in Classical Antiquity: Views and Controversies*, ed. M. I. Finley (Cambridge: Heffer & Sons, 1960), 172, 177. Cf. Stansbury, "Corinthian Honor," 163: "I suggest Corinth began to assume a leadership position in this market by the death of Augustus if not sooner." See further J. Albert Harrill, *The Manumission of Slaves in Early Christianity* (Tübingen: Mohr Siebeck, 1995), 72-73; Laura Salah Nasrallah, "'You Were Bought with a Price': Freedpersons and Things in 1 Corinthians," in Friesen, James, and Schowalter, *Corinth in Contrast*, 61.

48. Stansbury, "Corinthian Honor," 81; Harrill, *Manumission of Slaves*, 73-74.

49. Sherry C. Cox, "Health in Hellenistic and Roman Times: The Case Studies of Paphos, Cyprus and Corinth" in *Health in Antiquity*, ed. Helen King (New York: Routledge, 2005), 59-82.

50. Ibid., 62, 64, 77.

51. Ibid., 78.

52. Ibid., 79.

53. Ibid., 80.

54. IKorinthKent, 17: "It is difficult to think of any other ancient site where the inscriptions are so cruelly mutilated and broken."

the foundation of the colony to the end of the Julio-Claudian era.[55] From this period, the names of sixty-nine *duoviri* are known, among whom only thirty-three families seem to be represented.[56] For example, three Heii, C. Aristo, C. Pamphilus, and C. Polio, apparently freedmen of the same family in different generations, served as magistrates of Corinth during the reign of Augustus.[57] M. Antonius Theophilus, *duovir quinquennalis* in 30 BCE, succeeded in placing his son M. Antonius Hipparchus in the position of *duovir* twice in the last decade BCE.[58] The Spartan Euryclids, enfranchised by Octavian,[59] contributed another father-and-son pair to the Corinthian magistracy: C. Julius Laco was *duovir quinquennalis* probably in 17–18 CE,[60] while his son C. Julius Spartiaticus was *duovir quinquennalis* twice, most likely in 47–48 and 52–53 CE,[61] and was then ἀγωνοθέτης of the Isthmian and Caesarean games.[62] The epigraphic and numismatic record makes clear that Corinth was a city with an entrenched elite, a political oligarchy that perpetuated itself over generations by its control of wealth,

---

55. IKorinthKent, 67–86; Amandry, *Le Monnayage*.

56. Stansbury, "Corinthian Honor," 250–54; Benjamin W. Millis, "The Local Magistrates and Elite of Corinth," in *Corinth in Context: Studies in Inequality*, ed. Steven J. Friesen, Sarah A. James, and Daniel N. Schowalter (Leiden: Brill, 2014), 38–53, esp. 50–52.

57. Katherine N. Edwards, *The Coins, 1896–1929*, vol. 6 of *Corinth: Results of Excavations Conducted by the American School of Classical Studies at Athens* (Cambridge: Harvard University Press, 1933), §§25–26, 33–34, 36–39; Amandry, *Le Monnayage*, 38–39, 43–47, 47–49, 52–55, 140–42, 151–56; Andrew Burnett, Michel Amandry, and Pere Pau Ripollés, *From the Death of Caesar to the Death of Vitellius (44 BC–AD 69)*, vol. 1 of *Roman Provincial Coinage* (London: British Museum Press; Paris: Bibliothèque Nationale, 1992; rev. 2006 = *RPC* 1), §§1127–28, 1132, 1133, 1139–42; IKorinthKent §§150–51; Spawforth, "Roman Corinth," 178–79.

58. Amandry, *Le Monnayage*, 41–42, 49–50, 50–51; *RPC* 1, §§1129–31, 1134–35, 1136–37; cf. Spawforth, "Roman Corinth," 176; Millis, "Local Magistrates and Elite of Roman Corinth," 46–47, 49, 50.

59. Glen W. Bowersock, "Eurycles of Sparta," *JRS* 51 (1961): 112–18.

60. IKorinthWest §67; Lily Ross Taylor and Allen Brown West, "The Euryclids in Latin Inscriptions from Corinth," *AJA* 30 (1926): 389–400, esp. 389–93; Athanasios D. Rizakis and Sophie Zoumbaki, *Achaia, Argolis, Corinthia and Eleia*, vol. 1 of *Roman Peloponnese: Roman Personal Names in Their Social Context* (Athens: Research Centre for Greek and Roman Antiquity, 2001), 345.

61. IKorinthWest §68, p. 52; IKorinthKent, 25; Rizakis and Zoumbaki, *Achaia, Argolis, Corinthia and Eleia*, 353.

62. IKorinthWest §68, p. 52; IKorinthKent, 31.

office, and honor.[63] The maintenance of the system was facilitated by the fact that membership in the local senate was for life, unless a *decurion* was expelled for legal reasons.[64] The occasional admission of a new man to the *ordo* on the basis of wealth and connections actually served to strengthen the system by legitimizing the principle of the rule of the few.[65]

It has been suggested that the fact that freedmen might hold office at Corinth meant that the city's ruling class had a less oligarchic character, and that the Corinthian colony was somewhat egalitarian in terms of opportunity for political advancement.[66] The case of Cn. Babbius Philinus has often been adduced;[67] he is clearly recognizable as a freedman by his Greek cognomen and the omission of his filiation in all of the inscriptions that bear his name.[68] Despite his freedman status, Philinus gained the annual offices of aedile and *duovir*, and the lifetime position of *pontifex maximus*.[69] The extent of Philinus's wealth is demonstrated by two monuments that he erected in the forum: a fountain dedicated to Poseidon and a

---

63. Stansbury, "Corinthian Honor," 249-53; Millis, "Local Magistrates and Elite of Roman Corinth," 50-53.

64. Friedemann Quass, *Die Honoratiorenschicht in den Städten des griechischen Ostens: Untersuchungen zur politischen und sozialen Entwicklung in hellenistischer und römischer Zeit* (Stuttgart: Steiner, 1993), esp. 382-94.

65. On this dynamic in general, see H. W. Pleket, "Sociale stratificatie en sociale mobiliteit in de Romeinse Keizertijd," *TG* 84 (1971): 215-51; Quass, *Die Honoratiorenschicht*, 328-31.

66. Wayne A. Meeks, *The First Urban Christians: The Social World of the Apostle Paul* (New Haven: Yale University Press, 1983), 48; Donald W. Engels, *Roman Corinth: An Alternative Model for the Classical City* (Chicago: University of Chicago Press, 1990), 68-69; Benjamin W. Millis, "The Social and Ethnic Origins of the Colonists in Early Roman Corinth," in Friesen, Schowalter, and Walters, *Corinth in Context*, 13-36, here 34-35.

67. Meeks, *First Urban Christians*, 48; Stansbury, "Corinthian Honor," 258; Andrew D. Clarke, *Secular and Christian Leadership in Corinth: A Socio-historical and Exegetical Study of 1 Corinthians 1-6* (Leiden: Brill, 1993), 28.

68. IKorinthWest §132; IKorinthKent §§155, 176, 259, 323; cf. Meeks, *First Urban Christians*, 213 n. 268; Stansbury, "Corinthian Honor," 254.

69. IKorinthWest §132; IKorinthKent §155. Scranton, *Monuments in the Lower Agora*, 21-22, 32-36, 72; Charles K. Williams II, "A Re-evaluation of Temple E and the West End of the Forum at Corinth," in *The Greek Renaissance in the Roman Empire*, ed. Susan Walker and Averil Cameron (London: University of London, Institute of Classical Studies Press, 1989), 156-62, here 162 n. 14; Stansbury, "Corinthian Honor," 256; Millis, "Local Magistrates and Elite of Roman Corinth," 39.

circular aedicule bearing his name.[70] Nor was Philinus the only freedman who displayed his wealth in the city center: the Tiberian-era monument of the *Augustales* was erected by freedmen donors.[71] Another inscription honors C. Novius Felix, the freedman of a powerful family with business connections in the East, along with the freedman Q. Cispuleius Primus, described in the inscription as an *Augustalis*.[72] The career of Cn. Babbius Philinus demonstrates the possibility of status mobility at Corinth, an opportunity not available to freedmen elsewhere in the empire.[73] But one should not imagine that the prominence of freedmen in the epigraphic record of Corinth implies that the colony was more egalitarian in character.[74] Indeed, the fortune of Philinus probably exceeded that of his freeborn contemporaries. As Allen Brown West observed, "The name Cn. Babbius Philinus appears more frequently than any other in Corinthian inscriptions."[75]

The numerous inscriptions honoring Ti. Claudius Dinippus provide a final glimpse of both the wealth and power of a few and the poverty and vulnerability of the mass at Corinth.[76] Dinippus seems to have belonged to a Hellenized family of Roman businessmen (*negotiators*) that moved to Corinth from the East;[77] his vast fortune enabled him to meet the equestrian census.[78] Dinippus held all the high offices at Corinth, including those of *duovir quinquennalis* and ἀγωνοθέτης of the imperial games, and

---

70. Scranton, *Monuments in the Lower Agora*, 21–22, 32–36, 72; Williams, "A Reevaluation of Temple E"; Stansbury, "Corinthian Honor," 256; Millis, "Local Magistrates and Elite of Roman Corinth," 39.

71. Scranton, *Monuments in the Lower Agora*, 142–43, 150; IKorinthKent §53; cf. Stansbury, "Corinthian Honor," 280; Margaret L. Laird, "The Emperor in a Roman Town: The Base of the *Augustales* in the Forum at Corinth," in Friesen, Schowalter, and Walters, *Corinth in Context*, 67–116.

72. IKorinthWest §77, pp. 60–61; cf. Spawforth, "Roman Corinth," 180.

73. Susan Treggiari, *Roman Freedmen during the Late Republic* (Oxford: Clarendon, 1969), 52–64; Henrik Mouritsen, *The Freedman in the Roman World* (Cambridge: Cambridge University Press, 2011), 74–75.

74. Stansbury, "Corinthian Honor," 120; Millis, "Local Magistrates and Elite of Roman Corinth," 44, 50–53.

75. IKorinthWest, 5.

76. IKorinthWest §§86–90; IKorinthKent §§158–63.

77. Spawforth, "Roman Corinth," 177–78.

78. Hubert Devijver, *Prosopographia militiarum equestrium quae fuerunt ab Augusto ad Gallienum*, part 2 (Leuven: Symbolae Facultatis Litterarum et Philosophiae Louaniensis, 1977), C 139.

also served as priest and augur.[79] Under Claudius, Dinippus was appointed to the post of *curator annonae* for the colony,[80] probably in connection with the famines that affected portions of the Mediterranean at that time.[81] Dinippus's appointment to this position attests his substantial fortune and suggests influential connections with trading partners overseas, where the colony had to compete for grain.[82] But the need of Corinth for this office also attests a growing population whose lack of resources left them vulnerable to a crisis in the food supply.[83]

The case of Ti. Claudius Dinippus encourages us to attempt to construct a theoretical model capable of disclosing a correlation between the benefactions of the elite and the poverty of the mass. Such a framework has been articulated by Willem Jongman for the economy of Pompeii,[84] and more recently by Arjan Zuiderhoek for the cities of Asia Minor.[85] What results might obtain for the measure of inequality at Corinth from the application of such a model to the available evidence?

A neo-Ricardian model predicts that an increase in population such as Corinth experienced throughout the Julio-Claudian period would result in a scarcity of land relative to labor; the landowning urban elite would enjoy an increase in wealth from higher rents, while rural tenants and urban wage laborers would become progressively poorer.[86] Three fur-

---

79. Rizakis and Zoumbaki, *Achaia, Argolis, Corinthia and Eleia*, 170.

80. IKorinthWest, 73; Stansbury, "Corinthian Honor," 300.

81. IKorinthWest, 73; see further Barry N. Danylak, "Tiberius Claudius Dinippus and the Food Shortages in Corinth," *TynBul* 59 (2008): 231-70.

82. Stansbury, "Corinthian Honor," 301.

83. Ibid., 300.

84. Willem M. Jongman, *The Economy and Society of Pompeii* (Amsterdam: Gieben, 1991), esp. 85-98.

85. Arjan Zuiderhoek, *The Politics of Munificence in the Roman Empire: Citizens, Elites and Benefactors in Asia Minor* (Cambridge: Cambridge University Press, 2009).

86. For application of the neo-Ricardian model to Roman economic history, see Bruce W. Frier, "Demography," in *The High Empire, AD 70-192*, ed. Alan K. Bowman, Peter Garnsey, and Dominic Rathbone, vol. 11 of *The Cambridge Ancient History*, 2nd ed. (Cambridge: Cambridge University Press, 2000), 787-816, esp. 811-16; Frier, "More Is Worse: Some Observations on the Population of the Roman Empire," in *Debating Roman Demography*, ed. Walter Scheidel (Leiden: Brill, 2001), 139-59; Willem M. Jongman, "The Rise and Fall of the Roman Economy: Population, Rents and Entitlement," in *Ancient Economies and Modern Methodologies: Archaeology, Comparative History, Models and Institutions*, ed. Peter Bang, Mamoru Ikeguchi, and Harmut G. Ziche (Bari: Edipuglia, 2006), 237-54. See also Walter Scheidel, "Demo-

ther effects are predicted by this model. First, the base of the elite would have broadened, due to the general growth in prosperity of landowners and those who controlled ancillary resources.[87] Second, the elite would have become internally stratified, with a core group of supremely wealthy families standing over against a larger group of moderately wealthy ones.[88] Third, the segment of the nonelite population that provided services, such as shopkeepers, manufacturers, and traders, would have experienced a rise in incomes as a consequence of increased elite demand.[89] In general, the model predicts that during a period of rising population, the landowning elite would have become vastly richer, while a sizeable population of rural and urban poor would have endured increasing misery. Within this framework, elite munificence functioned to maintain social harmony and political stability in a time of unprecedented accumulation of wealth at the top.[90]

Is there concrete evidence from Paul's Corinth that would tend to confirm this model? That is to say, is there evidence of a substantial increase in wealth among the Corinthian elite and a corresponding decrease of resources among the poor? Is there evidence, in addition, of the internal oligarchization of the elite, such that a small group of super-wealthy families came to dominate Corinthian society? And finally, is there evidence of a proliferation of elite giving at Corinth as a palliative to social tensions arising from growing disparities within the population?

My brief survey of documentary sources already suggests answers to these questions. It is precisely during the reign of Claudius that the colony's first-known Roman knights, Ti. Claudius Dinippus and C. Julius Spartiaticus, appear in the epigraphic record.[91] Finally, we encounter two

---

graphic and Economic Development in the Ancient Mediterranean World," *Journal of Institutional and Theoretical Economics* 160 (2004): 743–57.

87. Willem Jongman, "The Roman Economy: From Cities to Empire," in *The Transformation of Economic Life under the Roman Empire*, ed. Lukas de Blois and John Rich (Amsterdam: Gieben, 2002), 28–47; Zuiderhoek, *Politics of Munificence*, esp. 53–60.

88. On the "internal oligarchization" of the bouleutic elite, see Pleket, "Sociale stratificatie in de Romeinse Keizertijd," 215–51; Zuiderhoek, *Politics of Munificence*, 54, 60–66, 134–37.

89. Jongman, "Rise and Fall," 245–46; Zuiderhoek, *Politics of Munificence*, 55.

90. Zuiderhoek, *Politics of Munificence*, 71–112, and passim.

91. Rizakis and Zoumbaki, *Achaia, Argolis, Corinthia and Eleia*, 170, 353; cf. Stansbury, "Corinthian Honor," 300.

individuals whose funds were substantial enough to meet the equestrian census, whose minimum (HS 400,000) exceeded that of an urban councilor by four times.[92] Dinippus and Spartiaticus differed from other Corinthian elites in the number and dignity of offices held: in addition to all the high magistracies at Corinth, both men held the *agonothesia*, the office of greatest prestige and financial responsibility.[93] Like Dinippus, Spartiaticus also held a number of priesthoods: he was *flamen* of the deified Julius, *pontifex*, and high priest of the house of Augustus in perpetuity.[94] The last named office, which climaxes Spartiaticus's *cursus honorum* on a Latin monument,[95] was a newly established position of great importance, as demonstrated by the fact that it is the only office mentioned in a Greek inscription in Spartiaticus's honor from Athens, which describes Spartiaticus as the first man to be chosen by the general assembly of Achaia as high priest for life in the imperial cult;[96] as such, Spartiaticus held the highest office in the province.[97]

The careers of Dinippus and Spartiaticus established and perpetuated the prominence of their families within the social and political hierarchy of Corinth. While the relationship of Dinippus to the numerous other Ti. Claudii attested at Corinth is difficult to determine,[98] it seems likely that he was a member of a dynasty that included two other *duoviri* in the first century.[99] As already noted, C. Julius Laco preceded his son in the office of *duovir*.[100] Laco was made the administrator (*procurator*) of imperial

---

92. Richard P. Duncan-Jones, *The Economy of the Roman Empire: Quantitative Studies*, 2nd ed. (Cambridge: Cambridge University Press, 1982), 4.

93. Spawforth, "Roman Corinth," 177–78; IKorinthWest, 52; IKorinthKent, 31. On the cost of the games and the burden of the office of ἀγωνοθέτης, see Daniel J. Geagan, "Notes on the Agonistic Institutions of Roman Corinth," *GRBS* 4 (1968): 69–80, esp. 69, 74; Wiseman, "Corinth and Rome I," 500.

94. IKorinthWest, 53; Taylor and West, "Euryclids in Latin Inscriptions," 394–95.

95. IKorinthWest §68, pp. 50–53.

96. *IG* 3.805 = *SIG* 2.790; see also Arthur Stein and Leiva Petersen, *Prosopographia Imperii Romani* (Berlin: de Gruyter, 1966), §587, 4:282. See further a Spartan dedication, *IG* 5.1.463.

97. Taylor and West, "Euryclids in Latin Inscriptions," 394.

98. Stansbury, "Corinthian Honor," 300.

99. Spawforth, "Roman Corinth," 177–78; Millis, "Local Magistrates and Elite of Roman Corinth," 43.

100. IKorinthWest §67, pp. 46–49.

estates in Greece;[101] he also served as *flamen Augusti*, setting his son an example of loyalty to the imperial house.[102] In sum, the families of Dinippus and Spartiaticus transcended in wealth and dignity other rich families at Corinth, as stunning examples of the phenomenon of the internal oligarchization of the elite in the first century.

The magnitude of the munificence of Dinippus and Spartiaticus is evident, even if all of the details of their benefactions cannot be established. As ἀγωνοθέτης of the imperial games, Dinippus, like Spartiaticus, would have been responsible for organizing and financing these spectacles at extraordinary expense.[103] The amounts Dinippus spent as superintendent of the grain supply are unknown, but must have been considerable, since no fewer than ten inscriptions in his honor were erected by various Corinthian tribes.[104] Whether Spartiaticus or his father Laco constructed the beautiful public baths on the Lechaion Road that are named after their ancestor Eurycles is not certain; in any case, the baths were remodeled in the second century by C. Julius Heraclanus.[105] The Latin inscription that preserves the record of Spartiaticus's public career concludes with praise of his "eager and all-encompassing munificence toward our colony" (*animosam fusissimamque erga coloniam nostrum munificientiam*).[106] That the amenities and even necessities of life provided by the big gifts of men such as Dinippus and Spartiaticus served to quiet the fears and soothe the tensions that brewed beneath the surface of society in first-century Corinth is indicated by the language of the honorific inscriptions dedicated to them. The nearly identical inscriptions honoring Dinippus by ten of the twelve Corinthian tribes suggest unanimity, if not spontaneity of gratitude.[107]

---

101. IKorinthWest §67, pp. 47, 49, 51; cf. K. M. T. Chrimes, *Ancient Sparta: A Re-examination of the Evidence* (Manchester: Manchester University Press, 1952), 184; Paul Cartledge and Antony J. S. Spawforth, *Hellenistic and Roman Sparta: A Tale of Two Cities* (London: Routledge, 2002), 102.

102. IKorinthWest §67, pp. 47, 49.

103. IKorinthKent, 30; Spawforth, "Roman Corinth," 178; Geagan, "Notes on the Agonistic Institutions," 69, 74; Wiseman, "Corinth and Rome I," 500.

104. IKorinthWest §§86–90; IKorinthKent §§158–63; cf. Danylak, "Tiberius Claudius Dinippus," 231–70.

105. Spawforth, "Roman Corinth," 179.

106. IKorinthWest §68; cf. Taylor and West, "Euryclids in Latin Inscriptions," 399–400.

107. Bruce W. Winter, *After Paul Left Corinth: The Influence of Secular Ethics and Social Change* (Grand Rapids: Eerdmans, 2001), 216.

The tribesmen of Calpurnia who dedicated an inscription to Spartiaticus proudly proclaim him their "patron."[108]

As noted earlier, the inscriptions of Corinth make no mention of non-elite individuals, that is, the poor and those of "middling" incomes who, according to the best estimates, accounted for 95 percent of the total population.[109] There would seem, then, to be an evidentiary limit to our ability to test key features of the economic model I am seeking to employ. How can we know whether urban wage laborers became progressively impoverished, or whether service providers, such as wine merchants and gem cutters, experienced a modest rise in incomes? At this point, Paul's extensive correspondence with the community of Christ believers at Corinth provides crucial, indeed invaluable, evidence. For Paul makes explicit statements about persons of low social status at Corinth, and describes tensions between the "haves" and the "have-nots." Moreover, a prosopography of Paul's Corinthian epistles affords glimpses of several persons who enjoyed middling incomes. Thus the data of Paul's epistolary archive make possible a more thorough assessment of a model that predicts a rise in social inequality.

In 1 Cor 1:26–28, Paul reminds his readers of their social condition, in order to illustrate the paradoxical character of the divine purpose: "For consider your calling, brothers and sisters, that not many of you were learned by worldly standards, not many were powerful, not many were nobly born; but God chose the foolish of the world to humiliate the learned, and God chose the weak of the world to humiliate the strong, and God chose the lowborn of the world and the despised, things that are nothing, to nullify the things that are, so that no human being might boast in the presence of God." Paul's studied use of litotes in this passage (οὐ πολλοί for ὀλίγοι) reveals that a few, if only a few, possessed the advantages that

---

108. IKorinthWest §68, p. 51.
109. Willem M. Jongman, "A Golden Age: Death, Money Supply, and Social Succession in the Roman Empire," in *Credito e moneta nel mondo romano: Atti degli Incontri capresi di storia dell'economia antica*, ed. Elio LoCascio (Bari: Edipuglia, 2003), 181-96; Jongman, "The Early Roman Empire: Consumption," in *The Cambridge Economic History of the Greco-Roman World*, ed. Walter Scheidel, Ian Morris, and Richard Saller (Cambridge: Cambridge University Press, 2007), 592–618; Keith Hopkins, "The Political Economy of the Roman Empire," in *The Dynamics of Ancient Empires*, ed. Ian Morris and Walter Scheidel (New York: Oxford University Press, 2009), 178–204; Walter Scheidel and Steven J. Friesen, "The Size of the Economy and the Distribution of Income in the Roman Empire," *JRS* 99 (2009): 61–91.

distinguished members of the upper class: education, wealth, and birth.[110] But Paul's statement leaves no doubt that the majority of Christ believers at Corinth were poor, perhaps very poor.[111]

Moreover, several passages in 1 Corinthians make clear that slaves belonged to the assembly of those in Christ at Corinth. Twice Paul reminds his readers: "You were bought with a price" (1 Cor 6:20, 7:22), evoking the experience of the large Roman slave market at Corinth.[112] In 1 Cor 7:21, Paul acknowledges, "You were called as a slave," then advises: "Do not worry about it. But if you can indeed become free, make use [of freedom] instead" (translating the brachylogy μᾶλλον χρῆσαι in an adversative sense).[113] In 1 Cor 7:22, Paul explains: "For the person who is a slave at the time when he or she was called in the Lord is the freedperson of the Lord," making use of the technical Greek term for a freedperson, ἀπελεύθερος.[114]

In 1 Cor 11:17-34, Paul deals with the problem of divisions that appeared when the Christ believers gathered to eat their communal meal, the Lord's Supper. Paul speaks of some who are "hungry" and others who are "satiated" (literally, "drunken"). Because several elements of the descriptive core of Paul's evaluation of the Corinthians' conduct in 1 Cor 11:21 are ambiguous, various reconstructions of what happened at the meal are possible.[115] Perhaps some (the rich) began to eat before others

---

110. On the litotes in 1 Cor 1:26 and its implications, see Edwin A. Judge, *The Social Pattern of the Christian Groups in the First Century* (London: Tyndale, 1960), 59; Theissen, *Social Setting*, 70, 72-73; Dale B. Martin, *The Corinthian Body* (New Haven: Yale University Press, 1995), 61.

111. On this implication of 1 Cor 1:26, see Theissen, *Social Setting*, 72-73. On the poverty of the majority of the Corinthian Christians in general, see Steven J. Friesen, "Poverty in Pauline Studies: Beyond the So-Called New Consensus," *JSNT* 26 (2004): 323-61, esp. 348-53; Friesen, "Prospects for a Demography of the Pauline Mission: Corinth among the Churches," in *Urban Religion in Roman Corinth*, ed. Daniel N. Schowalter and Steven J. Friesen (Cambridge: Harvard University Press, 2005), 351-70, esp. 367.

112. Nasrallah, "You Were Bought with a Price," 54-73.

113. For arguments in support of this translation, see Harrill, *Manumission of Slaves*, 76-121.

114. Nasrallah, "You Were Bought with a Price," 55.

115. Theissen, *Social Setting*, 145-74; Bruce W. Winter, "The Lord's Supper at Corinth: An Alternative Reconstruction," *RTR* 37 (1978): 73-82; Hans-Josef Klauck, *Herrenmahl und hellenistischer Kult. Eine religionsgeschichtliche Untersuchung zum ersten Korintherbrief* (Münster: Aschendorff, 1982), 285-332; Peter Lampe, "Das

(slaves and the poor) had arrived.[116] Or perhaps the rich feasted sumptuously while the poor looked on.[117] Perhaps the Lord's Supper at Corinth was a kind of "potluck" to which individual Christ believers contributed according to their means.[118] A better-grounded reconstruction suggests that a single patron supplied the meal for the group that met in his house, apportioning food to the guests as the patron saw fit.[119] In any case, Paul is concerned that inequity in the distribution of food and drink has resulted in the humiliation of the have-nots (1 Cor 11:22).[120] Some scholars have suggested that Paul's concern for the hunger of the poor in 1 Cor 11 should be set in the context of the food shortages in mid-first-century Corinth, which led to the appointment of Ti. Claudius Dinippus as the curator of the grain supply.[121] However that may be, Paul's description of the hunger of "those who have not" suggests that some in the community were living below subsistence level.[122] Indeed, Paul states that "many have become weak and sick and some have even died," on account of the failure of the Corinthians to discern the needs of members of the body of Christ (1 Cor 11:29–30).

Nine individuals are mentioned by name in 1 Corinthians and Rom 16 in connection with Corinth. We may proceed with our prosopography from lowest to highest in terms of social status. Tertius, the scribe of Paul's Epistle to the Romans (Rom 16:22), was probably a slave in the house of Gaius, where the epistle was composed (Rom 16:23).[123] The Latin name

---

korinthische Herrenmahl im Schnittpunkt hellenistischer Mahlpraxis und paulinischer Theologia Crucis (1 Kor 11,17–34)," *ZNW* 82 (1991): 183–213.

116. Günther Bornkamm, "Herrenmahl und Kirche bei Paulus," in *Studien zu Antike und Christentum: Gesammelte Aufsätze II* (Munich: Kaiser, 1959), 138–76, here 142; Theissen, *Social Setting*, 151; Lampe, "Das korinthische Herrenmahl," 198.

117. Winter, "The Lord's Supper at Corinth," 73–77.

118. Bornkamm, "Herrenmahl und Kirche bei Paulus," 143–44; Theissen, *Social Setting*, 148; Lampe, "Das korinthische Herrenmahl," 198–200.

119. Thomas Schmeller, *Hierarchie und Egalität: Eine sozialgeschichtliche Untersuchung paulinischer Gemeinden und griechisch-römischer Vereine* (Stuttgart: Katholisches Bibelwerk, 1995), 60, 71.

120. Meeks, *First Urban Christians*, 68.

121. Bruce W. Winter, "Secular and Christian Responses to Corinthian Famines," *TynBul* 40 (1989): 86–106; Winter, *After Paul Left Corinth*, 216–25; Danylak, "Tiberius Claudius Dinippus," 267–68.

122. Friesen, "Poverty in Pauline Studies," 349.

123. Theissen, *Social Setting*, 92; Meeks, *First Urban Christians*, 57; Robert Jewett, *Romans: A Commentary*, Hermeneia (Minneapolis: Fortress, 2007), 978–80.

Tertius means "third" and was often used for slaves.[124] Tertius's profession is a further indication of servile status, since amanuenses were often slaves.[125] Quartus's Latin name means "fourth" (Rom 16:22); like Tertius, it was a common name among slaves and freedmen.[126] Next, we meet Fortunatus and Achaicus, the two traveling companions of Stephanas (1 Cor 16:17); both names probably indicate servile origins.[127] Fortunatus ("lucky") was a common name, appropriate to a freedman. A cognomen such as Achaicus, derived from a place name or an ἔθνος, was generally associated with slaves or freedmen. The mention of Fortunatus and Achaicus along with Stephanas suggests that they were members of Stephanas's household, whether as slaves or freedmen clients.[128]

Moving up the social ladder, we come to Chloe, a woman of more than modest means, as demonstrated by the fact that she was able to provision members of her household, whether slaves or former slaves,[129] to travel to Ephesus, where they reported to Paul about divisions in the community of Christ believers at Corinth (1 Cor 1:11).[130] Twice in 1 Corinthians Paul mentions the "household" of Stephanas (1 Cor 1:16, 16:15); this household probably included slaves, in addition to family members.[131] Stephanas had the resources to travel from Corinth to Ephesus,[132] bringing a gift that

---

124. Heikki Solin, *Die stadtrömischen Sklavennamen: Ein Namenbuch* (Stuttgart: Steiner, 1996), 152–53, with many examples of Tertius as a slave name. Cf. Edwin Judge, "The Roman Base of Paul's Mission," in *The First Christians in the Roman World: Augustan and New Testament Essays*, ed. James R. Harrison (Tübingen: Mohr Siebeck, 2008), 562.

125. E.g., *ILS* 1514 in Robert K. Sherk, *The Roman Empire: Augustus to Hadrian* (Cambridge: Cambridge University Press, 1988), 237; see further G. H. R. Horsley, "The Distribution of a Deceased Man's Slaves," *NewDocs* 1:69–70.

126. Solin, *Die stadtrömischen Sklavennamen*, 154; cf. Judge, "Roman Base of Paul's Mission," 562.

127. Lily Ross Taylor, "Freedmen and Freeborn in the Epitaphs of Imperial Rome," *AJP* 82 (1961): 125; Judge, "Roman Base of Paul's Mission," 562.

128. Meeks, *First Urban Christians*, 56–57.

129. Theissen, *Social Setting*, 93: "Who were Chloe's people? ... Within the Pauline letters themselves the closest parallel would be groups of slaves addressed summarily (Rom. 16:10, 11; Phil. 4:22)"; Meeks, *First Urban Christians*, 59: "'Chloe's people' (*hoi Chloēs*, 1 Cor. 1:11) are slaves or freedmen or both."

130. Theissen, *Social Setting*, 91.

131. Ibid., 87–88, 92; Meeks, *First Urban Christians*, 56–58.

132. Theissen, *Social Setting*, 91; Meeks, *First Urban Christians*, 58.

alleviated Paul's lack.¹³³ A tantalizing, if tenuous, clue to Stephanas's occupation may be found in the locution Paul employs to describe Stephanas's function within the community: διακονίαν τάσσειν ἑαυτούς (1 Cor 16:15); elsewhere in Greek literature this phrase describes those who "appoint themselves to (a particular) service,"¹³⁴ "exchanging money for goods with those who wish to sell, and goods for money with those who desire to buy."¹³⁵ Perhaps Stephanas was a successful "shopkeeper" (κάπηλος) or, given his capacity for travel, a "merchant-trader" (ἔμπορος), like those whom Favorinus mentions in his Corinthian oration.¹³⁶

At the top of the social pyramid of Christ believers at Corinth are three individuals whose wealth is surprising. In 1 Cor 1:14, Paul names Crispus as one of the few whom he personally baptized at the beginning of his work in Corinth.¹³⁷ Acts 18:8 relates that "Crispus, the ruler of the synagogue, believed in the Lord, together with all his household." Because it is hardly possible to doubt the identity of the Crispus of Acts with the man named in 1 Corinthians,¹³⁸ the information of Acts that Crispus was the synagogue president is crucial for establishing his status and influence.¹³⁹ As the former ἀρχισυνάγωγος, Crispus would have had consider-

---

133. Theissen, *Social Setting*, 87–88; Meeks, *First Urban Christians*, 58.

134. LSJ, 1757–58 s.v. τάσσω II; BDAG, 1607 s.v. τάσσω. Cf. Andreas Lindemann, *Der erste Korintherbrief* (Tübingen: Mohr Siebeck, 2000), 384.

135. E.g., Plato, *Resp.* 2.371C; for further references, see Gerhard Delling, "τάσσω, κτλ.," *TDNT* 8:27–28, 28 n. 6.

136. Compare Sulpicius Cinnamus and Sulpicius Faustus, two freedmen *mercatores*, whose lives have been illuminated by the discovery of documents revealing their business activities at Murecine, a suburb of Pompeii, in Lucio Bove, *Documenti di operazioni finanziarie dall' archivio dei Sulpici* (Naples: Liguori, 1984); Andrew Wallace-Hadrill, *Houses and Society in Pompeii and Herculaneum* (Princeton: Princeton University Press, 1994), 175.

137. For the context of Paul's mention of Crispus, see Weiss, *Der erste Korintherbrief*, 19–21. For attestation of the name Crispus in the papyri, see Peter Arzt-Grabner, *1. Korinther. Papyrologische Kommentare zum Neuen Testament* (Göttingen: Vandenhoeck & Ruprecht, 2006), 74. For an estimate of the "social impressiveness" of the cognomen Crispus, see Judge, "Roman Base of Paul's Mission," 561–62.

138. The identity is assumed by Edwin A. Judge, "The Early Christians as a Scholastic Community," in Harrison, *First Christians*, 544-45; Theissen, *Social Setting*, 73–74; Abraham J. Malherbe, *Social Aspects of Early Christianity* (Philadelphia: Fortress, 1983), 72; Meeks, *First Urban Christians*, 57.

139. The importance of this datum for establishing the social status of Crispus is widely recognized: e.g., Theissen, *Social Setting*, 73–74; Meeks, *First Urban Christians*,

able wealth, since the position was that of benefactor and patron of the Jewish community, entailing responsibility for the construction, repair, and maintenance of the synagogue.[140]

Gaius, who is mentioned in the same breath with Crispus in 1 Cor 1:14, was also among the converts made by Paul on his first visit to Corinth.[141] In Rom 16:23, Paul sends greetings from a Gaius, whom he describes as "my host and the host of the whole assembly." Although Gaius was a common Latin praenomen,[142] especially common at Corinth, owing to the history of the colony,[143] there is no reason to doubt the identity of the two men of this name mentioned by Paul.[144] For evaluation of the social

---

57; Murphy-O'Connor, *St. Paul's Corinth*, 267. Meggitt (*Paul, Poverty and Survival*, 142–43) attempts to diminish the significance of Crispus's office as ἀρχισυνάγωγος; but see the counterarguments of Gerd Theissen, "The Social Structure of Pauline Communities: Some Critical Remarks on J. J. Meggitt, *Paul, Poverty and Survival*," *JSNT* 84 (2001): 81–82. It is puzzling that Crispus is omitted from the economic profile of Paul's assemblies in Friesen, "Poverty in Pauline Studies," 348–58, esp. 357.

140. Tessa Rajak and David Noy, "Archisynagogoi: Office, Title and Social Status in the Greco-Jewish Synagogue," *JRS* 83 (1993): 75–93; reprinted in Tessa Rajak, *The Jewish Dialogue with Greece and Rome: Studies in Cultural and Social Interaction* (Leiden: Brill, 2002), 393–430.

141. Theissen, *Social Setting*, 55, 89; Malherbe, *Social Aspects of Early Christianity*, 73; Meeks, *First Urban Christians*, 57.

142. Helmut Rix, *Römische Personennamen*, vol. 1 of *Namenforschung: Ein internationales Handbuch zur Onomastik* (Berlin: de Gruyter, 1995), 724–32; Olli Salomies, *Die römischen Vornamen: Studien zur römischen Namengebung* (Helsinki: Societas Scientiarum Fennica, 1987). It is possible that Gaius is a praenomen functioning as a cognomen in a Greek context; for this phenomenon, see Heikki Solin, "Latin Cognomina in the Greek East," in *The Greek East in the Roman Context*, ed. Olli Salomies (Helsinki: Finnish Institute at Athens, 2001), 189–202, esp. 191, 194–96. But the use of praenomens as cognomens did not become common until the second century CE, and then only in the less Romanized areas; see Salomies, *Die römischen Vornamen*, 164–65.

143. Corinth was refounded as a Roman colony by Gaius Julius Caesar in 44 BCE. Many of the colonists were Caesar's freedmen, and would have borne his praenomen. See Appian, *Punica* 136; Strabo, *Geogr.* 8.6.23; Plutarch, *Caes.*, 57.5; Dio Cassius, *Hist. rom.* 43.50.3–5. Cf. Edward T. Salmon, *Roman Colonization under the Republic* (Ithaca, NY: Cornell University Press, 1970), 135; Stansbury, "Corinthian Honor," 116–22.

144. So almost all commentators: e.g., Weiss, *Der erste Korintherbrief*, 21; Gordon Fee, *The First Epistle to the Corinthians*, NICNT (Grand Rapids: Eerdmans, 1987), 62, 82; Wolfgang Schrage, *Der erste Brief an die Korinther* (Neukirchen-Vluyn: Neukirchener Verlag, 1991), 1:155; Joseph A. Fitzmyer, *First Corinthians: A New Translation*

status of Gaius, Paul's description of him as "my host and the host of the whole assembly" is of utmost importance.[145] While it is possible that Gaius hosted the assembly in a meeting hall rented for that purpose,[146] the most natural construction of Paul's language suggests that Gaius placed his own house at the disposal of the community of Christ believers.[147] Gaius of Corinth is the only person in early Christianity who is said to have hosted all the believers of a given city in his house as a central meeting place,[148] which makes Gaius one of the wealthiest persons we know of from Paul's communities.[149]

Last, we come to Erastus, whom Paul describes in Rom 16:23 as "the financial manager of the city" (ὁ οἰκονόμος τῆς πόλεως). In inscriptions from Greece and Asia Minor, the title οἰκονόμος is applied to persons in a wide range of classes, embracing freeborn citizens on the one hand, and public slaves on the other.[150] But in seeking to ascertain what civic office

---

with *Introduction and Commentary*, AYB (New Haven: Yale University Press, 2008), 146.

145. Rightly, Theissen, *Social Setting*, 89; Malherbe, *Social Aspects of Early Christianity*, 73–74; Meeks, *First Urban Christians*, 57–58; Stansbury, "Corinthian Honor," 460-61; Friesen, "Poverty in Pauline Studies," 356.

146. As suggested by Craig Steven De Vos, *Church and Community Conflicts: The Relationship of the Thessalonian, Corinthian, and Philippian Churches with Their Wider Civic Communities* (Atlanta: Scholars Press, 1999), 204.

147. The distributive force of the articular noun ὁ ξένος in the phrase ὁ ξένος μου καὶ ὅλης τῆς ἐκκλησίας in Rom 16:23 implies that Gaius hosted the assembly in the place where Paul enjoyed his hospitality. See Theissen, *Social Setting*, 55, 89; Malherbe, *Social Aspects of Early Christianity*, 73–74; Murphy-O'Connor, *St. Paul's Corinth*, 156, 158; Meeks, *First Urban Christians*, 57; Stephen C. Barton, "Paul's Sense of Place: An Anthropological Approach to Community Formation in Corinth," *NTS* 32 (1986): 225–46, here 225; Theissen, "Social Structure," 83.

148. The point is well made by Peter Lampe, *From Paul to Valentinus: Christians at Rome in the First Two Centuries* (Minneapolis: Fortress, 2003), 192 n. 26; Lampe, "Paul, Patrons and Clients," in *Paul in the Greco-Roman World*, ed. J. Paul Sampley (Harrisburg, PA: Trinity Press International, 2003), 496; see already Meeks, *First Urban Christians*, 221 n. 7: "Gaius's role was unusual enough for Paul to single it out when mentioning him to the Roman Christians; it may have been unique."

149. Friesen, "Poverty in Pauline Studies," 356; cf. Theissen, "Social Structure," 83; Ekkehard Stegemann and Wolfgang Stegemann, *Urchristliche Sozialgeschichte: Die Anfänge im Judentum und die Christusgemeinden in der mediterranen Welt* (Stuttgart: Kohlhammer, 1995), 254.

150. Peter Landvogt, *Epigraphische Untersuchungen über den ΟΙΚΟΝΟΜΟΣ: Ein Beitrag zum hellenistischen Beamtenwesen* (Strassburg: Schauberg, 1908), esp.

Erastus might have held, it does not suffice to focus exclusively on the Greek expression,[151] because Corinth was a Roman colony whose official language was Latin.[152] Thus we must ask what Latin title would have corresponded to the Greek οἰκονόμος τῆς πόλεως. In his lexicon of Greek terms for Roman institutions, Hugh Mason judges that οἰκονόμος could designate the Roman municipal office of aedile, and adduces a number of inscriptions where this is the case.[153] John Kent, the principal epigrapher of Roman Corinth, argues that οἰκονόμος may have been an accurate description of the responsibilities of the aediles of Corinth, owing to the peculiarities of financial management in that city: "Corinth was a unique colony in that she controlled the management of the games which were internationally famous. She therefore administered the Isthmian festivals by means of a completely separate set of officials (the *agonothetai*), and the Corinthian aediles, thus relieved of all responsibilities for public entertainment, were in effect confined in their activities to local economic matters."[154] Thus Kent offers the explanation: "It is possibly for this reason that Paul does not use the customary word ἀγορανόμος to describe a Corinthian aedile, but calls him οἰκονόμος."[155] If the conclusions of Mason and Kent are valid, and Paul's Erastus was indeed an aedile of Corinth, this would have dra-

---

12-14. Landvogt's study is supplemented by the appendix on the status of *oikonomoi* in Dale B. Martin, *Slavery as Salvation: The Metaphor of Slavery in Pauline Christianity* (New Haven: Yale University Press, 1990), 174-77. The importance of Landvogt's study for an evaluation of the status of Erastus was already emphasized by Henry J. Cadbury, "Erastus of Corinth," *JBL* 50 (1931): 42-58, esp. 47; but the work has dropped out of some recent discussions: e.g., Meggitt, *Paul, Poverty and Survival*, 135-41; Steven J. Friesen, "The Wrong Erastus: Ideology, Archaeology, and Exegesis," in Friesen, Schowalter, and Walters, *Corinth in Context*, 231-56.

151. Rightly, Theissen, *Social Setting*, 78-79.

152. IKorinthKent, 18-19: "It will be noted that of the 104 texts that are prior to the reign of Hadrian 101 are in Latin and only three are in Greek, a virtual monopoly for the Latin language." On the Romanness of Corinth in the early empire, see Antony J. S. Spawforth, *Greece and the Augustan Cultural Revolution* (Cambridge: Cambridge University Press, 2012), 45, 48, 53, 54.

153. Hugh J. Mason, *Greek Terms for Roman Institutions: A Lexicon and Analysis* (Toronto: Hakkert, 1974), 71, 145, 175-76, referencing *IGRR* 4.813 (Hierapolis), 4.1435 (Smyrna), 4.1630 (Philadelphia). Friesen's judgment ("Wrong Erastus," 247 n. 48) that Mason's interpretation of these inscriptions is "clearly mistaken" ignores the arguments of Landvogt, *Epigraphische Untersuchungen*, 14, 26-27, 28, 47.

154. IKorinthKent, 27.

155. IKorinthKent, 27.

matic implications for our assessment of Erastus's social status: Erastus would then be a high-ranking official, one of only four annually elected magistrates, and consequently a *decurion*.

All in all, the ἐκκλησία of Christ believers at Corinth would seem to be a mirror and microcosm of the city itself. The majority were poor, lacking education, wealth, and birth, nobodies in terms of public honor; some had fallen below the level of subsistence and depended on the communal meals for nourishment. A few were persons of middling incomes, shopkeepers, perhaps, or merchant-traders. Surprising is only the presence of three rather wealthy individuals. But this finding is consistent with Paul's statements and representations elsewhere in his Corinthian correspondence. In a bitterly sarcastic passage in 1 Cor 4, Paul mocks the pretentions of the patrons of the community: "Already you have all you want! Already you have become rich! Quite apart from us you reign as kings!" (1 Cor 4:8).[156] Paul's use of the expression "reign like kings" is an unmistakable allusion to the role of some as patrons.[157] "King" (*rex*, βασιλεύς) is the satirists' term for a rich patron.[158] Similarly, in 1 Cor 11:22, Paul asks the rich, with biting irony, "Or don't you have houses in which to eat and drink?" seeking to prick their consciences over the humiliation of "those who have not."[159] Throughout all stages of the Corinthian correspondence, Paul anticipates the crucial role that the Corinthians will play in the success of the collection for the poor in Jerusalem, on account of their greater wealth. At the first mention of the collection project in 1 Cor 16:1–4, Paul adds to the instructions for accumulating monies a promissory incentive: "if [the collection] is sufficiently large [ἐὰν δὲ ἄξιον ᾖ]," he himself will

---

156. On the bitter sarcasm of this passage, see Weiss, *Der erste Korintherbrief*, 105–8; L. L. Welborn, *Paul, the Fool of Christ: A Study of 1 Corinthians 1–4 in the Comic-Philosophic Tradition* (London: T&T Clark, 2005), 115–16.

157. Martin, *Slavery as Salvation*, 210 n. 13; Welborn, *Paul, the Fool of Christ*, 232.

158. E.g., Horace, *Ep.* 1.7.37–38; Juvenal, *Sat.* 5.14, 130, 137, 161; 7.45; 10.161; cf. Gilbert Highet, "*Libertino Patre Natus*," *AJP* 94 (1973): 268–81, here 279; Peter White, *Promised Verse: Poets in the Society of Augustan Rome* (Cambridge: Harvard University Press, 1993), 29–30, 280 n. 47.

159. Guido O. Kirner, "Apostolat und Patronage (II) Darstellungsteil: Weisheit, Rhetorik und Ruhm in Konflikt um die apostolischen Praxis des Paulus in der frühchristlichen Gemeinde Korinth (1 Kor. 1–4 und 9; 2 Kor. 10–13," *ZAC* 6 (2002): 27–72, here 55; cf. James C. Walters, "Paul and the Politics of Meals in Roman Corinth," in Friesen, Schowalter, and Walters, *Corinth in Context*, 350–61, here 358–59.

convey it to Jerusalem.[160] In 2 Cor 8:14, Paul speaks of the "abundance" (περίσσευμα) of the Corinthians and contrasts it with the "lack" (ὑστέρημα) of the saints in Jerusalem. In 2 Cor 8:20, Paul seeks to reassure the Corinthians about the "large sum of money" (ἁδρότης) that they are entrusting to his administration.[161] I see no reason to believe that Paul's statements about the abundance of some at Corinth are rhetorical exaggerations.[162] Rather, it would seem that at Corinth, for the first time in his ministry, and for reasons that can only be conjectured, Paul succeeded in making a few converts from the upper class.[163]

In general, my analysis and prosopography of Paul's Corinthian epistles has provided impressive confirmation of the predictions of a neo-Ricardian model regarding social inequality at Corinth. In a period of increasing population in mid-first-century Corinth, extraordinary wealth accumulated in the hands of the few who owned land and houses, and who controlled ancillary resources (Crispus, Gaius, Erastus). A segment of the nonelite population that provided services, that is, merchants and traders (such as Chloe and Stephanas), experienced new prosperity as a consequence of increased elite demand. But for the great majority of urban wage laborers (the "nobodies" and "have-nots" of whom Paul speaks), the growing disparity in distribution of resources resulted in dangerous, even life-threatening levels of impoverishment.

A final respect in which Paul's Corinthian epistles confirm the predictions of a neo-Ricardian model is in the evidence they provide of social tensions in consequence of growing income disparities. Paul received more than one report of "divisions" (σχίσματα) in the assembly of Christ believers at Corinth. The first report in 1 Cor 11:18 is discreetly anonymous.[164] In this case, the cause of the conflict is clear: the failure of the patron of the community, in whose house the communal meal was celebrated, to fulfill the obligation to provide the amenities, indeed the neces-

---

160. Cf. Weiss, *Der erste Korintherbrief*, 382.

161. Hans Dieter Betz, *2 Corinthians 8 and 9: Two Administrative Letters of the Apostle Paul* (Philadelphia: Fortress, 1985), 77, observing that ἁδρότης is a *terminus technicus* of economic life.

162. Ibid., 45 nn. 15 and 68: "At the literal level, Paul certainly intended the material abundance of the Corinthians and the material poverty of the Jerusalem church."

163. De Vos, *Church and Community Conflicts*, 197–203.

164. Weiss, *Der erste Korintherbrief*, 277–79; L. L. Welborn, *Politics and Rhetoric in the Corinthian Epistles* (Macon, GA: Mercer University Press, 1997), 16–17.

sities of life. In other words, a display of oligarchic excess led to antagonism between the haves and the have-nots. The second report, in 1 Cor 1:10–12, is of noisy partisanship. It is significant that the report is brought by "Chloe's people."[165] In the discussion that follows (1 Cor 1:14–16), Paul takes pains to separate Stephanas, his strongest supporter at Corinth, from any connection with the outbreak of faction,[166] but treats the precedence of Crispus and Gaius with high irony.[167] It would seem that the two persons of middling income, Chloe and Stephanas, have turned to Paul to resolve the conflict, while the elite householders, Crispus and Gaius, have declared themselves partisans of the learned and eloquent Apollos.[168] The literature of the first and second centuries, especially the speeches of Dio Chrysostom and the letters of the younger Pliny, reveal that guilds, clubs, and voluntary associations were frequently the first places where the social tensions generated by economic disparities erupted into the open.[169]

BIBLIOGRAPHY

Amandry, Michel. *Le Monnayage des duovirs Corinthiens*. BCHSup 15. Athens: École française d'Athènes; Paris: de Boccard, 1988.
Anderson, J. G. C. "Some Questions Bearing on the Date and Place of Composition of Strabo's *Geography*." Pages 1–13 in *Anatolian Studies Presented to Sir W. M. Ramsay*. Edited by W. H. Buckler and W. M. Calder. Manchester: University of Manchester Press, 1923.
Arzt-Grabner, Peter. *1. Korinther: Papyrologische Kommentare zum Neuen Testament*. Göttingen: Vandenhoeck & Ruprecht, 2006.

---

165. On the possible interests and objectives of the lower classes in the assembly of Christ believers at Corinth, see Welborn, *Politics and Rhetoric*, 17, 27–28.

166. See the nuanced analysis of Paul's rhetoric in 1 Cor 1:14–16 by Weiss, *Der erste Korintherbrief*, 20–21.

167. On the unmistakable note of irony in 1 Cor 1:14 and its implications, see Weiss, *Der erste Korintherbrief*, 20–21; followed by L. L. Welborn, *An End to Enmity: Paul and the "Wrongdoer" of Second Corinthians*, BZNW 185 (Berlin: de Gruyter, 2011), 239–41.

168. Welborn, *An End to Enmity*, 240–41, 249, 251, 371–76.

169. Giovanni Salmeri, "Dio, Rome, and the Civic Life of Asia Minor," in *Dio Chrysostom: Politics, Letters, and Philosophy*, ed. Simon Swain (Oxford: Oxford University Press, 2000), 53–92, esp. 72–74; Arjan Zuiderhoek, "On the Political Sociology of the Imperial Greek City," *GRBS* 48 (2008): 417–45, esp. 436–40.

Barigazzi, Adelmo. *Favorino di Arelate, Opere: Introduzione, Testo Critica e comment.* Firenze: Felice le Monnier, 1966.

Bartchy, S. Scott. *ΜΑΛΛΟΝ ΧΡΗΣΑΙ: First-Century Slavery and the Interpretation of 1 Corinthians 7:21.* Atlanta: Scholars Press, 1985.

Barton, Stephen C. "Paul's Sense of Place: An Anthropological Approach to Community Formation in Corinth." *NTS* 32 (1986): 225–46.

Benner, A. R., trans. *The Letters of Alciphron.* LCL. Cambridge: Harvard University Press, 1962.

Betz, Hans Dieter. *2 Corinthians 8 and 9: Two Administrative Letters of the Apostle Paul.* Philadelphia: Fortress, 1985.

Bornkamm, Günther. "Herrenmahl und Kirche bei Paulus." Pages 138–76 in *Studien zu Antike und Christentum: Gesammelte Aufsätze II.* Munich: Kaiser, 1959.

Bove, Lucio. *Documenti di operazioni finanziarie dall' archivio dei Sulpici.* Naples: Liguori, 1984.

Bowersock, Glen W. "Eurycles of Sparta." *JRS* 51 (1961): 112–18.

Broneer, Oscar. *The South Stoa and Its Roman Successors.* Vol. 1.4 of *Corinth: Results of Excavations Conducted by the American School of Classical Studies at Athens.* Princeton: American School of Classical Studies at Athens, 1954.

Burnett, Andrew, Michel Amandry, and Pere Pau Ripollés. *From the Death of Caesar to the Death of Vitellius (44 BC–AD 69).* Vol. 1 of *Roman Provincial Coinage.* London: British Museum Press; Paris: Bibliothèque Nationale, 1992. Revised 2006.

Cadbury, Henry J. "Erastus of Corinth." *JBL* 50 (1931): 42–58.

Cartledge, Paul, and Antony J. S. Spawforth. *Hellenistic and Roman Sparta: A Tale of Two Cities.* London: Routledge, 2002.

Chrimes, K. M. T. *Ancient Sparta: A Re-examination of the Evidence.* Manchester: Manchester University Press, 1952.

Clarke, Andrew D. *Secular and Christian Leadership in Corinth: A Sociohistorical and Exegetical Study of 1 Corinthians 1–6.* Leiden: Brill, 1993.

Conzelmann, Hans. "Korinth und die Mädchen der Aphrodite: Zur Religionsgeschichte der Stadt Korinth." *NAWG* 8 (1967–1968): 247–61.

Cox, Sherry C. "Health in Hellenistic and Roman Times: The Case Studies of Paphos, Cyprus and Corinth." Pages 59–82 in *Health in Antiquity.* Edited by Helen King. New York: Routledge, 2005.

Danylak, Barry N. "Tiberius Claudius Dinippus and the Food Shortages in Corinth." *TynBul* 59 (2008): 231–70.

De Vos, Craig Steven. *Church and Community Conflicts: The Relationship of the Thessalonian, Corinthian, and Philippian Churches with Their Wider Civic Communities*. Atlanta: Scholars Press, 1999.

Devijver, Hubert. *Prosopographia militiarum equestrium quae fuerunt ab Augusto ad Gallienum*. Part 2. Leuven: Symbolae Facultatis Litterarum et Philosophiae Louaniensis, 1977.

Dio Chrysostom. Translated by J. W. Cohoon and H. Lamar Crosby. 5 vols. LCL. Cambridge: Harvard University Press, 1932–1940.

Duncan-Jones, Richard P. *The Economy of the Roman Empire: Quantitative Studies*. 2nd ed. Cambridge: Cambridge University Press, 1982.

Edwards, Katherine N. *The Coins, 1896–1929*. Vol. 6 of *Corinth: Results of Excavations Conducted by the American School of Classical Studies at Athens*. Cambridge: Harvard University Press, 1933.

Engels, Donald W. *Roman Corinth: An Alternative Model for the Classical City*. Chicago: University of Chicago Press, 1990.

Fee, Gordon. *The First Epistle to the Corinthians*. NICNT. Grand Rapids: Eerdmans, 1987.

Fitzmyer, Joseph A. *First Corinthians: A New Translation with Introduction and Commentary*. AYB. New Haven: Yale University Press, 2008.

Fobes, Francis H. Introduction. Pages 3–18 in *The Letters of Alciphron*. Translated by A. R. Benner. LCL. Cambridge: Harvard University Press, 1962.

Fowler, Harold N., and Richard Stillwell. *Introduction, Topography, Architecture*. Vol. 1.1 of *Corinth: Results of Excavations Conducted by the American School of Classical Studies at Athens*. Cambridge: Harvard University Press, 1932.

Fraser, P. M. and E. Matthews, *The Aegean Islands, Cyprus, Cyrenaica*. Vol. 1 of *A Lexicon of Greek Personal Names*. Oxford: Clarendon, 1987.

Frier, Bruce W. "Demography." Pages 787–816 in *The High Empire, AD 70–192*. Edited by Alan K. Bowman, Peter Garnsey, and Dominic Rathbone. Vol. 11 of *The Cambridge Ancient History*. 2nd ed. Cambridge: Cambridge University Press, 2000.

———. "More Is Worse: Some Observations on the Population of the Roman Empire." Pages 139–59 in *Debating Roman Demography*. Edited by Walter Scheidel. Leiden: Brill, 2001.

Friesen, Steven J. "Poverty in Pauline Studies: Beyond the So-Called New Consensus." *JSNT* 26 (2004): 323–61.

———. "Prospects for a Demography of the Pauline Mission: Corinth among the Churches." Pages 351–70 in *Urban Religion in Roman*

Corinth. Edited by Daniel N. Schowalter and Steven J. Friesen. Cambridge: Harvard University Press, 2005.

———. "The Wrong Erastus: Ideology, Archaeology, and Exegesis." Pages 231–56 in *Corinth in Context: Comparative Perspectives on Religion and Society*. Edited by Steven J. Friesen, Daniel N. Schowalter, and James C. Walters. Leiden: Brill, 2010.

Friesen, Steven J., Sarah A. James, and Daniel N. Schowalter, eds. *Corinth in Contrast: Studies in Inequality*. Leiden: Brill, 2014.

Friesen, Steven J., Sarah A. James, and Daniel N. Schowalter. "Inequality in Corinth." Pages 2–13 in *Corinth in Contrast: Studies in Inequality*. Edited by Steven J. Friesen, Sarah A. James, and Daniel N. Schowalter. Leiden: Brill, 2014.

Geagan, Daniel J. "Notes on the Agonistic Institutions of Roman Corinth." *Greek, Roman, and Byzantine Studies* 4 (1968): 69–80.

Gordon, Mary L. "The Nationality of Slaves under the Early Roman Empire." Pages 171–89 in *Slavery in Classical Antiquity: Views and Controversies*. Edited by M. I. Finley. Cambridge: Heffer & Sons, 1960.

Harrill, J. Albert. *The Manumission of Slaves in Early Christianity*. Tübingen: Mohr Siebeck, 1995.

Highet, Gilbert. "*Libertino Patre Natus*." *AJP* 94 (1973): 268–81.

Hopkins, Keith. "The Political Economy of the Roman Empire." Pages 178–204 in *The Dynamics of Ancient Empires*. Edited by Ian Morris and Walter Scheidel. New York: Oxford University Press, 2009.

Horsley, G. H. R. "The Distribution of a Deceased Man's Slaves." *NewDocs* 1:69–70.

Jewett, Robert. *Romans: A Commentary*. Hermeneia. Minneapolis: Fortress, 2007.

Jongman, Willem M. "The Early Roman Empire: Consumption." Pages 592–618 in *The Cambridge Economic History of the Greco-Roman World*. Edited by Walter Scheidel, Ian Morris, and Richard Saller. Cambridge: Cambridge University Press, 2007.

———. *The Economy and Society of Pompeii*. Amsterdam: Gieben, 1991.

———. "A Golden Age: Death, Money Supply, and Social Succession in the Roman Empire." Pages 181–96 in *Credito e moneta nel mondo romano: Atti degli Incontri capresi di storia dell'economia antica*. Edited by Elio LoCascio. Bari: Edipuglia, 2003.

———. "The Rise and Fall of the Roman Economy: Population, Rents and Entitlement." Pages 237–54 in *Ancient Economies and Modern Methodologies: Archaeology, Comparative History, Models and Institutions*.

Edited by Peter Bang, Mamoru Ikeguchi, and Harmut G. Ziche. Bari: Edipuglia, 2006.

———. "The Roman Economy: From Cities to Empire." Pages 28–47 in *The Transformation of Economic Life under the Roman Empire*. Edited by Lukas de Blois and John Rich. Amsterdam: Gieben, 2002.

Judge, Edwin A. "The Early Christians as a Scholastic Community." Pages 526–52 in *The First Christians in the Roman World: Augustan and New Testament Essays*. Edited by James R. Harrison. Tübingen: Mohr Siebeck, 2008.

———. "The Roman Base of Paul's Mission." Pages 553–67 in *The First Christians in the Roman World: Augustan and New Testament Essays*. Edited by James R. Harrison. Tübingen: Mohr Siebeck, 2008.

———. *The Social Pattern of the Christian Groups in the First Century*. London: Tyndale, 1960.

Kent, John Harvey. *The Inscriptions, 1926–1950*. Vol. 8.3 of *Corinth: Results of Excavations Conducted by the American School of Classical Studies at Athens*. Princeton: American School of Classical Studies at Athens, 1966.

Kirner, Guido O. "Apostolat und Patronage (II) Darstellungsteil: Weisheit, Rhetorik und Ruhm in Konflikt um die apostolischen Praxis des Paulus in der frühchristlichen Gemeinde Korinth (1 Kor. 1–4 und 9; 2 Kor. 10–13." *ZAC* 6 (2002): 27–72.

Klauck, Hans-Josef. *Herrenmahl und hellenistischer Kult. Eine religionsgeschichtliche Untersuchung zum ersten Korintherbrief*. Münster: Aschendorff, 1982.

Kyle, Donald G. *Spectacles of Death in Ancient Rome*. New York: Routledge, 1998.

Laird, Margaret L. "The Emperor in a Roman Town: The Base of the *Augustales* in the Forum at Corinth." Pages 67–116 in *Corinth in Context: Comparative Studies on Religion and Society*. Edited in Steven J. Friesen, Daniel N. Schowalter, and James C. Walters. Leiden: Brill, 2010.

Landvogt, Peter. *Epigraphische Untersuchungen über den ΟΙΚΟΝΟΜΟΣ: Ein Beitrag zum hellenistischen Beamtenwesen*. Strassburg: Schauberg, 1908.

Lampe, Peter. *From Paul to Valentinus: Christians at Rome in the First Two Centuries*. Minneapolis: Fortress, 2003.

———. "Das korinthische Herrenmahl im Schnittpunkt hellenistischer Mahlpraxis und paulinischer Theologia Crucis (1 Kor 11,17–34)." *ZNW* 82 (1991): 183–213.

———. "Paul, Patrons and Clients." Pages 488–523 in *Paul in the Greco-Roman World*. Edited by J. Paul Sampley. Harrisburg, PA: Trinity Press International, 2003.

Lindemann, Andreas. *Der erste Korintherbrief*. Tübingen: Mohr Siebeck, 2000.

Malherbe, Abraham J. *Social Aspects of Early Christianity*. Philadelphia: Fortress, 1983.

Martin, Dale B. *The Corinthian Body*. New Haven: Yale University Press, 1995.

———. *Slavery as Salvation: The Metaphor of Slavery in Pauline Christianity*. New Haven: Yale University Press, 1990.

Mason, Hugh J. *Greek Terms for Roman Institutions: A Lexicon and Analysis*. Toronto: Hakkert, 1974.

———. "Lucius at Corinth." *Phoenix* 25 (1971): 160–65.

Meeks, Wayne A. *The First Urban Christians: The Social World of the Apostle Paul*. New Haven: Yale University Press, 1983.

Meggitt, Justin J. *Paul, Poverty and Survival*. Edinburgh: T&T Clark, 1998.

Millis, Benjamin W. "The Local Magistrates and Elite of Corinth." Pages 38–53 in *Corinth in Context: Studies in Inequality*. Edited by Steven J. Friesen, Sarah A. James, and Daniel N. Schowalter. Leiden: Brill, 2014.

———. "The Social and Ethnic Origins of the Colonists in Early Roman Corinth." Pages 13–36 in *Corinth in Context: Comparative Studies on Religion and Society*. Edited by Steven J. Friesen, Daniel N. Schowalter, and James C. Walters. Leiden: Brill, 2010.

Mouritsen, Henrik. *The Freedman in the Roman World*. Cambridge: Cambridge University Press, 2011.

Murphy-O'Connor, Jerome. *St. Paul's Corinth: Texts and Archaeology*. Collegeville, MN: Glazier, 1983.

Nasrallah, Laura Salah. "'You Were Bought with a Price': Freedpersons and Things in 1 Corinthians." Pages 54–73 in *Corinth in Contrast: Studies in Inequality*. Edited by Steven J. Friesen, Sarah A. James, and Daniel N. Schowalter. Leiden: Brill, 2014.

Pais, Ettore. "The Time and Place in Which Strabo Composed His Historical Geography." Pages 379–430 in *Ancient Italy*. Translated by C. Densmore Curtis. Chicago: University of Chicago Press, 1908.

Pleket, H. W. "Sociale stratificatie en sociale mobiliteit in de Romeinse Keizertijd." *TG* 84 (1971): 215–51.

Quass, Friedemann. *Die Honoratiorenschicht in den Städten des griechischen*

Ostens: Untersuchungen zur politischen und sozialen Entwicklung in hellenistischer und römischer Zeit. Stuttgart: Steiner, 1993.
Rajak, Tessa. *The Jewish Dialogue with Greece and Rome: Studies in Cultural and Social Interaction.* Leiden: Brill, 2002.
Rajak, Tessa, and David Noy. "Archisynagogoi: Office, Title and Social Status in the Greco-Jewish Synagogue." *JRS* 83 (1993): 75–93.
Ridgway, Brunilde Sismonde. "Sculpture from Corinth." *Hesperia* 50 (1981): 432–33.
Rix, Helmut. *Römische Personennamen.* Vol. 1 of *Namenforschung: Ein internationales Handbuch zur Onomastik.* Berlin: de Gruyter, 1995.
Rizakis, Athanasios D., and Sophie Zoumbaki. *Achaia, Argolis, Corinthia and Eleia.* Volume 1 of *Roman Peloponnese: Roman Personal Names in Their Social Context.* Athens: Research Centre for Greek and Roman Antiquity, 2001.
Romano, David Gilman. "Post-145 B.C. Land Use in Corinth, and Planning of the Roman Colony of 44 B.C." Pages 9–30 in *Corinthia in the Roman Period.* Edited by Timothy E. Gregory. Ann Arbor: University of Michigan Press, 1993.
———. "Urban and Rural Planning in Roman Corinth." Pages 25–59 in *Urban Religion in Roman Corinth: Interdisciplinary Approaches.* Edited by Daniel N. Schowalter and Steven J. Friesen. Cambridge: Harvard University Press, 2005.
Salmeri, Giovanni. "Dio, Rome, and the Civic Life of Asia Minor." Pages 53–92 in *Dio Chrysostom: Politics, Letters, and Philosophy.* Edited by Simon Swain. Oxford: Oxford University Press, 2000.
Salmon, Edward T. *Roman Colonization under the Republic.* Ithaca, NY: Cornell University Press, 1970.
Salomies, Olli. *Die römischen Vornamen: Studien zur römischen Namengebung.* Helsinki: Societas Scientiarum Fennica, 1987.
Scranton, Robert L. *Monuments in the Lower Agora and North of the Archaic Temple.* Vol. 1.3 of *Corinth: Results of Excavations Conducted by the American School of Classical Studies at Athens.* Princeton: American School of Classical Studies at Athens, 1951.
Scheidel, Walter. "Demographic and Economic Development in the Ancient Mediterranean World." *Journal of Institutional and Theoretical Economics* 160 (2004): 743–57.
Scheidel, Walter, and Steven J. Friesen. "The Size of the Economy and the Distribution of Income in the Roman Empire." *JRS* 99 (2009): 61–91.

Schmeller, Thomas. *Hierarchie und Egalität: Eine sozialgeschichtliche Untersuchung paulinischer Gemeinden und griechisch-römischer Vereine*. Stuttgart: Katholisches Bibelwerk, 1995.

Schrage, Wolfgang. *Der erste Brief an die Korinther*. Vol. 1. Neukirchen-Vluyn: Neukirchener Verlag, 1991.

Sherk, Robert K. *The Roman Empire: Augustus to Hadrian*. Cambridge: Cambridge University Press, 1988.

Solin, Heikki. "Latin Cognomina in the Greek East." Pages 189–202 in *The Greek East in the Roman Context*. Edited by Olli Salomies. Helsinki: Finnish Institute at Athens, 2001.

———. *Die stadtrömischen Sklavennamen: Ein Namenbuch*. Stuttgart: Steiner, 1996.

Spawforth, Antony J. S. *Greece and the Augustan Cultural Revolution*. Cambridge: Cambridge University Press, 2012.

———. "Roman Corinth: The Formation of a Colonial Elite." Pages 167–82 in *Roman Onomastics in the Greek East: Social and Political Aspects*. Edited in Athanasios D. Rizakis. Athens: Research Center for Greek and Roman Antiquity, 1996.

Stansbury, Harry A. "Corinthian Honor, Corinthian Conflict: A Social History of Early Roman Corinth and Its Pauline Community." PhD diss., University of California Irvine, 1990.

Stegemann, Ekkehard, and Wolfgang Stegemann. *Urchristliche Sozialgeschichte: Die Anfänge im Judentum und die Christusgemeinden in der mediterranen Welt*. Stuttgart: Kohlhammer, 1995.

Stein, Arthur, and Leiva Petersen. *Prosopographia Imperii Romani*. Vol. 4. Berlin: de Gruyter, 1966.

Stillwell, Richard. *The Theatre*. Vol. 2 of *Corinth: Results of Excavations Conducted by the American School of Classical Studies at Athens*. Princeton: American School of Classical Studies at Athens, 1952.

Stillwell, Richard, Robert L. Scranton, and Sarah Elizabeth Freeman. *Architecture*. Vol. 1.2 of *Corinth: Results of Excavations Conducted by the American School of Classical Studies at Athens*. Cambridge: Harvard University Press, 1941.

Taylor, Lily Ross. "Freedmen and Freeborn in the Epitaphs of Imperial Rome." *AJP* 82 (1961): 113–32.

Taylor, Lily Ross, and Allen B. West. "The Euryclids in Latin Inscriptions from Corinth." *AJA* 30 (1926): 389–400.

Theissen, Gerd. *The Social Setting of Pauline Christianity: Essays on Corinth*. Philadelphia: Fortress, 1982.

———. "Social Stratification in the Corinthian Community: A Contribution to the Sociology of Early Hellenistic Christianity." Pages 69–119 in *The Social Setting of Pauline Christianity: Essays on Corinth*. Philadelphia: Fortress, 1982.

———. "The Social Structure of Pauline Communities: Some Critical Remarks on J. J. Meggitt, *Paul, Poverty and Survival*." *JSNT* 84 (2001): 65–84.

———. "Soziale Schichtung in der korinthischen Gemeinde: Ein Beitrag zur Soziologie des hellenistischen Urchristentums." *ZNW* 65 (1974): 232–72.

Treggiari, Susan. *Roman Freedmen during the Late Republic*. Oxford: Clarendon, 1969.

Tumolesi, Patrizia Sabbatini. *Gladiatorum parie: Annunci di spettacoli gladiatorii a Pompeii*. Rome: Edizion da storia e letteratura, 1980.

Veyne, Paul. "Apulée a Cenchrées." *RevPhil* 39 (1965): 241–51.

Ville, Georges. *La gladiature en Occident des origins à la mort de Domitien*. Rome: École française de Rome, 1981.

Waele, Ferdinand J. de. "The Roman Market North of the Temple at Corinth." *AJA* 34 (1930): 432–54.

———. *Theater en Amphitheater te oud Korinthe*. Utrecht: Dekker, 1928.

Walbank, Mary E. Hoskins. "Pausanias, Octavia and Temple E at Corinth." *ABSA* 84 (1989): 361–94.

Wallace-Hadrill, Andrew. *Houses and Society in Pompeii and Herculaneum*. Princeton: Princeton University Press, 1994.

Walters, James C. "Paul and the Politics of Meals in Roman Corinth." Pages 350–61 in *Corinth in Context: Comparative Studies on Religion and Society*. Edited by Steven J. Friesen, Daniel N. Schowalter, and James C. Walters. Leiden: Brill, 2010.

Weinberg, Saul S. "Roman Twins: Basilicas at Corinth." *Arch* 13 (1960): 137–43.

———. *The Southeast Building, the Twin Basilicas, the Mosaic House*. Vol. 1.4 of *Corinth: Results of Excavations Conducted by the American School of Classical Studies at Athens*. Princeton: American School of Classical Studies at Athens, 1960.

Weiss, Johannes. *Der erste Korintherbrief*. Göttingen: Vandenhoeck & Ruprecht, 1910.

Welborn, L. L. *An End to Enmity: Paul and the "Wrongdoer" of Second Corinthians*. BZNW 185. Berlin: de Gruyter, 2011.

———. *Paul, the Fool of Christ: A Study of 1 Corinthians 1–4 in the Comic-Philosophic Tradition*. London: T&T Clark, 2005.

———. *Politics and Rhetoric in the Corinthian Epistles*. Macon, GA: Mercer University Press, 1997.

Welch, Katherine E. "Negotiating Roman Spectacle Architecture in the Greek World: Athens and Corinth." Pages 125–45 in *The Art of Ancient Spectacle*. Edited by Bettina Ann Bergmann and Christine Kondoleon. New Haven: Yale University Press, 1999.

West, Allen Brown. *Latin Inscriptions, 1896–1926*. Vol. 8 of *Corinth: Results of Excavations Conducted by the American School of Classical Studies at Athens*. Cambridge: Harvard University Press, 1931.

White, Peter. *Promised Verse: Poets in the Society of Augustan Rome*. Cambridge: Harvard University Press, 1993.

Wiedemann, Thomas E. J. *Emperors and Gladiators*. London: Routledge, 1992.

Williams, Charles K., II. "Corinth, 1983: The Route to Sicyon." *Hesperia* 53 (1984): 97–100.

———. "Corinth and the Cult of Aphrodite." Pages 12–24 in *Corinthiaca: Studies in Honor of Darrell A. Amyx*. Edited by Mario Aldo Del Chiaro and William R. Biers. Columbia: University of Missouri Press, 1986.

———. "A Re-evaluation of Temple E and the West End of the Forum at Corinth." Pages 156–62 in *The Greek Renaissance in the Roman Empire*. Edited by Susan Walker and Averil Cameron. London: University of London, Institute of Classical Studies Press, 1989.

Winter, Bruce W. *After Paul Left Corinth: The Influence of Secular Ethics and Social Change*. Grand Rapids: Eerdmans, 2001.

———. "The Lord's Supper at Corinth: An Alternative Reconstruction." *RTR* 37 (1978): 73–82.

———. "Secular and Christian Responses to Corinthian Famines." *TynBul* 40 (1989): 86–106.

Wiseman, James. "Corinth and Rome, I: 228 BC–AD 267." *ANRW* 7.1:491–96.

Ziegler, Konrat. "Plutarchos." *RE* 22.1 (1964): 636–962.

Zuiderhoek, Arjan. "On the Political Sociology of the Imperial Greek City." *GRBS* 48 (2008): 417–45.

———. *The Politics of Munificence in the Roman Empire: Citizens, Elites and Benefactors in Asia Minor*. Cambridge: Cambridge University Press, 2009.

Negotiating Multiple Modes of Religion and Identity in Roman Corinth

Cavan Concannon

In this essay I offer an oblique reading of Paul's references to the spirit, baptism (for the living and dead), and the Israelite wanderings in the wilderness in 1 Cor 10 and 2 Cor 3. I say oblique because I am not looking to uncover Paul's own intentions in these invocations of the past; rather, I read Paul as one among many in Corinth speaking of the past. I argue that we might hear something of this conversation by treating Paul obliquely, reading him at a slant, refusing to engage images of Israelite wandering, spirits, and baptism on Paul's own terms.[1] I read Paul obliquely in order to offer an imagining of *some* Corinthians, a phrase I borrow from Merrill Miller and Ron Cameron, as im/migrants negotiating multiple modes of religion and identity in Roman Corinth.[2] By placing *some* Corinthi-

---

1. In suggesting that we read Paul "obliquely," I am building on earlier attempts by feminist biblical scholars to read Paul "against the grain." For examples of this approach, see, in particular, Antoinette Clark Wire, *The Corinthian Women Prophets: A Reconstruction through Paul's Rhetoric* (Minneapolis: Fortress, 1990), and Elisabeth Schüssler Fiorenza, *In Memory of Her: A Feminist Theological Reconstruction of Christian Origins*, 10th anniversary ed. (New York: Crossroad, 1994); Schüssler Fiorenza, *Rhetoric and Ethic: The Politics of Biblical Studies* (Minneapolis: Fortress, 1999). While such readings are important ways of leveraging Paul's rhetoric, I also think that it is worth exploring other directions that might be more oblique than oppositional to Paul. For other examples of how one might read obliquely, see Cavan W. Concannon, *"When You Were Gentiles": Specters of Ethnicity in Roman Corinth and Paul's Corinthian Correspondence* Synkrisis (New Haven: Yale University Press, 2014).

2. Ron Cameron and Merrill P. Miller, "Redescribing Paul and the Corinthians," in *Redescribing Paul and the Corinthians*, ed. Ron Cameron and Merrill P. Miller, ECL 5 (Atlanta: Society of Biblical Literature, 2011), 245–57. I use the word *im/migrants* to differentiate the Corinthians whom I hope to conjure in this paper from modern

ans within the larger landscape of Corinth, I conjure im/migrants making meaning, discerning leaders, and negotiating identity in ways that were shaped by trade, movement, and mobility. I do this by redescribing conversations about baptism, spirits, and the Israelites as negotiations of cult and ancestors, ritual and identity, geography, distance, and absence.

Such negotiations were not merely isolated acts of individuals but social acts carried out both in community and over geographic distance, lived space, and time. More to the point, we should expect such negotiations to be complex, contextual, and prone to misunderstanding. As such, this is not a quest for Paul's "opponents" among the Corinthians; rather, I want to conjure what some Corinthians did with and through, against and around, even despite, Paul's writings, a search that privileges plurality rather than univocity and presumes that Paul was one among many in Corinth finding ways to make connections between history, cultic practice, and identity.[3] By attending to Paul obliquely rather than simply reading against the grain or mirror-reading his arguments, I hope to summon the complexities of an association of Corinthians in a city "on the move" by intertwining Israelite and Corinthian history, spirits, and baptisms as ways of negotiating multiple modes of religion and ethnicity in Corinth.

From Paul's letters, we know that he was one among a number of Jewish authority figures who made their way to, from, and through Corinth.[4] We also know from Paul's scattered references that the history and sacred

---

assumptions about immigrants and migrants moving between and among the bounded spaces of the modern nation state and the globalized, neocapitalist landscape.

3. This is not to say that looking for *opponents* is itself a flawed endeavor. Such work has been an important part of shaping and refining reading strategies in scholarship on the Corinthian correspondence. See, for example, Dieter Georgi, *The Opponents of Paul in Second Corinthians: A Study of Religious Propaganda in Late Antiquity* (Philadelphia: Fortress, 1986); and Jerry L. Sumney, *Identifying Paul's Opponents: The Question of Method in 2 Corinthians*, JSNTSup 40 (Sheffield: JSOT Press, 1990). While such work is interesting in itself, I am not looking here for one, singular group of opponents but trying to think about diverse responses to Paul that may or may not overlap with the groups that other scholars have identified.

4. In 2 Cor 11:22 we learn that the "super apostles" (οἱ ὑπερλίαν ἀπόστολοι [2 Cor 11:5]) claimed that they were Hebrews, Israelites, and descendants of Abraham. Among other Jews in Corinth were Cephas (1 Cor 1:12; 3:22; 9:5; 15:5) and Apollos (1 Cor 1:12; 3:4–6, 22; 4:6; 16:12), if we take Acts 18:24 as accurately reflecting the latter's Judean background.

scriptures of Israel were invoked by and for the Corinthians.[5] The interest among some Corinthians in an ancient history like that of the Israelites might have come from a desire to finds new ways to negotiate identity in motion. As a hub for regional and international commerce, Corinth was a place in motion.[6] With its two ports of Lechaion and Kenchreai and its strategic location along the land routes connecting mainland Greece to the interior of the Peloponnese, Corinth was a vital hub for communication and movement and a major emporium for the distribution of goods, people, and ideas in the eastern Mediterranean.

Im/migrants to Corinth, brought by larger patterns of trade and mobility, would find themselves in a landscape bereft of extended familial and patronage networks, ancestral traditions, the familiar cults of the homeland, or access to family burial sites. Such dislocations might inspire precisely the kinds of experimentation that one hears echoing against Paul's rhetoric (like those baptizing for the dead in 1 Cor 15:29 or those who feel comfortable being monotheists while eating in the temples of the local gods in 1 Cor 8–10). We might hear another kind of experimentation in this epitaph put up by Apollonius, who uses a Latin formula in Greek and advertises his im/migrant status:

Ζῶν Π. Ἐγ[νάτιος] Ἀπολλ[ώνιος] Ἐφέσιος [ἑαυτῷ κ]αὶ Μοσχ[ίνῃ (?) γυνα-][κὶ] καὶ το[ῖς ἐκγόοις] ("While still living P. Egnatios Apollonios from Ephesos [purchased this] for himself and for his wife Moschine . . . and for his parents").[7]

We do not know why Apollonius came to Corinth from Ephesos with his extended family, but the geographic and civic translations that were doubtless required to find a new home on the slopes of Acrocorinth are hinted at by the merging of a Latin funerary formula with Greek in the epitaph.[8] For

---

5. The best discussion I have seen of the use of the scriptures of Israel in Corinth can be found in Christopher D. Stanley, *Arguing with Scripture: The Rhetoric of Quotations in the Letters of Paul* (New York: T&T Clark, 2004), 75–113.

6. On Corinth's role as a hub of trade in the eastern Mediterranean, see Concannon, *When You Were Gentiles*, 51–56.

7. John Harvey Kent, *The Inscriptions, 1926–1950*, vol. 8.3 of *Corinth: Results of Excavations Conducted by the American School of Classical Studies at Athens* (Princeton: American School of Classical Studies at Athens, 1966 = IKorinthKent), §303.

8. This kind of linguistic switching was not uncommon in bilingual environments. On Delos the Italian *negotiatores* ("trading families") occasionally made use of Greek

other im/migrant Corinthians, the stories of Israel and practices related to baptism and the spirit might offer ways of negotiating between home and away, ways of connecting across distance and time.

In order to account for a Corinthian concern with the homeland, it is important to note the importance of place for ancient religious practices and identity. Identity was often tied to how one negotiated relationships between family, city, and the gods through cultic practices in the home(land). Travelers and im/migrants mediated absence and distance, in part, by the construction of civic and cultic landscapes of travel.[9] So, a traveler leaving home on business would find cultic sites along the roads, such as herms and shrines, linking the city to a broader network of territory or marking boundaries between one region and another. The same traveler might bring with her objects that connected her with the patronage of deities from home or who were known for watching over travelers. She might expect to be approached by a deity in a vision or through an

---

grammatical forms in their inscriptions. One example of this trend is the adoption by the Italici of the Greek practice of referring to the honorand of an inscription in the accusative. In Greek inscriptions it is common to place the name of the honorand in the accusative case, with the implied verb being one of honoring. In Latin inscriptions the honorand is named in the dative with a different verb implied or used (such as the common *fecit* or *posuit*) See James N. Adams, "Bilingualism at Delos," in *Bilingualism in Ancient Society: Language Contact and the Written Text*, ed. James N. Adams, Mark Janse, and Simon Swain (New York: Oxford University Press, 2002), 115. At Delos all of the honorific inscriptions associated with the Italici employ the accusative for the honorand (116). This suggests a Greek influence on the Italians, who clearly accommodated their linguistic tendencies to their Greek neighbors. The accusative of the honorand is employed consistently by other Italians in Greek-speaking cities, which suggests that "there is a convention deliberately adopted by the Italici at work here" (116). That we find similar interaction between Greek and Latin inscriptional practices at Corinth suggests that "a significant percentage of the population was capable of drawing upon both Greek and Roman traditions and of effecting a combination of the two" (Benjamin W. Millis, "The Social and Ethnic Origins of the Colonists in Early Roman Corinth," in *Corinth in Context: Comparative Studies on Religion and Society*, ed. Steven Friesen, Daniel N. Schowalter, and James Walters [Leiden: Brill, 2010], 25).

9. David Frankfurter, "Traditional Cult," in *A Companion to the Roman Empire*, ed. David S. Potter (Malden, MA: Blackwell, 2007), 547–52; Steven Muir, "Religion on the Road in Ancient Greece and Rome," in *Travel and Religion in Antiquity*, ed. Philip A. Harland, Studies in Christianity and Judaism 21 (Waterloo, ON: Wilfred Laurier University Press, 2011), 33–45. On the religion of mobility in the Mediterranean, see Peregrine Horden and Nicholas Purcell, *The Corrupting Sea: A Study of Mediterranean History* (Oxford: Wiley-Blackwell, 2000), 438–49.

omen and might have begun and ended the trip with an augury, a vow, or a sacrifice. Because travel put the individual into a situation where one was separated from the webs of meaning that were a major part of one's social identity, travel was envisioned and experienced as a negotiated movement through a landscape populated by a variety of divine beings.

Though operating with a slightly different metaphysical paradigm, Paul certainly saw his travel experiences as movement through divinely ordered space. Paul's travel plans can be contingent on the permission of God (e.g., 1 Cor 16:7; 2 Cor 2:12–13). In 2 Cor 2:14–16, Paul can describe his own movements as God's triumphal or festal procession.[10] Those Corinthians who traveled as part of their work or to maintain communication between Paul and the community, such as "Chloe's people" (1 Cor 1:11) or Phoebe (Rom 16:1–3), would also see their movements within the network of relationships (divine, human, and material) that structured the landscape through which they moved.

For Corinthian im/migrants, the question of distance and geography would be inflected differently. Some Corinthians may have been temporary residents of Corinth who traveled to and from the city on periodic business or for particular seasons, moving between town and country as different kinds of work were available. Others may have come to Corinth permanently as part of forced or economically necessary migration. Lack of employment, famine, or a blighted harvest in a nearby village may have pushed some to look for help in the Corinthian metropolis. Others may have come to advance their careers in the provincial capital, others as slaves shipped alongside other commodities. Still others who had long been residents in the city may have told stories of their ancestors' arrivals to the newly founded colony. In each of these situations, im/migrants would be looking to connect gods and traditions to (home)lands new and old in a city shaped by movement and flux.[11]

---

10. For an excellent analysis of the intertwining of travel and cult in this passage, see Timothy L. Marquis, "At Home or Away: Travel and Death in 2 Corinthians 1–9" (Ph.D. diss., Yale University, 2008), 133–66.

11. Philip A. Harland ("Pausing at the Intersection of Religion and Travel," in Harland, *Travel and Religion in Antiquity*, 4–23) offers a number of categories for why people might travel from one place to another in the ancient world: honoring the gods, promoting a deity or way of life, encountering foreign cultures, migrating, making a living. David Noy (*Foreigners at Rome: Citizens and Strangers* [London: Duckworth, with the Classical Press of Wales, 2000], 53–55) identifies several different motivations for why people might have migrated to Rome: local movement to connect with mar-

One way of negotiating home and away was to invoke the patronage of deities from one's homeland. Travelers to and from Corinth might have invoked the patronage of any number of deities. For example, the Sarapias who carved his name on the side of the Corinthian bema alongside his Syrian friend Alexas may have looked to the gods of Egypt (particularly his namesake Sarapis) as part of negotiating his own identity in Corinth.[12] Isis was worshiped in both Corinth and Kenchreai, where she was associated with the sea and with sea travel. She famously had a shrine at the end of a mole in the harbor at Kenchreai (Pausanias, *Descr.* 2.4.6).[13] More specifically related to deities "from home" may be the temple of Sarapis "in Canopus" mentioned by Pausanias as being one of two temples to the god on Acrocorinth.[14] Though commonly associated with the Egyptian cult, the imagery of Canopus, however idealized or orientalized, would remind devotees of the power of the Egyptian gods across distance and space. As patrons of travelers and as deities associated with particular geographic

---

kets in the city; seasonal, temporary migration; chain migration along various social networks; and career advancement.

12. "Alexas and Sarapias are lovers of merriment" (Φίλοι | Ἀλεξᾶς | Σαραπιᾶς | εὐφροσύνης [IKorinthKent §361]). Besides being written in Greek, the inscription is interesting for the names that it records, which are Syrian and Egyptian, respectively. The inscription was carved on what "seems to have been used either as an orthostate slab or as a backer for one of the benches in the eastern schola of the Bema" (IKorinthKent, 141). Kent notes that the original publishers of the inscription read Ἀλιζᾶς instead of Ἀλεξᾶς and interpreted the graffiti to mean that two men were lovers of a woman named Euphrosune. Kent notes that Σαραπιᾶς is a woman's name and Ἀλιζᾶς is otherwise unattested. Ἀλεξᾶς is a masculine name that is attested in Syria. One is tempted to see behind these names Greek speakers from areas on the fringes of the Hellenistic world.

13. We know something of this from Apuleius's description of Isiac worship at Kenchreai in book 11 of the *Metamorphoses*.

14. As Dennis Edwin Smith has pointed out, Canopus was a city near Alexandria with a temple of Sarapis that was famous for being both an oracle and a place of healing ("The Egyptian Cults at Corinth," *HTR* 70 [1977]: 227–28). With three cult sites associated with Sarapis in the city (two on Acrocorinth and one in the South Stoa), the shrine associated explicitly with Canopus may have been a place where Corinthians might expect healing in the midst of a medical crisis. On the Acrocorinth sanctuaries, see Smith, "Egyptian Cults at Corinth," 210–12. On the chapel in the South Stoa, see Oscar Broneer, *The South Stoa and Its Roman Successors*, vol. 1.4 of *Corinth: Results of Excavations Conducted by the American School of Classical Studies at Athens* (Princeton: American School of Classical Studies at Athens, 1954), 132–45; Smith, "Egyptian Cults at Corinth," 212–16.

regions, the Egyptian cults may have been useful for *some* Corinthians in linking Corinth with their homelands.[15]

Other local traditions point to connections between geography and water, a theme to which I will return later. The Peirene Fountain just to the north of the forum along the Lechaion road was one of the first buildings remodeled after Corinth was refounded.[16] It marks the location for the events of the myth of Bellerophon's taming of Pegasos, a famous Corinthian story that is retold on other monuments in and around the city. While the myth can be localized in Corinth, it is also a story of movement. Bellerophon and Pegasos connect places across the geographic expanse of the Mediterranean, appearing as far afield as at Aphrodisias, where the two formed part of that city's foundation myth.[17] Pegasos was something of a fertile airplane, creating new fountains, cities, and memories wherever he touched down. Similarly with another major fountain near the Corinthian forum: the fountain of Glauke, named for the daughter of King Kreon, who is killed tragically in the Medea cycle, visible today as a freestanding block of oolithic limestone that is the last remnant of the hill into which it was carved.[18] Here Corinth is not the starting point but the terminus in a larger tragic story of travel, movement, jealousy, and betrayal.[19] In both

---

15. We might note the Syrian freedman of the Iulii, C. Iulius Syrus, who made a dedication to Isis and Sarapis in the Corinthian theater in the first century CE (IKorinthKent §57).

16. On the fountain, see Betsey A. Robinson, "Fountains and the Culture of Water at Roman Corinth," (Ph.D. diss., University of Pennsylvania, 2001); Robinson, "Fountains and the Formation of Cultural Identity at Roman Corinth," in *Urban Religion in Roman Corinth: Interdisciplinary Approaches*, ed. Daniel N. Schowalter and Steven J. Friesen (Cambridge: Harvard University Press, 2005); Robinson, *Histories of Peirene: A Corinthian Fountain in Three Millennia*, Ancient Art and Architecture in Context (Athens: American School of Classical Studies at Athens, 2011); and Concannon, *When You Were Gentiles*, 119–22.

17. Bellerophon and Pegasos have been found on Aphrodisian coins and in relief sculptures of Flavian date from the Basilica (discovered in 1978). See C. P. Jones, *Kinship Diplomacy in the Ancient World*, Revealing Antiquity 12 (Cambridg.: Harvard University Press, 1999), 139–43. For further examples, see Robinson, "Fountains and the Culture of Water," 166–84.

18. On the fountain, its history, and its connection to the myth of Medea and Jason, see Robinson, "Fountains and the Culture of Water," 207–42; and Concannon, *When You Were Gentiles*, 122–27.

19. Favorinus even suggests that the prow of Jason's ship, the Argo, that conveyed them to Corinth was still memorialized at Isthmia ("Corinthian Oration," §15). Favo-

cases, these fountains represent stories that connect Corinth with other places and spaces and speak about the perils and possibilities of travel and movement.

In a similar way, we might see traditions of divine ordering and presence in the stories of the Israelites as another set of mobile constructions by which some Corinthians might have negotiated their own experiences of movement. Christopher Stanley notes that Paul assumes that the Corinthians to whom he writes have knowledge of the creation account in Gen 1–3 (1 Cor 8:6; 11:8–9, 12; 15:21–22, 44–45; 2 Cor 4:6; 11:3) and the exodus narrative (1 Cor 10:1–10; 2 Cor 3:3–18).[20] Paul invokes the Genesis creation stories to address concerns and debates about gendered and resurrected bodies, but the divine ordering of creation is also assumed behind the Corinthian "slogan" in 1 Cor 8:6 that evokes a single god who brings all things into being and sustains them. Divine control over the cosmos might be useful in thinking about how to connect movement to place for *some* Corinthians. Similarly, the wilderness narratives that appear in 1 Cor 10 and 2 Cor 3 highlight God's presence as it accompanies the Israelites on their wanderings. Paul's use of these traditions presumes that his Corinthian audience might be persuaded to follow his moral and cultic authority by the promise of divine presence and blessing similar to that experienced by their Israelite "fathers."[21]

We can usefully compare these historical allusions to those found in the fountains of Peirene and Glauke around the Corinthian forum. At each of these fountains mythological events (the taming of Pegasos by Bellerophon and the killing of Glauke by Medea, respectively) were sited within the landscape of Roman Corinth. Peirene, in particular, places the story

---

rinus implies that it was still there when he visited the city in the second century CE. It is doubtful that such a landmark would have survived the sack of Corinth and the Isthmian sanctuary by Mummius. It may be that another version of the Argo was set up in Isthmia by Favorinus's day. Aristides associates the building of the Argo with Corinth and says that the ship set out from there ("Regarding Poseidon," in Aristides, *Aristides in Four Volumes*, 29). There is also a duoviral coin from P. Aebutius and C. Pinnius dating to 39–36 BCE that pictures a prow on the reverse (*RPC* 1, §1124).

20. Stanley, *Arguing with Scripture*, 76–77. He also notes that Paul presumes some knowledge of some Torah commands (1 Cor 5:1, 7–8; 14:34), christological interpretations of the Hebrew scriptures (1 Cor 15:3–4, 27), and Jewish ideas and practices (1 Cor 1:30; 2:1, 6–7; 3:13; 7:18; 8:13; 16:8; 2 Cor 3:6, 14; 5:21)

21. For more on Paul's use of the Israelites in 1 Cor 10 and 2 Cor 3, see Concannon, *When You Were Gentiles*, 97–116.

of Pegasos within a remodeled and monumental fountain complex that evokes Roman architectural grandeur, with a two-story façade of Doric and Ionic columns fronting the deep reservoir caves carved out of the hillside. Peirene translates the Greek history of Corinth in a Roman idiom. Similarly, stories about Israelite fathers in the wilderness might offer Corinthians a way of translating an ancient history for their own interests. Both Peirene and the wilderness narratives offer ways of asserting antiquity amidst newness, stability while in motion.

Paul's own rhetoric of mobile structures (the community as a body [1 Cor 12:12–27] and the individual as a portable temple where the spirit dwells [1 Cor 3:16; 6:19]) might be made to address Corinthian questions about their own movement and the issues that would arise as a result of mobility. Though away from home, the community and its traditions become ways for reaffirming the presence and patronage of the god who ordered the cosmos and who blessed the Israelites in their wanderings. Paul's invocations of the group as a "body" suggest how the community itself might create new ways of negotiating identity for im/migrants in Corinth. As Philip Harland has noted, associations were a means by which immigrants found ways to negotiate "acculturation and continual attachments to the homeland."[22] To see how the community might be a site for negotiating between home and away, we have to remain open to the possibility of mistranslation between Paul and the Corinthians about the spirit itself.

As biblical scholars who have access to, and a great facility with, printed (and searchable digital) Bibles, we often make the assumption that terms such as *spirit* (πνεῦμα) were clearly understood by Paul's audiences. In a context of low rates of literacy, the prevalence of verbal communication, and the vagaries of distance in epistolary communication, we cannot assume that Paul's definitions were heard, understood, or accepted in Corinth. Dale Martin has shown some of the complexity associated with *spirit* and how it might be heard among Corinthians attuned to ancient medical literature.[23] Jonathan Z. Smith has further suggested that the definition of *spirit* might be an important site of miscommunication between

---

22. Philip A. Harland, *Dynamics of Identity in the World of the Early Christians: Associations, Judeans, and Cultural Minorities* (New York: T&T Clark, 2009), 101.

23. Dale B. Martin, *The Corinthian Body* (New Haven: Yale University Press, 1995).

Paul and his Corinthian audience.[24] In fact, 2 Cor 11:4 suggests that there was debate or disagreement between Paul, the Corinthians, and other itinerant missionaries over what the spirit actually was: "For if someone comes heralding another Jesus than the one we heralded, or you receive a different spirit than the one you received, or a different gospel than the one you accepted, you gladly suffer it."[25] The assumption here is that there are different notions of the spirit floating around Corinth, the result of multiple authorities offering multiple definitions and experiences to a discerning Corinthian audience.

Rather than seeing these multiple spirits and Christs in Corinth as the heretical doctrines promulgated by Pauline "opponents," we can redescribe this multiplicity as a reflection of the capacity within Greek modes of religious practice to hold multiple perspectives on the names of deities. Take, for example, Pausanias's observation that there were three statues of Zeus in the forum of Corinth: one with no epithet, one called Chthonios, and a third called Hypsistos (*Descr.* 2.2.8). Are these the same god in different modes or different deities? As H. S. Versnel has provocatively argued, gods with the same name but different epithets "may but need not" be the same deity: "Gods bearing the same name with different epithets were and were not one and the same, depending on their momentary registrations in the believer's various layers of perception."[26] Those who walked through the Corinthian forum had a choice that they could make each time they approached one or all of the three statues of Zeus, and they may not have made the same choice on different days. Similarly, the Corinthians who interacted with the multiple missionaries of Jesus and the spirit would need to decide: Were these the same deity that Paul preached or different ones? More to the point, they may have been quite content to make no theoretical decisions on the matter, open to different manifesta-

---

24. Jonathan Z. Smith, "Re: Corinthians," in *Redescribing Paul and the Corinthians*, ed. Ron Cameron and Merrill P. Miller, ECL 5 (Atlanta: Society of Biblical Literature, 2011), 17–34.

25. εἰ μὲν γὰρ ὁ ἐρχόμενος ἄλλον Ἰησοῦν κηρύσσει ὃν οὐκ ἐκηρύξαμεν, ἢ πνεῦμα ἕτερον λαμβάνετε ὃ οὐκ ἐλάβετε, ἢ εὐαγγέλιον ἕτερον ὃ οὐκ ἐδέξασθε, καλῶς ἀνέχεσθε. Unless noted otherwise, all biblical translations are mine.

26. H. S. Versnel, *Coping with the Gods: Wayward Readings in Greek Theology*, RGRW 173 (Leiden: Brill, 2011), 82–83. He notes that the Greeks "had an extensive range of divine images in store, and boasted an uncommon capacity of evoking different identities of a god in rapidly shifting perspectives, generating (seemingly) incompatible statements to the distress of the modern observer" (6–7).

tions of Christ and the spirit "depending on their momentary registrations in the believer's various layers of perception."[27] Paul may have been less concerned with doctrinal difference than with convincing some Corinthians that they needed to make a choice between competing gods and that his was the only correct choice.[28]

In speaking of and experiencing spirits, some im/migrant Corinthians may have imagined themselves as connecting to the ancestral spirits of their ancestors and homelands, while Paul may have heard their tongues as failed or dangerous prophecy, imagining the incoherent speech of the Delphic oracle.[29] As Burton Mack puts it, following Jonathan Z. Smith, Paul's discussion of meals, bodies, and the spirit "indicates that the Corinthians may have been at work on 'translating' modes of remembering and relating to their ancestors now that they no longer had access to their tombs and the proper performance of their festivals in the districts from which they had come.[30] The spirit as a vehicle for connecting with one's ancestral spirits would be useful for Corinthians "on the move" to negotiate connections between Corinth and their homelands.

One can perhaps hear something of the logic involved here in Paul's own rhetoric of the spirit in the Corinthian letters. The divine presence with the Corinthians' Israelite fathers is characterized by a variety of "spiritual" objects: food, drink, and a rock that was Christ (1 Cor 10:3). The spiritual food and drink of the Israelites parallels and creates a histori-

---

27. Versnel further notes that, when the micro meets the macro, when the local meets the national or regional, there are always questions and negotiations. As a result, the "Greek gods suffer from multiperspectiveness," participating in both pan-Hellenic and local pantheons (*Coping with the Gods*, 114). Both the local gods and the geography that they mark (polis, houses, graves, boundary stones, cultic sites) "*together* construct the lived identity of the local population" (118, emphasis original).

28. As Stanley K. Stowers ("Kinds of Myth, Meals, and Power: Paul and the Corinthians," in Cameron and Miller, *Redescribing Paul and the Corinthians*, 122) notes, "Many of the passages that the Christian church has cherished as theological are less anachronistically described as Paul appealing to the interests of aspirants to *paideia* by 'showing his stuff' in intellectualizing issues that were 'practical' and strategic for most of the Corinthians."

29. Jonathan Z. Smith, "Re: Corinthians," in *Relating Religion: Essays in the Study of Religion*, ed. Jonathan Z. Smith (Chicago: University of Chicago Press, 2004), 350. What I find interesting about Smith's reading of the Corinthian situation is the possibility that the Corinthians and Paul may have been operating on different wavelengths.

30. Burton Mack, "Rereading the Christ Myth: Paul's Gospel and the Christ Cult Question," in Cameron and Miller, *Redescribing Paul and the Corinthians*, 52.

cal continuity with the eating practices of the Corinthians, which are the focus of Paul's discussion of meat sacrificed to idols in 1 Cor 8:1–11:1. The image of drinking the spirit returns in Paul's discussion of the community as a body in which all drink of one spirit (πάντες ἓν πνεῦμα ἐποτίσθημεν [1 Cor 12:13]). Spiritual food and spiritual drink and a spiritual rock that was Christ create "spiritual" connections between past and present. Similarly, the spirit mediates distance between Paul and the Corinthians. Though absent from discussions about the man who is sleeping with his stepmother (1 Cor 5), Paul is nevertheless present in the spirit (5:3–4). The spirit thus can, among other things, connect past and present, near and far.

The spirit is also implicated in how Paul speaks about baptism. In baptism members of the community are made into one body in the spirit (1 Cor 12:12–13). Like the spirit, baptism also links past and present. Paul parallels the Corinthians' baptism with the Israelites, who undergo a mysterious baptism into Moses in the wilderness (1 Cor 10:2). Baptism connected people together through the ritual act itself, beyond the idealized body envisioned by Paul. Paul's report from Chloe's people suggests that some in Corinth envisioned baptism as a ritual that linked the baptized to the baptizer (1 Cor 1:13). In each of these cases, baptism acts as a means of linking people together across time and space.

Baptism could also function as a way of mediating relationships with the dead. Paul's reference to a baptism "on behalf of/for/because of" the dead in 1 Cor 15:29 has been a puzzle for many exegetes, who seem concerned that such a practice bordering on the superstitious could ever be associated with Paul.[31] In his work on this ambiguous passage, Richard DeMaris has rightly situated baptism for the dead, and baptism more generally, within the larger context of water use in Corinth.[32] As part of "a spectrum of water use" in Corinth, baptism for the dead allowed *some*

---

31. On the confusions of scholars and the possibilities for translating the verse, see Richard E. DeMaris, *The New Testament in Its Ritual World* (New York: Routledge, 2008), 57–59.

32. Ibid., 57–71. In two parallel articles, DeMaris has made a compelling case for thinking about the role of mystery cults in the landscape of Corinthian religion: Richard E. DeMaris, "Demeter in Roman Corinth: Local Development in a Mediterranean Religion," *Numen* 42 (1995): 105–17; and DeMaris, "Corinthian Religion and Baptism for the Dead (1 Corinthians 15:29): Insights from Archaeology and Anthropology," *JBL* 114 (1995): 661–82.

Corinthians to use ritual practice as a way of maintaining connections to ancestors and homeland.[33]

Water was an important part of the civic landscape of Corinth.[34] The abundant local aquifers in the Corinthia brought more water to the city than to other sites in the arid region. It is from these aquifers and the fountains and wells that they made possible that the city was known as "well-watered."[35] The abundant water supply allowed the Romans to construct a civic landscape around water, its use, collection, and dispersal. In the Corinth of Pausanias's day, we have evidence for many waterworks: Hadrian's aqueduct that brought water from Lake Stymphalos (*Descr.* 8.22.3); the refurbished port of Lechaion;[36] a series of fountains, the most prominent of which were Peirene, Glauke, and the fountain of Poseidon on the west terrace of the forum;[37] and a number of baths (2.3.5),[38] including new baths built at Isthmia.[39] Despite the role that water played in structuring the civic landscape of Corinth, DeMaris notes the strange absence of water from cultic rituals after the Roman refounding, a marked shift from Corinth's Greek past, when a number of cults made use of water in their rituals.[40] The exception to the lack of water in Corinthian ritual is

---

33. DeMaris, *The New Testament in Its Ritual World*, 37.

34. On water and cult more generally in Mediterranean religion and geography, see Horden and Purcell, *The Corrupting Sea*, 412–13.

35. For references to this nickname, see Bert Hodge Hill, *The Springs: Peirene, Sacred Spring, Glauke*, vol. 1.6 of *Corinth: Results of Excavations Conducted by the American School of Classical Studies at Athens* (Princeton: American School of Classical Studies at Athens, 1964), 1–4.

36. Richard M. Rothaus, "Lechaion, Western Port of Corinth: A Preliminary Archaeology and History," *OJA* 14 (1995): 293–306.

37. Robinson, "Fountains and the Culture of Water."

38. On Corinthian baths, see also Jane C. Biers, *The Great Bath on the Lechaion Road*, vol. 17 of *Corinth: Results of Excavations Conducted by the American School of Classical Studies at Athens* (Princeton: American School of Classical Studies at Athens, 1985).

39. DeMaris, *The New Testament in Its Ritual World*, 46.

40. Ibid., 48–49. We might imagine this alongside the other changes to cultic practice in Corinth that came with Roman colonization. On these, see Christine M. Thomas, "Greek Heritage in Roman Corinth and Ephesos: Hybrid Identities and Strategies of Display in the Material Record of Traditional Mediterranean Religions," in *Corinth in Context: Comparative Studies on Religion and Society*, ed. Steven Friesen, Daniel N. Schowalter, and James Walters (Leiden: Brill, 2010), 119–23; and Concannon, *When You Were Gentiles*, 69–73.

baptism; however, it was still one of many uses to which water was put in the Corinthian landscape. Though a ritual that certainly had a life before Paul arrived in Corinth, the meaning, practice, and utility of baptism were negotiated within a civic context in which water was present in myriad ways. As such, "baptism represents an act of creative interaction with the complex cultural situation that typified life" in Corinth.[41]

Although baptism for the dead was part of the spectrum of water use in Corinth, it was also part of the spectrum of practices associated with death and burial in the Corinthia. Elsewhere Paul links baptism with the individual's participation in the death and burial of Jesus in Rom 6:3–4. The evidence for Corinthian mortuary practices is admittedly scant, but it does offer us some insight into the local funerary practices that are relevant to think with in imagining how baptism for the dead might function as one among many Corinthian negotiations with ancestors and the homeland.

Burial sites in the region were not isolated from daily life but were designed to be visited and seen. Clustered on the east and north of the city, most graves were placed along major roads in and out of the city.[42] Often their layout was constructed in such a way as to maximize the visibility and accessibility of the site to the road. The funerary assemblage from the Corinthia also suggests that grave sites were not only visible monuments to the deceased and their families but also places where Corinthians might gather for meals and other rituals connected with the dead.[43] Death and

---

41. DeMaris, *The New Testament in Its Ritual World*, 50. DeMaris goes further and suggests that baptism was a use of water that was subversive, even as it mimicked Roman bathing practices, because it was a use of water that evaded Roman control (49).

42. In his systematic study of mortuary practices in the Corinthia, Joseph L. Rife, "Death, Ritual, and Memory in Greek Society during the Early and Middle Roman Empire" (Ph.D. diss., University of Michigan, 1999), catalogues 426 individuals buried at twenty-eight discrete sites from the first three centuries after the colonization of Corinth. On the location of graves in the Corinthia, see 210–18.

43. In her forensic examination of human remains from Corinth in the early Roman Empire, Sherry Fox has shown that, when compared with remains from Paphos in Crete, mortality rates for children were higher in Corinth, though life expectancy was higher for those who lived past adulthood (Sherry C. Fox, "Health in Hellenistic and Roman Times: The Case Studies of Paphos, Cyprus and Corinth, Greece," in *Health in Antiquity*, ed. Helen King [New York: Routledge, 2005], 59–82). Fox's study was based on the remains of ninety-four individuals isolated from thirty-

burial in Corinth would have been a public process, with funeral processions moving through the city and out through gates on either the north or east toward the major burial sites.[44] Once the body was deposited in a grave site (although with cremations there would have been an intermediary step before depositing the remains), a whole host of public rituals would have attended the process, and family members would likely continue to meet at the burial site at various times thereafter.[45] As social sites, burials in the Corinthia would be the locus of a variety of ritual actions by which Corinthians negotiated their relationships with the dead.

As part of a "culture in which aiding the dead was all-important and which assumed that the world of the living could affect the world of the dead,"[46] it makes sense that *some* Corinthians might adapt a ritual such as baptism, itself a water ritual introduced in a well-watered town, as a way of negotiating relationships with the dead, both within the community and back home. There is evidence to suggest that already in the first century CE Corinthians were changing how they commemorated the dead. One finds in Corinthian burials the use of both cremation and inhumation at this time and adaptations continue into the second century CE.[47] What one did with the dead was up for debate and scrutiny in Corinth.

---

three bone lots excavated from throughout the city. Of these, eighteen could be identified as female and twenty-three as male. For these, the average age at death for men was 42.3 years and for women 39.6. Fox also notes that Corinthians were, on average, shorter than those from Paphos and more prone to exhibit enamel hypoplasia, which may have come from dietary stress or disease during development (78–79).

44. Rife, "Death, Ritual, and Memory," 290.

45. Rife notes that the most frequently attested ceramic vessels found among graves are those related to drinking and eating (ibid., 270–71). This suggests that, much as at other places in the Mediterranean, Corinthians often dined at the grave site. Some of the larger tombs in the region were equipped with benches or other architectural features that would have made dining and sacrificial rites possible, both at the time of death and at various points afterward (292–95, 99).

46. DeMaris, *The New Testament in Its Ritual World*, 59.

47. By the end of the second century, burial in tombs had become a more common practice in the Corinthia. The tombs of this period are both more crowded with human remains and less expensive in their production, suggesting that by this time "a larger proportion of the Corinthian population was concerned to identify itself not only as prosperous and eminent members but also as belonging to a specific descent group" (Rife, "Death, Ritual, and Memory," 331). This trend is part of a larger homogenization of burial practices (328–32). The arrival of the Romans introduced the practice of cremation into the landscape of Corinth, which was practiced alongside traditional forms

Baptism for the dead represents another Corinthian negotiation with the dead. Whatever the ritual looked like in practice, Paul's admittedly opaque description suggests that the ritual involved some form of benefit that was provided to the dead and an element of vicarious participation.[48] DeMaris suggests that the Corinthian practice of the ritual developed as a way of helping deceased members of the community negotiate their transition between the world of the living and the world of the dead.[49]

While this was quite likely one use to which the ritual might have been put, it seems equally possible that it may also have been a vehicle with which some Corinthians connected with the ancestral spirits of their homeland. Lacking access to the burial sites of their ancestors, the lararia of their former homes, or the shrines of familiar local deities, some Corinthians may have viewed baptism for the dead as a way of connecting with traditions, family, and other "spirits" across geographic space. Like the Israelites who were baptized into Moses during their own wanderings (1 Cor 10:3), some Corinthians may have seen baptism for the dead as a practice that ameliorated the dislocations of life on the road by connecting themselves and their distant and departed relatives to the spirit and to the Israelites. A similar explanation is offered by Stowers, who links baptism for the dead to Abraham through the spirit and a concern on the part of some Corinthians that their own baptisms might cut them off from a connection to the ancestors.[50]

---

of inhumation (254–55). By the end of the second century, cinerary urns containing the cremated remains were found strictly inside tombs, a combination of Greek and Roman forms of burial practice (331). See also DeMaris, *The New Testament in Its Ritual World*, 70.

48. DeMaris (*The New Testament in Its Ritual World*, 62–64) notes examples of funerary rites that could involve surrogacy and substitution, as when a body needed to be buried but could not be acquired. He also shows how the notion of the dead benefiting from a funerary ritual was quite common. Baptism for the dead functions like a rite carried out for a person in absentia (64). Paul certainly suggests a similarly vicarious interpretation of baptism in Rom 6:3–4.

49. "As an entry rite, baptism on behalf of the dead would have confirmed the departure of deceased community members from the circle of the living and enabled their entry into the community of the dead" (ibid., 64). DeMaris further argues that such a focus on the dead was related to broader Corinthian interest in chthonic cults (66–71). On this, see also DeMaris, "Demeter in Roman Corinth," 105–17; DeMaris, "Baptism for the Dead," 661–82.

50. Stowers, "Myth, Meals, and Power," 125: "Paul taught [the Corinthians] that they could share in the *pneuma* of the *pneuma*-bringer, Christ, and that the divine

If some Corinthians were indeed asking questions about how to connect with their ancestors and homelands while in motion, it makes some sense of how Paul might have been initially received in Corinth. As Mack suggests,

> That the Corinthians had bothered to give him [Paul] a hearing at all can only be understood as their reception of a traveling teacher/philosopher, with something of interest to say about "wisdom," "spirits," group identities, and meals in memory of ancestors. ... It seems that the Corinthians received him just as they would have entertained others and debated some of his ideas without having to assent to his gospel.[51]

As a traveling teacher/philosopher, Paul may have offered some Corinthians new ideas about how to reconcile the problems occasioned by distance from home. Paul offered a way that those already interested in how to connect with the spirits of their families and ancestors back home might think about spirit that could link people together across distance and space. Similarly, having introduced baptism as an entry rite to the community, some Corinthians may have adapted the practice to connect to their ancestors, as one among many practices around water and burial that were being negotiated in the Corinthian landscape. Such practices may not have ultimately been what Paul intended for his Corinthian audience, but this does not mean that they would not have been fitting theological and cultic responses to the challenges faced in a Corinth where movement to and fro required new solutions to how identity might be maintained far from home.

Works Cited

Adams, James N. "Bilingualism at Delos." Pages 103–27 in *Bilingualism in Ancient Society: Language Contact and the Written Text*. Edited by James N. Adams, Mark Janse, and Simon Swain. New York: Oxford University Press, 2002.

---

pneuma would connect them to the renowned ancient ancestor, Abraham. They saw another ritual means for improving the lot of their more immediate ancestors. Baptism for the dead would incorporate those dead into the distinguished lineage and ancestry. Without baptism for the dead, their own baptisms might cut them off from their extended families of the significant dead."

51. Mack, "Rereading the Christ Myth," 52.

Aelius Aristides. *Aristides in Four Volumes*. Edited and Translated by C. A. Behr. LCL. Cambridge: Harvard University Press, 1973.

Biers, Jane C. *The Great Bath on the Lechaion Road*. Vol. 17 of *Corinth: Results of Excavations Conducted by the American School of Classical Studies at Athens*. Princeton: American School of Classical Studies at Athens, 1985.

Broneer, Oscar. *The South Stoa and Its Roman Successors*. Vol. 1.4 of *Corinth: Results of Excavations Conducted by the American School of Classical Studies at Athens*. Princeton: American School of Classical Studies at Athens, 1954.

Cameron, Ron, and Merrill P. Miller. "Redescribing Paul and the Corinthians." Pages 245–302 in *Redescribing Paul and the Corinthians*. Edited by Ron Cameron and Merrill P. Miller. ECL 5. Atlanta: Society of Biblical Literature, 2011.

Concannon, Cavan W. *"When You Were Gentiles": Specters of Ethnicity in Roman Corinth and Paul's Corinthian Correspondence*. Synkrisis: Comparative Approaches to Early Christianity in Greco-Roman Culture. New Haven: Yale University Press, 2014.

DeMaris, Richard E. "Corinthian Religion and Baptism for the Dead (1 Corinthians 15:29): Insights from Archaeology and Anthropology." *JBL* 114 (1995): 661–82.

———. "Demeter in Roman Corinth: Local Development in a Mediterranean Religion." *Numen* 42 (1995): 105–17.

———. *The New Testament in Its Ritual World*. New York: Routledge, 2008.

Fox, Sherry C. "Health in Hellenistic and Roman Times: The Case Studies of Paphos, Cyprus and Corinth, Greece." Pages 59–82 in *Health in Antiquity*. Edited by Helen King. New York: Routledge, 2005.

Frankfurter, David. "Traditional Cult." Pages 543–64 in *A Companion to the Roman Empire*. Edited by David S. Potter. Malden, MA: Blackwell, 2007.

Georgi, Dieter. *The Opponents of Paul in Second Corinthians: A Study of Religious Propaganda in Late Antiquity*. Philadelphia: Fortress, 1986.

Harland, Philip A. *Dynamics of Identity in the World of the Early Christians: Associations, Judeans, and Cultural Minorities*. New York: T&T Clark, 2009.

Harland, Philip A. "Pausing at the Intersection of Religion and Travel." Pages 1–26 in *Travel and Religion in Antiquity*. Edited by Philip A. Harland. Studies in Christianity and Judaism 21. Waterloo, ON: Wilfred Laurier University Press, 2011.

Hill, Bert Hodge. *The Springs: Peirene, Sacred Spring, Glauke*. Vol. 1.6 of *Corinth: Results of Excavations Conducted by the American School of Classical Studies at Athens*. Princeton: American School of Classical Studies at Athens, 1964.

Horden, Peregrine, and Nicholas Purcell. *The Corrupting Sea: A Study of Mediterranean History*. Oxford: Wiley-Blackwell, 2000.

Jones, C. P. *Kinship Diplomacy in the Ancient World*. Revealing Antiquity 12. Cambridge: Harvard University Press, 1999.

Kent, John Harvey. *The Inscriptions, 1926–1950*. Vol. 8.3 of *Corinth: Results of Excavations Conducted by the American School of Classical Studies at Athens*. Princeton: American School of Classical Studies at Athens, 1966.

Mack, Burton. "Rereading the Christ Myth: Paul's Gospel and the Christ Cult Question." Pages 35–73 in *Redescribing Paul and the Corinthians*. Edited by Ron Cameron and Merrill P. Miller. ECL 5. Atlanta: Society of Biblical Literature, 2011.

Marquis, Timothy L. "At Home or Away: Travel and Death in 2 Corinthians 1–9." PhD diss., Yale University, 2008.

Martin, Dale B. *The Corinthian Body*. New Haven: Yale University Press, 1995.

Millis, Benjamin W. "The Social and Ethnic Origins of the Colonists in Early Roman Corinth." Pages 13–36 in *Corinth in Context: Comparative Studies on Religion and Society*. Edited by Steven Friesen, Daniel N. Schowalter, and James C. Walters. Leiden: Brill, 2010.

Muir, Steven. "Religion on the Road in Ancient Greece and Rome." Pages 29–47 in *Travel and Religion in Antiquity*. Edited by Philip A. Harland. Studies in Christianity and Judaism 21. Waterloo, ON: Wilfred Laurier University Press, 2011.

Noy, David. *Foreigners at Rome: Citizens and Strangers*. London: Duckworth; Classical Press of Wales, 2000.

Rife, Joseph L. "Death, Ritual, and Memory in Greek Society during the Early and Middle Roman Empire." PhD diss., University of Michigan, 1999.

Robinson, Betsey A. "Fountains and the Culture of Water at Roman Corinth." PhD diss., University of Pennsylvania, 2001.

———. "Fountains and the Formation of Cultural Identity at Roman Corinth." Pages 111–40 in *Urban Religion in Roman Corinth: Interdisciplinary Approaches*. Edited by Daniel N. Schowalter and Steven J. Friesen. Cambridge: Harvard University Press, 2005.

———. *Histories of Peirene: A Corinthian Fountain in Three Millennia*. Ancient Art and Architecture in Context. Athens: American School of Classical Studies at Athens, 2011.
Rothaus, Richard M. "Lechaion, Western Port of Corinth: A Preliminary Archaeology and History." *OJA* 14 (1995): 293–306.
Schüssler Fiorenza, Elisabeth. *In Memory of Her: A Feminist Theological Reconstruction of Christian Origins*. 10th anniversary ed. New York: Crossroad, 1994.
———. *Rhetoric and Ethic: The Politics of Biblical Studies*. Minneapolis: Fortress, 1999.
Smith, Dennis Edwin. "The Egyptian Cults at Corinth." *HTR* 70 (1977): 201–31.
Smith, Jonathan Z. "Re: Corinthians." Pages 17–34 in *Redescribing Paul and the Corinthians*. Edited by Ron Cameron and Merrill P. Miller. ECL 5. Atlanta: Society of Biblical Literature, 2011.
———. "Re: Corinthians." Pages 340–61 in *Relating Religion: Essays in the Study of Religion*. Edited by Jonathan Z. Smith. Chicago: University of Chicago Press, 2004.
Stanley, Christopher D. *Arguing with Scripture: The Rhetoric of Quotations in the Letters of Paul*. New York: T&T Clark, 2004.
Stowers, Stanley K. "Kinds of Myth, Meals, and Power: Paul and the Corinthians." Pages 105–50 in *Redescribing Paul and the Corinthians*. Edited by Ron Cameron and Merrill P. Miller. ECL 5. Atlanta: Society of Biblical Literature, 2011.
Sumney, Jerry L. *Identifying Paul's Opponents: The Question of Method in 2 Corinthians*. JSNTSup 40. Sheffield: JSOT Press, 1990.
Thomas, Christine M. "Greek Heritage in Roman Corinth and Ephesos: Hybrid Identities and Strategies of Display in the Material Record of Traditional Mediterranean Religions." Pages 117–47 in *Corinth in Context: Comparative Studies on Religion and Society*. Edited by Steven Friesen, Daniel N. Schowalter, and James C. Walters. Leiden: Brill, 2010.
Versnel, H. S. *Coping with the Gods: Wayward Readings in Greek Theology*. RGRW 173. Leiden: Brill, 2011.
Wire, Antoinette Clark. *The Corinthian Women Prophets: A Reconstruction through Paul's Rhetoric*. Minneapolis: Fortress, 1990.

Between Polis, Oikos, and Ekklesia: The Challenge of Negotiating the Spirit World (1 Cor 12:1–11)

Kathy Ehrensperger

Most members of the Corinthian ἐκκλησία were accustomed to a context in which numerous deities and spiritual beings were seen as responsible for diverse aspects of life. Entrenched in their *habitus* was the perception that each and every aspect of life required the appropriate relationship to a specific deity or spiritual being. This permeated public life but to an even greater and more significant extent kin group and household on an everyday basis. Those directly addressed in 1 Cor 12:1–11 certainly were embedded in Roman, Greek and possibly other cult practices. Having joined the Christ-movement, these Corinthian practitioners of diverse cults needed to work out how this formerly life-assuring and meaning-generating *habitus* related to their new loyalty, as is evident in issues such as marriage and meat eating dealt with earlier in the letter. They were obviously also concerned about issues pertaining to pneumatic things (τὰ πνευμάτικα) and had asked for Paul's advice and views. The general translation of τὰ πνευμάτικα as "spiritual gifts" is questionable because it is based on the presupposition that Paul speaks here generally of "gifts" imparted by the Spirit, due to the occurrence of χαρίσματα in 12:9. However, there is no indication in this section that the "gift" character of the aspects mentioned in 12:3–11 is the focus of Paul's clarifications. The fact that τὰ πνευμάτικα is translated as "spiritual things" (1 Cor 2:13), "spiritual good" (1 Cor 9:11), "spiritual blessing" (Rom 15:27), or, when referring to people, as "those who are spiritual" (1 Cor 2:13, 15; 3:1), those who have "spiritual powers" (1 Cor 14:37) or "who have received the Spirit" (Gal 6:1) clearly indicates that what is at stake here is not primarily a gift but something related to the "spirit world."[1] Thus I will

---

1. The passage from Eph 6:12 could prove illuminating here in that τὰ πνευμάτικα

explore in this essay what Paul might be talking about here, whether spiritual gifts or, more likely, spiritual things or spiritual powers. Since the spirit world was a key aspect of life in antiquity, it should not surprise us that Paul replies at length about these πνευμάτικα. Issues concerning pneumatic things are addressed throughout chapters 12–14, including the "body" section, the "love" song of chapter 13, and the detailed discussion of "tongues" in chapter 14. All these important topics are dealt with under the heading περὶ δὲ τῶν πνευματικῶν (issues concerning pneumatic things). My concern here is the first section (12:1–11), where the key aspects/components of τὰ πνευμάτικα to be addressed are initially mentioned. The passage indicates the challenge the Corinthians are facing when it comes to things of a pneumatic kind. Thus here I will focus on (1) the challenge of separation from cults and their idols (12:2), (2) Paul's explanatory preamble (12:3), and (3) Paul's reassurance concerning the "spiritual things" (12:4–11).

1. The Challenge of Separation from Cults and Their Idols (1 Cor 12:2)

Before discussing anything in further detail, Paul reminds the addressees who they were before they joined the Christ-movement: they were ἔθνη entirely led by what Paul calls speechless idols (τὰ εἴδωλα τὰ ἄφωνα). Concerning the past tense in the reference to the Corinthians as ἔθνη, I follow those who do not take this as an indication that Paul considers them as no longer ethnically distinct people, that is, as "former" ἔθνη. Paul, in my view, here clearly qualifies them as the kind of ἔθνη they were in the past in relation to their trust and loyalty to τὰ εἴδωλα τὰ ἄφωνα. They *were* ἔθνη who followed and sought guidance from τὰ εἴδωλα τὰ ἄφωνα, but they *now* ἔθνη follow Christ. This specific aspect of their former life should have been left in the past—not their cultural and ethnic diversity. (What else would they have become? Paul certainly could not regard them as Jews, not even as honorary Jews, and to my knowledge there were no other categories available, as it is widely acknowledged that the Christ-followers at

---

are clearly specified as τῆς πονηρίας. This implies that there are most likely other πνευμάτικα that would be charaterized differently. On the spirit world generally, see Guy J. Williams, *The Spirit World in the Letters of Paul the Apostle: A Critical Examination of the Role of Spiritual Beings in the Authentic Pauline Epistles*, FRLANT 231 (Göttingen: Vandenhoeck & Ruprecht, 2009), 19–29.

that time were not a "third kind" of ἔθνη.²) The question arises why Paul reminded them at this point of this aspect of their past lives. He had only referred to "some" who had previously been accustomed to idols (8:7) and are thus still influenced by this affiliation, in a context where he provided guidance to what did and did not constitute idolatry. Here, however, they are *all* reminded of this dimension of their past lives. (It is obvious that the addressees are not Jews!)

1.1. Τὰ Πνευμάτικα—Life Essentials

The specific reminder must have something to do with the topic: τὰ πνευμάτικα. These pneumatic things and following τὰ εἴδωλα τὰ ἄφωνα must be interfering with each other in an even wider sense than just the eating of meat where only some are reminded that they formerly had been accustomed to εἴδωλα. With regard to τὰ πνευμάτικα, their past following of εἴδωλα might cause problems for all of the ἐκκλησία when it comes to the appropriate understanding and handling of the pneumatic things in Christ. It needs to be noted that not all aspects of the Corinthians' previous life are considered problematic by Paul, as he confidently affirms that "all things are lawful" (6:12; 10:23). I will come back to this aspect later. Moreover, as in 8:5, Paul does not deny the existence of εἴδωλα, but here he particularly emphasizes that they are ἄφωνα, mute, speechless. Although there must be room in the ἐκκλησία for previous life experience, this aspect of their life is to be relegated to the past. Paul has already tried to clarify this with regard to the eating of meat or other food prepared in the context of pagan sacrifices, when he orders them to "shun the worship of idols" (10:14b) and states "I do not want you to be partners with demons" (10:20b NRSV). It seems he should have made his point clear there. But the issue concerning the pneumatic things is most likely of similar if not higher importance than the partaking in pagan sacrifices. Paul indicates this by noting the power by which they had been drawn to seek guidance and follow in the paths of these deities (ἤγεσθε ἀπαγόμενοι, 12:2).

Following the guidance of the gods was no minor aspect of their previous lives: this was the core to their being in and perceiving the world. It was the social and symbolic universe of the ἔθνη. This was not just an

---

2. For discussion, see my "Paul, His People and Racial Terminology," *JECH* 3 (2013): 17–33.

additional practice that could be followed or not but rather something that permeated all aspects of their life. No dimension of life was outside the realm of deities and spiritual beings.[3] The lives of humans and gods were intertwined, and the only variation was the hierarchy of priorities in which one participated in the cult of particular deities. Thus Aelius Aristides tells of a dream in which he refused to honor the emperor with the required kiss, explaining to the ruler that he was a follower of Asclepius.[4] Similarly, not all Corinthians would have participated in all cult practices of all the deities that were relevant to the city during the first century. Although it cannot be ascertained with certainty which cults were practiced at the time of Paul's visits and thereafter, there seem to have been Roman and Greek, possibly also Egyptian, cults present in the first century CE.

1.2. Aspects of Public Cult in Roman Corinth

1.2.1. Roman Cults

The establishment of Corinth as a Roman colony privileged Roman deities as the officially practiced cults. The *Colonia Laus Iulia Corinthiensis* was organized according to Roman patterns—not as a variation of a Greek πόλις—and this certainly included the organization and status of Roman cults. As a Roman colony, the civic and cultic institutions of Rome would have been replicated in Corinth, and the colonists would have been

---

3. Stanley K. Stowers, "Greeks Who Sacrifice and Those Who Do Not: Toward an Anthropology of Greek Religion," in *The Social World of the First Christians: Essays in Honor of Wayne A. Meeks*, ed. L. Michael White and O. Larry Yarborough (Minneapolis: Fortress, 1995), 293–333; Jörg Rüpke, *The Religion of the Romans* (Cambridge: Polity Press, 2007); Markus Öhler, "Das ganze Haus: Antike Alltagsreligiosität und die Apostelgeschichte," *ZNW* 102 (2011): 201–34.

4. Προσειπόντος δὲ κἀμοῦ καὶ στάντος ἐθαύμασεν ὁ αὐτοκράτωρ ὡς οὐ καὶ αὐτὸς προσελθὼν φιλήσαιμι. Κἀγὼ εἶπον ὅτι ὁ θεραπευτὴς εἴμην ὁ τοῦ Ἀσκληπιοῦ τοσοῦτον γάρ μοι ἤρεσκεν εἰπεῖν περὶ ἐμαθτοῦ. Πρὸς οὖν τοῖς ἄλλοις ἔφην καὶ τοῦτο ὁ θεός μοι παρήγγελειν μὴ φιλεῖν οὑτωσί καὶ ὅς ἀρκεῖ ἔφη κἀγὼ ἐρίγησα. καὶ μὴν θεραπεύειν γε παντὸς κρείττων ὁ Ἀσκληπιός: "When I too saluted him and stood there, the Emperor wondered why I too did not come forward and kiss him. And I said that I was a worshipper of Asklepius. For I was content to say so much about myself. 'In addition to other things,' I said, 'the god has also instructed me not to kiss in this fashion.' And he replied, 'I am content.' I was silent. And he said, "Asklepius is better than all to worship'" (*Or.* 47.23 [Behr]).

expected to be "Roman" in recognizing the Roman gods and participating in their cults.[5] Archaeological evidence shows that the Roman cults were laid out around the periphery of the lower forum.[6] There is evidence for Roman cults of Fortuna, Neptune, Clarion Apollo, Venus, Mercury, Diana, and Bacchus. The imperial cult seems to have been present in the city during the first century as well. As Nancy Bookidis affirms, the cults of the forum were closely linked to Rome, and the cults were performed according to Roman practice and calendar. The issue of the calendar reminds us of the importance of time and the life-structuring dimension of calendars. The rhythm of life ticked according to the official calendar of a city, and a Roman colony clearly ticked according to the Roman calendar in all aspects of its official organization.[7] Cult was performed in the Roman vein at the official temples, organized and supervised by the Ordo Decurionum, the city council.[8] Valerius Maximus (writing during the reign of Tiberius, 14–37 CE) described Roman cult practices as follows: "Our ancestors desired that fixed and formal annual ceremonies be regulated by the knowledge of the *pontifices*; that sanction of the good governance of affairs be marshalled by the observation of augurs; that Apollo's prophecies be revealed by the books of the seers" (*Fact.* 1.1a–b).[9] Proper regard for the gods served the purpose of addressing problems in the here and now. Rituals were performed to have a desired effect and, if effective, were conducted in exactly the same way until a change was required due to changed circumstances. The key factor for Roman piety was knowledge. It was essential to know how to give to the gods what they were due: *scientia colendorum deorum* was considered key in all Roman

---

5. Mary Beard, John North, and S. R. F. Price, *The Religions of Rome: A History* (Cambridge: Cambridge University Press, 1998), 1:315–17; see also James C. Walters, "Civic Identity in Roman Corinth and Its Impact on Early Christianity," in *Urban Religion in Roman Corinth*, ed. Daniel N. Schowalter and Steven J. Friesen (Cambridge: Harvard University Press, 2005), 410.

6. Nancy Bookidis, "Religion in Corinth 146 BCE–100 CE," in Schowalter and Friesen, *Urban Religion in Roman Corinth*, 152.

7. Ibid., 157.

8. Greg Woolf, *Becoming Roman: The Origins of Provincial Civilization in Gaul* (Cambridge: Cambridge University Press, 1998), 224–25.

9. Similarly Cicero, *Nat. d.* 3.2.5: "The *religio* of the Roman people comprises ritual, auspices, and the third additional division consisting of all such prophetic warnings as the interpreters of the Sybil or the *haruspices* have derived from portents and prodigies" (Rackham).

activities. The grace and generosity of the gods depended on such accurate knowledge and meticulous performance of rituals. Only if one was able to give to them what they were due in the right way would one be blessed with their gifts. Correct communication with the gods was thus vital for the well-being of the city. However, peculiarly, the Roman gods did not speak: they were mute, ἄφωνος. They did not speak either to priests or to magistrates during rituals or otherwise. Verbal communication was restricted to the prophecies of the officially sanctioned Sibylline books. The only way of understanding their communication and of responding appropriately was through *haruspices* (observation and interpretation of bird flight, entrails of victims of sacrifices, the smoke formation during sacrificing) performed by *auguri*. It was thus vital to perform the rituals in exactly the right way: one had to have knowledge/*scientia* to that effect and also to know how to interpret the flight of birds, the entrails of victims of sacrifices, and the smoke formation of sacrifices. Thus Cicero notes: "Moreover we receive a number of warnings by means of signs and of the entrails of victims, and by many other things that long-continued usage has noted in such a matter as to create the art of divination. Therefore no great man ever existed who did not enjoy some portion of divine inspiration" (*Nat. d.* 2.166–167 [Rackham]). Divine inspiration here is understood as practical knowledge, the key for communicating accurately with the gods and giving them their due so they would grant favor and success to one's actions. Roman colonists would most likely adhere to these cults, and the Greek elite, as far as they were present in the city, would probably do so as well in so far as they cooperated with the colonizers, whereas locals are considered to have adhered to the indigenous Greek cults.[10]

1.2.2. Greek Cults

While the Roman cult practice must have had a dominating impact on the daily rhythm of life in Corinth, there is also evidence that Greek cults reemerged after the destruction of the city, even if they might not have been in direct continuity with the pre-Roman period. It is at least a question as to whether all of the above-mentioned deities were merely worshiped in their Roman vein or also in their Greek identity, but this is difficult to assess.

---

10. Beard, North, and Price note "local élites in the provinces showing greater interest in ostensibly *Roman* deities than their poorer compatriots" (*Religions of Rome*, 1:314).

Outside the forum there seem to have been cultic activities at the temple of Asclepius, which was repaired by a Roman official, Marcus Antonius Milesius, and thus most likely operated under some form of Roman supervision. Bookidis further refers to the worshiping of Jupiter Capitolinus possibly also outside the forum district, which could be an indication that there was a Greek cult at the same site where Zeus Olympios might have also been worshiped. The sanctuary of Demeter and Kore was reestablished.[11] The character of the cult of Demeter and Kore cannot be clearly confirmed, but it may well be that there was a continuing or, as Jorunn Økland has argued,[12] a reemerging Greek aspect to this important cult in Corinth. The temple of Aphrodite on Acrocorinth was officially revived shortly after the establishing of the Roman colony, but again this says little about possible ongoing significance at the local level even in the interim period after the destruction of the city. Although Bookidis believes that the cults of Asclepius, Jupiter Capitolinus/Zeus Olympios, Demeter and Kore, and Aphrodite were established or reestablished upon Roman initiative and thus were under Roman supervision and control, their *local* significance cannot be denied, and a particularly Greek aspect of worshiping that may not have taken on official guise cannot be ruled out.[13] All of these cults would have been considered of decisive significance for the well-being of the city in Roman as well as Greek perspective.

Thus participation in cult practice was not only normal but was essential for the well-being of individuals as well as for the community, at the level of the πόλις/*oppida*/*colonia*, *provinicia*, and *imperium*. The coherence and prosperity depended on the right and accurate performance of cult, the accurate communication between gods and humans, and the accurate interpretation and understanding of the deities' communication. How this was done had to do with accurate performance of cults: the sacrifices at temples, including meals associated with these. Thus public performance of cult practices was a decisively important aspect of civic life in πόλεις/ *oppida* and *colonia* throughout the empire, hence also in the *colonia* of

---

11. Bookidis, "Religion in Corinth," 160.
12. Jorunn Økland, "Ceres, Kore, and Cultural Complexity: Divine Personality Definitions and Human Worshippers in Roman Corinth," in *Corinth in Context: Comparative Studies on Religion and* Society, ed. Steven Friesen, Daniel N. Schowalter, and James C. Walters (Leiden: Brill 2010), 199–229.
13. See also Walters, "Civic Identity," 410.

Corinth. Paul had addressed issues arising from the public cult participation in chapters 8–10.

However, cult practice was not only important at the *official* level, visible on a grand scale in temple ceremonies, sacrifices, and festivals. The other possibly more important aspect was that of a more *private* nature: the role and function of cults in households and families, which governed daily life and provided help and orientation.[14] This may have been more significant for early Christ-followers, since this is where they encountered cult practice in relation to "mute idols" on a daily basis. It is to this context that we now turn in order to gain an impression of what the separation that Paul required of them actually meant.

1.3. In the House and at the Crossroads: The Significance of Domestic Cults

Small neighborhood shrines at crossroads and fountains and altars at the entrance of houses were scattered throughout any ancient πόλις/*oppidum*. With regard to the family and household cults, not only the great deities of the official cult were important but also in-between spiritual beings. The world was not only populated by humans on earth and deities in heaven; there were divine powers of a middle nature who "sinuate in this interval of the air between highest ether and earth below through whom our aspirations and our deserts are conveyed to the Gods. The Greeks call them 'daimons' (*De DeoSoc* 6)."[15] They existed in such a diversity and multitude that there was no situation for which they were not responsible.[16] According to Plutarch, they were fundamental parts of the hierarchy of the cosmos, structurally indispensible in that they were the "interpretative and ministering nature" between gods and humans. To remove them would mean to "make the relations between gods and men alien and remote" or else "force us to a disorderly confusion of all things, in which we bring the

---

14. Peter Foss, "Watchful Lares: Roman Household Organization and the Rituals of Cooking and Dining," in *Domestic Space in the Roman World*, ed. Ray Laurence and Andrew Wallace-Hadrill, Journal of Roman Archaeology Supplement Series 22 (Portsmouth, RI: JRA, 1997), 196–216; Andrew Wallace-Hadrill and Stanley K. Stowers, "Kinds of Myth, Meals, and Power," in *Redescribing Paul and the Corinthians*, ed. Ron Cameron and Merrill P. Miller, ECL 5 (Atlanta: Society of Biblical Literature 2011), 111; Öhler, "Das ganze Haus."

15. Naomi Janowitz, *Magic in the Roman World: Pagans, Jews, and Christians* (London: Routledge, 2001), 34.

16. Ibid., 29.

god into men's emotions and activities, drawing him down to our needs" (*Def. orac.* 13.52–53 [416F] [Babbitt]). There were ways and means via which one related to these "spiritual powers": one had to know the rites, when and where to do them, in order to maintain the relationship not only with them but also with the deity to whom they were subject. A differentiated hierarchical system ordered the cosmos and thus every aspect of daily life. Daimons were part of one's life as much as family members and neighbors. In as much as the spheres of deities and mediatory spiritual beings were differentiated but interrelated, so were the cultic dimensions. Thus when we distinguish between civic and domestic cult practices, these should not been seen as separate or oppositional spheres but as part of a cosmic network. In sum, encounter with and separation from "mute idols" would have been most frequent. I will present a broad overview of aspects of domestic cults relevant for Roman Corinth, being aware that these spirits, demons, and deities were relevant not only at this level in the domestic sphere but for other contexts as well.

These spiritual beings were differentiated by Greeks and Romans in various ways. Only the Romans know of Penates, Lares, and genii. For classical Greece, although no such specific designations existed, there is still clear evidence for domestic cults as well. Since Greek public cults continued to be practiced after the destruction of Corinth or reemerged after its constitution as a Roman colony, it is likely that Greek domestic cults continued to play a certain role in houses and among kin groups as well.

1.3.1. Aspects of Domestic Cults in Classical Greece

Recently Christopher A. Faraone has argued for a distinction between οἶκος- and γένος-related cults, both relevant in the domestic sphere. The former included all members of a particular house and was thus a locative cult; the latter was specifically related to those who claimed descent from a common ancestor. It appears that the οἶκος-related cult was a kind of replication of civic cults on a smaller scale, as the deity most frequently mentioned in this respect is Zeus Herkeios or Zeus Ktesios. They represent "a fairly common characteristic of Greek domestic religion, and one of the ways in which it intersects with the practices of larger communities: household cults can be smaller versions of civic cults."[17] But of course these

---

17. Deborah Boedeker, "Family Matters: Domestic Religion in Classical Greece,"

two were not the only ones. Another key deity of the house was Hestia, probably the most widespread of the domestic deities, despite her low key presence in civic cult and mythology. The daily life of the house centered around the hearth, so Hestia was the center of daily life.[18]

Distinct from such locative cults were ancestral cults. Indications for the distinction between the two in classical Greece can be found in the questions candidates for public office in Athens had to answer. It was thus decisive that they could name their Apollo Patroos and Zeus Herkeios and confirm the location of their shrines, thus demonstrating that they were godfearing citizens, in order to be eligible for an office in the polis.[19] Plato has Socrates refer to his βωμοὶ καὶ ἱερὰ οἰκεῖα καὶ πατρῷα and thus, in Faraone's view, clearly distinguishing between altars and shrines of the household and of the kin group.[20]

In addition to the parallelization with civic cults, household and kin-group rites focused on aspects that were not well represented by the former. They had to do with immediate needs and life transitions such as birth, illness, weddings, death, with female household members playing key roles in these rites. As such, the distinction advocated by Faraone may not always have been clearly maintained, as such rites could have involved all those living in the house or only those of the specific kin group. Many of these particular rites circled around the hearth, that is, Hestia, when, for example, a bride was welcomed by the groom's mother and introduced by her to the household deities or when a newborn child was accepted by the father in the *amphidromia,* a rite that included "running around the hearth" and whereby the child was placed under the protection of Hestia.[21] Children generally had to be protected from ill fate by numerous measures, including charms and amulets, as were women safeguarded during pregnancy and childbirth.[22] Although these are examples from classical Greece, there is little doubt that such household and kin-group cults con-

---

in *Household and Family Religion in Antiquity: Contextual and Comparative Perspectives,* ed. John Bodel and Saul M. Olyan (Oxford: Blackwell, 2008), 233.

18. Ibid., 234.
19. Ibid., 212.
20. Plato, *Euthyd.* 302C. See also the discussion by Christopher A. Faraone, "Household Religion in Ancient Greece," in Bodel and Olyan, *Household and Family Religion in Antiquity.*
21. Boedeker, "Family Matters," 241.
22. Ibid., 240–42.

tinued to be of core significance for the Greek population of Corinth in their daily lives into the first century CE.

1.3.2. Aspects of Roman Domestic Cults

This is certainly the case for the Penates, Lares, and genii of Roman tradition. As with the Roman public cult, Roman domestic cults would have made their way into the *colonia* of Corinth. There is wide evidence from different parts of the Roman Empire for domestic deities and spiritual beings. They figure prominently in literary and visual sources, as well as in material culture in the form of statuettes and small shrines and altars in and near houses. Similar, although not identical, to the pattern found in classical Greece, the domestic deities were either those of the *domus*, that is, of all who lived in the house (the Lares), or those of the clan or gens (the Penates). Without a Greek equivalent is the *genius*, the guardian spirit of the head of the household. Although often found together in niches or shrines, the two groups were distinct, as John Bodel emphasizes. The Lares "were represented iconographically in a remarkably consistent way and in paintings were seldom accompanied by depictions of other gods. The other embraced collectively a stylistically heterogeneous and conceptually diverse assortment of aniconic and iconic objects representing individual deities, demi-gods, and heroes."[23] Their material difference is evidence for their distinction in terms of role and function.

Although both could move with the respective household and clan, the Penates were normally only honored at one place in the house, whereas the Lares could have diverse locations where they would be worshiped. Although the Lares were more communal in their worship focus, they did not bind the slave and free members of the household together in one worshiping community. Rather, it appears that the Lares of the freeborn kin group were also the Lares of the slaves of this kin group, with the result that the Lares were worshiped in separate groups. Cicero maintains that the Lares were "handed down by our ancestors both to masters and to slaves" (*cum dominis tum famulis*, *Leg.* 2.27; also 2.19.5), but significantly he refers to their role for slaves and masters separately. Similarly, Columella advises villa owners to get their agricultural slaves to have their

---

23. John Bodel, "Cicero's Minerva, *Penates*, and the Mother of the *Lares*: An Outline of Roman Domestic Religion," in Bodel and Olyan, *Household and Family Religion in Antiquity*, 258.

meals "around the household hearth and the master's *Lar.*" Most likely this envisages a scene where master and slaves are in sight of each other but are not eating together. Thus commensality is reserved for rare special occasions if at all (Columella, *Rust.* 11.1.19). Archaeological findings from Pompeii indicate a similar segregation in terms of domestic worshiping communities between slaves and freeborn members of the kin group, even though the cult activities are related to the same Lares within the one and the same house. Although the Lares slaves were included in domestic daily cult activities, nevertheless as slaves they were denied any protection by Penates, since they legally were considered to have no ancestors and thus were not part of a kin group/clan. Thus the Lares also had somehow the function of being the deities of the slave families (*dis famulis*).[24] Bodel concludes that in ancient Rome "'household' religion and 'family' religion, like the conditions of slave and free generally, were separate and interdependent, but not equal categories."[25]

The numerous archaeological finds of niches and shrines in houses and shops, and the diversity of statuettes and other objects found there, are indications of the significance of these *private* forms and places of devotion in Roman tradition. Even if it is difficult to establish precisely what meaning was attributed to these statuettes and objects in a particular context, the fact that these were part of the house demonstrates that a sacred or spiritual function was affirmed for them, and correct performance of worship, that is, of giving them what one owed, was vital for the well-being of the house and those who lived in it.[26] It was here at these shrines, small altars, and niches in houses that all inhabitants of the empire related to the spirit world of gods, half-gods, demons, and spirits. This is the place and form through which people communicated with this world by performing rites and offering sacrifices and prayers for their daily needs that were intertwined with the powers and needs of these spiritual beings. Although the practice of "official" cults dominated public life in many ways, probably

---

24. See ibid., 265–67.

25. Ibid., 267. This is a significant insight that has important implications for understanding how slave members of a pagan household could become Christ-followers. If there were separate cult communities within one and the same household, this might have opened a niche for alternative cult activities for slaves, something that seems to have been feared and was discouraged. See Bodel, "Cicero's Minerva," 274–75 n. 56.

26. Bodel, "Cicero's Minerva," 261–63.

the most important cult practice happened low-key and small-scale in the realm of daily life. As noted already, these deities, spirits, or demons were of decisive importance for daily life, and it was inconceivable from the life experience in the first century to ignore or consider these powers as nonexistent. They were part of their lives and required due attention through cult practice.

1.3.3. Forms of Jewish Domestic Piety

Since Corinth was a Roman colony in Greece, it can be assumed that both Greek and Roman forms of domestic cults were prevalent there and permeated the context of daily life in the πόλις for all its inhabitants. For Jewish inhabitants, the situation would have been different. They were, of course, not part of this world of domestic and public cults. However, it should not be assumed that this "spiritual" world did not play an important role in Jewish tradition.[27] Since the major form of public cult practice was performed in the temple in Jerusalem, this was, although of central relevance, not part of the daily form of worshiping practice for Jews in the diaspora. Although Sabbath communal prayer and Torah reading and teaching were undeniably important communal practices, it is evident that, with regard to the spirit world, there must have been ways and means to relate to it also for Jews, although in distinction from their pagan neighbors. Without being able to provide much detail in a contribution of this length, the key difference between Jewish and pagan perceptions of these spiritual beings lies in them being seen by Jews as subordinate to the One. Only God was to be given glory through worshiping. This is what decisively distinguishes Jews from their pagan neighbors: the latter honor these as deities. This is what Paul refers to when he accuses pagans that they do not honor God as God (Rom 1:21) and instead worshiped and served the creature rather than the Creator (1:25). The problem is not the existence of the spirit world as such but how to relate to it appropriately. Also in the Jewish perception, the world, heaven, and earth and the realm in between is populated by

---

27. Jack Lightstone (*The Commerce of the Sacred: Mediation of the Divine among Jews in the Greco-Roman World* [New York: Columbia University Press, 2006], 36) notes that "in the Greco-Roman diaspora, at the very least, belief in demons seems everywhere, and in all periods."

spiritual beings, but the power of these is clearly subordinated to, and distinguished from, the power of God.[28]

There is clear evidence for "holy men," or magicians, in numerous magic texts who could specifically relate to these beings; in addition, spells from the period in question attest to the numerous practices through which Jews, similar to their pagan neighbors, related to this world. Although from the late third or early fourth century, the Sefer Harazim is evidence for known magical practices to relate to this in-between world of demons, spirits, and the dead. Those who are able to relate to this world are men of particular charismatic power, knowledgeable and wise mediators. They know how to compel such spirits to exert positive effects through "offerings, and other ritual actions, magical syllables, adjuration of one power in the name of its superior, prayer and praise."[29] Key to "handling" such spiritual powers was the necessity to have power over them rather than being taken over by their power. Authority from God and protection or immunity from these lesser powers were requisites of holy men. Intimacy with God or union with the divine realm were decisive for mastering those inferior spirits and demons. What is evident from magical texts is that "the Jewish communities of the Hellenistic world had recourse to sacred creative power from the heavenly angelic realms."[30] There certainly were other ways to relate to this world on a daily basis or to express belonging to God in specific ways, but little is actually known about the domestic piety of diaspora Judaism. Their pagan neighbors noted the lighting of candles on the Sabbath, commented on by Seneca as something that should be forbidden, "since the gods do not need light, neither do men take pleasure in soot."[31] As for the Torah scrolls, they were attributed some kind of sacredness, and keeping them in specific niches in synagogue buildings attributed sacredness to them. Nevertheless, synagogue assemblies, although they met regularly on Sabbath, were not the places of daily life generally for Jews. What happened in the homes of Jewish families in the diaspora is difficult to assess, given the rarity of material findings. The fact that tefillin and mezuzoth have been found or are mentioned by Philo (*Spec.* 4.137–139) and Josephus (*Ant.* 4.213) is evidence for the existence of small items

---

28. See ibid., 15–16.
29. Ibid., 29.
30. Ibid., 35.
31. Seneca, *De superstitione* (*Ep.* 95.47), cited in Lightstone, *Commerce of the Sacred*, 66.

of piety, but how widespread these were and how exactly they were used cannot be established with any degree of certainty.³²

Nevertheless, the example of magical texts demonstrates that the spirit world with its demons and other spiritual beings was as real for Jews in the diaspora of the first century as it was for their polytheistic contemporaries throughout the Roman Empire. Such a reality had to be dealt with: one needed knowledge, practical knowledge, to relate to this world accurately on a daily basis one way or another. For Jews in the diaspora as much as for their pagan neighbors, the kin group and household provided the most important dimension of their social and symbolic world. In this realm the relationship to the spirit world was lived through daily practices and traditions that protected the members against risks and dangers and affirmed their identity and sense of belonging.³³ This is the world to which Paul refers with the term τὰ πνευμάτικα. Jewish communities in the diaspora obviously had developed ways and means to relate to the spirit world in a manner that was in accordance with their loyalty to their One God. The separation Paul requires affects the Christ-followers from the nations, and it is inconceivable that the space this separation requires could remain vacant.

1.3.4. Separated from "Mute Idols"—What Now?

Issues pertaining to the public cult had already been addressed by Paul in 1 Cor 8–11. There he emphasized that for Christ-followers abstinence from any form of cult practice associated with deities other than the God of Israel was a nonnegotiable requirement. Although this seems to be clear, it apparently raised questions among the Corinthians. It seems it was not obvious to them what did and did not constitute participation in such cults.³⁴ Paul's reminder of their former loyalty indicates the enhanced importance of this fact when pneumatic things, τὰ πνευμάτικα, are addressed. The extent of this dissociation cannot be underestimated: given the all-permeating nature of cult practices at all levels and in all and every context of life, to abstain from any such activity was an enormously

---

32. See Öhler, "Das ganze Haus," 217.
33. Ibid., 226.
34. For a detailed discussion of this aspect, see my *Paul at the Crossroads of Cultures: Theologizing in the Space-Between*, LNTS 456 (London: T&T Clark 2013), 189–213.

challenging and possibly dangerous endeavor. It would have been challenging in that daily cult practices in the domestic realm had to be given up, including the security they provided.³⁵ It would have been difficult in a context of multiple small shrines, niches, and altars dedicated to Lares and Penates or Greek domestic deities in every house. It is difficult to imagine how this requirement could have been fulfilled if an entire household had not joined the Christ-movement. Thus if you did not live in the house of Stephanas (1 Cor 1:16) but as a woman were possibly married to an unbeliever (7:13), how could you avoid being involved at all? How, as a slave (7:21), could you not have followed the cult practice of your master? It might have been possible for slaves, women, or possibly freedmen and freedwomen to avoid participating in some of the official Roman or public Greek cult practices without drawing attention to themselves, but not to participate in any cultic practice would most likely have been regarded as antisocial behavior at least, more likely as endangering the well-being of at least the household, if not of the community/city. In the worst case, it could have been seen as an act of more or less open resistance to Roman domination. It would have been considered an expression of ἀσέβεια, which could have severe repercussions. "Roman authorities moved to suppress (or 'emend') religious forms that seemed to be a focus of opposition to Roman rule—whenever and wherever they found them."³⁶

At the macro-social level, to abstain from cultic practice would have been a difficult position; at the micro-social level it would have been almost impossible. In terms of *normal* communication with the deities, it deprived Christ-followers of the familiar means of daily communication to and from deities. It also deprived them of the guidance and support on which they relied in their daily lives. Where could one get support and help when one was sick, pregnant and giving birth, traveling, and so on? Since all these aspects were vital in the people's daily lives, these had to

---

35. Mark D. Nanos (*The Irony of Galatians: Paul's Letter in First-Century Context* [Minneapolis: Fortress, 2002], 265) has emphasized the significance of this concerning the situation in Galatia, noting, "The pagan networks of support into which they were born and raised would begin to break down ... bringing shame and fear, creating the need to provide for themselves and any family members in their trust by appeal to the network of those whom they perceive to share in this new identity."

36. Beard, North, and Price, *Religions of Rome*, 1:339. Concerning Egypt, they note, "even where existing religious institutions were not abolished by the Romans, there is a clear trend towards increasing Roman supervision, if not direct control" (340).

be covered in the context of their new loyalty to Christ. Since they obviously had some expertise on how to communicate with the realm of the divine, what would be more logical than to draw on this experience? But Paul explicitly denies that their former familiarity with cult practices and forms of communication were of any use; they had to be abandoned when it came to communicating with the God of Israel.[37] With regard to τὰ πνευμάτικα, they could not draw on their previous experience, and there was nothing "lawful" in this respect that could be "transformed" in Christ. With regard to τὰ πνευμάτικα, they had to learn afresh how to relate to and communicate with the divine sphere.

2. Paul's Preamble (1 Cor 12:3)

After establishing that their loyalty and attraction to deities was to be a dimension of their previous lives that had no room in their lives in Christ, Paul adds an explanatory note that seems in some sense to be superfluous. Oscar Cullmann suggested that this could have related to persecution situations,[38] others that this is merely clarifying what can and cannot be expected from the perspective of Christ with a clear line of demarcation being drawn between the Spirit of God and any other spirits. These may be possible aspects, but they do not provide an explanation for these rather strong expressions. If the Roman presence is as significant in Corinth as has been suggested, then an allusion to Rome in this verse should not be excluded: the dichotomy between ἀνάθεμα and κύριος applied to Jesus could indicate a reversal of an imperial perception of Jesus: one convicted and crucified as an enemy of the Roman state would certainly be declared ἀνάθεμα, whereas no one loyal to Roman claims would dare to declare anyone else except the emperor to be his or her lord. Given the emphasis on the cross in 1:18–2:2, the reference to the rulers of this age who do not understand and thus crucified the Lord (2:6-8) and the role of the spirit in knowing and understanding God's wisdom (2:9-16) provide links to 12:3, which, in light of these previous passages, then sounds like a summary reminder of the longer explanations earlier in the letter. Paul already stated that wisdom, knowledge, and understanding in relation to the God

---

37. Roy E. Ciampa and Brian S. Rosner, *The First Letter to the Corinthians* (Grand Rapids: Eerdmans, 2010), 564.
38. Oscar Cullman, *The Earliest Christian Confessions* (London: Lutterworth, 1949), 22–23.

of Israel are available only through the Spirit. An understanding of Jesus crucified is impossible through the channels of divine communication with which the Corinthians had been familiar in their lives thus far. One could not perceive Jesus as a criminal convicted and thus declared ἀνάθεμα by Rome and at the same time be loyal to him as Lord. These two perceptions were mutually exclusive.

A different interpretation of ἀνάθεμα in this verse has been proposed by Kenneth L. Waters. He draws attention to the fact that ἀνάθεμα in Greek and Jewish literature of the period does not mean "curse" but rather refers to an offering to a deity: a dedicatory gift. Rather than referring to a practice of cursing Jesus, Paul is here correcting a Corinthian misunderstanding of Jesus's life and death as a dedicatory offering in a sense with which the Corinthians had been familiar from their pagan past.[39] I cannot discuss this proposal in any detail here, but it deserves further consideration as a viable interpretive option. Whatever the precise meaning, 1 Cor 12:3 could be Paul's summary reminder of the fundamental difference between the Corinthians' former life, as those drawn to τὰ εἴδωλα τὰ ἄφωνα, and their present life in Christ, before providing reassurance in light of the challenge that the abandonment of anything related to idolatry means for the Corinthians.

3. Paul's Reassurance concerning the "Spiritual Things" (1 Cor 12:4–11)

At the outset Paul reassures his addressees that, within the sphere of the Lord, communication with God is possible. The diversity of gifts needed to communicate with, and relate to, the spirit world and to God were freely given to them, but the source of these χαρίσματα, διακονίαι, and ἐνεργήματα for them were no longer the plurality of deities and diverse spirits but the one Spirit, Lord and God. The parallel construction of 1 Cor 12:4–5 is noteworthy here, and it is possible that Paul refers here in some kind of "technical" vocabulary to relevant "skills" and ways and means to communicate with the divine world. Thus Paul here confirms the diversity of gifts (χαρίσματα) they receive, the diversity of mediating practices (διακονίαι), and the diversity of real effects (ἐνεργήματα) in their lives, but he affirms

---

39. Kenneth L. Waters, "No Cursing in the Church: *Anathema* in the Corinthian Congregation (1 Corinthians 12:3) and the Letters of Paul," paper presented at the Society of Biblical Literature International Meeting, Rome, 2009.

in no uncertain terms that all of these were actually granted, exercised, and effected by one and the same Spirit, Lord, and God. It is the oneness of God in which this diversity is rooted and held together. The diversity of their life experiences and needs is not abrogated or downplayed but acknowledged. However, this diversity does not require a diversity of deities, spirits, and demons.

3.1. Mediating Powers and the One Spirit: Transforming Cultural Practice

In their previous lives the addressees were not only used to a diversity of deities who were the guarantors of good life if addressed and looked after properly, but in conjunction with these there were numerous mediators who were able to communicate on their behalf with the deities, spirits, and demons, if they could not or were not supposed to do so themselves. In addition to those involved in the performance of sacrifices were those designated to communicate with the deities: augurs, sacerdotes, diverse priests of diverse cults, and the *pontifex maximus*, that is, the emperor. Of no less importance were all those specialists needed for issues of a more ordinary kind, relevant in daily life, the *sortileges, vates, harioloi, coniectores, interpretes somniorum, psychomanteis, magi, astrologi, chaldaei* (Cicero, *Nat. d.* 1.55–56; *Div.* 1.128). For transitions during the life cycle, specialists of specifically designated members of the kin group took care of the relevant communication with the spirit world.[40]

Thus in as much as the world was inhabited by deities, spirits, demons, and the like, there were equally high numbers of specialists who had knowledge (γνῶσις), wisdom (σοφία), and effective power (ἐνεργήματα δυνάμεων), to mediate appropriately between this world and the world of humans. The absence of all of these practices, along with distancing oneself from any such mediators, would have possibly been challenging if not frightening for anyone whose well-being relied on the right means to relate to and communicate with the spirit world. Here Paul steps in and assures the Corinthians that all essential aspects of communicating with the divine are provided for through manifestations of the Spirit in members of the community.

---

40. Mauruzio Bettini, *Anthropology and Roman Culture: Kinship, Time, Images of the Soul*, trans. John van Sickle (Baltimore: John Hopkins University Press, 1991).

Thiselton has noted that Paul seems to change the term probably used by the Corinthians, πνευμάτικα, to χαρίσματα. This may indicate an emphasis on Paul's part that the means to relate to the spirit world were not special qualities that were self-acquired or "earned" in reciprocity to a service for a deity.[41] In their diversity the χαρίσματα were all granted in Christ as gifts from the one God. They were not qualities that elevated the status of any individual bearer in the community. Their only purpose was to contribute to the well-being of the community as a whole. Within the diversity of these gifts, the one source of all of them is emphasized, thus countering any attempts to enhance individual status at the expense of the unity of the community.[42]

The list Paul presents here seems to be rooted in the Jewish tradition of the messianic age, but at the same time it reflects aspects of divine communication from a Greek and Roman perspective. The point here is not whether this list is Greek/Roman or Jewish in essence but that it most likely resonated with both worlds. Paul and Jewish Christ-followers drew on the Jewish scriptural tradition, in which wisdom and knowledge, the strength of trust and loyalty (Isa 11:1–5), the power of healing (Isa 61:1; 2 Kgs 2:15–16), and the power to effect peaceful life, prophecy, and visions (Joel 2:28) are signs of the world to come. The fulfillment of these prophecies and visions is seen as having been inaugurated through the Christ-event. Thus for Paul as for other Jewish Christ-followers, the Scriptures and Jewish tradition of their times provided the context for understanding the pouring out of the Spirit. The effects of the Spirit were decisive, not its nature or essence. Not what it consisted of or how it worked but that it worked was decisive. For Paul and his fellow Jews, it was obvious that all of these events and effects had nothing to do with the "rulers of this age" nor the power of any deities or demons but exclusively with the power of God. To impart this to an audience that probably was only partially familiar with the Jewish social and symbolic universe (if these gentiles were former sympathizers of Judaism or godfearers) would have been an uphill struggle. This is especially so when it is taken into account that the God of Israel relates to "human desire, aspirations, and emotions in a way quite

---

41. Anthony C. Thiselton, *The First Epistle to the Corinthians: A Commentary on the Greek Text*, NIGTC (Grand Rapids: Eerdmans, 2000), 929–30.

42. Dale B. Martin, *Slavery as Salvation: The Metaphor of Slavery in Pauline Christianity* (New Haven: Yale University Press, 1990), 87.

different from Greek and Roman deities," as Stowers notes.[43] For these Christ-followers from the nations, who had not previously been embedded in the Jewish scriptural tradition and the Jewish social world, it would have been normal to draw on their previous experience and knowledge, that is, Greek and Roman understandings of τὰ πνευμάτικα.

The transformation of the *habitus* of people is a challenging endeavor, and Paul does not generally require that these Christ-followers from the nations give up everything of their former lives. "All things are lawful," he agrees with the Corinthians, but he advises the Thessalonians to "test everything; hold fast to what is good" (1 Thess 5:21). But that which probably was most relevant to them—their embeddedness in the world of their domestic and public cults and the practices with which they were familiar for relating to the spirit world—had to be given up. That difficulties would arise here in terms of their understanding and with regard to their relations with the city and the empire could almost be anticipated.[44]

The aspects Paul mentions in 1 Cor 12:8–10 could provide an indication to realms or practices that were central in daily relations to the spirit world. I assume that they resonated with both, the Greek and Roman, as well as with the Jewish social and symbolic universe.

3.2. Essential Manifestations of the One Spirit

For Christ-followers, wisdom and knowledge are no longer in the hand of *auguri*, who would only know how to read the flight of the birds or be able to understand the ruling power of Rome as ordained by the will of deities, thereby promoting appropriate behavior and thus peace and prosperity. Talk of wisdom (λόγος σοφίας) and of knowledge (λόγος γνώσεως) are now nothing but expressions of the Spirit of God. It is a kind of wisdom and knowledge associated with weakness and the cross, as Paul already referred to in 1 Cor 1:18–2:5 and which he exemplifies further in chapter 13. It has nothing to do with the dominating power for which Jesus is ἀνάθεμα but with everything relating to wisdom and knowledge, which is inseparably intertwined with trust, hope, and love. This wisdom and knowledge is embedded in Jewish tradition, as noted above, and has nothing to do with the accurate performance of cult practice and the correct

---

43. Stowers, "Kinds of Myth," 119, n. 35.
44. The difficulties addressed in Galatians seem to be caused by this very same problem, as Nanos has convincingly demonstrated (*Irony of Galatians*, 265–71).

interpretation of entrails. The real purpose of wisdom and knowledge is to contribute to the empowerment of all members of the ἐκκλησία.

The next manifestation of the Spirit, πίστις (12:9a), has caused problems for interpreters in that it is strange that a core aspect of being in Christ for all Christ-followers should be a special gift to some in the ἐκκλησία.[45] It may refer to a special aspect of trust and loyalty within the community, or by the "mature" in Christ, or to a technical form of loyalty the allusion of which is lost to us.

There can hardly be any doubt that the gift of healing (12:9b) was of vital importance for everyone in the first century. Paul confirms this, but the source of the gift is neither Asclepius nor any other deity or spirit but the one Spirit. Jewish tradition links the healing of the sick and wounded as a core dimension associated with the messianic age. The prophecies of Isaiah most prominently refer to this aspect in relation to messianic hopes.

In 1 Cor 12:10 a whole cluster of manifestations of the One Spirit is listed, and it is unclear whether Paul considers these to be inherently related to each other. The working of miracles and discernment of spirits, in my view, are evidence that it is not the spirit world as such that is being rejected here but rather the existence of this world and the taking of these spiritual beings and powers as self-evident. Now the ability to discern the character or nature of these beings is provided as a manifestation of the One Spirit rather than through one of the numerous deities or spirits with which the Corinthians had been accustomed. Prophecy is a means of communication known in both the Greek and Roman as well as in the Jewish world. Prophets were entrusted in the present with a message from a deity, a spokesperson on behalf of a god, and they could be related to a particular place, the place of an oracle or a temple. Prophetic utterances seem to have been responsive to specific issues, circumstances, or needs; they seem to have been taken for granted in both worlds. Later on in 1 Cor 14 Paul provides his understanding of prophecy as speech, which was intelligible without the need for further clarification. This distinguishes his understanding of prophecy to some extent from the Greek and Roman understanding: the Sibylline books as well as the oracle in Delphi required interpretation for being understandable; the message had to be translated into intelligible language by specialists. This kind of prophecy may have resembled what Paul mentions under γλώσσῃ, which is speech that requires interpretation,

---

45. For a discussion, see Ciampa and Rosner, *First Corinthians*, 577–78.

whereas Paul assumes that prophecy in the Spirit of God would be intelligible in itself.

The only aspect that Paul mentions here that does not lead to immediate understanding is the γένη γλωσσῶν (12:10). The γλῶσσαι require interpretation, and again in 1 Cor 14 Paul explains why this is so. The issue here is not the nature of these γλῶσσαι but their effects. I find Martin's arguments with regard to this aspect of the passage convincing.[46] Given the recurrence of the term γλῶσσαι at the beginning of chapter 13 with the additional distinction between γλῶσσαι of humans and γλῶσσαι of angels, it could well be that Paul has such a language in mind here that might have been perceived by some as a particularly well-suited means of communication with the divine realm. Martin demonstrates that in the Greek and Roman world deities were perceived as having a special language, a language that some humans have heard or seem to know. Since this was the language of higher beings, humans with experience with this higher language were attributed higher status. The daughters of Job who, instead of inheriting property like their brothers, were provided with angelic language certainly do not suffer from a diminishing of their status through this gift (T. Job 49.1–50.3). Martin argues that the length of Paul's discussion of issues related to γλῶσσαι indicates that the Corinthians must have misunderstood the significance of this particular means of communication with God. Mentioning it at the end of this section of the letter, together with its downplaying later in 1 Cor 13 and 14, and the emphasis in the body metaphor of the significance of the less-honorable parts all point in the direction of status reversal. The gift of γλῶσσαι cannot be associated in any way with an enhanced status in the community. If speaking "out of one's senses" was a sign of divine speech, as understood in Greek tradition, this would possibly be perceived as the closest possible communication with the divine realm. Paul plays down the significance of this not by denying its existence or importance but by stressing that its importance does not consist in an individual's close link to the deity but in its relevance for the well-being of the community.

---

46. Dale B. Martin, *The Corinthian Body* (New Haven: Yale University Press, 1995), 87–103.

4. Conclusions: Cultural Translation as Transformation of Cultural Practice

Paul assured the Corinthians that the challenge that their turning away from idols implied—the loss of the means of communication with the spiritual realm—was compensated for by the gifts imparted to them through the Spirit. He reminded them that they could not rely in any way on their previous experience for the communication with, and relation to, this realm, as there was an insurmountable difference between mute idols and the God of Israel, and they were to have nothing to do with the former. What sounds clear and nonnegotiable in theory must have been very difficult in practice in a context in which every aspect of life in the πόλις and οἶκος, in the *colonia* and *domus*, was permeated by cultic practice. Thus issues pertaining to the realm of *public* cult practice were addressed by Paul in 1 Cor 8–11, followed by the issues of cult practice and communication with the spirit world in the context of daily life in 12:1–11.

Paul tried at length to cover all aspects of life that seemed important when it came to communicating with the divine sphere. He acknowledged the diversity of these aspects and the experiences to which they were related. But the source of the diversity of gifts and practices required to relate to, and deal with this sphere, was the Spirit of God, not numerous spirits and deities. It was not important to conduct the numerous rituals in a correct way, because such knowledge was not necessary; one did not need to know the right deity or the right name to ensure a particular area of life was actually covered. This did not imply that one was at risk of attracting the anger of a god or had to go without protection or help. The source for life was the one God of Israel, Paul assured them: all gifts for life come from this very same source through the very same Spirit. Paul's perception of relating to God and the spirit world were Jewish, and although certain aspects of this spirit world were shared with their neighbors from the nations, there was only one God in this spiritual hierarchy. To communicate this intelligibly to people from the nations was no incidental aspect of the transmission of the gospel. It involved a process of cultural translation that required of the Christ-followers from the nations a transformation of essential cultural practices. The issue was not the belief system, whether the beings that populated the spirit world existed or not. The issue was how to relate to this world, now as a member of τὴν ἐκκλησίαν τοῦ θεοῦ τὴν οὖσαν ἐν Κορίνθῳ. In sum, it was an issue of practice. The implications at every level of life for Christ-followers from the nations were enormous and potentially dangerous in that refusing to participate in cultic practices could have been seen as posing a risk to the πόλις and the οἶκος, depriving them of prosperity and harmony, or attracting the anger of deities or neighbors. Paul does not consider the wider implications of this separation from cult practice for the ἐκκλησία in relation to πόλις/*colonia* and οἶκος/*domus*, nor does he provide any assurance to the Corinthians in this respect. The dimension of the πόλις/*colonia* does not seem to be in view in Paul's guidance here, although what is required had wide-ranging consequences for Christ-followers from the nations. Paul's concern was with the building up and well-being of the ἐκκλησία. This was the key focus of his assurance. The manifestations of the Spirit themselves provided the community with those aspects that were vital for sustaining life (from the perspective of former adherents of Roman and Greek deities), but at the same time their significance was considered only in relation to the good of the community. They were not supposed to lead to any status enhancement and were nothing to boast about. This not only applied to the gift of γλῶσσαι, as Martin has demonstrated, but to the other gifts as well. It is in tune with the theme of the letter with its emphasis on status change. The gifts provided the Corinthians assurance and challenged them to grow in their learning of Christ, in their building up a community that was "not of this world," socializing into an ethos that was rooted in their relationship to the God of Israel through Christ, an ethos that was strongly associated with the Jewish social and symbolic universe but resonated with aspects of the identity of people from the nations as well. The passage 1 Cor 12:1–11 provides a glimpse into the challenges of a cultural translation process through which Paul attempted to transmit an ethos and practices embedded in the Jewish world to the world of the nations.[47] It demonstrates the challenge former pagan members of the ἐκκλησία faced within the context of a πόλις/*colonia* that was structured around an entirely different ethos. The notion of well-being might have provided a trajectory that enabled Christ-followers to expand the well-being of the ἐκκλησία to the πόλις/*colonia*, as hinted at in Rom 12:18. But the separation from all aspects of cult practice that were considered vital for the well-being of the οἶκος and πόλις community certainly made it difficult for Christ-followers not to be seen as undermining civic society itself. The cultural translation of the

---

47. For more details on the process of cultural translation in Paul's letters see my *Paul at the Crossroads of Cultures*, esp. 175–213.

message of the gospel into the daily practices of the social and symbolic universe of the nations was a challenging task not least for the Christ-followers from the nations themselves.

Works Cited

Aelius Aristides. *Aristides in Four Volumes.* Edited and Translated by C. A. Behr. LCL. Cambridge: Harvard University Press, 1973.
Beard, Mary, John North, and S. R. F. Price. *The Religions of Rome: A History.* Vol. 1. Cambridge: Cambridge University Press, 1998.
Bettini, Mauruzio. *Anthropology and Roman Culture: Kinship, Time, Images of the Soul.* Translated by John van Sickle. Baltimore: John Hopkins University Press, 1991.
Bodel, John. "Cicero's Minerva, *Penates,* and the Mother of the *Lares*: An Outline of Roman Domestic Religion." Pages 248–75 in *Household and Family Religion in Antiquity.* Edited by John Bodel and Saul M. Olyan. Oxford: Blackwell, 2008.
Boedeker, Deborah. "Family Matters: Domestic Religion in Classical Greece." Pages 229–47 in *Household and Family Religion in Antiquity: Contextual and Comparative Perspectives.* Edited by John Bodel and Saul M. Olyan. Oxford: Blackwell, 2008.
Bookidis, Nancy. "Religion in Corinth 146 BCE–100 CE." Pages 141–64 in *Urban Religion in Roman Corinth: Interdisciplinary Approaches.* Edited by Daniel N. Schowalter and Steven J. Friesen. Cambridge: Harvard University Press, 2005.
Ciampa, Roy E., and Brian S. Rosner. *The First Letter to the Corinthians.* Grand Rapids: Eerdmans, 2010.
Cicero. *De natura deorum; Academica.* Edited and translated by H. Rackham. LCL. London: Heinemann; New York: Putnam's Sons, 1933.
Cullman, Oscar. *The Earliest Christian Confessions.* London: Lutterworth, 1949.
Ehrensperger, Kathy. *Paul at the Crossroads of Cultures: Theologizing in the Space-Between.* LNTS 456. London: T&T Clark, 2013.
———. "Paul, His People and Racial Terminology," *JECS* 3 (2013): 17–33.
Faraone, Christopher A. "Household Religion in Ancient Greece." Pages 210–28 in *Household and Family Religion in Antiquity: Contextual and Comparative Perspectives.* Edited by John Bodel and Saul M. Olyan. Oxford: Blackwell, 2008.

Foss, Peter. "Watchful Lares: Roman Household Organization and the Rituals of Cooking and Dining." Pages 196–216 in *Domestic Space in the Roman World*. Edited by Ray Laurence and Andrew Wallace-Hadrill. Journal of Roman Archaeology Supplement Series 22. Portsmouth, RI: JRA, 1997.

Janowitz, Naomi. *Magic in the Roman World: Pagans, Jews, and Christians*. London: Routledge, 2001.

Lightstone, Jack. *The Commerce of the Sacred: Mediation of the Divine among Jews in the Greco-Roman World*. New York. Columbia University Press, 2006.

Martin, Dale B. *The Corinthian Body*. New Haven: Yale University Press, 1995.

———. *Slavery as Salvation: The Metaphor of Slavery in Pauline Christianity*. New Haven: Yale University Press, 1990.

Nanos, Mark D. *The Irony of Galatians: Paul's Letter in First-Century Context*. Minneapolis: Fortress, 2002.

Økland, Jorunn. "Ceres, Kore, and Cultural Complexity: Divine Personality Definitions and Human Worshippers in Roman Corinth." Pages 199–229 in *Corinth in Context: Comparative Studies on Religion and Society*. Edited by Steven Friesen, Daniel N. Schowalter, and James C. Walters. Leiden: Brill, 2010.

Öhler, Markus. "Das ganze Haus: Antike Alltagsreligiosität und die Apostelgeschichte." *ZNW* 102 (2011): 201–34.

Plutarch. *Moralia*. Vol. 5. Translated by Frank Cole Babbitt. LCL. Cambridge: Harvard University Press, 1936.

Rüpke, Jörg. *The Religion of the Romans*. Cambridge: Polity Press 2007.

Stowers, Stanley K. "Greeks Who Sacrifice and Those Who Do Not: Toward an Anthropology of Greek Religion." Pages 293–333 in *The Social World of the First Christians: Essays in Honor of Wayne A. Meeks*. Edited by L. Michael White and O. Larry Yarborough. Minneapolis: Fortress, 1995.

Thiselton, Anthony C. *The First Epistle to the Corinthians: A Commentary on the Greek Text*. NIGTC. Grand Rapids: Eerdmans, 2000.

Wallace-Hadrill, Andrew, and Stanley K. Stowers. "Kinds of Myth, Meals, and Power." Pages 105–49 in *Redescribing Paul and the Corinthians*. Edited by Ron Cameron and Merrill P. Miller. ECL 5. Atlanta: Society of Biblical Literature, 2011.

Walters, James C. "Civic Identity in Roman Corinth and Its Impact on

Early Christianity." Pages 397–417 in *Urban Religion in Roman Corinth: Interdisciplinary Approaches*. Edited by Daniel N. Schowalter and Steven J. Friesen. Cambridge: Harvard University Press, 2005.

Waters, Kenneth L. "No Cursing in the Church: *Anathema* in the Corinthian Congregation (1 Corinthians 12:3) and the Letters of Paul." Paper presented at the Society of Biblical Literature International Meeting, Rome, 2009.

Williams, Guy J. *The Spirit World in the Letters of Paul the Apostle: A Critical Examination of the Role of Spiritual Beings in the Authentic Pauline Epistles*. FRLANT 231. Göttingen: Vandenhoeck & Ruprecht, 2009.

Woolf, Greg. *Becoming Roman: The Origins of Provincial Civilization in Gaul*. Cambridge: Cambridge University Press, 1998.

Brother against Brother: *Controversiae* about Inheritance Disputes and 1 Corinthians 6:1–11*

Michael Peppard

> Don't you know that wrongdoers will not inherit God's kingdom? (1 Cor 6:9)[1]

The metaphor of inheritance is relatively rare in Paul's epistles. Its appearances during crucial arguments in Galatians and Romans have garnered well-deserved scholarly attention, though, because Paul's expositions of who may rightfully claim the inheritance of the Abrahamic promise are among his most important contributions to nascent Christianity.[2] By contrast, the inheritance metaphor in 1 Cor 6:9 has not been the subject of much interest, despite the intense focus of scholarship on that verse. Scholars have been more interested—and justifiably so—in the subsequent "vice list" and its implications for contemporary views on human sexuality. Still, the opening question of that verse—"Don't you know that wrongdoers will not inherit God's kingdom?"—is worth close consideration for two reasons: first, because of the relative rarity of inheritance and kingdom of God metaphors in the Pauline corpus; second, because the connection

---

* A shorter version of this research was presented at the 2012 Annual Meeting of the Society of Biblical Literature. I am grateful for feedback from Allan Georgia, Larry Welborn, Dale Martin, Alan Mitchell, James Harrison, and the anonymous readers for *JBL*.

1. Unless otherwise indicated, all biblical translations are mine.

2. Among many excellent treatments of these issues, two are Caroline E. Johnson Hodge, *If Sons, Then Heirs: A Study of Kinship and Ethnicity in the Letters of Paul* (Oxford: Oxford University Press, 2007); and James C. Walters, "Paul, Adoption, and Inheritance," in *Paul in the Greco-Roman World*, ed. J. Paul Sampley (Harrisburg, PA: Trinity Press International, 2003), 42–76.

between this verse and the preceding section about lawsuits (6:1-8) still remains to be clarified.

This essay offers a presentation of fraternal lawsuits and inheritance disputes in Greco-Roman society—based primarily on the corpus of extant *controversiae* (legal case-studies)—as a way of explaining Paul's rhetorical move from verses 1-8 to verses 9-11 in its social context. The ubiquity of actual fraternal lawsuits in the πόλις gave Paul an opportunity to comment on the social reality in Corinth by means of a favorite ecclesial metaphor: the ἐκκλησία as a new family under God. That is to say, the crucial unstated premise that connects verses 1-8 with 9-11 is the fact that fraternal lawsuits were often inheritance disputes. I conclude that this understanding of what normally happened when legally defined brothers went to court against one another thus allows Paul to draw from social reality in order to reorient the focus of the discussion: Paul wants to emphasize the new family of "brothers" and their "inheritance" in the Spirit.

Scholarship on 1 Cor 6:1-11 has not often emphasized the passage's familial language, presumably because of the prevalence of such language in the Pauline corpus and early Christianity generally.[3] Forms of the sibling word group (ἀδελφ-) are used so often in the New Testament that they usually go unnoticed.[4] In addition, familial language has sometimes been translated out of existence by a widely used inclusive-language version (NRSV): in the passage under consideration here (6:5-8), ἀδελφός is rendered "believer." Such a translation accentuates the contrast with ἀπίστων ("unbelievers," 6:6), and elsewhere in the NRSV it can serve as an inclusive-language marker of membership in an early Christian community. One might endorse the inclusive-language goal of the NRSV overall and nonetheless criticize the particular choices made.[5] In another proximate

---

3. Notable exceptions include Wolfgang Schrage, *Der erste Brief an die Korinther, Teil. 1*, EKKNT 7.1 (Zürich: Benziger; Neukirchen-Vluyn: Neukirchener Verlag, 1991), 402-19; Raymond F. Collins, *First Corinthians*, SP (Collegeville, MN: Liturgical Press, 1999), 228-29; section 6 of Bruce W. Winter, "Civil Law and Christian Litigiousness (1 Corinthians 6:1-8)," ch. 4 in *After Paul Left Corinth: The Influence of Secular Ethics and Social Change* (Grand Rapids: Eerdmans, 2001), 70-71; and Brian S. Rosner, *Paul, Scripture and Ethics: A Study of 1 Corinthians 5-7*, AJGU 22 (Leiden: Brill, 1994), 108.

4. In what follows, I use "brother(s)" and "son(s)" to emphasize the familial inheritance imagery in its original social and rhetorical context, but I do not mean to imply that women were not authoritative members of Pauline communities.

5. A similar lament is issued by Richard B. Hays, *First Corinthians*, IBC (Louisville: John Knox, 1997), 95.

example, the translation of 1 Cor 8:11-12 renders ἀδελφός as "believers" (8:11) but ἀδελφούς as "members of your family" (8:12). The original resonance of Paul's paraenesis in 1 Cor 8—heard through a sustained familial metaphor—is thus lost for readers of the NRSV, and I argue that such is also the case with 1 Cor 6:1-11. To meet the goal of inclusive-language translation, "brother(s) and sister(s)" is far preferable to "believer(s)," so that readers without access to Greek may nonetheless have access to the ubiquitous and crucial familial metaphors in the New Testament.

New Testament scholars do have access to Greek, of course, and our lack of interest in the familial language in the passage is likely due to other questions that have occupied the field. What was the social problem that led to litigation at Corinth?[6] What, if anything, was the connection between this problem and the previous one in 1 Cor 5?[7] In Paul's argument, from what scriptural resources might he have been drawing?[8] Finally, what exactly—and I do mean *exactly*—was meant by the terms μαλακοί and ἀρσενοκοῖται?[9] Setting those questions aside, let us turn our focus to the characterization of plaintiff and defendant in our courtroom drama: they go to court "brother with brother" (ἀδελφὸς μετὰ ἀδελφοῦ,

---

6. Alan C. Mitchell, "Rich and Poor in the Courts of Corinth: Litigiousness and Status in 1 Corinthians 6.1-11," *NTS* 39 (1993): 562-86; based on Alan C. Mitchell, "1 Corinthians 6:1-11: Group Boundaries and the Courts of Corinth" (PhD diss., Yale University, 1986); Winter, "Civil Law and Christian Litigiousness," 58-75; Andrew D. Clarke, *Secular and Christian Leadership in Corinth: A Socio-historical and Exegetical Study of 1 Corinthians 1-6*, AGJU 18 (Leiden: Brill, 1993), 59-71; David G. Horrell, *The Social Ethos of the Corinthian Correspondence: Interests and Ideology from 1 Corinthians to 1 Clement*, SNTW (Edinburgh: T & T Clark, 1996), 137-42.

7. Peter Richardson, "Judgment in Sexual Matters in 1 Corinthians 6:1-11," *NovT* 25 (1983): 37-58; J. Duncan M. Derrett, "Judgment and 1 Corinthians 6," *NTS* 37 (1991): 22-36. In the words of Richard A. Horsley, "The context of this paragraph, sandwiched between two discussions of '(sexual) immorality,' suggests that the case had to do with marital relations, perhaps in some economic way such as inheritance" (*1 Corinthians*, ANTC [Nashville: Abingdon, 1998], 86).

8. Rosner, "Moses and Paul Appointing Judges," ch. 4 in his *Paul, Scripture and Ethics*.

9. Robin Scroggs, *The New Testament and Homosexuality: Contextual Background for Contemporary Debate* (Philadelphia: Fortress, 1983); John H. Elliott, "No Kingdom of God for Softies? Or, What Was Paul Really Saying? 1 Corinthians 6:9-10 in Context," *BTB* 34 (2004): 17-40; Dale B. Martin, "*Arsenokoitēs* and *Malakos*: Meanings and Consequences," ch. 3 in his *Sex and the Single Savior: Gender and Sexuality in Biblical Interpretation* (Louisville: Westminster John Knox, 2006), 37-50.

6:6). Paul speaks figuratively of "brothers," using a preferred first-century term for those "in Christ."[10] But Paul's familial metaphors are usually rooted in concrete social practices, and those social practices can illuminate the meaning of the metaphors (as in Gal 3:15–5:1). Then we might ask: What happened when—*not* speaking figuratively—a brother went to court against a brother in Greco-Roman society?

1. Brother against Brother in the *Controversiae*

Ancient evidence for fraternal lawsuits comes frequently from declamations, some of which are preserved completely (many in Latin, fewer in Greek).[11] Specifically, many examples come from the *controversiae*, or legal case-studies, which preserve some full speeches, along with outlines of arguments, talking points, and epigrams. They were collected primarily to train men in forensic rhetoric. Declamations were also performed in public as ways for the best orators to express their skills and attract students (and their tuition-paying parents).[12] Many who were not teachers or students of rhetoric "continued to declaim in adulthood," and thus "declamation, as well as being an educational tool, was also a hobby, a public entertainment, a competitive sport, and a literary genre."[13]

Certain aspects of the *controversiae* might raise doubts about our ability to use them as resources for social history.[14] They are frequently

---

10. Alan C. Mitchell has also analyzed this passage in terms of philosophy and rhetoric about friendship ("Friends Do Not Wrong Friends: Friendship and Justice in 1 Corinthians 6.8," in *The Impartial God: Essays in Biblical Studies in Honor of Jouette M. Bassler*, ed. Calvin J. Roetzel and Robert L. Foster [Sheffield: Sheffield Phoenix, 2007], 134–44).

11. For summary of the Latin evidence, see Stanley F. Bonner, *Roman Declamation in the Late Republic and Early Empire* (Berkeley: University of California Press, 1949). On the Greek evidence, see D. A. Russell, *Greek Declamation* (Cambridge: Cambridge University Press, 1983).

12. See Bruce W. Winter, *Philo and Paul among the Sophists: Alexandrian and Corinthian Responses to a Julio-Claudian Movement*, 2nd ed. (Grand Rapids: Eerdmans, 2002), 19–39; and Bonner, *Roman Declamation*, 42–43.

13. D. H. Berry and Malcolm Heath, "Oratory and Declamation," in *Handbook of Classical Rhetoric in the Hellenistic Period 330 B.C.–A.D. 400*, ed. Stanley E. Porter (Leiden: Brill, 2001), 408.

14. It is also possible to use papyrological evidence to do social history of fraternal relationships regarding inheritance. For example, *SB* 18.13301 (second–third century; = P.Cair. 10575) concerns the dividing of an estate between two brothers,

dramatic and sometimes hyperbolic in their characterizations of plaintiffs and defendants. They often embark on fantastic tales involving poison, prostitution, or pirates. (They were meant to keep listeners—mostly young men—interested in their learning.) Roman historian Erik Gunderson "remind[s] the reader of the arduousness of deriving any positive statements about Roman reality from these willful fictions and from speeches where the advocate is likely soon to reverse himself and to claim the contrary."[15] Historians approach declamations with requisite caution, therefore, just as one might approach novels, comedies, or hagiographies from antiquity.

Nevertheless, *social history* can still be gleaned from all these genres. When one focuses on general trends in the genre, the *controversiae* are especially useful in reconstructing the most frequent motifs to be found in the courtroom, the kinds of relationships expected between potential litigants, the common tensions between members of a household, and how stock characters were imagined and deployed in arguments. Gunderson thus qualifies his reticence: "If any given statement is not necessarily earnest, one nevertheless does notice tendencies when related topics, themes, or treatments are collected."[16] Finally, the declamations are full of epigrams or "commonplaces," pithy one-liners that can be applied to

---

since the elder brother was away when the father died and the younger brother was left in charge of the inheritance (see Jean Bingen, "Documents de l'Egypte romaine," *BASP* 22 [1985]: 15–23). In the case of the present essay, I have not incorporated papyrological evidence for two reasons. First, the legal conventions of Greco-Roman Egypt often followed localized common-law traditions that were not necessarily applicable to other parts of the Roman Empire. With regard to inheritance practices and fraternal relationships specifically, Egyptians differed from most of the Greco-Roman world and may have even used these differences as a marker of distinctive ethnic identity in the Roman era (see Jane Rowlandson and Ryosuke Takahashi, "Brother-Sister Marriage and Inheritance Strategies in Greco-Roman Egypt," *JRS* 99 [2009]: 104–39, especially 120–26). Second, while the papyrological evidence preserves a record of Egyptian cases and/or their resolutions, it rarely offers a glimpse of the rhetoric involved in such cases. The present study examines rhetorical conventions and argumentation related to brothers and inheritance.

15. Erik Gunderson, *Declamation, Paternity, and Roman Identity* (Cambridge: Cambridge University Press, 2003), 17. See also Mary Beard, "Looking (Harder) for Roman Myth: Dumézil, Declamation and the Problems of Definition," in *Mythos in mythenloser Gesellschaft: Das Paradigma Roms*, ed. Fritz Graf (Stuttgart: Teubner, 1993), 44–64.

16. Gunderson, *Declamation, Paternity, and Roman Identity*, 17.

multiple situations of forensic (the *controversiae*) or deliberative (the *suasoriae*) rhetoric. These epigrams were designed to appeal to what social theorist Pierre Bourdieu might call the "epistemological unconscious" shared by the declaimers and their audiences.[17] The declamations play on (and prey on) various cultural ideologies and can reveal to us a glimpse of what might be called, more simply, a culture's common sense.

Scholarly interest in Roman declamation can be credited to Stanley F. Bonner, whose *Roman Declamation in the Late Republic and Early Empire* presented the declamations of the Elder Seneca as an underutilized resource in the study of Roman law and society.[18] These featured "no mere gatherings of schoolboys," he writes, but "men of standing who found therein a means of sharpening their wits, elaborating and exhibiting their legal knowledge, and spending their leisure hours in a friendly, amusing, and by no means futile intellectual exercise."[19] More recently, Mary Beard and especially Erik Gunderson have shown how "declamation involves thinking through what it means to be Roman ... beyond mere social practice and into the space where society and psyche intersect. Thus this playing at being a Roman also becomes believing in the contents of one's own dramas."[20] Gunderson summarizes the most prominent theme of declamations as "social inequality and how to negotiate it," and he isolates the cases involving fathers and sons as most ripe for analysis. However, one might also highlight the *controversiae* about brothers or inheritance, and to some of these examples we now turn.

To get a sense of the prominence of fraternal lawsuits and inheritance disputes in the *controversiae*, one can begin on the very first page of the Elder Seneca's declamations.[21] The declaimers are to argue about the case study, "A Man Who Disinherited His Nephew" (or literally, "A Disinheriting Uncle," *patruus abdicans*):

---

17. Pierre Bourdieu and Loïs J. D. Wacquant, *An Invitation to Reflexive Sociology* (Chicago: University of Chicago Press, 1992), 41.

18. The summary in this paragraph bears some resemblance to my treatment of the same material in Michael Peppard, *The Son of God in the Roman World: Divine Sonship in Its Social and Political Context* (New York: Oxford University Press, 2011), 55–56.

19. Bonner, *Roman Declamation*, 40.

20. Gunderson, *Declamation, Paternity, and Roman Identity*, 233.

21. Michael Winterbottom, *The Elder Seneca*, 2 vols., LCL (Cambridge: Harvard University Press, 1974).

Two brothers were in a disagreement. One had a son. The uncle fell into need. Against his father's wishes, the youth supported the uncle. As a result the youth was disinherited, without protest. He was adopted by his uncle. The uncle then received a bequest and became rich. Then the [biological] father fell into need, and the youth supported him against his uncle's [adoptive father's] wishes. Now the youth is being disinherited [by his uncle/adoptive father].[22]

What happens when *duo fratres inter se dissidebant*, when brother litigates against brother? Frequently the brothers argue about the proper destination and division of inheritance, a subject that often brings strife, enmity, and division within a family. In this case, they are not arguing about their own inheritances from their father but rather about the personal enmity between themselves, which has caused the young man of the family to have been disinherited twice—first by his biological father, then by his uncle/adoptive father.

In well-preserved cases, the *controversiae* capture the following components: a citation of the law (if any) on which the case is based; the "theme" (*thema*) to be debated (e.g., the paragraph quoted above); reports of epigrams (*sententiae*) and talking points from famous declaimers; the "division" (*divisio*), which lays out possible frameworks for arguing different sides of the theme; and, finally, "colors" (*colores*), that is, examples of rhetorical flourish, "often pithily expressed, which threw a different light on the actions of the defendant or accuser…; by a slight shift of argument, by an added insinuation, or a guileless plea, they tone down the guilt or represent it in even more glaring colors."[23] The *controversia* under consideration here preserves all these features and is, in fact, one of the longest of all the *controversiae*. Of note for our purposes are two details. Like the Christians in Corinth, these brothers are repeatedly encouraged to come to reconciliation, concord, or harmony, and the language of "grace" (*gratia*)

---

22. Elder Seneca, *Contr.* 1.1. Trans. modified from LCL to make clear exactly who the characters are. Latin: "Duo fratres inter se dissidebant; alteri filius erat. Patruus in egestatem incidit; patre vetante adulescens illum aluit; ob hoc abdicatus tacuit. Adoptatus a patruo est. Patruus accepta hereditate locuples factus est. Egere coepit pater: vetante patruo alit illum. Abdicatur."

23. This summary of the *controversiae* is indebted to Winterbottom, *Elder Seneca*, vii–xxiv; Bonner, *Roman Declamation*, 51–70. Quotation from Bonner, *Roman Declamation*, 55–56.

is often used (*redite in gratiam* = "be reconciled with").²⁴ In addition, one of the declaimers uses the following epigram (*sententia*) on behalf of the disinheritor to "great applause": "Who are you," he says to the youth, "to pass judgment on your fathers' action? ... We do not send our quarrels for you to settle them. For judges we have the gods."²⁵ A different *controversia* echoes that epigram, invoking the gods to judge between brothers, after their father's judgment was not honored (*Di, judicate post patrem!*).²⁶ When brothers argue, they are to be adjudicated either by their father or the gods.

Many of the extant *controversiae* feature cases about brothers or inheritance—or both. By my count of the *controversiae* of the Elder Seneca, (1) six concern brothers but not inheritance, (2) twelve concern inheritance but not brothers, and (3) eleven concern both brothers and inheritance.²⁷ That is to say, twenty-nine (or almost 40 percent) of Seneca's seventy-four extant *controversiae* have something to do with brothers or inheritance, and eleven (or about 15 percent) of them present a case about brothers *and* family inheritance.²⁸ The many cases about disinheritance (*abdicatio*) present, at first glance, a quandary for the social historian, since *abdicatio* was not permitted by Roman law (as it was by the Greeks).²⁹ However, Bonner has used Quintilian's discussion of forensic rhetoric about disinheritance to show that these plentiful declamatory exercises would have real-life applications when lawsuits were brought against a father's will after his death.³⁰ In the *controversiae*, the father is still alive for dramatic

---

24. Elder Seneca, *Contr.* 1.1.3, 1.1.6, 1.1.7, 1.1.10.
25. Elder Seneca, *Contr.* 1.1.23. Trans. LCL modified.
26. Elder Seneca, *Contr.* 7.1.25.
27. (1) Elder Seneca, *Contr.* 1.7, 4.6, 7.5, 9.3, 9.4, 9.5. In some of these cases, the brothers are just part of the plot and not main characters. (2) *Contr.* 1.4, 1.6, 1.8, 2.2, 2.7, 3.4, 4.3, 4.5 (= Lucian, *Abdic.*), 5.2, 7.3, 8.5, 10.2; (3) *Contr.* 1.1, 2.1, 2.4, 3.3, 5.3, 5.4, 6.1, 6.2, 6.3, 7.1, 8.3.
28. In the corpus of declamations from Calpurnius Flaccus, nos. 14, 18, 19, 30, 31, 37, and 48 deal with inheritance, and some of these (e.g., 14) concern both brothers and inheritance (Lewis A. Sussman, *The Declamations of Calpurnius Flaccus: Text, Translation, and Commentary*, Mnemosyne 133 [Leiden: Brill, 1994]). There are also some in the corpus ascribed to Quintilian (Michael Winterbottom, *The Minor Declamations Ascribed to Quintilian*, TK 13 [Berlin: de Gruyter, 1984]).
29. Cod. justin. 8.46.6: "Abdicatio, quae Graeco more ad alienandos liberos usurpabatur et apoceryxis [ἀποκήρυξις] dicebatur, romanis legibus non comprobatur."
30. Quintilian, *Inst.* 7.4.10–12; Bonner, *Roman Declamation*, 102.

effect—to enable a face-to-face confrontation of the disinheritor with his heir or heirs—but the arguments are meant to be used during posthumous inheritance disputes.[31]

Some other examples can further illuminate our understanding of what happened when brother went to court with a brother in the late republic and early empire. Sometimes brothers were on the same side of a case, as in the case of a young boy who defended his brother in a trial: "If you want to know the power of natural ties," said the declaimer, "even a baby boy [*infans*] is ready to speak on behalf of his brother."[32] In another case, after being neglected by his father but saved by his younger brother, an older brother adopts the younger and the father disinherits the older. The brothers looked out for each other, but the father considered the older son to have been a cancer in the family: "Let us use the inescapable medicine," says a declaimer on behalf of the father: "as is the way with dangerous wounds, the evil must be cut away from the body."[33] The resonances with Paul's paternal rhetoric in 1 Cor 4 and the surgical recommendation in 5:13 are easy to note, although medical analogies were used often in rhetorical education.[34] In his treatise on "brotherly love" (φιλαδελφία)—whose addressees, Nigrinus and Quietus, were probably noble brothers in Achaia—Plutarch would agree with the declaimers' sentiment about brothers vis-à-vis their father.[35] When a wrong has been done to a father, brothers should do whatever possible to restore one another to a state of

---

31. See also Sussman, *Declamations of Calpurnius Flaccus*, 150.

32. Elder Seneca, *Contr.* 7.5.1: "vis scire quantum natura possit? etiam infans pro fratre loquitur."

33. Elder Seneca, *Contr.* 3.3.1: "utamur medicina qua cogimur: quod in vulneribus fieri periculosis solet, ut malum cum ipso corpore exsecetur."

34. Another occurs at Elder Seneca, *Contr.* 9.5.6.

35. This was proposed in Edmund Groag, *Die römischen Reichsbeamten von Achaia bis auf Diokletian* (Vienna: Hölder-Pichler-Tempsky, 1939), cols. 42–45. The argument relies first on evidence from Pliny the Younger (*Ep.* 10.65.3; 10.66.2) that a certain Avidius Nigrinus was proconsul under Domitian (although those letters do not say in which province). In addition, a certain Avidius Quietus is attested as proconsul (ἀνθύπατος) of Achaia in an inscription from Delphi (Corpus des inscriptions de Delphes [CID] 4.143.2–3 [91/92 CE]). Groag lines up this evidence to suggest that these brothers were proconsuls of Achaia in the late first century. As such, Plutarch's exhortation to them about how best to resolve their disputes without contentious litigation (*Frat. amor.* 17 [488B–C]) provides real evidence of noble brothers who might have been tempted toward fraternal lawsuits in first-century Corinth.

χάρις with their father.³⁶ Brothers "ought to rejoice and to pride themselves on having surpassed their brothers in fairness and χάρις."³⁷

Brothers were usually not on the same side of an inheritance dispute, though, and the likelihood of conflict increased if they were only half-brothers. Consider this case:

> A man disinherited one of his sons. The disinherited son took in with a prostitute and acknowledged a son by her. The disinherited son fell ill and sent for his father. When his father came, the disinherited son entrusted his son to his father and then died. After his death the father adopted the boy. Now the father is accused of insanity by his other surviving son.³⁸

The case concerns the anger of a biological son toward his biological nephew (by a prostitute) who had become his legal half-brother (by adoption) and thus a coheir. Why should the biological, older son be expected to share his inheritance with a bastard nephew? The history of this *controversia* was reported by Seneca in some detail because of an instance in which Latro, an expert declaimer, made a faux pas of imperial proportions.³⁹ In his discussion and critique of how adoption raises up the lowborn to higher status, Latro forgot for a moment that he was declaiming in the presence of none other than Augustus and Marcus Agrippa, who themselves were in the process of negotiating biological and adoptive statuses.⁴⁰ (Latro's opponent made sure to point out his mistake.) Seneca thinks the scene exemplifies Augustus's clemency, since Latro was not punished for his slipup.

---

36. Plutarch, *Frat. amor.* 8 (482E).

37. Plutarch, *Frat. amor.* 11 (483F). A summary of the treatise for scholars of early Christianity can be found in Hans Dieter Betz, "De Fraterno Amore (Moralia 478A–492D)," in *Plutarch's Ethical Writings and Early Christian Literature*, ed. Hans Dieter Betz, SCHNT 4 (Leiden: Brill, 1978), 231–63. Betz notes 1 Cor 6:7 on p. 257.

38. Elder Seneca, *Contr.* 2.4, trans. LCL modified to make clear exactly who the characters are. Latin: "Abdicavit quidam filium; abdicatus se contulit ad meretricem; ex illa sustulit filium. Aeger ad patrem misit: cum venisset, commendavit ei filium suum et decessit. Pater post mortem illius adoptavit puerum; ab altero filio [pater] accusatur dementiae."

39. I discuss this case further in Peppard, *Son of God*, 57.

40. Elder Seneca, *Contr.* 2.4.13.

Another case uses the language of fraud, thus resembling the situation set before Paul in Corinth: "A man with a legitimate son acknowledged another by a slave, and then the father died. The elder brother made a division by which he put the whole estate in one part and the mother of the bastard in the other part. The younger son chose his mother and accuses the older brother of fraud."[41] The *controversia* is based on the enduring principle of fairness, "I cut, you choose," which Bonner argues may go all the way back to the Twelve Tables of 449 BCE.[42] But it also concerns the characteristic disdain felt by sons for half-brothers and stepmothers in the *controversiae*, especially when inheritances were at stake.[43] The older brother made an ingenious division, but the younger accuses him of "fraud" or "cheating" (*circumscriptio*). Plutarch would not be pleased: he admits that other writers use the topic of a "father's inheritable goods" as the "starting-point for a treatise" about fraternal relationships, but he hopes that brothers can refrain from enmity over their inheritances, lest they lose "the greatest and most valuable part of their inheritances, the friendship [φιλία] and fidelity [πίστις] of a brother."[44] The πίστις, fidelity or faithfulness, shared between brothers must not be lost to enmity through an inheritance dispute that has to be settled by ἄπιστοι, untrustworthy judges.

All these examples are suggestive, even tantalizing, as means by which to understand the social situation at Corinth and Paul's own rhetorical education. There is even a case involving a disinheritance and incest with a stepmother, which may be fodder for further reflection on how the issues of 1 Cor 5 and 6 might have been related.[45] In summary, though, the primary point is a simple one: the declamations of the late republic and early

---

41. Elder Seneca, *Contr.* 6.3, trans. LCL, modified to make clear exactly who the characters are. Latin: "Quidam, cum haberet legitimum filium, alium ex ancilla sustulit et decessit. Maior frater sic divisit ut patrimonium totum ex una parte poneret, ex altera matrem nothi. Minor elegit matrem et accusat fratrem circumscriptionis."

42. Bonner, *Roman Declamation*, 130. Latin: "maior frater dividat patrimonium, minor eligat."

43. Inheritance disputes between sons and stepmothers are also evidenced by the papyrological record, e.g., P.Turner 34 (216 CE).

44. Plutarch, *Frat. amor.* 9, 11 (482D, 483E).

45. Elder Seneca, *Contr.* 6.7. This case has been raised as an aid to understanding 1 Cor 5; see, e.g., Robert M. Grant, *Paul in the Roman World: Conflict at Corinth* (Louisville: Westminster John Knox, 2001), 116–17. Cf. Richardson, "Judgment in Sexual Matters."

empire demonstrate the prominence of fraternal lawsuits and disputed inheritances amid the "common sense" of what happened when people went to civil court. Hearing about brothers in court would have called to mind the theme of inheritance.

2. "Brother" against "Brother" Endangers the Family "Inheritance"

Returning now to the New Testament, one might raise the point that Paul uses the inheritance metaphor in other places, so there is no need to probe the social context of 1 Cor 6 to justify his using it there. However, Paul uses the metaphor rarely and not capriciously; in each case it serves a specific argument. For example, Paul spends large parts of Galatians (3:15–5:1) and Romans (4:1–25) discussing inheritance in order to justify the possibility of gentiles' spiritual descent from Abraham.[46] In related usages, inheritance signifies the eschatological reward for the spiritual, adoptive sonship conferred at baptism (Gal 3:23–4:7; Rom 8:1–30). Paul reminds the "brothers" in 1 Cor 15:50 that such an eschatological inheritance comes only through spiritual sonship and not a lineage of "flesh and blood." In all these cases, the inheritance metaphor stands very close to at least one familial metaphor.[47]

A final example occurs near the end of Galatians, when Paul uses the metaphor (Gal 5:21) during the presentation of the "works of the flesh" and the "fruit of the Spirit" (Gal 5:16–26). This usage is the one that most resembles our target for exegesis, 1 Cor 6:9–11. Paul has already concluded the argument about sonship and inheritance (Gal 3–4), which offered a rationalization of how Jews and gentiles can be coheirs of God's promise to Abraham through the Spirit in baptism. But Gal 5 still emphasizes the imagery of the spiritual family: they were called to "freedom" as "brothers" but ought to become "slaves" to one another (5:13). The "works of the flesh" define those who live as in natural families, who might inherit earthly things but "will not inherit the kingdom of God" (5:21). On the

---

46. For a bold, new reading of Paul's argument about descent and inheritance from Abraham, see Joshua D. Garroway, *Paul's Gentile-Jews: Neither Jew Nor Gentile, but Both* (New York: Palgrave Macmillan, 2012).

47. In a similar way, Paul's uses of the "kingdom [of God]" metaphor, although infrequent, stand close to familial metaphors: 1 Cor 4:20; 15:24–25; 1 Thess 2:11–12; Rom 14:15–21.

contrary, those called to a spiritual family do the "fruit of the Spirit" and are not to be "conceited" or "envious" toward their "brothers" (5:22–6:1).

These uses of the metaphor of inheritance in Paul's undisputed letters (and almost all of those in the disputed letters) stand proximate to familial metaphors in their literary contexts.[48] To explain the toughest cases of Gal 5:21 and 1 Cor 6:9, both of which accompany a vice list, Günter Haufe has proposed that such a list of vices describing those who will not inherit the kingdom of God was part of the κήρυγμα Paul received from the oral traditions about Jesus; perhaps, he argues, it constituted part of the inchoate, pre-Pauline rituals of baptism and initiation.[49] This is an attractive hypothesis, but even so, the example of 1 Cor 6:9 can also be understood cogently in light of the social context of fraternal lawsuits and inheritance disputes. Even if Paul received such a κήρυγμα, he still had to make choices about when and how to apply the oral traditions in his written arguments.

In this case, Paul did so by drawing on the cultural common sense about fraternal lawsuits. First, they were almost always about money or property. Recently Larry Welborn has shown that the verb ἀδικέω, the term calling out the "wrongdoers" of 1 Cor 6:9, normally implies a fraudulent use of money in the Corinthian correspondence.[50] When used in the portion of the deutero-Pauline *Haustafeln* about slaves, it implies fraud or embezzlement specifically toward one's anticipated inheritance (Col 3:24–25). The simplest explanation of the lawsuit in Corinth was a financial dispute that involved "wrongdoing" (ἀδικέω) and "fraud" (ἀποστερέω). Since these are so-called "brothers" going to court about a financial matter, the theme of

---

48. In the disputed Pauline corpus, the two usages in Ephesians are juxtaposed with references to the Spirit (Eph 1:13–14, 17–18) or near a vice list (5:5), as in Gal 5:21 and 1 Cor 6:9. The usage at Col 3:24 is clearly drawing on the household metaphors of the *Haustafeln* (Col 3:18–25).

49. There seem to be moral exhortations about who will and will not inherit/enter the kingdom of God that cluster around discussions of baptism and inheritance: Mark 10:13–31 and parr.; John 3:5; 1 Cor 6:9; Gal 5:21. Günter Haufe ("Reich Gottes bei Paulus und in der Jesustradition," *NTS* 31 [1985]: 467–72) also points to the Didache, which refers to the "two ways" tradition of life/virtue and death/vice that constituted the things said prior to baptism (ταῦτα πάντα προειπόντες, Did. 7.1). Others agree that the verses draw on pre-Pauline tradition: Hans Conzelmann, *1 Corinthians*, trans. James W. Leitch, Hermeneia (Philadelphia: Fortress, 1975), 106; Collins, *First Corinthians*, 229.

50. L. L. Welborn, *An End to Enmity: Paul and the "Wrongdoer" of Second Corinthians*, BZAW 185 (Berlin: de Gruyter, 2011), 52–58.

inheritance comes to mind.⁵¹ Second, taking family matters outside the family is an action worthy of shame, a point made well by Bruce Winter: "Paul's intention in [the] lengthy discussion on conflict over teachers in the Christian community had not been to shame but rather to admonish them as 'beloved children' (4:14). By way of contrast, on the issue of civil litigation he declared that this was precisely what he had intended to do."⁵² "I say this for your shame," Paul writes; or, "You should be ashamed of yourselves," as we might now say (6:5). Furthermore, judges outside the family would not be trustworthy, as many ancient examples attest, even about Corinth specifically.⁵³ Thus Paul's reference to external judges as ἄπιστοι (6:6) works in two senses: as those outside the community of faith, they were "unbelievers" (the word's ἐκκλησία meaning); as those outside the "family," they were "untrustworthy" (the word's πόλις meaning).

If not external judges, then who should judge this intrafamily dispute? One of the other brothers or sisters, Paul says, but from where does that person derive authority to judge? Here, too, the social context is helpful. Paul asks if there is not anyone σοφός among them who could resolve a dispute between brothers (6:5). A σοφός would have been just the type to have studied declamation, a form of education that was eminently popular and available in first-century cities such as Corinth.⁵⁴ Indeed, Winter has argued that Paul's Corinthian opponents judged specifically his declamatory abilities as insufficient (2 Cor 10:10).⁵⁵ Normally in a dispute between brothers (whose father was alive), their father, the *paterfamilias*, should judge between them.⁵⁶ In Paul's understanding of the ἐκκλησία as family, without a father on earth, it would be the divine *paterfamilias* who would do the judging, that is to say, the πνεῦμα of the divine *paterfamilias* alive in the community. That "spirit," which already demonstrated its judicial

---

51. I do not intend here to determine what exactly caused the lawsuit(s) about which Paul wrote. Paul uses the occasion of lawsuits between spiritual brothers in order to make a point about spiritual inheritance, but that does not necessarily mean that the actual lawsuit(s) concerned inheritance.
52. Winter, *After Paul Left Corinth*, 71–72.
53. See references in ibid., 62.
54. Winter, *Philo and Paul*, 22–24; cf. Winter, *After Paul Left Corinth*, 73.
55. Winter, *Philo and Paul*, 204–23. The "sophists' preference for extempore oratory over the written form, and their preoccupation with declamation, control the judgement against Paul in 10.10b" (223).
56. See Winter, *After Paul Left Corinth*, 70.

power by having "judged them as righteous" in their baptismal initiation as sons (6:11), ought to be the judge over the brothers.

As representative of the power of a *paterfamilias*, the Spirit shares some of the qualities attributed to the *genius* in the traditional conception of the Roman family.

> In the general Roman worldview, a *genius* is an unseen spiritual power, often personified as an object of worship, which unifies the members of a family (*gens*). Though each member of a family has a share in the family *genius*, it is manifested uniquely by the head of the family, the *paterfamilias*, and ultimately his preeminent son and heir. Overall, the *genius* has two chief functions: it is a life-force that enables the continuation of a family (passed on by both procreation and adoption) and also a tutelary spirit that guards over its members while they are alive.[57]

Like the *genius*, the Spirit marks and unifies for Paul the family inaugurated by the resurrection of God's Son and heir. The Spirit permeates the family as a paternal life force and guardian. According to the Gospel of Mark, the Spirit even speaks for Christians specifically during times of trial (Mark 13:11). In short, the Spirit is the manifest presence of the Father's will in this family, and thus only it should do the judging.

This connection helps us to see the fatherly rhetoric of 1 Cor 4:14–5:13 in a new light. The presumed social context from the πόλις and οἶκος was that a father had the right to judge and, if necessary, exclude members of a family. In Paul's ἐκκλησία, he had acted as a kind of father because he had "begotten" the Corinthian part of the family into existence (4:14–15). Then as the preeminent living representative of the paternal God's πνεῦμα on earth, Paul had the paternal power to constitute and reconstitute the family structure (5:3–4). Stated another way, Paul had the power, through the Spirit, to judge. He demonstrates this power of judgment in 5:1–13. But regarding lawsuits among brothers in 6:1–11, Paul wants the Corinthians to "imitate" him (4:16). They themselves should become judges through the power of the fatherly πνεῦμα (6:11)—like a *genius* that both constitutes and guards a family.

In turn, the vice list (6:9–10) takes on a slightly different meaning. The ten sins listed are not just individual faults but are precisely the kinds

---

57. Peppard, *Son of God*, 113.

of acts that threaten to break apart a family.[58] In Paul's understanding, the vices derive from self-centeredness and thus inhibit love, justice, and familial cohesion. Such a reading is corroborated by Paul's paraenesis to the Thessalonians, in which he warns against πορνεία as a form of πλεονεξία ("exploitation") against one's brother or sister (1 Thess 4:3–8), thus bringing sexual and financial sins together as threats to familial unity. It is only "brotherly love" (φιλαδελφία, 1 Thess 4:9) that will keep the Thessalonian community together as a family until the eschaton. These interpretations are also supported by what are probably the earliest quotations and interpretations of 1 Cor 6:9. In his letter to the Philadelphians, Ignatius of Antioch begins with several exhortations to ecclesial unity, among which is, "Do not be deceived, my brothers: anyone who follows someone creating a schism will not inherit the kingdom of God."[59] In his letter to the Ephesians, he writes, "Do not be deceived, my brothers: those who corrupt households [οἰκοφθόροι] will not inherit the kingdom of God" (Ignatius, *Eph.* 16.1). Both instances support the argument that inheritance metaphors were closely tied to familial metaphors in earliest Christianity: Ignatius inserts the vocative "brothers" (ἀδελφοί) in his quotation of 1 Cor 6:9 in each case, even though he does not often use that vocative elsewhere in his letters.[60] Earlier in the letter to the Ephesians, Ignatius had introduced "brothers" language as a way to encourage "gentleness" (ἐπιείκεια, one of Plutarch's signs of φιλαδελφία) and thus to avoid "wrongdoing" (ἀδικέω) and "defrauding" (ἀποστερέω), the exact issues attested in 1 Cor 6:1–8 (*Eph.* 10.3). From these examples, we can conclude that Ignatius interpreted Paul's vice list in 1 Cor 6:9 as a catalog of sins against unity and community. Moreover, it is probable that Ignatius offers the "family cohesion" reading of the vice list, since he summarizes the list's sinners simply as οἰκοφθόροι, "corrupters of the household." We might call them "homewreckers," in the parlance of our times. Greedy brothers and predatory homewreckers are disinherited in real life, say a city's legal declaimers; so also in the kingdom of God, say Paul and Ignatius.

---

58. See Elliott, "No Kingdom of God for Softies," 35.

59. Ignatius, *Phil.* 3.3. "Schism" was, of course, a chief concern of 1 Corinthians overall (1:10, 11:18, 12:25).

60. The other usage at *Phil.* 5.1 is very near to the introduction of the language in 3.3, and it also begins a section where Ignatius talks about his "lot" (κλῆρος). The use at *Rom.* 6.2 comes just after a birth metaphor (6.1).

In conclusion, like the psalmist before him, Paul concerns himself with the ideal of "brothers dwelling together in unity" (Ps 133:1).[61] Paul's chief concern throughout 1 Corinthians is to bring the brothers and sisters in Christ forward to the eschaton together as a cohesive family. Toward that end, he counsels the family to stop taking each other to court over financial matters, as if they were brothers wrangling over their father's inheritable goods. The understanding of what normally happened when legally defined brothers went to court against one another thus allows Paul to draw from social reality in order to reorient the focus of the discussion: he emphasizes the new family of brothers and their inheritance in the Spirit.

The baptismal reference that concludes the exhortation reminds them that they are part of a new family and that these are their real, spiritual brothers. In the language of Paul's other letters, they are all adopted children, and through adoption they received a new lord and a new family spirit under their new father. This father's inheritance is divine and is not a zero-sum commodity. Indeed, more and more brothers and sisters could be brought into the family, without ever needing to litigate or defraud one another over it (6:8). The inheritance is, to use another economic metaphor, χάρις or *gratia* in abundance.

Works Cited

Beard, Mary. "Looking (Harder) for Roman Myth: Dumézil, Declamation and the Problems of Definition." Pages 44–64 in *Mythos in mythenloser Gesellschaft: Das Paradigma Roms*. Edited by Fritz Graf. Stuttgart: Teubner, 1993.

Berry, D. H. and Malcolm Heath. "Oratory and Declamation." Pages 394–420 in *Handbook of Classical Rhetoric in the Hellenistic Period 330 B.C.–A.D. 400*. Edited by Stanley E. Porter. Leiden: Brill, 2001.

Betz, Hans Dieter. "De Fraterno Amore (Moralia 478A–492D)." Pages 231–63 in *Plutarch's Ethical Writings and Early Christian Literature*. Edited by Hans Dieter Betz. SCHNT 4. Leiden: Brill, 1978.

Bingen, Jean. "Documents de l'Egypte romaine." *BASP* 22 (1985): 15–23.

---

61. Although this essay has not treated the role of law in the self-regulation of Jewish families and communities in the diaspora, it is likely that Paul knew about the possibilities for such self-regulation of a πολίτευμα that existed within a πόλις (such as at Alexandria and Sardis). On these and related matters, see ch. 3 of Mitchell, "1 Corinthians 6:1–11."

Bonner, Stanley F. *Roman Declamation in the Late Republic and Early Empire*. Berkeley: University of California Press, 1949.
Bourdieu, Pierre, and Loïs J. D. Wacquant. *An Invitation to Reflexive Sociology*. Chicago: University of Chicago Press, 1992.
Clarke, Andrew D. *Secular and Christian Leadership in Corinth: A Sociohistorical and Exegetical Study of 1 Corinthians 1–6*. AGJU 18. Leiden: Brill, 1993.
Collins, Raymond F. *First Corinthians*. SP. Collegeville, MN: Liturgical Press, 1999.
Conzelmann, Hans. *1 Corinthians*. Translated by James W. Leitch. Hermeneia. Philadelphia: Fortress, 1975.
Derrett, J. Duncan M. "Judgment and 1 Corinthians 6." *NTS* 37 (1991): 22–36.
Elliott, John H. "*No Kingdom of God for Softies*? Or, What Was Paul Really Saying? 1 Corinthians 6:9–10 in Context." *BTB* 34 (2004): 17–40.
Garroway, Joshua D. *Paul's Gentile-Jews: Neither Jew Nor Gentile, but Both*. New York: Palgrave Macmillan, 2012.
Grant, Robert M. *Paul in the Roman World: Conflict at Corinth*. Louisville: Westminster John Knox, 2001.
Groag, Edmund. *Die römischen Reichsbeamten von Achaia bis auf Diokletian*. Vienna: Hölder-Pichler-Tempsky, 1939.
Gunderson, Erik. *Declamation, Paternity, and Roman Identity*. Cambridge: Cambridge University Press, 2003.
Haufe, Günter. "Reich Gottes bei Paulus und in der Jesustradition." *NTS* 31 (1985): 467–72.
Hays, Richard B. *First Corinthians*. IBC. Louisville: John Knox, 1997.
Hodge, Caroline E. Johnson. *If Sons, Then Heirs: A Study of Kinship and Ethnicity in the Letters of Paul*. Oxford: Oxford University Press, 2007.
Horrell, David G. *The Social Ethos of the Corinthian Correspondence: Interests and Ideology from 1 Corinthians to 1 Clement*. SNTW. Edinburgh: T&T Clark, 1996.
Horsley, Richard A. *1 Corinthians*. ANTC. Nashville: Abingdon, 1998.
Martin, Dale B. *Sex and the Single Savior: Gender and Sexuality in Biblical Interpretation*. Louisville: Westminster John Knox, 2006.
Mitchell, Alan C. "1 Corinthians 6:1–11: Group Boundaries and the Courts of Corinth." PhD diss., Yale University, 1986.
———. "Friends Do Not Wrong Friends: Friendship and Justice in 1 Corinthians 6.8." Pages 134–44 in *The Impartial God: Essays in Biblical*

Studies in Honor of Jouette M. Bassler. Edited by Calvin J. Roetzel and Robert L. Foster. Sheffield: Sheffield Phoenix, 2007.

———. "Rich and Poor in the Courts of Corinth: Litigiousness and Status in 1 Corinthians 6.1–11." *NTS* 39 (1993): 562–86.

Peppard, Michael. *The Son of God in the Roman World: Divine Sonship in Its Social and Political Context*. New York: Oxford University Press, 2011.

Richardson, Peter. "Judgment in Sexual Matters in 1 Corinthians 6:1–11." *NovT* 25 (1983): 37–58.

Rosner, Brian S. *Paul, Scripture and Ethics: A Study of 1 Corinthians 5–7*. AGJU 22. Leiden: Brill, 1994.

Rowlandson, Jane, and Ryosuke Takahashi, "Brother-Sister Marriage and Inheritance Strategies in Greco-Roman Egypt," *JRS* 99 (2009): 104–39.

Russell, D. A. *Greek Declamation*. Cambridge: Cambridge University Press, 1983.

Schrage, Wolfgang. *Der erste Brief an die Korinther, Teil. 1*. EKKNT 7.1. Zürich: Benziger; Neukirchen-Vluyn: Neukirchener Verlag, 1991.

Scroggs, Robin. *The New Testament and Homosexuality: Contextual Background for Contemporary Debate*. Philadelphia: Fortress, 1983.

Sussman, Lewis A. *The Declamations of Calpurnius Flaccus: Text, Translation, and Commentary*. Mnemosyne 133. Leiden: Brill, 1994.

Walters, James C. "Paul, Adoption, and Inheritance." Pages 42–76 in *Paul in the Greco-Roman World*. Edited by J. Paul Sampley. Harrisburg, PA: Trinity Press International, 2003.

Welborn, L. L. *An End to Enmity: Paul and the "Wrongdoer" of Second Corinthians*. BZNW 185. Berlin: de Gruyter, 2011.

Winter, Bruce W. *After Paul Left Corinth: The Influence of Secular Ethics and Social Change*. Grand Rapids, 2001.

———. *Philo and Paul among the Sophists: Alexandrian and Corinthian Responses to a Julio-Claudian Movement*. 2nd ed. Grand Rapids: Eerdmans, 2002.

Winterbottom, Michael. *The Elder Seneca*. 2 vols. LCL. Cambridge: Harvard University Press, 1974.

———. *The Minor Declamations Ascribed to Quintilian*. TK 13. Berlin: de Gruyter, 1984.

The Changing Rural Horizons of Corinth's First Urban Christians

David K. Pettegrew

The Problem of the Essential Countryside

In an edited series dedicated to the first urban churches, it is natural that territory should occupy a place in the conversation. An ancient Greek polis, after all, denoted both an urban center (*astu*) and its countryside (*chora*), and free land-owning males living in scattered farms and satellite communities had as much claim to citizenship as residents in the urban center.[1] Roman colonies such as Corinth, founded in the eastern Greek provinces during the first centuries BCE and CE, likewise formed a unified administrative unit of town and surrounding territory (*territorium*) that was apportioned to founding citizens for sustenance and civic participation.[2] Across the Roman Mediterranean, the segment of the population that did not reside in exurban farms and villas regularly encountered the countryside through land investment, seasonal labor needs, sacred rites, mortuary practices, transport, and travel. Even the residents of the largest cities of the Roman Empire were constantly enmeshed in their territories through the complex patterns of human mobility, exchange, and social networks. As ancient historians, classicists, and archaeologists have come to recognize, rural landscapes were of fundamental significance to Greek and Roman economies, social worlds, and culture.

---

1. Mogens Herman Hansen and Thomas Heine Nielsen, "Meaning and Reference of the Word *Polis*," in *An Inventory of Archaic and Classical Poleis*, ed. Mogens Herman Hansen and Thomas Heine Nielsen (Oxford: Oxford University Press, 2004), 39–46.

2. Edward T. Salmon, *Roman Colonization under the Republic* (Ithaca, NY: Cornell University Press, 1970), 13–39.

This fact of the countryside's value prompts questions about the longstanding view among early Christian scholars that the earliest ekklesiai were predominantly, if not exclusively, urban-oriented. William H. C. Frend's seminal article on the Christian countryside, for example, described and predicated a wholly urban world of Christians: the rural regions were the last to convert to Christianity.[3] Closer to home, Wayne A. Meeks's influential work on first-century Christians represented Paul and his associates as exclusively urban: the changeless countryside lay outside the sphere of interest or influence of upwardly mobile believers.[4] Yet, the recognition of the significance of the countryside in ancient studies more generally encourages us to reconsider the potential intersections of the *chora* with polis and ekklesia.

The region of Corinth offers a particularly interesting case study in the potential value of the territory for an understanding of the first urban Christians. New Testament scholars have typically neglected Corinthian territory in favor of urban depictions, even as they have in other cities of the Mediterranean. The late Jerome Murphy-O'Connor's popular and useful *St. Paul's Corinth: Texts and Archaeology*, for example, made accessible a set of Roman literary texts that imaged Corinth as an urban center uniquely shaped by its maritime environment, but the countryside was practically absent.[5] Biblical commentaries and historical overviews of Pauline Christianity have usually depicted Corinth as simply its urban center, even though this colony included a vast surrounding territory. The reasons for such neglect make sense in light of the assumption, noted above, that early Christians had little concern for the countryside. They signal also the urban bias of American archaeological investigations in the region, which have unearthed mainly the Roman forum and led to hundreds of technical reports on finds and buildings exclusively from ancient Corinth. Finally, they reflect a broader body of Corinthian scholarship that has either overlooked territory or deliberately undercut its relevance to the Roman city, the most dramatic example being Donald Engels's problematic monograph

---

3. William H. C. Frend, "The Winning of the Countryside," *JEH* 18 (1967): 1–14.

4. Wayne A. Meeks, *The First Urban Christians: The Social World of the Apostle Paul* (New Haven: Yale University Press, 1983), especially 9–16.

5. Jerome Murphy-O'Connor, *St. Paul's Corinth: Texts and Archaeology*, 3rd ed. (Collegeville, MN: Liturgical Press, 2002).

on Roman Corinth, which rejected agriculture as an important economic activity in favor of urban trade and services.[6]

In another respect, however, New Testament scholars have long been interested in Corinth's famous eastern territory, the Isthmus, and the important places there, as indicators of a timeless regional connectivity. Since the early eighteenth century, the narrow neck of land linking southern and central Greece, together with its portage road (the diolkos) and three principal sites (Kenchreai, Lechaion, Isthmia), has appeared in countless biblical prefaces and introductions to explain the Pauline mission to Corinth and the divisive ekklesia there. Adam Clarke's prefatory comments on 1 Corinthians, for example, argued that Corinth's favorable position on the Isthmus was responsible for the city's inherent dispositions to trade, wealth, and immorality. In its central maritime position, with its harbors Kenchreai and Lechaion receiving the wealth of the nations, Corinth gained riches, "riches produced luxury, and luxury a total corruption of manners.... it is no wonder that, in its heathen state, it was exceedingly corrupt and profligate."[7] In the mid-nineteenth century, Conybeare and Howson's masterful biography of Saint Paul placed the apostle against the essential backdrop of a connecting land bridge of harbors and the diolkos, which shaped both the history and character of the Corinthians:

> We are thus brought to that which is really the characteristic both of Corinthian geography and Corinthian history, its close relation to the commerce of the Mediterranean... A narrow and level isthmus, across which smaller vessels could be dragged from gulph to gulph, was of inestimable value to the early traders of the Levant. And the two harbours, which received the ships of a more maturely developed trade, — Cenchrea on the Eastern Sea, and Lechaeum on the Western, with a third and smaller port, called Schoenus, where the isthmus was narrowest, — form an essential part of our idea of Corinth.[8]

---

6. Donald W. Engels, *Roman Corinth. An Alternative Model for the Ancient City* (Chicago: University of Chicago Press, 1990).

7. See preface to *1 Corinthians* in vol. 2 of Adam Clarke, *The New Testament, of Our Lord and Saviour Jesus Christ: Containing the Text, Taken from the Most Correct Copies of the Present Authorised Translation, Including the Marginal Readings and Parallel Texts, with a Commentary and Critical Notes; Designed as a Help to a Better Understanding of the Sacred Writings* (London: Butterworth, 1817).

8. W. J. Conybeare and J. S. Howson, *The Life and Epistles of St. Paul*, 2 vols. (London: Longman, Brown, Green, & Longmans, 1852), 1:442-43.

Interpretations such as these, with their emphasis on the region's connective landscape, reflected both the logic of nineteenth-century geographical determinism and knowledge of ancient literary texts about the region, especially the geographer Strabo's influential overview of Corinthian wealth and immorality (Strabo, *Geogr.* 8.6.20). While today scholars have become more critical of projecting the source material about the Greek city onto the Roman colony, the Strabonic view of Corinth has continually led scholars to underplay the region's agriculture and natural resources and overplay the city's destiny and tendencies toward markets, banking, and wealth—and a motley, mobile, transient, and immoral population.[9] In this essentially connective land bridge with good harbors, a portage road, and cosmopolitan population, scholars have found a reason for Paul's visits as well as the economic, social, and moral problems of the Christian community planted there.

Neither of these broad sets of approaches to Corinthian territory is fruitful. It is no longer reasonable, on the one hand, to assume that territory was simply irrelevant or unimportant to the urban inhabitants, given the corpus of scholarship that has shown how central agriculture and land were to the developing Roman colony. The old view that the Roman city

---

9. See, for example, the constant role of essential geography in modern scholarship in establishing the "commercial" Corinth of Paul's day, usually to the exclusion of agriculture. Examples are numerous: Hans Conzelmann, *1 Corinthians: A Commentary on the First Epistle to the Corinthians*, trans. James W. Leitch, Hermeneia (Philadelphia: Fortress, 1975), 11–12; Meeks, *The First Urban Christians*, 47–48; Scott J. Hafemann, *2 Corinthians*, NIV Application Commentary (Grand Rapids: Zondervan, 2000), 22–28; Ben Witherington III, *Conflict and Community in Corinth: A Socio-rhetorical Commentary on 1 and 2 Corinthians* (Grand Rapids: Eerdmans, 1995), 9–11; Scott Hahn and Curtis Mitch, *The First and Second Letters of Saint Paul to the Corinthians, with Introduction, Commentary, and Notes*, Ignatius Catholic Study Bible (San Francisco: Ignatius Press, 2004), 13; David G. Horrell and Edward Adams, "Introduction: The Scholarly Quest for Paul's Church at Corinth: A Critical Survey," in *Christianity at Corinth: The Quest for the Pauline Church*, ed. Edward Adams and David G. Horrell (Louisville: Westminster John Knox, 2004), 1–8; Craig S. Keener, *1–2 Corinthians*, New Cambridge Bible Commentary (Cambridge: Cambridge University Press), 2005, 7; Robert Scott Nash, *1 Corinthians*, Smyth & Helwys Bible Commentary (Macon, GA: Smyth & Helwys, 2009), 5–6; Mitzi L. Minor, *2 Corinthians*, Smyth & Helwys Bible Commentary (Macon, GA: Smyth & Helwys, 2009), 6–9; Roy E. Ciampa and Brian S. Rosner, *The First Letter to the Corinthians*, Pillar New Testament Commentary (Grand Rapids: Eerdmans, 2010), 2–3; George T. Montague, *First Corinthians*, Catholic Commentary on Sacred Scripture (Grand Rapids: Baker Academic, 2011), 16–19.

was wholly oriented to commerce and had little dependence on agriculture, for example, has been disproven through systematic analysis of land division patterns in aerial photographs and the documentation of a network of rural farms and villas in regional archaeological survey.[10] The urban and rural worlds were both vital to the Roman city despite the neglect of literary sources. On the other hand, one can also no longer approach the territory as if it were the static and changeless backdrop to a dynamic city. Recent archaeological and historical investigations have shown that the countryside, like the urban center, underwent major developments between the colony's foundation in 44 BCE and the late second century CE and beyond.[11] The rural world was less a timeless entity than a contingent countryside that developed in spurts that marked the energies of both the imperial state and local elite.

In this essay I consider how two features of Corinthian territory, the diolkos and canal, highlight both the importance of the territory and its changing character in the Roman era.[12] These two exurban features have frequently appeared in New Testament scholarship as a way to set the (maritime) scene for the Pauline mission and religious communities in Corinth. The pair has often been regarded as two sides of the same coin about the region's maritime connectedness in antiquity: the diolkos a symbol of a complex but difficult transport business, the canal a sign of the region's potential connectivity in long-distance trading networks. Each has been used to support a timeless view of Corinthian territory that has acted as the backdrop to discussions of polis and ekklesia. My discussion will highlight the deficiencies of these conventional views and advance

---

10. See, for example, David Gilman Romano, "Roman Surveyors in Corinth," *Proceedings of the American Philosophical Society* 150 (2006): 62–85; Romano, "City Planning, Centuriation, and Land Division in Roman Corinth: *Colonia Laus Iulia Corinthiensis* and *Colonia Iulia Flavia Augusta Corinthiensis*," in *Corinth, the Centenary: 1896–1996*, ed. Charles K. Williams II and Nancy Bookidis (Princeton: American School of Classical Studies at Athens, 2003), 279–301; David K. Pettegrew, "Corinthian Suburbia: Patterns of Roman Settlement on the Isthmus," in *The Bridge of the Untiring Sea: The Corinthian Isthmus from Prehistory to Late Antiquity*, ed. Elizabeth R. Gebhard and Timothy E. Gregory, Hesperia Supplement (Princeton: American School of Classical Studies at Athens, 2015).

11. Pettegrew, "Corinthian Suburbia."

12. The following arguments are outlined in fuller form in David K. Pettegrew, *The Isthmus of Corinth: Crossroads of the Mediterranean World* (Ann Arbor: University of Michigan Press, 2016).

perspectives of a changing countryside. The first case study surveys new scholarship about the diolkos portage road and the shifting east–west networks of people and goods in the first century CE and concludes that the diolkos was relatively unimportant for the Corinth of Paul's day; the harbors, not the diolkos, had become the vital points of regional connectivity in the mid-first century CE due to the specific geopolitical factors of the previous century. The second case study rejects the view that potentates throughout Corinthian history desired to canalize the Isthmus and focuses on the reasons for the Roman state's sudden involvement in this Corinthian project in the 60s CE. Both case studies emphasize a contingent and dynamic countryside rather than an essential and static backdrop and the broader social, economic, and political networks that shaped the development of the territory over time. Moreover, each draws attention to the transformation of the region's maritime infrastructure and its implications for the developing ekklesia.

The Diolkos

Our first case study is the diolkos of Corinth, the famous portage road that connects the Saronic Gulf with the Corinthian Gulf via the narrow Isthmus (figs. 1 and 2).[13] Scholars long regarded the diolkos as a great portage highway used to trans-ship enormous volumes of goods between the eastern and western Mediterranean. As its effects were imagined, traders arriving from Italy/Asia Minor disembarked at the western/eastern end, unloaded their cargoes, and moved the ships and freights via wheeled carts over 6 km to the opposite gulf, where they continued to the coastal cities of Asia Minor/Italy. Merchants benefited by this shortcut in long-distance trade, while Corinth received revenues on the tolls, transport fees, and services to passengers in transit. As a mechanism for the movement of ships, cargoes, and people between gulfs, the diolkos allegedly made the Isthmus a great zone of trans-shipment and turned Corinth into a populous city of visitors and transients. It also influenced (as noted above) the Chris-

---

13. This discussion summarizes and updates previous arguments made in David K. Pettegrew, "The Diolkos and the Emporion: How a Land Bridge Framed the Commercial Economy of Roman Corinth," in *Corinth in Contrast: Studies in Inequality*, ed. Steven J. Friesen, Sarah James, and Daniel Schowalter, NovTSup 155 (Leiden: Brill, 2013), 126–42; and Pettegrew, "The *Diolkos* of Corinth," *AJA* 115 (2011): 549–74. For an even fuller view, see Pettegrew, *Isthmus of Corinth*.

Figure 1. A section of the excavated diolkos road along the modern canal, facing northwest toward the Corinthian Gulf.

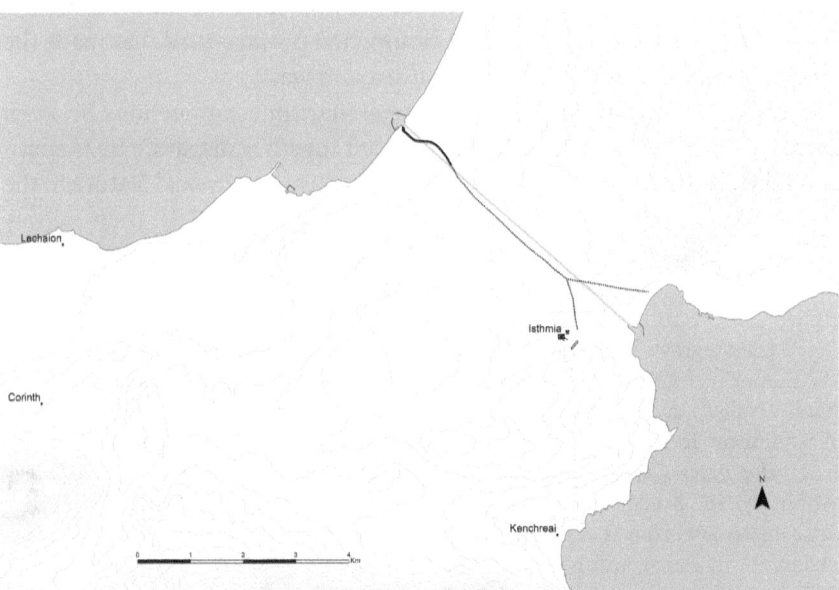

Figure 2. Map of the Isthmus showing locations of major Roman sites, the line of the modern canal with breakwaters on both gulfs. The dark line overlying the canal represents the part of the diolkos uncovered through excavation. The dashed line marks one reconstruction of the path of the remainder of the road over the Isthmus.

tian communities toward commerce, the accumulation of wealth, and, ultimately, community conflict. The diolkos has tremendously shaped the popular image of Roman Corinth as a commerce town whose population was wholly engaged in constant trade between east and west.

A number of recent studies have problematized the traditional view.[14] Most especially, scholars have shown that the diolkos, as we know it today, was the creation of mid-nineteenth-century travelers and educated Europeans, who imagined ancient Corinth as a great sea lane between east and west.[15] In a progressive era when new European and American capitalists applied the machines of the industrial age to excavate the modern world's major canals—Suez (1869), the Corinthian Isthmus (1893), and eventually Panama (1914)—scholars imagined that the Isthmus also functioned as a bridge of the sea. The word *diolkos* was, of course, a term of great antiquity, but its ancient meaning denoted a toponym rather than a portage road. Strabo, who applied the term to Corinthian territory (*Geogr.* 8.2.1, 8.6.4, 8.6.22), used it exclusively to refer to the narrowest part of the Corinthian Isthmus visible from Acrocorinth, where the temple of Poseidon was located and ships were once dragged from sea to sea. Ancient and medieval writers referred to the portaging of ships over the land bridge, but no ancient writer imagined a monumental portage road that made the Isthmus a major trade route between east and west.

Influenced by an age of greater global maritime connections between Europe and Asia, modern scholars cobbled together disparate texts spanning the classical age to the Byzantine era to create a physical feature in the landscape. Translated first as land carriage (Cramer 1828), then railway (Mott 1842) and railroad (Finley 1841), then slipway (Koeppen 1856),[16]

---

14. Pettegrew, "The *Diolkos* of Corinth," 549–74; Pettegrew, "The Diolkos and the Emporion," 126–42; Pettegrew, *Isthmus of Corinth*. Cf. Despina Koutsoumba and Yannis Nakas, "Δίολκος: Ένα Σημαντικό Τεχνικό Έργο Της Αρχαιότητας [The Diolkos: A Significant Technical Achievement of Antiquity]," in *The Corinthia and the Northeast Peloponnese: Topography and History from Prehistoric Times until the End of Antiquity*, ed. Konstantin Kissas and Wolf-Dietrich Niemeier (Munich: Hirmer, 2013), 191–206; Hans Lohmann, "Der Diolkos von Korinth—Eine Antike Schiffsschleppe?" in Kissas and Niemeier, *The Corinthia and the Northeast Peloponnesus*, 207–30.

15. Pettegrew, "The *Diolkos* of Corinth," 550–52.

16. J. A. Cramer, *A Geographical and Historical Description of Ancient Greece: With a Map, and a Plan of Athens*, vol. 3 (Oxford: Clarendon, 1828); Valentine Mott, *Travels in Europe and the East* (New York: Harper, 1842); George Finlay, *The History*

the diolkos soon became synonymous with a celebrated road used for the overland conveyance of maritime vessels well before a physical road was even seen in the landscape. When sections of an ancient limestone road across the Isthmus were discovered in the territory in the late nineteenth century, and then excavated in the 1950s, scholars claimed to have found that very monumental road that made the Isthmus a central trade route in the ancient Mediterranean. As the diolkos became linked in scholarly literature to a physical road, it lost its specific ancient connotation as a geographic district of the Isthmus visible from Acrocorinth.

From this paved road, archaeologists found support for the view that the land bridge functioned as a trans-shipment zone throughout antiquity. Excavated by the Greek archaeologist Nikolaos Verdelis, the section of road ran eastward for a kilometer from the Corinthian Gulf.[17] Although the pavements could not be traced beyond a certain point, Verdelis surmised that they continued to the opposite sea.[18] The excavator dated the road to the archaic age, specifically the reign of the Corinthian tyrant Periander in the late seventh century, based on associated pottery and cut stone blocks with inscribed early Corinthian alphabetic characters and the belief that Periander had desired to cut the canal. Verdelis held that the diolkos remained in use through the end of antiquity as a great portage for moving military ships and commercial vessels and cargoes. This image of the region's essential maritime properties—formed in the nineteenth century and materialized through archaeological investigations of the twentieth century—eventually became part of the introductory scholarship to early Christianity in Corinth.

---

of Greece: From Its Conquest by the Crusaders to Its Conquest by the Turks and of the Empire of the Trebizond 1204-1461 (Edinburgh: Blackwood, 1851); A. L. Koeppen, "Sketches of a Traveler from Greece, Constantinople, Asia Minor, Syria and Palestine—My Travels in Peloponnesus," *Mercersburg Quarterly Review* 8 (1856): 350–83.

17. For a fuller review of the archaeological evidence, see Pettegrew, "The *Diolkos* of Corinth," 549–74; Koutsoumba and Nakas, "Διολχος," 191–206; and Lohmann, "Der Diolkos von Korinth," 207–30. Most of Verdelis's results were published in Greek in the journals *Archaiologikon Deltion* and *Praktika*, but a convenient English summary is available in N. M. Verdelis, "How the Ancient Greeks Transported Ships over the Isthmus of Corinth: Uncovering the 2550-Year-Old *Diolcos* of Periander," *Illustrated London News* (19 October 1957), 649–51.

18. Verdelis "How the Ancient Greeks Transported Ships," 649.

Over the last decade, a new body of scholarship has undercut every tenet of the old orthodoxy.[19] Archaeologists have underscored that the road is actually an amalgamation of different phases of construction that may have begun as early as the seventh century, as Verdelis suggested, but that are not necessarily any earlier than the fifth century BCE. Different styles of construction and the reuse of architecture such as column capitals indicate at least one phase later than the early fourth century BCE. There remains some disagreement about the dating of the road. Despina Koutsoumba and Yannis Nakas, for example, have accepted Verdelis's archaic date but noted that Nero's canal trenches decisively ended the life of the road in 67 CE.[20] Hans Lohmann has proposed that the reuse of archaic architecture in the road indicates a postarchaic date, possibly even after the destruction of Corinth in 146 BCE, when numerous temples in the district lay derelict, destroyed, and accessible for mining and when Corinth's harbors were out of use.[21] For reasons I will present below, I believe that the laying of pavements occurred in the sixth or early fifth centuries BCE and that the road played almost no role in portaging goods, let alone ships, in the Roman period.

Scholars have also convincingly overturned older views about the form and extent of the paved diolkos. Whereas archaeologists and classicists once imagined that limestone pavements ran all the way across the Isthmus, Lohmann, Koutsoumba, and Nakas have underscored that limestone blocks were placed only in the loosest sandy sediments near the coast and stop at higher elevations, where rockier ground provides a sufficient foundation for the movement of heavy cargoes.[22] In short, only a quarter of the road was paved, and some three-quarters ran over earth or shallow bedrock. The road may have been important in its day, but it was not the "largest ship trackway in ancient times," as one scholar once described it,[23]

---

19. Pettegrew, "The *Diolkos* of Corinth," 549–74; Pettegrew, "The Diolkos and the Emporion," 126–42; Pettegrew, *Isthmus of Corinth*; Koutsoumba and Nakas, "Δiολκος," 191–206; Lohmann, "Der Diolkos von Korinth," 207–30.

20. Koutsoumba and Nakas, "Διολκος," 203–4.

21. Lohmann, "Der Diolkos von Korinth," 207–30.

22. Koutsoumba and Nakas, "Διολκος"; Lohmann, "Der Diolkos Von Korinth," 207–30.

23. Walter Werner, "The Largest Ship Trackway in Ancient Times: The Diolkos of the Isthmus of Corinth, Greece, and Early Attempts to Build a Canal," *International Journal of Nautical Archaeology* 26 (1997): 98–119.

and it did not require, as another scholar estimated,[24] 40,000 m² of stone pavement and 60,000 man days to lay it. Such revision problematizes older interpretations of the road as the great ancient railway open for business from the seventh century BCE to the fifth century CE.

A critical piece in this new scholarship has been the systematic reinterpretation of a dozen ancient and medieval texts related to the transfer of ships over the Isthmus. Most of these texts reference the portaging of military galleys during times of war, but the passing comments of Aristophanes (*Thesm.* 647–648), Strabo (*Geogr.* 8.2.1), and Pliny the Elder (*Nat.* 4.9–10) had suggested that commercial ships were also portaged frequently. I have argued elsewhere that the "general passages" reference the same unusual portages of military galleys noted in the other texts.[25] The fifth-century BCE playwright Aristophanes, who has a character voice a sexual innuendo about the Corinthian Isthmus, is specifically referencing the dramatic Peloponnesian portage of 412 BCE that surprised the Athenians (cf. Thucydides, *Pelop.* 8.7–10). Pliny the Elder's comment in the late 70s CE about smaller ships (*porthmeia*) portaged over the Isthmus marks a summary of historical ship portages (cf. Polybius, *Hist.* 5.101). Strabo's denotation of the diolkos as a district associated with ship portaging (*Geogr.* 8.2.1) is not contemporary observation but a summary of the famous portages of ancient times. Strabo and Pliny are not contemporary witnesses to ship transfers but secondary sources referencing the earlier histories of Thucydides and Polybius; their passing comments reflect an interest and educational background in the historical geography of the Mediterranean.

The second key interpretive shift concerning the texts has been the recognition that even the episodes of generals and admirals carting ships overland do not reflect ordinary or commonplace military portage activity. Recent scholarship has emphasized the rhetorical character of these accounts.[26] The narratives, for example, assume a common form in describing covert and decisive military stratagems signifying remarkable

---

24. R. M. Cook, "A Further Note on the Diolkos," in *Studies in Honor of T. B. L. Webster I*, ed. J. H. Betts, J. T. Hooker, and J. R. Green (Bristol: Bristol Classical, 1986), 65–68.

25. Pettegrew, "The *Diolkos* of Corinth," 566, 569–70.

26. Koutsoumba and Nakas ("Δίολκος") have noted, for instance, that the military portages are always described in the language of secretive and rapid attack. See further Pettegrew, "The *Diolkos* of Corinth," 565–69.

achievement that required some explanation. The historians explain why the generals decide to portage—as a stealth naval offense, a sign of ambition, or a hasty retreat during an emergency[27]—as well as how the portage occurs—as a costly and involved activity requiring significant expenditures of resources and manpower. The explanations indicate that the historians had to convince their readers of there being a need for portage that outweighed the difficulty involved.

Collectively the specific historical instances of ship carting and the three general references all indicate the unusual stratagems of ancient history that were worthy of mention precisely because the movement of enormous, multi-ton military galleys was logistically extraordinary. Scholars have consequently rejected the view that commercial vessels were carried over the Isthmus and even undercut the role of the diolkos in the occasional ship transfers of military vessels. In the articles previously cited, Lohmann, Koutsoumba, and Nakas have argued, in fact, that fleets were transferred over felled trees or greased wooden beams. As those authors note, such techniques are known from other accounts of portaging in antiquity and correspond well to the textual accounts of portaging that survive.

If the diolkos was never central to a grand operation of conveying commercial vessels and military fleets, other interpretations of the road have proven equally problematic. Since Cook and MacDonald debated the subject in the 1980s,[28] scholars have accepted that the portage road was used primarily for the transfer of cargoes and freights.[29] Some have interpreted the road as a portage for moving divisible commodities such as grain, oil, and wine transported in baskets and amphoras during the Hellenistic and Roman eras, but the argument has not convinced everyone because of logistical difficulties: breaking down several entire cargo ships, after all, would have required numerous porters, hundreds of ox-drawn carts, and many days' time. Moreover, the ceramic evidence from excava-

---

27. Stealth offense: Thucydides, *Pelop.* 3.8–16 (428 BCE) and 8.1–10 (412 BCE); Polybius, *Hist.* 4.19.7-9 for Demetrius of Pharos (220 BCE). Ambition: Polybius, *Hist.* 5.101.4 on Philip V (217 BCE). Hasty retreat: Livy, *Ab urbe cond.* 42.16 on King Eumenes's haste (172 BCE).

28. R. M. Cook, "Archaic Greek Trade: Three Conjectures," *JHS* 99 (1979): 152-55; Brian R. MacDonald, "The Diolkos," *JHS* 106 (1986): 191–95.

29. For fuller discussion with references, see Pettegrew, "The *Diolkos* of Corinth," 549–74.

tions and surveys in the Corinthia and neighboring regions of the Corinthian and Saronic Gulfs simply does not bear out the view that the land bridge facilitated the westward and eastward flows of commodities. Other scholars have more plausibly argued that the road was used for the movement of heavy construction material such as timber, building stone, and marbles, destined for monumental buildings in the Panhellenic sanctuaries, but even this scenario proves logistically problematic when one thinks through the operation necessary to lift multi-ton columns and stones into and out of ships and transfer overland. Would the trip around Malea not have been the easier operation?

In my view, the principal purpose of the road in late archaic to Hellenistic times had less to do with shipping goods through the region than moving goods to a particular place, the Panhellenic sanctuary of Poseidon at Isthmia.[30] This site was the major destination in Corinthian territory when Corinth was an independent polis and during the period of Macedonian rule. It functioned as the site of biennial athletic contests and religious festivals and occasional large-scale military encampments. Provisioning the population gathered there on a semiregular basis required initial investments in physical roads by which carts laden with provisions could move through the sandy coastal region of the Isthmus. The roads would also have facilitated the movement of heavy building materials for investments in the monumental buildings at Isthmia.

Read in this light, the diolkos was a feature of the territory of the Greek polis that functioned within a regional system of provisioning and marketing to repeated temporary swells in population in encampments in the Isthmian district. The termination of the Greek polis by the Romans in 146 BCE permanently altered this regional network, ended the contests and festival at the Isthmus for two centuries, and terminated the functional value of the road. By the time the apostle Paul arrived on the scene, the road that scholars call the diolkos had not serviced crowds at the Isthmus for two centuries. The limestone pavements visible at the Corinthian Gulf may have continued to facilitate some direct cross-Isthmus traffic, but the road was already an "ancient" monument in the landscape that had little adaptive value for the new colony. The diolkos, in this view, has no place in

---

30. Pettegrew, "The *Diolkos* of Corinth," 562–63; developed most fully in Pettegrew, *Isthmus of Corinth*.

setting the scene for Pauline Corinth except as an interesting and curious feature of a vanished set of regional relationships.

The Corinthia, however, was a transit zone for goods throughout the first century CE, although not in the way that scholars have imagined. Cargoes never moved over and beyond the Isthmus in a kind of constant voluminous flow, for example.[31] Ceramic studies have highlighted how the Isthmus hindered more intergulf trade than it facilitated,[32] as regions west of Corinth generally participated in the western markets of Italy and the Ionian and Adriatic Seas, while eastern regions largely exchanged goods produced in the Saronic Gulf and Aegean basin. The narrowness of the Isthmus clearly facilitated westward movements of luxury products for consumption in Rome, but exchanges of this sort formed a tiny proportion of the main trade in bulk commodities such as oil, wine, and grain. The limited presence of western goods in eastern regions arguably reflects the movement and tastes of Roman citizens, who resided in cities east of Corinth and desired table wares over eastern ones. Most of the traffic in commodities and luxuries, however, was destined for consumption in the growing urban center at Corinth and passed through the well-built harbors Lechaion and Kenchreai, not the terminal nodes of the diolkos. Goods that moved beyond the region to distant destinations were purchased in the marketplaces of Corinth, Lechaion, Kenchreai, and Isthmia, not transferred over the diolkos through a putative trans-shipment business. Finally, the movements of eastern and western goods were never a constant flow, as the geographer Strabo's description of Corinth may imply, but shifted frequently in the early history of the colony.[33]

---

31. Pettegrew, "The *Diolkos* of Corinth," 549–74.

32. E.g., John W. Hayes, "Notes on Roman Pottery in Greece and the Aegean," *Rei Cretariae Romanae Fautorum acta* 5–6 (1963): 31–36; Mark L. Lawall, "Consuming the West in the East: Amphoras of the Western Mediterranean in the Aegean before 86 BC," in *Old Pottery in a New Century: Innovating Perspectives on Roman Pottery Studies*, ed. Daniele Malfitana, Jeroen Poblome, and John Lund (Catania: Ibam, 2006), 265–85.

33. Kathleen W. Slane, "Corinth's Roman Pottery: Quantification and Meaning," in Williams and Bookidis, *Corinth, the Centenary*, 321–35; Slane, "East-West Trade in Fine Wares and Commodities: The View from Corinth," *Rei Cretariae Romanae Fautorum Acta* 36 (2000): 299–312; and Slane, "Corinthian Ceramic Imports: The Changing Patterns of Provincial Trade in the First and Second Centuries A.D.," in *The Greek Renaissance in the Roman Empire*, ed. Susan Walker and Averil Cameron (London: Institute of Classical Studies, 1989), 219–25.

In all probability, the only thing that moved over the Isthmus constantly and in considerable volume in the first century CE was human traffic between Italy and the provinces of the east.[34] These human patterns of movement, however, were neither timeless nor essential features of Corinthian geography, as ancient and modern writers have imagined, but had been established through the Roman conquest and incorporation of the territories of the eastern Mediterranean. In the lands of Greece, the foundation of Roman colonies at Patrai, Dyme, and Corinth in the later first century BCE and early first century CE created a string of nodes linking Italians traveling between their motherland and the eastern provinces. The populations of these colonies had strong interest at first in maintaining connections with their homeland, and Roman elites who traveled eastward to govern provinces moved along a chain of Italian connection, familiar culture and language, and comfortable places for repose. As these colonies grew in the mid- to late first century CE, of course, they became truly cosmopolitan centers of population and social complexity that also created niche communities of eastern people, such as Greeks, Jews, Egyptians, and Phoenicians, as well as particular occupational groups such as craftsmen and artisans. Corinth was experiencing a new moment of growth in the 50s CE as the tent maker from Tarsus was establishing his churches in the city. It was also at that moment that the elite of the region began to make their initial preparations for the visit of another outsider, the emperor of Rome.

The Canal

The emperor Nero's canal project of 66–68 CE has received surprisingly little attention in the literature of the early Christian communities of Corinth. Scholars have occasionally noted the canal project as another indicator of the region's potential connectivity and commercial character,[35] but most have simply overlooked the enterprise as irrelevant to the apos-

---

34. See Pettegrew, *Isthmus of Corinth*.
35. As noted earlier, the canal has functioned to illustrate what the region *might* have been for east–west travel and trade. E.g., Edwin H. Robertson, *Corinthians 1 and 2*, J. B. Phillips' Commentaries 7 (New York: Macmillan, 1973), 12; C. K. Barrett, *A Commentary on the Second Epistle to the Corinthians*, BNTC (New York: Harper & Row, 1973), 1; Jerome Murphy-O'Connor, *St. Paul's Corinth*, 88–89; Ciampa and Rosner, *First Letter to the Corinthians*, 2.

tle's Corinthian correspondence. This is striking, considering that the canal enterprise marked one of the most dramatic moments in the history of the city and territory in the first century CE and no doubt had enormous effects on horizons of the early Christian churches at Corinth. The emperor's presence in the small community of Corinth for an extensive period would have presented the first Christian communities there with a range of problems.

The eclipse of the canal project in contemporary scholarship owes much, of course, to the generally negative treatment of the enterprise in the first and second centuries CE. According to later historians and biographers, Nero's enterprise to cut a canal through the Isthmus of Corinth was an impulsive and unplanned project that was doomed to failure from the start. As later writers such as the historian Dio Cassius imagined it, Nero came to Greece in the final years of his reign on a pleasure tour to perform in the Greek athletic festivals through singing, acting, and the chariot race. Beholding the Isthmus, Nero became seized by a sudden lust to cut it, and he immediately set to work to penetrate the land using thousands of slaves (Dio Cassius, *Hist. rom.* 63.16.1). Dramatic portents such as bleeding earth, phantoms, and loud groans across the territory should have shown Nero that the project was sacrilege, but the emperor instead doggedly committed himself to an enterprise that would prove impossible. Contemporary and later writers could hardly miss that the Corinth canal project was the last major engineering endeavor of Nero's reign before his suicide in June 68 CE: the canal marked a fitting, ultimate rapacious act to a life of extravagance, impiety, and megalomania.

Modern scholars once followed the ancient sources in imagining Nero "at play" in a project that was wasteful and unrealistic, carried out simply for "the love of the impossible" (Tacitus, *Ann.* 15.42),[36] but the material evidence—500,000 m^3 of earth and stone removed during the extraction (see below)—speaks to a seriousness of motivation and enterprise. Recent studies, in fact, have seen the enterprise as an expression of the emperor's philhellenism, a conscious move to promote trade for the sake of Greek merchants, and an act of emulation of powerful men such as Periander, Demetrius Poliorcetes, Julius Caesar, and Caligula, who had consid-

---

36. See discussion in Susan E. Alcock, "Nero at Play? The Emperor's Grecian Odyssey," in *Reflections of Nero*, ed. Jaś Elsner and Jamie Masters (Chapel Hill: University of North Carolina Press, 1994), 98–111.

ered, planned, or attempted the feat.[37] This interpretation highlights the endeavor as a serious one but is based on the same problematic, essentialist vision of the Corinthian Isthmus outlined earlier; in the timeless view, a highly connective territory constantly tempted men of power to pierce it to create a superhighway for east–west trade. The interpretation that I propose here—the historically contingent view—considers the material record of the Isthmus and draws attention to the particular historical contexts that demanded, generated, and supported this major imperial enterprise.

The material evidence for the canal project derives from Béla Gerster's record of the ancient remains made before the modern Corinth canal project commenced in 1882 and from geological studies of the Isthmus (fig. 3). Gerster was an engineer from Hungary who produced a careful account of the physical remains of the cuts and mounds left by Nero's work crews. As

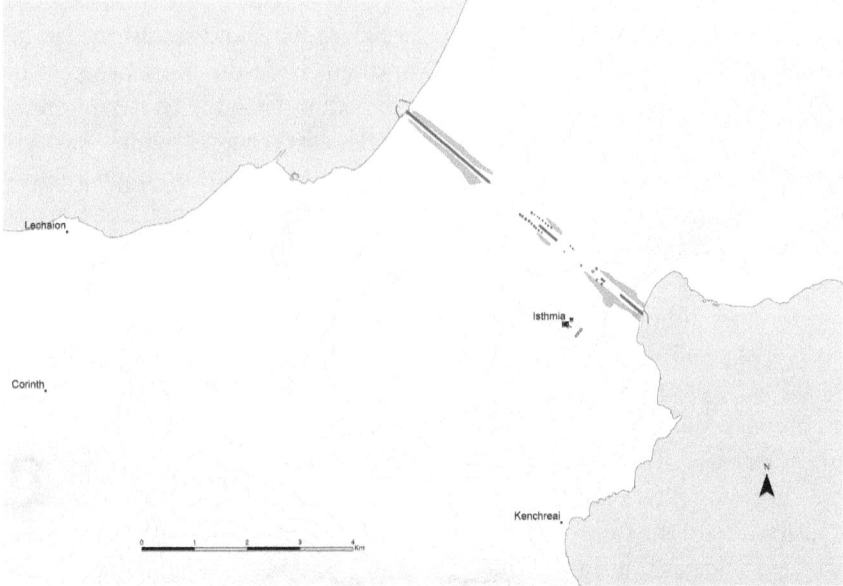

Figure 3. Map of the Isthmus showing the remains of Nero's canal recorded by Gerster. Dark lines and circles represent trenches and pits left by the ancient excavators. Light gray shade marks the parallel spoil heaps.

---

37. E.g., Engels, *Roman Corinth*, 59–60; Edward Champlin, *Nero* (Cambridge: Harvard University Press, 2003), 136–37; Jürgen Malitz, *Nero* (Malden, MA: Blackwell, 2005), 93–94; David C. A. Shotter, *Nero* (London: Routledge, 2005), 55.

the chief engineer of the modern canal project, Gerster concerned himself with recording the traces of the ancient remains before they were obliterated by the modern canal. In 1882, he wrote a brief article about his investigation that he later revised for his 1896 book on the modern canal.[38] Between the article and the book, he included a detailed summary of the ancient cuttings, a map of the Isthmus, photos of ancient discoveries, and computations of the volume of debris removed. The careful record of the ancient works sheds significant light on the nature of the ancient enterprise, especially when considered against our knowledge of the geological strata of the territory.

Gerster's description and plan of the emperor's canal shows that the cuts, pits, and spoil mounds extended over two-thirds of the Isthmus.[39] The trenches and pits were uneven. Many were as wide as 40–50 m, but some were narrower; most reached shallow depths of 2–3 m, but some penetrated 30–40 m down. Since the Isthmus is mainly a rocky massif of 80 m above sea level (masl) consisting of thick strata of blue and pale marl and overlying deposits of limestone, conglomerate, and sandstone, some zones were easier to excavate. The workmen made the most progress in the alluvial and sandy coastal zones of the Isthmus; in the western trench, excavation even cut a kilometer-long canal below sea level (which was evidently inundated with water at the time of construction). In higher elevations of rocky limestone, sandstone, conglomerate, and marl, the crews made slow progress removing the stone. Across the ridgetop, where the elevation of 60–80 masl runs over the course of several kilometers, the work crews did not cut any trenches but sunk twenty-eight pits in parallel lines spaced 45–50 m north and south of the intended canal's central axis.

The physical evidence suggests that the work crews clearly made an impressive start to their initiative but had an enormous amount of work ahead of them. They removed over 500,000 m^3 of debris, over half of which was limestone, sandstone, conglomerate, and marl. The consistent maximum width of the canal cuts at 40 m across (twice the width of the modern canal) indicates that the engineers had in mind a channel of at least that

---

38. Béla Gerster, "L'isthme de Corinthe: Tentatives de percement dans l'antiquité," *BCH* (1884): 225–32; Gerster, *L'isthme de Corinthe et son percement* (Budapest: Márkus, 1896).

39. The following summarizes an argument developed fully in Pettegrew, *Isthmus of Corinth*. All of the following numerical figures are derived from chapter 7 of that work, which relates Gerster's description (1884) to the local geology of the region.

width that would allow plentiful room for ships of substantial size to pass. A trench 40 m wide running 5 m below sea level would have required the removal of about 10,000,000 m³ of spoil. In this case, the 500,000 m³ of earth and stone removed by ancient crews formed only 5 percent of the total volume. The amount of time necessary to remove the remaining 4.2 million m³ of stone depends largely on the work force gathered. The historian Josephus notes that Nero's general Vespasian sent six thousand Jewish male prisoners to Nero after the capture of Taricheae in the Galilee in September 67 (Josephus, *B.J.* 3.540). Since the Praetorian Guard was also evidently involved, as were gangs of political prisoners (Suetonius, *Nero* 19.2; Philostratus, *Vit. Apoll.* 5.19; *Nero* 3–4), the work force at full capacity may have reached eight to ten thousand individuals, including prisoners, soldiers, and local paid or conscripted laborers. A work force of eight thousand might have excavated the remaining debris in about twenty years of constant work.

Other evidence speaks to the longevity of the work at the Isthmus. Gerster documented twenty-eight shafts across the ridge of the Isthmus that were typically 3 m in dimension and spaced at intervals of 40–45 m. Gerster excavated two of them and found they plunged 40 m into the rock. The engineer later calculated, on the basis of the method of picking and the character of material extracted (sandstone, limestone, conglomerate, marl, and marly limestone), that these shafts would have required at least four months of continuous work to excavate and, if workers were given some time to rest and recover, six or seven months.[40] Gerster's estimate of four months is based on a faster rate of quarrying and mining through limestone and sandstone than is typically used today (.37–.47 m³ of stone/person/day).[41] Accepting the more conservative figures for cutting soft limestone, a team of four excavating in a shaft of 3 x 3 m could have reached a depth of 40 m in about eight months.

---

40. Gerster, *L'isthme de Corinthe*, 44–45.
41. A. Trevor Hodge, "Engineering Works," in *Handbook of Ancient Water Technology*, ed. Örjan Wikander (Leiden: Brill, 2000b), 70; Klaus Grewe, *Licht am Ende des Tunnels: Planung und Trassierung im antiken Tunnelbau* (Mainz am Rhein: von Zabern, 1998), 290–93; Grewe, "Tunnels and Canals," in *Oxford Handbook of Engineering and Technology in the Classical World*, ed. John Peter Oleson (Oxford: Oxford University Press, 2008), 323, 319–36. For full discussion with references, see Pettegrew, *Isthmus of Corinth*.

In Gerster's final opinion, Nero's engineers determined a good course of action for excavating the canal.[42] They worked inward from the coasts, gradually attacking the higher elevations and leaving the central ridge intact. Gerster documented twenty-eight shafts on the ridge, located for the most part where the trenches stop, and they appear in elevations over 60 m above sea level. Spaced at intervals of 40–45 m from one another and from the central axis of the canal path, they most likely represent a line of vertical shafts intended to create two underground horizontal tunnels deep within the rocky Isthmus. The *qanat* method, or the "manhole" approach to tunneling, was widely adopted in the ancient Mediterranean and Near East and employed frequently by Roman engineers for digging aqueduct, road, and drainage tunnels in Italy and the provinces.[43] On the Corinthian Isthmus, as the enormous work force gradually attacked the ridge from each side, working toward one another, tunnelers were planning to dig down and then out to link the western canal trench with the eastern one, probably at or just above sea level. Tunneling was a good way of eliminating uncertainties in the project by establishing control over the local geology, determining the presence of subterranean water sources such as springs, connecting the eastern and western work sites of the Corinth canal, facilitating the movement of debris at ground level, and providing a more accurate estimate of the difference in sea level between the Corinthian and Saronic Gulfs. However, the decision to tunnel may have also been part of an even more ambitious plan to create parallel ship tunnels through the rockiest plateau of the Isthmus. Canal tunnels over a distance of a kilometer and a half would have eliminated 50 percent of the material needing excavation, saving 4.8 million m^3, or about eleven years of excavation.

Gerster rightly concluded that the extensive zones of quarried stone and the total quantity of spoil proved that Nero's canal attempt marked a concerted and well-planned attack on the Isthmus that pointed to a serious purpose. The extensive planning, the creation of massive work crews, the

---

42. Gerster, "L'isthme de Corinthe," 229; Gerster, *L'isthme de Corinthe*, 41–42, 54–57. Nero's canal line was the most efficient, for it required the removal of the least amount of debris.

43. See, for example, A. Trevor Hodge, "Qanats," in Wikander, *Handbook of Ancient Water Technology*, 35–38; Grewe, "Tunnels and Canals," 323–33; Andrew I. Wilson, "Hydraulic Engineering and Water Supply," in Oleson, *Oxford Handbook of Engineering*, 290–93.

establishment of work camps, and the coordination of fresh water and provisions indicate a dedication of resources over an extended period of planning and execution of six months to a year or more. Scholars have found a serious motivation that matches the magnitude of the project within the context of the emperors' interest in improving food supply routes to provision Rome.[44] Nero himself was concerned with supplying Rome with grain from the east in the wake of the loss of corn ships to storms in 62 CE and grain supplies in the disastrous fire of Rome in 64. Indeed, the Black Sea region was just beginning to supply Rome with grain in the early 60s CE, and the Corinth canal was clearly intended to make this trade easier.[45] The emperor's decision to canalize the Isthmus, in short, was neither a whimsical move nor an act to fulfill or emulate predecessors but a carefully planned enterprise carried out for the specific reason of food supply in the 60s CE.[46]

The project's cessation soon after the emperor's departure to Rome in the year 67 CE inevitably branded the enterprise a colossal and tragic failure that mangled and marred a sacred landscape at the heart of Greece.[47] The work crews left behind a series of gouges in the territory, sometimes 30 m deep, dangerous shafts over the central ridge, and towering mounds of debris rising 20 to 30 m. The canal project even changed the main routes into and out of the Peloponnese. It sliced through the path of the old diolkos road on the Corinthian Gulf (as well as ancient cemeteries of the Greek period) and bisected the coastal road on the Saronic Gulf. All pedestrians now had to wind their way around trenches and mounds that marked the "tangible symbols of imperial domination."[48]

---

44. K. R. Bradley, *Suetonius' Life of Nero: An Historical Commentary* (Brussels: Latomus, 1978), 115–16; Miriam T. Griffin, *Nero: The End of a Dynasty* (New Haven: Yale University Press, 1985), 108–9, 262–63; Werner Johannowsky, "Appunti Su Alcune Infrastrutture Dell'annona Romana Tra Nerone e Adriano," *Bollettino di Archeologia* 4 (1990): 1, 10; Alcock "Nero at Play," 102.

45. Griffin, *Nero*, 108; Peter Garnsey, *Famine and Food Supply in the Graeco-Roman World: Responses to Risk and Crisis* (Cambridge: Cambridge University Press, 1988), 224, 230.

46. I cannot agree with Murphy-O'Connor (*St. Paul's Corinth*, 117–18) that Nero was uninterested in the canal project or that the project was initiated by local aristocrats.

47. Later ancient writers consistently criticized the project, for example, Pausanias, *Descr.* 2.1.5.

48. Alcock, "Nero at Play," 102.

Yet, the emperor's visit and his canal project also developed the landscape through large-scale investment in specific places on the Isthmus and patterns of intensive settlement.[49] In the decade leading up to Nero's arrival, a number of spaces at the site of Isthmia were newly constructed or repaired and expanded, such as the shrine to Palaimon, the stadium, and the theater.[50] In the same period, work crews evidently revamped the main Corinth–Megara road at Isthmia and erected a massive triple arch to serve as a highly visible monument articulating a new boundary to the Peloponnese.[51] The presence of a massive force of at least ten thousand laborers for a year, moreover, demanded reliable food and water supply, camps, and infrastructure to support their work. The enlargement and expansion of the basins at the harbor of Lechaion probably date to this period, as Romano has suggested from his study of the planned settlement at the harbor with its *insulae* and wide roads, as well as a new centuriation of the entire territory.[52] Patterns of settlement across the countryside dating to the mid- to late first century CE point to explosive growth of population in comparison with the previous century.[53] Whether these patterns represent the settlement of Jewish slaves in the territory,[54] the growth of villa culture, or the settlement of veterans in the Flavian period, the rural population seems to have swelled beginning in the third quarter of the first century.

---

49. Romano has summarized some of this evidence ("City Planning, Centuriation, and Land Division," 294–95, 298; "Roman Surveyors in Corinth," 76–81) for new construction in the region the late 60s or 70s in the context of Nero's visit to Corinth and Flavian settlement and centuriation of the land. For further discussion, see Pettegrew, *The Isthmus of Corinth*.

50. Elizabeth R. Gebhard, "The Isthmian Games and the Sanctuary of Poseidon in the Early Empire," in *The Corinthia in the Roman Period: Including the Papers Given at a Symposium Held at The Ohio State University on 7–9 March, 1991*, ed. Timothy E. Gregory (Ann Arbor: Journal of Roman Archaeology, 1993), 78–94; Gebhard, *The Theater at Isthmia* (Chicago: University of Chicago Press, 1973); Elizabeth R. Gebhard, Frederick P. Hemans, and John W. Hayes, "University of Chicago Excavations at Isthmia, 1989: III," *Hesperia* 67 (1998): 416–33, 444–46.

51. Gebhard, Hemans, and Hayes, "University of Chicago Excavations," 408–22; Timothy E. Gregory and Harrianne Mills, "The Roman Arch at Isthmia," *Hesperia* 53 (1984): 426–29.

52. Romano, "City Planning, Centuriation, and Land Division," 297.

53. Pettegrew, "Corinthian Suburbia."

54. David Gilman Romano, "Urban and Rural Planning in Roman Corinth," in *Urban Religion in Roman Corinth : Interdisciplinary Approaches*, ed. Daniel N. Schowalter and Steven J. Friesen (Cambridge: Harvard University Press, 2005), 53.

The emperor had come to town, and the region would never again be the same. The emperor's grand ambition to canalize the Isthmus of Corinth and change the nature of east–west concourse ultimately failed, but not for lack of trying. In fact, the project sparked a range of new building projects in town and territory either in preparation for Nero's visit, in conjunction with the canal enterprise, or in the reign of Vespasian. Many of these new construction projects, such as those at Isthmia, were intended to be part of a large-scale remaking of the landscape. The failure left ugly scars across the region but also brought new life to the countryside through scattered farms, population increase, and the monumentalization of Isthmia.

Territory, Polis, and Ekklesiai

Our discussion to this point has highlighted the problems of conceiving the diolkos and the canal as changeless features of Corinthian territory. Each has functioned in modern scholarship as a prop to underpin conventional views of the Isthmus as a timeless landscape oriented toward commercial enterprise through a constant geographic position and Corinth as a city destined for commercial greatness. The unfinished ancient canal has signaled the full *potential* of the landscape for long-distance travel and trade—only realized in the completion of the modern canal in 1896—while the diolkos has embodied the region's *actual* role in facilitating commerce. Among New Testament scholars, the diolkos especially and the canal less commonly have been used to set the scene for the apostle's mission to Corinth, the maritime character of the Christian communities, and the problems of division faced by the community of believers. Geographic determinism lurks behind many depictions of the polis and ekklesia in the first century.

The contingent perspective, on the other hand, substitutes a static view of the *landscape as backdrop* with a dynamic vision of *territory in change* and thereby offers a fresh perspective on the relationship between city, territory, and Christian community. Viewed historically, the diolkos was constructed and functioned within the regional framework of the classical and Hellenistic polis, not the long-distant trade networks of the early Roman Empire; trade, as we have noted, passed through the harbors of Lechaion and Kenchreai. The Corinth canal project was intended to meet a particular problem, shoring up the grain supply to Rome in the 60s CE. A historical approach to regional connectivity inverts previous interpretations of territory by showing that the famous diolkos has no bearing on the early Christian communities of the first century, while the overlooked canal project must have influenced the experience and outlook of the early Christian communities.

A historical approach to territory also provides perspective on a range of issues related to the early Christian ekklesiai at Corinth. To touch on several of the obvious ones, Paul's reasons for coming to Corinth had less to do with the imagined timeless geographic characteristic of the location than the city's particular place within the network of redefined networks of trade and human movements in the Roman Empire. The Isthmus lay on maritime and pedestrian routes between east and west that had gained newfound value since the Augustan age as the regular path of movement of Roman citizens and provincials between Italy and the eastern provinces. Corinth's advantageous position, in other words, had less to do with its timeless geographic centrality between east and west than the developing networks of travel and trade in the early Roman Empire. Corinth occupied a critical transition zone especially in the movement of people, but also in a trickle of goods, to the province of Italy and the capital at Rome. Nero sought to open up this same axis of movement in his failed canal project a decade later.

The city that Paul and his associates inhabited, moreover, was itself undergoing an important period of change in the mid-first century and was soon to be transformed through the emperor's visit. This was not the fully developed and populous city of the second century CE, but it was also no longer a baby colony. Had Paul's mission to Corinth occurred a generation earlier, he would have found a very small urban community; a generation later, a developed provincial capital. The apostle's stay occurred just at the moment the city was shedding its colonial garb and taking on the appearance of a provincial capital through new construction and a growing population. The presence of Paul, his associates, and a diverse population of Greeks, Jews, Italians, and Phoenicians were themselves indications of new urban growth and greater cosmopolitan character. This backdrop of change established both the missionaries within the city through their occupations and the social networks in which the company moved.

The territory that Paul encountered also had a long history that had gained new value within a Roman context. The trans-Isthmus road known as the diolkos, for example, may have been defunct and had little place in the new regional economy—we should no longer name it as part of the cultural backdrops of the early Christian community. The Panhellenic site of Isthmia had just become the site of athletic contests in the 40s CE but was still a pale shadow of the site it had been in the archaic to Hellenistic periods; its full revival would begin only in the 50s–60s CE, largely in conjunction with Nero's visit. Besides the growing urban center, the principal sites in the landscape in the mid-first century CE were the harbors Lechaion and Kenchreai.[55] The former was so close to Corinth that its development was overshadowed by the urban center, but the latter was just becoming a notable community that hailed some autonomy from Corinth as a satellite harbor-town based in Aegean trade networks.[56] At a three-hour walk from Corinth, it is Kenchreai that developed its own Christian community with some distinct identity. The value of eastern trade for the Roman city, however, constantly united that harbor with the urban center through the daily movements of laborers, farmers, construction workers, porters, and traders. The development of the region in the 40s–60s CE dispersed Christian believers across the territory through settlement, trade, labor, and movement.

Finally, the historical approach advocated in this paper raises new questions about the meanings of the imperial presence for the region's nascent Christian communities. What did it mean to have the emperor in town with his Praetorian Guard and retinue immediately following the persecution of Christians in Rome (Suetonius, *Nero* 16.2; Tacitus, *Ann.* 15.54)? What did it mean to the Jews and Christ-followers of Corinth to have thousands of Jewish slaves from the Galilee laboring in the countryside to construct the emperor's canal? How did Corinthian believers read Paul's teachings about the rich and poor, powerful and weak, privilege and the cross, the humble and exalted, Christ the judge, sexual immorality, worship and idolatry, freedom and slavery, and affliction and persecution in light of the emperor's visit in 66–67 CE? While such questions await further study, it is clear that the rural world must become a more central part of our explorations of polis and ekklesia. It is no longer acceptable to

---

55. Pettegrew "The Diolkos and the Emporion," 126–42.

56. For recent discussion, see Jospeh L. Rife, "Religion and Society at Roman Kenchreai," in *Corinth in Context: Comparative Studies on Religion and Society*, ed. Steven J. Friesen, Daniel Schowalter and James C. Walters, NovTSup 134 (Leiden: Brill, 2010), 391–432; Elena Korka and Jospeh L. Rife, "Systematic Excavations Undertaken by the Ministry of Culture and the American School of Classical Studies at Athens to Promote the Roman Cemetery on the Koutsongila Ridge at Kenchreai," in *The Corinthia and the Northeast Peloponnese: Topography and History from Prehistory until the End of Antiquity*, ed. Konstantin Kissas and Wolf-Dietrich Niemeier (Munich: Hirmer, 2013), 285–97.

ignore the territory as irrelevant to the concerns of the first urban Christians, but our views of the territory must also allow ample room for contingency, change, and historical developments.

Works Cited

Alcock, Susan E. "Nero at Play? The Emperor's Grecian Odyssey." Pages 98–111 in *Reflections of Nero*. Edited by Jaś Elsner and Jamie Masters. Chapel Hill: University of North Carolina Press, 1994.

Barrett, C. K. *A Commentary on the Second Epistle to the Corinthians*. BNTC. New York: Harper & Row, 1973.

Bradley, K. R. "Nero's Retinue in Greece, A.D. 66/67." *Illinois Classical Studies* 4 (1979): 152–57.

———. *Suetonius' Life of Nero: An Historical Commentary*. Brussels: Latomus, 1978.

Champlin, Edward. *Nero*. Cambridge: Harvard University Press, 2003.

Ciampa, Roy E., and Brian S. Rosner. *The First Letter to the Corinthians*. Pillar New Testament Commentary. Grand Rapids: Eerdmans, 2010.

Clarke, Adam. *The New Testament, of Our Lord and Saviour Jesus Christ: Containing the Text, Taken from the Most Correct Copies of the Present Authorised Translation, Including the Marginal Readings and Parallel Texts, with a Commentary and Critical Notes; Designed as a Help to a Better Understanding of the Sacred Writings*. Vol. 2. London: Butterworth, 1817.

Conybeare, W. J., and J. S. Howson. *The Life and Epistles of St. Paul*. 2 vols. London: Longman, Brown, Green, & Longmans, 1852.

Conzelmann, Hans. *1 Corinthians: A Commentary on the First Epistle to the Corinthians*. Translated by James W. Leitch. Hermeneia. Philadelphia: Fortress, 1975.

Cook, R. M. "Archaic Greek Trade: Three Conjectures." *JHS* 99 (1979): 152–55.

———. "A Further Note on the Diolkos." Pages 65–68 in *Studies in Honor of T. B. L. Webster I*. Edited by J. H. Betts, J. T. Hooker, and J. R. Green. Bristol: Bristol Classical, 1986.

Cramer, J. A. *A Geographical and Historical Description of Ancient Greece: With a Map, and a Plan of Athens*. Vol. 3. Oxford: Clarendon, 1828.

Engels, Donald W. *Roman Corinth: An Alternative Model for the Ancient City*. Chicago: University of Chicago Press, 1990.

Finlay, George. *The History of Greece: From Its Conquest by the Crusaders to Its Conquest by the Turks and of the Empire of the Trebizond 1204–1461.* Edinburgh: Blackwood, 1851.
Frend, William H. C. "The Winning of the Countryside." *JEH* 18 (1967): 1–14.
Garnsey, Peter. *Famine and Food Supply in the Graeco-Roman World: Responses to Risk and Crisis.* Cambridge: Cambridge University Press, 1988.
Gebhard, Elizabeth R. "The Isthmian Games and the Sanctuary of Poseidon in the Early Empire." Pages 78–94 in *The Corinthia in the Roman Period: Including the Papers Given at a Symposium Held at The Ohio State University on 7–9 March, 1991.* Edited by Timothy E. Gregory. Ann Arbor: Journal of Roman Archaeology, 1993.
———. *The Theater at Isthmia.* Chicago: University of Chicago Press, 1973.
Gebhard, Elizabeth R., Frederick P. Hemans, and John W. Hayes. "University of Chicago Excavations at Isthmia, 1989: III." *Hesperia* 67 (1998): 405–56.
Gerster, Béla. *L'isthme de Corinthe et son percement.* Budapest: Márkus, 1896.
———. "L'isthme de Corinthe : Tentatives de percement dans l'antiquité." *BCH* (1884): 225–32.
Gregory, Timothy E., and Harrianne Mills. "The Roman Arch at Isthmia." *Hesperia* 53 (1984): 407–45.
Grewe, Klaus. "Tunnels and Canals." Pages 319–36 in *Oxford Handbook of Engineering and Technology in the Classical World.* Edited by John Peter Oleson. Oxford: Oxford University Press, 2008.
———. *Licht am Ende des Tunnels: Planung und Trassierung im antiken Tunnelbau.* Mainz am Rhein: von Zabern, 1998.
Griffin, Miriam T. *Nero: The End of a Dynasty.* New Haven: Yale University Press, 1985.
Hafemann, Scott J. *2 Corinthians.* NIV Application Commentary. Grand Rapids: Zondervan, 2000.
Hahn, Scott, and Curtis Mitch. *The First and Second Letters of Saint Paul to the Corinthians, with Introduction, Commentary, and Notes.* Ignatius Catholic Study Bible. San Francisco: Ignatius Press, 2004.
Hansen, Mogens Herman, and Thomas Heine Nielsen. "Meaning and Reference of the Word *Polis.*" Pages 39–46 in *An Inventory of Archaic and Classical Poleis.* Edited by Mogens Herman Hansen and Thomas Heine Nielsen. Oxford: Oxford University Press, 2004.

Hayes, John W. "Notes on Roman Pottery in Greece and the Aegean." *Rei Cretariae Romanae Fautorum acta* 5–6 (1963): 31–36.

Higgins, Michael D., and Reynold A. Higgins. *A Geological Companion to Greece and the Aegean.* London: Duckworth, 1996.

Hill, Herbert. *The Roman Middle Class in the Republican Period.* Oxford: Blackwell, 1952.

Hodge, A. Trevor. "Engineering Works." Pages 67–93 in *Handbook of Ancient Water Technology.* Edited by Örjan Wikander. Leiden: Brill, 2000.

———. "Qanats." Pages 35–38 in *Handbook of Ancient Water Technology.* Edited by Örjan Wikander. Leiden: Brill, 2000.

Horrell, David G., and Edward Adams. "Introduction: The Scholarly Quest for Paul's Church at Corinth: A Critical Survey." Pages 1–47 in *Christianity at Corinth: The Quest for the Pauline Church.* Edited by Edward Adams and David G. Horrell. Louisville: Westminster John Knox, 2004.

Johannowsky, Werner. "Appunti Su Alcune Infrastrutture Dell'annona Romana Tra Nerone e Adriano." *Bollettino di Archeologia* 4 (1990): 1–13.

Keener, Craig S. *1–2 Corinthians.* New Cambridge Bible Commentary. Cambridge: Cambridge University Press, 2005.

Koeppen, A. L. "Sketches of a Traveler from Greece, Constantinople, Asia Minor, Syria and Palestine—My Travels in Peloponnesus." *Mercersburg Quarterly Review* 8 (1856): 350–83.

Korka, Elena, and Joseph L. Rife. "Systematic Excavations Undertaken by the Ministry of Culture and the American School of Classical Studies at Athens to Promote the Roman Cemetery on the Koutsongila Ridge at Kenchreai." Pages 285–97 in *The Corinthia and the Northeast Peloponnese: Topography and History from Prehistory until the End of Antiquity.* Edited by Konstantin Kissas and Wolf-Dietrich Niemeier. Munich: Hirmer, 2013.

Koutsoumba, Despina, and Yannis Nakas. "Διολκος: Ενα Σημαντικο Τεχνικο Εργο Της Αρχαιοτητας [The Diolkos: A Significant Technical Achievement of Antiquity]." Pages 191–206 in *The Corinthia and the Northeast Peloponnese: Topography and History from Prehistory until the End of Antiquity.* Edited by Konstantin Kissas and Wolf-Dietrich Niemeier. Munich: Hirmer, 2013.

Lawall, Mark L. "Consuming the West in the East: Amphoras of the Western Mediterranean in the Aegean before 86 BC." Pages 265–85 in *Old*

Pottery in a New Century: Innovating Perspectives on Roman Pottery Studies. Edited by Daniele Malfitana, Jeroen Poblome, and John Lund. Catania: Ibam, 2006.

Lohmann, Hans. "Der Diolkos von Korinth—Eine Antike Schiffsschleppe?" Pages 207–30 in *The Corinthia and the Northeast Peloponnese: Topography and History from Prehistory until the End of Antiquity*. Edited by Konstantin Kissas and Wolf-Dietrich Niemeier. Munich: Hirmer, 2013.

MacDonald, Brian R. "The Diolkos." *JHS* 106 (1986): 191–95.

Malitz, Jürgen. *Nero*. Malden, MA.: Blackwell, 2005.

Meeks, Wayne A. *The First Urban Christians: The Social World of the Apostle Paul*. New Haven: Yale University Press, 1983.

Meiggs, R. *Roman Ostia*. 2nd ed. Oxford: Oxford University Press, 1973.

Minor, Mitzi L. *2 Corinthians*. Smyth & Helwys Bible Commentary. Macon, GA: Smyth & Helwys, 2009.

Montague, George T. *First Corinthians*. Catholic Commentary on Sacred Scripture. Grand Rapids: Baker Academic, 2011.

Mott, Valentine. *Travels in Europe and the East*. New York: Harper, 1842.

Murphy-O'Connor, Jerome. *St. Paul's Corinth: Texts and Archaeology*. 3rd ed. Collegeville, MN: Liturgical Press, 2002.

Nash, Robert Scott. *1 Corinthians*. Smyth & Helwys Bible Commentary. Macon, GA: Smyth & Helwys, 2009.

Pettegrew, David K. "Corinthian Suburbia: Patterns of Roman Settlement on the Isthmus." Pages 289–310 in *The Bridge of the Untiring Sea: The Corinthian Isthmus from Prehistory to Late Antiquity*. Edited by Elizabeth R. Gebhard and Timothy E. Gregory. Hesperia Supplement. Princeton: American School of Classical Studies at Athens, 2015.

———. "The Diolkos and the Emporion: How a Land Bridge Framed the Commercial Economy of Roman Corinth." Pages 126–42 in *Corinth in Contrast: Studies in Inequality*. Edited by Steven J. Friesen, Sarah James, and Daniel Schowalter. NovTSup 155. Leiden: Brill, 2013.

———. "The *Diolkos* of Corinth." *AJA* 115 (2011): 549–74.

———. *The Isthmus of Corinth: Crossroads of the Mediterranean World*. Ann Arbor: University of Michigan Press, 2016.

Rickman, Geoffrey. *The Corn Supply of Ancient Rome*. Oxford: Clarendon; New York: Oxford University Press, 1980.

Rife, Jospeh L. "Religion and Society at Roman Kenchreai." Pages 391–432 in *Corinth in Context: Comparative Studies on Religion and Society*.

Edited by Steven J. Friesen, Daniel Schowalter and James C. Walters. NovTSup 134. Leiden: Brill, 2010.

Robertson, Edwin H. *Corinthians 1 and 2*. J. B. Phillips' Commentaries 7. New York: Macmillan, 1973.

Romano, David Gilman. "City Planning, Centuriation, and Land Division in Roman Corinth: *Colonia Laus Iulia Corinthiensis* and *Colonia Iulia Flavia Augusta Corinthiensis*." Pages 279–301 in *Corinth, the Centenary: 1896–1996*. Edited by Charles K. Williams II and Nancy Bookidis. Princeton: American School of Classical Studies at Athens, 2003.

———. "Roman Surveyors in Corinth." *Proceedings of the American Philosophical Society* 150 (2006): 62–85.

———. "Urban and Rural Planning in Roman Corinth." Pages 25–59 in *Urban Religion in Roman Corinth: Interdisciplinary Approaches*. Edited by Daniel N. Schowalter and Steven J. Friesen. Cambridge: Harvard University Press, 2005.

Salmon, Edward T. *Roman Colonization under the Republic*. Ithaca, NY: Cornell University Press, 1970.

Shotter, David C. A. *Nero*. London: Routledge, 2005.

Slane, Kathleen W. "Corinth's Roman Pottery: Quantification and Meaning." Pages 321–35 in *Corinth, the Centenary: 1896–1996*. Edited by Charles K. Williams II and Nancy Bookidis. Princeton: American School of Classical Studies at Athens, 2003.

———. "Corinthian Ceramic Imports: The Changing Patterns of Provincial Trade in the First and Second Centuries A.D." Pages 219–25 in *The Greek Renaissance in the Roman Empire*. Edited by Susan Walker and Averil Cameron. London: University of London, Institute of Classical Studies, 1989.

———. "East-West Trade in Fine Wares and Commodities. The View from Corinth." *Rei Cretariae Romanae Fautorum Acta* 36 (2000): 299–312.

Verdelis, N. M. "How the Ancient Greeks Transported Ships over the Isthmus of Corinth: Uncovering the 2550-Year-Old *Diolcos* of Periander." Pages 649–51 in *Illustrated London News* (19 October 1957).

Werner, Walter. "The Largest Ship Trackway in Ancient Times: the Diolkos of the Isthmus of Corinth, Greece, and Early Attempts to Build a Canal." *International Journal of Nautical Archaeology* 26 (1997): 98–119.

Wilson, Andrew I. "Hydraulic Engineering and Water Supply." Pages 285–318 in *Oxford Handbook of Engineering and Technology in the Classical World*. Edited by John Peter Oleson. Oxford: Oxford University Press, 2008.

Witherington, Ben, III. *Conflict and Community in Corinth: A Socio-rhetorical Commentary on 1 and 2 Corinthians*. Grand Rapids: Eerdmans, 1995.

Mixed-Language Inscribing at Roman Corinth

Bradley J. Bitner

1. Introduction

On 23 November of an unknown year sometime in the second century CE, a letter of the governor of Achaia was read out from the *rostra* in the urban center of Roman Corinth.[1] Sometime later, the text by which we know the rescript was inscribed on a limestone block. Fully thirty-one of the thirty-two lines of extant text—those contextualizing and reproducing the text of the rescript itself—are in Greek; only the final line—recording the place and date of the reading out—is in Latin. At least in this instance, the things written (or proclaimed) in Roman Corinth were recorded in Greek but were punctuated by a concluding Latin postscript.

What are we to make of this "bilingual" inscription? Is it an epigraphic glimpse into larger cultural and linguistic currents in Roman Corinth? Would we, for example, be justified in drawing the conclusion that the proconsul actually drafted the decree in Greek?[2] Did a herald (*praeco*) or assistant (*apparitor*) read it out in Greek to a crowd assembled in the forum? Could we go further and surmise that he knew that more of the Corinthian auditors/readers would understand Greek than Latin so he composed it in Greek? Who commissioned the inscription and why? Where was it displayed? Why is the final line in Latin? Is this simply a holdover from the early days of the colony when Latin predominated in

---

1. IKorinthKent §306, 119–21, places this text with four others under the heading "Decrees and Rescripts," calling it "part of an official letter" with no further discussion of genre (nor any comment on the bilingual nature of the text); I use *rescript* throughout, for which, see commentary below.
2. Or had it read out for him in Greek; see below.

public administration and officially inscribed texts?[3] Or are there perhaps other ways to interpret the evidence from a Roman colony in Greece where the Greek and Latin languages, not to mention "Greek-ness" and "Roman-ness," interacted in ways that were complex linguistically, politically, materially, and culturally?

This inscription—and these questions—point us toward an overlooked yet important investigation that addresses the complex interplay of "Greek" and "Roman" in early Roman Corinth. That is, a thorough study is called for that treats the bilingual and mixed-language Corinthian inscriptions, one that systematically analyzes them in terms of archaeological and historical context(s), epigraphic genre, language use, and performative function(s).[4] In this essay I outline the shape such a study might take, first by a summary of methodological issues and then by an exploratory, detailed treatment of a few inscriptions. I begin by providing a descriptive typology that guides us to representative selection of mixed-language inscriptions. Next I define important methodological terminology and rehearse important studies of the sociolinguistic context of Roman Corinth. Then, with regard to a sample of carefully chosen mixed-language inscriptions,

---

3. "In official documents ... we might expect the Latin language would be used exclusively for some time after the language spoken in the city was largely Greek, and that Latin would never be completely supplanted by Greek as long as the Roman provincial government lasted, or at any rate until the second half of the second century" (IKorinthKent, 18).

4. I borrow the phrase "mixed language inscriptions" from Rosalinde Kearsley, with Trevor V. Evans, *Greeks and Romans in Imperial Asia: Mixed Language Inscriptions and Linguistic Evidence for Cultural Interaction until the End of AD III*, IGSK 59 (Köln: Habelt, 2001), 1–2, 147. I use "mixed language" rather than "bilingual" in order to highlight the varieties of language contact observable in this set of texts. Other important studies on multilingual inscriptions include Johannes Touloumakos, "Bilingue [Griechisch-Lateinische] Weihinschriften der römischen Zeit," Τεκμήρια 1 (1995): 79–129; James N. Adams, Mark Janse, and Simon Swain, eds., *Bilingualism in Ancient Society: Language Contact and the Written Text* (Oxford: Oxford University Press, 2002); James N. Adams, *Bilingualism and the Latin Language* (Cambridge: Cambridge University Press, 2003); Jonathan J. Price and Shlomo Naeh, "On the Margins of Culture: The Practice of Transcription in the Ancient World," in *From Hellenism to Islam: Cultural and Linguistic Change in the Ancient Near East*, ed. Hannah Cotton (Cambridge: Cambridge University Press, 2009), 257–88; Jennifer Larson, "Bilingual Inscriptions and Translation in the Ancient Mediterranean World," in *Complicating the History of Western Translation: The Ancient Mediterranean in Perspective*, ed. Siobhán McElduff and Enrica Scarrino (New York: Routledge, 2011), 50–74.

I begin the task of thorough analysis. Finally, I offer preliminary conclusions that are relevant to studies of sociolinguistics, Roman Corinth, as well as the New Testament Corinthian correspondence and research on other early Christian texts related to Corinth.

2. Typology and Selection of Inscriptions

The inscriptions discussed below as well as those incorporated in the appendix take account of published Corinthian inscriptions of which I am aware, but given the nature of Corinthian epigraphy these must be considered merely indicative rather than exhaustive.[5] The selection includes inscriptions that evince *language contact* according to the following typology in which the first three categories embrace the linguistic and physical features and the latter two relate more to performative aspects. Thus, there is some natural overlap among the categories.

1. Dual-language: a comprehensive set of inscriptions preserving text in more than one language, where both languages were inscribed as part of the same communicative act (usually Latin-Greek; varieties of more or less explicit language contact and code-switching).
2. Monolingual: inscriptions in a single language manifesting some sign of language mixture (loanwords, calques, more or less mechanical translations, or linguistic interference).[6]

---

5. Besides gathering many "stray" Corinthian inscriptions not included in IKorinthMeritt, IKorinthWest, and IKorinthKent, a thorough study must account for much unpublished material such as stamped tiles and graffiti (see further below) as well as important recent and forthcoming publications: Ronald S. Stroud, *The Sanctuary of Demeter and Kore: The Inscriptions*, vol. 18.6 of *Corinth: Results of Excavations Conducted by the American School of Classical Studies at Athens* (Princeton: American School of Classical Studies at Athens, 2013); Nancy Bookidis and Elizabeth G. Pemberton, *The Sanctuary of Demeter and Kore: The Greek Lamps and the Offering Trays*, vol. 18.7 of *Corinth: Results of Excavations Conducted by the American School of Classical Studies at Athens* (Princeton: American School of Classical Studies, 2016); and the forthcoming fascicle 3 of *IG* 4 (2nd ed.), edited by E. Sironen.

6. On loanwords and calques, see n. 9 below. Some scholars distinguish between explicit and implicit bilingualism. See James N. Adams and Simon Swain, "Introduction," in Adams, Janse, and Swain, *Bilingualism in Ancient Society*, 2 n. 8, where they

3. Multiple-use: inscriptions preserving text in more than one language but with evident reuse (and thus presumably inscribed and displayed at different times and for distinct purposes). These may evince partial erasure in a "palimpsest" final form or may be inscribed on multiple, separate surfaces.
4. Graffiti and minor objects: examples of inscribed materials (not usually included in Corinthian epigraphic corpora) in one or more languages but relevant to our conception of language contact in the Roman colony. These are highlighted separately because they are only sporadically published and are therefore often hidden from scholarly view.
5. Dual-perspective: inscriptions (each stone monolingual in itself) that offer a dual-language perspective on the same person or event.

3. Terminology

Several sociolinguistic terms appear throughout, the most important of which I define at the outset. *Linguistic interference* refers broadly to any phenomenon whereby a feature of one language is transferred to another.[7] Such interference may be observable at a variety of levels—whether phonological, lexical, or syntactical—and in inscribed texts at Corinth may occasionally be deliberate but usually appears to be unintentional. A related phenomenon is the *loanword*, namely, the result of lexical borrowing whereby a word from one language is adopted into another.[8] Between Latin and Greek in the Corinthian inscriptions this usually occurs by means of transliteration.[9]

---

associate the latter with a text that "on the face of it [is] in a single language, but there is reason to think that another language played a part in its formation."

7. Ibid., 3–7.

8. Cf. Hans Henrich Hock and Brian D. Joseph, "Lexical Borrowing," in Hock and Joseph, *Language History, Language Change, and Language Relationship: An Introduction to Historical and Comparative Linguistics* (Berlin: de Gruyter, 1996), 253–91. Martti Leiwo ("From Contact to Mixture: Bilingual Inscriptions from Italy," in Adams, Janse, and Swain, *Bilingualism in Ancient Society*, 170) draws a sharp distinction between *borrowing* and *interference* in terms of contact situation and linguistic results.

9. Adoption by transliteration distinguishes a *loanword* (e.g., THEOCOLUS → θεόκολος in IKorinthKent §§152, 194–96, 198) from a *calque* (e.g., AMICVS CAESARIS → φιλόκαισαρ in IKorinthWest §15), in which adoption by sense translations occurs.

Code-switching is an important discourse feature that may be cautiously applied to epigraphical texts.[10] It refers to instances where the same speaker (or author) within the same conversation (or text) shifts from one language to another.[11] Shifts of this kind may be key indicators of conventional or ideological pressures on language choice[12] and may create, not merely reflect, social dynamics.[13] *Diglossia*, a related notion, refers to the practice of choosing from among two possibilities a particular language when dealing with a specific *linguistic domain*, or genre of speech or writing.[14] Such domains are tacitly acknowledged within an *epigraphic community*, a group representing those members of a speech community who are involved in the inscribing of texts. Texts produced and displayed in such communities may, therefore, reflect some discourse features of spoken-language usage.[15]

See the caution on defining the term *loanword* in Jorma Kaimio, *The Romans and the Greek Language*, CHL 64 (Helsinki: Societas Scientiarum Fennica, 1979), 295–97.

10. But see G. H. R. Horsley, "The Fiction of 'Jewish Greek,'" *New Docs* 5:8–9.

11. Adams and Swain, "Introduction," 2: "the practice of using two or more languages in the same utterance"; Leiwo, 169 n. 3: "The main categories of code-switching are intersentential [at clause or sentence boundaries] and intrasentential [within a clause or phrase]." See also Martti Leiwo, "The Mixed Languages in Roman Inscriptions," in *Acta Colloquii Epigraphici Latini, Helsingiae 3–6 September 1991*, ed. Heikki Solin, Olli Salomies, and Uta-Maria Liertz, CHL 104 (Helsinki: Societas Scientiarum Fennica, 1995), 300–301.

12. James N. Adams, "Bilingualism at Delos," in Adams, Janse, and Swain, *Bilingualism in Ancient Society*, 126: "code-switching is an *ad hoc* change of languages within an utterance or piece of writing." He also uses the term *accommodation* to describe a phenomenon implied by code-switching wherein, for example, "one speaker switches from time to time into another's language as an act of solidarity or politeness" or to "project an identity."

13. Peter Auer (*Bilingual Conversation*, Pragmatics and Beyond 8 [Philadelphia: Benjamins, 1984], 20) argues that, in conversation, code-switching can be a contextualizing strategy. The pragmatics of inscribed texts might be better conceptualized in terms of performative function; see, e.g., John Ma, "Seleukids and Speech-Acts: Performative Utterances, Legitimacy and Negotiation in the World of the Maccabees," *Scripta Israelica Classica* 19 (2000): 71–112; Peter Keegan, "Texting Rome: Graffiti as Speech-Act and Cultural Discourse," in *Ancient Graffiti in Context*, ed. Jennifer A. Baird and Claire Taylor (London: Routledge, 2010), 165–90.

14. Leiwo, "Mixed Languages," 295.

15. Leiwo, "From Contact to Mixture," 170, 192–93.

Each of these sociolinguistic phenomena is relevant to aspects of language use and "identity" in Corinth and Achaia and should figure in a study of the mixed-language inscribed material of Roman Corinth.

4. The Sociolinguistic Context of Roman Corinth

From the Hellenistic era onward Corinth was an important site for the complex interaction between Greece and Rome. Polybius relates the electrifying proclamation of Greek freedom by T. Quinctius Flamininus at the Isthmian Games of 196 BCE (Polybius, *Hist.* 18.46). However, the excitement of the thronging crowds that day was followed a half-century later by the decisive reprisal to Corinthian participation in the revolt of the Achaian League. *Corinthus deletus est* was the result of Rome's response in 146 BCE, in the person of L. Mummius (Pausanias, *Descr.* 7.16.8). Nevertheless, the ruined and sparsely populated site on the Isthmus presented itself to Caesar a century later as a prime location for a Roman colonial foundation.[16] Shortly after Caesar's assassination, colonists were led out to the site by commissioners, and the new city was planted within its *territorium*, one of many such Roman colonies in Greece that would follow in the next several decades (Pausanias, *Descr.* 2.1.2; Strabo, *Geogr.* 8.6.23).

From the moment of its foundation as an iconic Caesarian colony in 44 BCE, the institutions and public administration of Corinth operated within a framework chartered by its Roman constitution.[17] For this reason, scholars rightly speak of *Roman* Corinth. Thus, public and administrative documents occur overwhelmingly and unsurprisingly in Latin. Still, as a colony near the center of Old Greece, we may also place the accent on Roman *Corinth*, especially as we take into account unofficial texts and the varieties of people composing the population.

---

16. G. D. R. Sanders, "Urban Corinth: An Introduction," in *Urban Religion in Roman Corinth*, ed. Daniel N. Schowalter and Steven J. Friesen, HTS 53 (Cambridge: Harvard University Press, 2005), 22: "at best an almost-deserted ghost town." See most recently Sarah A. James, "The Last of the Corinthians? Society and Settlement from 146 to 44 BCE," in *Corinth in Contrast: Studies in Inequality*, ed. Steven J. Friesen, Sarah A. James, and Daniel N. Schowalter, NovTSup 155 (Leiden: Brill, 2014), 17–37.

17. The growing consensus is that Corinth's constitution must have been quite close to the pattern preserved in the *leges Ursonennsis* and *Irnitana*, Flavian municipal charters found in Spain that reflect the Caesarian model for colonial foundations. See now Bradley J. Bitner, *Paul's Political Strategy in 1 Corinthians 1–4: Constitution and Covenant*, SNTSMS 163 (Cambridge: Cambridge University Press, 2015).

The works of three authors who treat the social, ethnic, and linguistic matrix of Roman Corinth provide a helpful backdrop to our consideration of language contact in the inscriptions. First, Antony Spawforth concluded that, among the Julio-Claudian colonial elite, Roman freedmen and businessmen (*negotiatores*) predominated.[18] Many had strong links to Italy, but some also had long experience and personal networks in the Greek East, particularly in places such as Delos. Despite certain aspects of "hellenization," however, Spawforth emphasizes the Romanness of the early colony and argues that the integration of Corinth as a "Roman enclave" into the larger life of the Greek region took a "significant step" forward only from the reign of Claudius onward.[19] As Spawforth acknowledges, it is problematic to generalize from the prosopography of the colonial elite to firm conclusions concerning the mixture of cultural elements in Roman Corinth.[20] This is all the more true for generalizations from officially inscribed public documents to language use in the colony and its *territorium*.

Second is a series of important studies by Benjamin M. Millis,[21] who has challenged overly simplistic views of the Corinth's Romanness and is among those who have sought to nuance the traditional emphasis on the colony's discontinuity with its Greek past.[22] His work is particularly valuable because he draws not only on the relatively well-known public inscriptions and coins but also on epitaphs, graffiti, and *dipinti*, as well as mason's and other manufacturer's marks in order to begin to sketch a more robust portrait of the Roman Corinthian population.[23] On the

---

18. Antony J. S. Spawforth, "Roman Corinth: The Formation of a Colonial Elite," in *Roman Onomastics in the Greek East: Social and Political Aspects; Proceedings of the International Colloquium on Roman Onomastics, Athens, 7–9 September 1993*, ed A. D. Rizakis, Μελητήματα 21 (Athens: Κέντρος Ἑλληνικῆς καὶ Ρωμαϊκῆς Ἀρχαιότητος τοῦ Ἐθνικοῦ Ἱδρύματος Ἐρευνῶν, 1996), 174–75. See also Spawforth, *Greece and the Augustan Cultural Revolution* (Cambridge: Cambridge University Press, 2012).

19. Spawforth, "Roman Corinth," 175.

20. But see now Jean-Sébastien Balzat and Benjamin M. Millis, "M. Antonius Aristocrates: Provincial Involvement with Roman Power in the Late 1st Century B.C.," *Hesperia* 82 (2013): 651–72.

21. Benjamin M. Millis, "The Social and Ethnic Origins of the Colonists in Early Roman Corinth," in *Corinth in Context: Comparative Studies on Religion and Society*, ed. Steven J. Friesen, Daniel N. Schowalter, and James C. Walters, NovTSup 134 (Leiden: Brill, 2010), 13–35.

22. Ibid., 13–17.

23. Ibid., 23–30, but see 27 n. 45, 28 n. 51, 29 n. 56. Millis notes (21 n. 26), that

basis of this diverse evidence,[24] Millis argues that, when private, nonelite inscribed texts are taken into account, we glimpse a broad social spectrum of the populace using Greek as their language of choice, even in the early Roman period, and this despite the use of Latin in most extant public inscriptions.[25] This use of Greek in many areas of colonial life, therefore, adds another layer of complexity to our understanding of what it means to speak of *Roman* Corinth.

Third, a recently published study by Cavan W. Concannon connects debates about identity in Roman Corinth both to the epigraphic material and the Pauline Corinthian correspondence.[26] Building on the work of Millis, Concannon emphasizes the predominance of Greek in the non-public inscribed material and among the nonelite populace.[27] He judges, "In all likelihood it was the local elite who were the most bilingual part of the population, as this flexibility allowed them to better negotiate the complicated trade routes on which Corinth sat, while the non-elite, the craftsmen, builders, merchants, farmers, and others sitting at or below the poverty line were primarily Greek speakers."[28] Importantly, for the purposes of the kind of project proposed here, Concannon places the epigraphic evidence from Roman Corinth within an adaptive and "hybrid" rhetorical framework of cultural and ethnic identity. Especially with regard to interpreting the Pauline letters to Corinth, Concannon argues that the composite picture of colonial identity to which the inscriptions contribute suggests a dynamic plurality and multiculturalism that cuts against easy categorizations of Greek or Roman.[29]

In terms of the present investigation of mixed-language inscriptions, the studies of Spawforth, Millis, and Concannon highlight the need for care

---

together with Ronald S. Stroud, he is engaged in a larger, long-term project related to a comprehensive prosopography of Corinth.

24. Millis ("Social and Ethnic Origins," 25–26) is one of few among epigraphists and ancient historians who also takes into account the early Christian Pauline correspondence with the *ekklēsia* at Corinth when thinking about language use in the colony.

25. Ibid., 27–30.

26. Cavan W. Concannon, *"When You Were Gentiles": Specters of Ethnicity in Roman Corinth and Paul's Corinthian Correspondence* (New Haven: Yale University Press, 2014).

27. Ibid., 64–74.

28. Ibid., 65.

29. Ibid., 73–74.

in handling the evidence in debates concerning language use and identity in Roman Corinth. The scholarly consensus of the late twentieth century, rightly emphasizing the Romanness of Corinth, relied almost exclusively on official, public, elite evidence. Because of this, most scholars have followed Kent in assuming a very *Roman* Roman Corinth, primarily on the basis of the use of Latin in public inscribed texts, from its foundation until the time of Hadrian. At that stage, when Greek seems to make an appearance among public inscriptions, the colony is presumed to have become in some sense more Greek.[30] Such a reliance on official texts and exclusively political and legal categories certainly evokes particular domains of public life in Corinth. In sociolinguistic terms, this is the intersection of linguistic domains (genres) and epigraphic communities. But Millis and others have shown that it is no longer possible to speak in such an unqualified manner of the Roman identity of early Roman Corinth up to Hadrian's principate, followed by a shift toward a Greek identity in the colony.

As a result, a growing stream of recent Corinthian scholarship has sought to improve on this overly simplistic model. In this stream there has been a drift toward employing the mixed metaphors of ethnicity, hybridity, negotiation, and adaptation as categories for analyzing various sets of evidence for what they might tell us about Corinthian identity.[31] To what extent these categories, drawn largely from cultural studies, are helpful depends on how the move is made from a given set of evidence to claims about identity. Sociolinguistic categories may complement these analyses by bringing new perspectives to shared sets of evidence. One highly relevant but neglected set of evidence is the bilingual and mixed language inscriptions of Roman Corinth.[32] A systematic analysis of salient features

---

30. IKorinthKent, 18–19. Cf. Millis, "Social and Ethnic Origins," 16–17. Kent's brief comments are more qualified than the statements of many historians and New Testamen scholars who have depended on him.

31. Apart from Concannon's important monograph, see also Betsey A. Robinson, "Fountains and the Formation of Cultural Identity at Roman Corinth," in Schowalter and Friesen, *Urban Religion in Roman Corinth*, 111–40; Christine M. Thomas, "Greek Heritage in Roman Corinth and Ephesos: Hybrid Identities and Strategies of Display in the Material Record of Traditional Mediterranean Religions," in Friesen, Schowalter, and Walters, *Corinth in Context*, 117–47; Millis, "Social and Ethnic Origins," 30–35.

32. Another is the colonial coinage of Roman Corinth, on which see Bradley J. Bitner, "Coinage and Colonial Identity: Corinthian Numismatics and the Corinthian Correspondence," in *The First Urban Churches 1: Methodological Foundations*,

of this evidence must act as one control in theories of linguistic, political, and cultural identity in the Roman colony. My hope is that the present exploratory analysis of epigraphical texts will serve such a grounding function in future discussions of Corinthian identity and language use.

5. Texts and Commentary

In this section I adduce representative inscriptions. With the first two dual-language texts I have made every attempt to include inventory and excavation data, measurements (in the form height x width x thickness; all measurements in meters), and full bibliography (exhaustive for editions and significant for commentary). Descriptions are taken from published reports and editions.[33] Only significant variants in readings or restorations have been included in an *apparatus criticus*. A brief analysis and commentary follows each text, with overall reflections and conclusions in the final section. Following the first two texts, I point briefly to several other inscriptions that fit the other typological categories suggested above and that would repay close attention in future studies.

5.1. Language Contact in Dual-Language Inscriptions

5.1.1. Dedication (?) and Artist's Signature from the Theater, 44 BCE–ca. 150 CE

Fragment A: I-251 (IKorinthMeritt §71) + Fragment B: I-2294 (IKorinthKent §41). Fine-crystalled white marble fragment (A) found in Theater trench "near the centre of the orchestra," 20 May 1902 during initial excavations of the Theater supervised by Dr. Samuel Bassett.[34] Joined in 1998

---

ed. James R. Harrison and L. L. Welborn, WGRWSup 7 (Atlanta: SBL Press, 2015), 151–87.

33. I have not been able to examine these stones by autopsy nor to study the excavation notebooks except in scanned form generously made available online by the American School of Classical Studies at Athens.

34. Corinth excavation notebook 16 (http://corinth.ascsa.net/id/corinth/notebook/16), p. 50, and notebook 13 (http://corinth.ascsa.net/id/corinth/notebook/13), p. 26. The excavation notebooks record associated finds such as the sculpted head of the so-called Monteverde youth, on which, see Mary C. Sturgeon, *Sculpture: The Assemblage from the Theater*, vol. 9.3 of *Corinth: Results of Excavations Conducted by*

Figure 1. Corinth I-251 (IKorinthKent §41 + IKorinthMeritt §71). Photograph by Ino Ioannidou and Lenio Bartzioti. American School of Classical Studies at Athens, Corinth Excavations. Used by permission.

by Mary C. Sturgeon to slab of white marble (B) found May 1926 "in the cavea of the Theater." Both together are now Corinth I-251.

Measurements: .313 x .425 x .05; letter height: .055 (Latin, preserved height); .017 (Greek); space of .081 between lines; clamp cutting in bottom, 0.148 m. from left edge.

Bibliography: K. K. Smith, "Greek Inscriptions from Corinth II," *AJA* 23 (1919): 381, no. 88; IKorinthMeritt §71; IKorinthKent §41; P. M. Fraser and E. Matthews, eds., *The Peloponnese, Western Greece, Sicily, and Magna Graecia*, vol. 3A of *Lexicon of Greek Personal Names* (Oxford: Clarendon, 1997), nos. 7, 32; Mary C. Sturgeon, *Sculpture: The Assemblage from the*

the American School of Classical Studies at Athens (Athens: American School of Classical Studies at Athens, 2004), 114–17, pl. 19.

Theater, vol. 9.3 of *Corinth: Results of Excavations Conducted by the American School of Classical Studies at Athens* (Athens: American School of Classical Studies at Athens, 2004), 22–25; SEG 55.383.

5.1.1.1. Text

---]ṾỊ[---
vacat
Θεόδοτος Ἀθηναῖος ἐποίει[---?

Apparatus: line 1: [*dedica*]VI[*t*], Smith and Meritt; [*cura*]VI[*t*], [*restit*]VI[*t*], [*instaura*]VI[*t*], [*orna*]VI[*t*], Sturgeon; outsize M, rejected (without argument) by Smith.

5.1.1.2. Translation

... dedicated? it ...
vacat
Theodotos Athenaios made it

5.1.1.3. Archaeological and Historical Context

A fascinating instance of the problems and potential of Corinthian mixed-language epigraphy, these fragments from the Roman Theater preserve parts of (apparently) two Latin letters[35] above an artist's signature in Greek. Sturgeon's work with the epigraphical fragments and associated finds from the Theater is a model of the painstaking effort required by the disturbed stratigraphy and sherdlike nature of the epigraphical remains.[36] Kent's ini-

---

35. K. K. Smith ("Greek Inscriptions from Corinth II." *AJA* 23 [1919]: 331–93) (followed by Meritt and Sturgeon) rejected the restoration of a single Latin M, arguing that "the proportions would be monstrous." Given the nature of the fragment, one ought perhaps to keep open the possibility of a larger letter such as M.

36. Sturgeon, *Sculpture*, "Appendix: The Inscriptions from the Corinth Theater," 211–13. Cf. IKorinthKent §§374–500: "Fragments Too Small to Classify." See also Louis Robert, "Inscriptions de l'antiquité et du bas-empire a Corinthe," in *Épigraphie et antiquités grecques*, vol. 6 of *Opera Minora Selecta* (Amsterdam: Hakkert, 1989), nos. 148, 552, "On le voit par le grand écart des provenances de fragments qui se rejoignent pour former un seul texte.... A ce point de vue, chaque champ de fouilles peut offrir un tableau différent et toujours instructif."

tial judgment of the fragment with only Theodotus's name in Greek placed it in the second century BCE. But here he was clearly misled by assumptions related to Greek language epigraphy and letter forms at Corinth. Sturgeon's 1998 join, connecting Theodotus to an inscription that also bears Latin text, demonstrates the inadequacy of dating by letter forms[37] and should lead us to reconsider the dating of small Corinthian fragments with only Greek or Latin visible.[38] It adds as well to the challenge mounted by Millis and others to the consensus view of language use in the phases of Corinth's history.[39] The completion of the sculptor's name calls for updates to the *Lexicon of Greek Personal Names* and the online text of the Packard Humanities Institute's Greek inscriptions database.[40]

Sturgeon notes correctly, on the basis of *comparanda* from other Roman theater contexts, that several restorations are possible for the final (?) Latin line in such a dedication. Theodotos appears to have been a craftsman involved in work on the *scaenae frons*,[41] probably during the phase of

---

37. IKorinthKent §41: "The lettering suggests a date in the second century B.C."

38. Cf., e.g., IKorinthKent §44, another sculptor's signature dated II BC on the basis of letter forms alone.

39. IKorinthKent, 18–19, illustrates this consensus whereby Greek inscriptions are presumed to be either from before 146 BC or post-Hadrianic. Kent admits, "In some cases the letter forms seem to be reasonably reliable, *especially when they are virtually identical with the forms of a second text whose date is assured*. In many other cases, however, the criterion is so unavoidably subjective that any assigned date is little better than an educated guess" (IKorinthKent, 19 n. 7, emphasis added).

40. Cf. IKorinthKent §41 in P. M. Fraser and E. Matthews, eds., *The Peloponnese, Western Greece, Sicily, and Magna Graecia*, vol. 3A of *Lexicon of Greek Personal Names* (Oxford: Clarendon, 1997), s.v. Θεόδοτος, no. 32; and IKorinthKent §139 in Fraser and Matthews, *The Peloponnese*, s.v. Ἀθήναιος, no. 7; text 178919 in the Packard Humanities Institute's Greek inscriptions database, http://epigraphy.packhum.org/text/178919.

41. Sturgeon, *Sculpture*, 1: "the *scaenae frons* was impressively embellished with painted marble reliefs beneath the columns, with painted statuary between the columns and in the niches, and with painted busts in the pediments. The *scaenae frons* contained a sculptural complex that evoked the Theater's political, religious, and cultural functions as well as the self-identification of the city." Sturgeon (*Sculpture*, 23) rejects the possibility of an architect's signature and argues for the probability that Theodotos was a sculptor. An architect should not be ruled out, however; cf. Marie-Christine Hellmann, "Les signatures d'architectes en langue grecque: Essai de mise au point," *ZPE* 104 (1994): 155, no. 8 [= IDelos 5.2342, 110–109 BCE], for one of several inscriptions mentioning the Delian "architecte-sculpteur" Menandros (Μένανδρος Μέλανος Ἀθηναῖος ἐποίει). The absence of the designation ἀρχιτεκτῶν in a dedication cannot rule out such a role for the named person; see, further Hellmann, "Les signa-

construction undertaken during Hadrian's time.[42] His ethnic, the genitive Athenaios,[43] combined with other evidence for craftsmen's signatures in the period, suggest he may have been part of an Attic or Peloponnesian workshop providing contracted labor in Roman Corinth.[44]

5.1.1.4. Convention, Language Use, and Performative Function

Although the formula *name* + *ethnic* + ἐποίει is common in Greece from an early date,[45] the only other certain occurrence in relation to a sculptural assemblage connected with a theater façade is found in a dedication at Side in Pamphylia.[46] So while the artisan's signature in Greek is itself conventional in terms of genre and language use (an unsurprising linguistic domain), its juxtaposition with a Latin inscription in such a setting is

---

tures d'architectes," 175. This possibility is not discussed by Michael Donderer in his sections dealing with signatures, *Die Architekten der späten römischen Republik und der Kaiserzeit: Epigraphische Zeugnisse* (Erlangen: Universitätsbund Erlangen-Nürnberg, 1996), 24–34, although see, e.g., his no. D1.

42. For the phases of the Roman theater, see Sturgeon, *Sculpture*, 4–7.

43. Ethnic: *from Athens*; patronymic: *son of Athenaios*. This was a common name among contractors and craftsmen in the Peloponnese and surrounding areas. See, e.g., *IG* 4.1.431 (Epidauros); 4.698 (Sparta); Wilhelm Dittenberger and Karl Purgold, *Die Inschriften von Olympia* (Berlin: Asher, 1896), 646–48 (Olympia); *IG* 2.4313 (Athens). ΑΘΗΝΑΙΟΥ is stamped on an amphora handle (?) found in 1902 in the back of Shop XV at Corinth (see Corinth notebook 15 [http://corinth.ascsa.net/id/corinth/notebook/15], p. 48).

44. Sturgeon, *Sculpture*, 22–25. She notes the appearance of the ethnic *Korinthios* in such artists' signatures, pointing to the difficult-to-date *IG* 11.4.1173 from Delos. See also the earlier study Mary C. Sturgeon, "Roman Sculptures from Corinth and Isthmia: The Case for a Local 'Workshop,'" in *The Greek Renaissance in the Roman Empire: Papers from the Tenth British Museum Classical Colloquium*, ed. Susan Walker and Averil Cameron, BICSSup 55 (London: University of London, Institute of Classical Studies, 1989), 114, 117–19.

45. The aorist ἐποίησε/ἐπόησε gave way gradually to the imperfect ἐποίει until the latter "predominated in the imperial period," according to Bradly M. McLean, *An Introduction to Greek Epigraphy of the Hellenistic and Roman Periods from Alexander the Great down to the Reign of Constantine (323 BC–AD 337)* (Ann Arbor: University of Michigan Press, 2002), 208. See also Margherita Guarducci, *Epigrafi di carattere private*, vol. 3 of *Epigrafia Greca* (Rome: Instituto Poligrafico, 1974), 398; Emanuel Loewy, *Inschriften Griechischer Bildhauer* (1885; repr., Chicago: Ares, 1976), xii.

46. Sturgeon, *Sculpture*, 49. Cf. Loewy, *Inschriften Griechischer Bildhauer*, no. 382 (= *CIL* 6.1.857 = *CIG* 3.6174 = *IG* 14.1264).

remarkable. It is an example of intersentential code-switching, or better, of *accommodation* with a view to multiple layers of audience and self-presentation (both colonial and individual).

In a wide-ranging study of theater inscriptions, Sturgeon observes that Corinth "stands out" for its continued practice of Latin inscribing on public structures, even in the second century CE. Elsewhere Greek dedications are found paired with Greek signatures, even when associated with "Roman" structures. In this respect, Corinth's Romanness in terms of public life persisted strongly even when expressed in a construction project oriented toward the hellenophile Hadrian.[47] Sturgeon notes further that funding for theater construction in the East shifted from the cities in the first century to wealthy individuals in the second.[48] In addition, she finds that theater dedications frequently attest benefactions contributing to certain limited areas of the entire monumental complex and suggests that a Corinthian *agonothētes* may have been responsible for the construction phase of which our inscription was a part.[49] If this were so, it is possible to conceive of an elite Roman Corinthian, holding the highest colonial liturgy (itself represented in local inscriptions as a Latinized Greek loanword),[50] commissioning a sculptural assemblage with a Latin dedication from a Greek artisan. The complexity of linguistic, social, political, and cultural layers is evident, but it is unclear whether a notion such as *hybridity* adequately interprets these phenomena, or if *accommodation* or *contextualization* may be helpful as well.

Finally, if we consider the performative space of which this inscription was but one small part, we see that even in the Corinth of Hadrian's day the colony cultivated a "Roman" profile and discourse without abandoning either the Greek language or aspects of Greek culture. Sturgeon argues,

---

47. Sturgeon, *Sculpture*, 1–2.

48. Mary C. Sturgeon, "Dedications of Roman Theaters," in *ΧΑΡΙΣ: Essays in Honor of Sara A. Immerwahr*, ed. Anne P. Chapin, Hesperia Supplements 33 (Princeton: American School of Classical Studies at Athens, 2004), 411–29.

49. IKorinthKent §§336 and 433, found in different phases and locations of the Theater excavations, recording, respectively, s]CAEN[a and ornam]ENTA(?); see Sturgeon, "Dedications of Roman Theaters," 413, 425–26. Cn. Publicius M. f. Rusticus (IKorinthKent §176; Athanasios D. Rizakis, Sophia B. Zoumbaki, and Maria Kantirea, *Roman Peloponnese I: Roman Personal Names in Their Social Context* [Paris: de Boccard, 2001], 507) was voted agonothetic honors, possibly in the time of Hadrian; see IKorinthKent, 31.

50. On *agonothētes*, see below.

the use of Latin in the dedicatory inscriptions in the entablature and on revetment plaques highlights Corinth's status as a Roman colony. Both image and text convey important messages, which can be read singly, in segments, and as a whole. As one of the most important places in the city for large gatherings of people, citizens and foreigners alike, the Theater provided an excellent locale for such propagandistic statements and for the display of substantial public benefactions. Moreover, the multifaceted decoration of the *scaenae frons* exhibits a constructed iconography. The different forms, subjects, and scale of the Theater facade sculptures provided the setting for the religious, political, and dramatic spectacles that were likely to have been featured on this stage.[51]

Many of those from Corinth and its environs passing through the Theater space and viewing the various spectacles of *politeia* enacted there would have been adept at switching between the encoded messages embedded in the impressive iconographical and inscribed fabric of which we have but a trace in this bilingual inscription.[52]

---

51. Sturgeon, *Sculpture*, 2: "In the proposed reconstruction, the highly articulated decoration of the Corinth Theater facade is a vehicle for the self-presentation of Corinth as a Roman city, as a Roman colony, and as the prosperous capital of the province of Achaia. Both the selection of subjects and their location on the facade are deliberate, such that the sculptures are thematically interrelated both vertically and horizontally. The sculptural program celebrates the *virtus* of the reigning emperor and of past Roman emperors, while it also emphasizes the importance of military triumphs and hereditary right to rule. The ideas are promoted of Corinth as an important political and cultural center and as a city situated at the crossroads of East and West, populated by people of many ethnic backgrounds."

52. Sturgeon (*Sculpture*, 1) notes that the Theater was striking with its "three-storied columnar facade made of multicolored marble. The polychrome architecture, composed of multicolored stones, did not stand alone, for the *scaenae frons* was impressively embellished with painted marble reliefs beneath the columns, with painted statuary between the columns and in the niches, and with painted busts in the pediments. The *scaenae frons* contained a sculptural complex that evoked the Theater's political, religious, and cultural functions as well as the self-identification of the city." Although the comments here concerning the presence and legibility of layered Roman and Greek codes is particularly true of the Hadrianic phase (Phase 4 of the Roman Theater), they would seem consistent with what is known from earlier phases, on which see Sturgeon, *Sculpture*, 4–6.

5.1.2. Stela Honoring P. Licinius Priscus Iuventianus, Second Century CE

Fragment A: Corinth I-2194 (IKorinthKent §306, lines 14–32) + Fragment B: Isthmia I-261 (lines 1–14). Large limestone fragment (A) found in colonnade of South Stoa on 28 May 1934.[53] Additional fragment (B) found 7 June 1954 in the Fortress of Justinian at Isthmia, subsequently found to join atop fragment A.[54] Inventory record mentions seven additional small fragments of the stela (not all inscribed). Top is still missing. Both together now Corinth I-2194.

Measurements: 1.17 x .65 x .28; letter height: .028 (Geagan); lines 15–33, .15–17; line 34, .013 (Kent).

Bibliography: Oscar Broneer, "An Official Rescript from Corinth," *Hesperia* 8 (1939): 181–90; *AE* 1939.110; Louis Robert, "Un edifice du sanctuaire de l'Isthme dans une inscription de Corinthe," *Hellenica* I (1940): 43–53; *AE* 1947.198; IKorinthKent §306; Louis Robert, "Inscriptions de l'antiquité et du bas-empire à Corinthe," *REG* 79 (1966): 754–56, repr. as pages 572–74 in Robert, *Épigraphie et antiquités grecques*, vol. 6 of *Opera Minora Selecta* (Amsterdam: Hakkert, 1989); L'Institut Fernand-Courby, *Nouveau choix d'inscriptions grecques* (Paris: Belles lettres, 1971); *SEG* 26.410, 35.264; Daniel J. Geagan, "The Isthmian Dossier of P. Licinius Priscus Iuventianus," *Hesperia* 58 (1989): 349–60; *SEG* 37.263; *BE* 1990.103; *SEG* 38.293, 39.340, 53.283; A. d'Hautcourt, "Corinthe: Financement d'une colonization et d'une reconstruction," in *Constructions publiques et programmes éditilaires en Grèce entre le IIe siècle av. J.-C. et le Ier siècle ap. J.-C.: Actes du colloque organisé par l'École française d'Athènes et le CNRS, Athènes, 14–17 mai 1995*, ed. J.-Y. Marc and J.-C. Moretti, BCHSup 39 (Athens: École française d'Athènes; de Boccard, 2001), 427–38; full prosopography for Priscus: P. M. Fraser and E. Matthews, eds., *The Peloponnese, Western Greece, Sicily, and Magna Graecia*, vol. 3A of *Lexicon of Greek Personal Names* (Oxford: Clarendon, 1997), Corinthia 378.

---

53. Corinth excavation notebook 141 (http://corinth.ascsa.net/id/corinth/notebook/141), pp. 81–83.

54. The join was first reported by Daniel J. Geagan ("The Isthmian Dossier of P. Licinius Priscus Iuventianus," *Hesperia* 58 [1989]: 349–60), but it is unclear precisely by whom (one assumes by Geagan himself) or when it was made.

Figure 2. Corinth I-2194 (IKorinthKent §306 + Isthmia I-261). Photography by Ino Ioannidou and Lenio Bartzioti. American School of Classical Studies at Athens, Corinth Excavations. Used by permission.

5.1.2.1. Text[55]

[--] 1
[----------------- traces of two lines -----------------]
---]α[.]ο[.]νεπια[---
[....]του[..]ο[..]σ[.]τος ἀνθύπατος [---
---]ανο[--- 5
--]α[.....]τανευ[---
---]ς τῆς σ[τοᾶ]ς [---
---]Ν[...]ΝΩ ὑετη[---
[......] ἀπ[ο]δέχεσθαι ᵛ Λικίνιον Π[ρ]είσ[κον ἄνδρα]
[πε]πολιειτευμένον φιλοτειμότατα καὶ τὰ [μὲν κα] 10
[τ]ὰ στάδιον ὑπὸ σεισμῶν ἐσκυλμένα τὰ δὲ [ὑπὸ πα]-
[λ]α[ι]ότητος δ[ε]δαπανημένα ἀποκαθεστ[ότα ---]
[...]θα ὑπὸ το[ῦ] δήμου [..]τε φημ[---
[..] τοῖς χρίοσι ἀθλητ[άς --- ---]ωΙ[.]ΪΙμ[---
---]ος [συ]νᾶραι ἐρείπια στοᾶς 15
τῆς Ῥήγλ[ο]υ [.]α[.]μάρας οὕτως ὥστε ποιῆ[σ]αι οἴκους
πεντήκ[ο]ντα ᵛ ἐπεὶ οὖν καὶ ἐν τούτῳ φι[λ]οτείμως
ὁ Πρεῖ[σ]κ[ο]ς ἀναστρέφεται ὥστε ὑπὲρ τῆς τειμῆς
τοῦ προδηλουμένου τόπου δοῦναι τοῖς πολείταις
ἑκάστῳ δηνάριον ἕν ᵛ οὐ μόνον συνκατατίθεμαι 20
τῇ τε τῆς [β]ουλῆς καὶ τοῦ δήμου γνώμῃ ἀλλὰ καὶ ἀ-
ποδέχομαι τὸν ἄνδρα οὕτως ἐν ἅπασιν ἀναστρε-
φόμενον φιλοτείμως καὶ ἐπιτρέπω τὸν προ-
δηλούμενον τόπον ταύτῃ τῇ αἱρέσει αὐτῷ πρα-
θῆναι ᵛ οὕτως μέντοι ὥστε τοὺς γεινομένους 25
οἴκους τοῖς ἀθληταῖς προῖκα τῷ καιρῷ τῶν ἀγώ-
νων σχολάζειν εἰς τὸ διηνεκὲς ἔχοντος τοῦ κα-
τὰ καιρὸν ἀγωνοθέτου ἐξουσίαν διανέμειν
τὰς ξενίας αὐτοῖς ᵛ εἰ μέντοι τις πρὸς τοῦτο ἀν-
τιλέγει δυνήσεται διδάξαι με ἐντὸς Καλανδῶν 30

---

55. Text reproduced from the edition of Geagan (ibid.), with minor variation in presentation and a single corrected breathing (ἕν, l. 20). Only the text of lines 15–32 (= IKorinthKent §306) is available on the Packard Humanities Institute Greek inscriptions database (http://epigraphy.packhum.org/text/179293). The same incomplete text is found on the *Epigraphische Datenbank Heidelberg* database (http://edh-www.adw.uni-heidelberg.de/edh/inschrift/HD022605). Both should be updated.

Ἰανουαρίων τῶν ἔνγιστα ᵛ ἐρρῶσθαι ὑμᾶς εὔχομαι
[data -]IIIIK · Decembr ᵛ et · pro rostris lecta pr. * Decembr'

Apparatus: line 15: ---]ναρ[.]ι , Broneer and Kent; line 16: ...ε.ηρια or [Εὐ]ε[τ]ηρία, Broneer; [τῆ]ς ['Ρ]ηγλ[ιανῆς], Robert; ['Ρ]ήγλ[ο]υ, Kent; [κα]μάρας, Broneer; [μαρ]μάρας, Kent[56]; line 19: πολήταις, Broneer; πο[λ]ίταις, Kent; line 21: τῆσδε τῆς βουλῆς, Kent;

5.1.2.2. Translation

```
--- 1
---
?
... proconsul[57] ...
?[58] 5
?[59]
... of the stoa? ...
?
... to approve.[60] Licinius Priscus a man
who has conducted himself most generously in civic life and        10
restored both the structures beneath
the stadium torn apart by earthquakes as well as the things
    destroyed by age ...
--- by the People ... ?
for those rubbing oil athletes? ...
```

---

56. Robert ("Inscriptions de l'antiquité et du bas-empire à Corinthe," *REG* 79 [1966]: 755) corrected Kent's translation (not his restoration, *contra* Geagan, "Isthmian Dossier," 352]), pointing out that μαρμάρας (if correct) should be taken as a participle and not an adjective. Given the uncertainty of the reading, I leave it untranslated below.

57. Geagan notes ("Isthmian Dossier," 354–55) that this Greek word for *proconsul* remains quite legible because it was cut more deeply than the surrounding letters.

58. Among other possibilities, Ἀδρι]άνο[υ or Τραι]άνο[υ *vel sim* are conceivable.

59. Given Geagan's reading, ---]τανευ[--- is quite possibly from the verb πρυτανεύω.

60. For this translation of ἀποδέχομαι, see the remarks of Louis Robert ("Un edifice du sanctuaire de l'Isthme dans une inscription de Corinthe," *Hell* 1 [1940]: 44–45). In the case of this word and several others, Robert connects the "technical" terminology of this rescript with the Opramoas dossier, on which see now Christina Kokkinia, *Die Opramoas-Inschrift von Rhodiapolis: Euergetismus und soziale Eliten in Lykien* (Bonn: Habelt, 2000).

... ? ruins of the stoa 15
of Regulus ... ? in the same manner so that he might make fifty
    chambers.
Since then also in this
Priscus is acting generously so that, as the price
of the previously mentioned site, he may give to each citizen
one denarius. Not only do I sanction[61] 20
the proposed decree of the Council and the People but also
I approve of the man [who], in all things, is
acting so generously, and I permit the
previously mentioned site on this condition[62]
to be sold to him: In this manner, however, so that the resulting 25
chambers, for the athletes freely in the time of the games,
may be devoted in perpetuity—the *agonothetes* having
each time authority to assign
the guest rooms to them. If, however, anyone opposes this
he will be able to instruct[63] me before the Kalends 30
of the coming January. I pray that you are well.
[Given?] four days before the Kalends of December and read from
    the rostra the
day before the Kalends of December.

5.1.2.3. Archaeological and Historical Context

In stark contrast to our earlier example from the theater, these joining pieces give us one of the longest extant epigraphical texts from Roman Corinth.[64] Considered as a single stela, it also exemplifies the interplay of

---

61. See Robert, "Un edifice du sanctuaire," 47–48.
62. See Robert, "Un edifice du sanctuaire," 47; ταύτῃ τῇ αἱρέσει could also signify "for this purpose."
63. For διδάσκειν as "instruct" or "explain" before a magistrate, see Louis Robert, *Hellenica: Recueil d'épigraphie de numasmatique et d'antiquités grecques* (Paris: Librairie d'amérique et d'orient, Adrien-Maisoneuve, 1960), 11–12:252–54; Joyce Reynolds, *Aphrodisias and Rome*, Journal of Roman Studies Monographs 1 (London: Society for the Promotion of Roman Studies, 1982), 138–39. See also Ernst Kalinka, *Tituli Lyciae linguis Graeca et Latina conscripti*, vol. 2 of *Tituli Asiae Minoris*, 3 fasc. (Vienna: Hölder, 1920–1944), 2.905, col. VII.24.1 (Opramoas inscription); IGBulg 4.2263.4–5.
64. Geagan, "Isthmian Dossier," remains the most detailed and comprehensive treatment.

Greek and Latin, of "Greek" and "Roman," in the early Roman colony and its *territorium*, which extended to Isthmia. Discovered in Corinth's South Stoa in 1934, the text of the lower half of the stela was published by Broneer in 1939 and again by Kent in 1966. Although Kent labeled it a proconsul's letter, that is only part of the picture in terms of the linguistic domain, or genre, of the inscription. It should be considered part of a larger monument honoring a local benefactor from the regional Greek elite by the name of Publius Licinius Priscus Iuventianus (see further below).[65] This fact was confirmed when in 1989 Geagan made a join that added fourteen more lines of text. More surprising, however, than the new text was its find spot. The pieces preserving the upper text were found at Isthmia, not in the urban center of Corinth, where the lower text had been discovered. Geagan has argued that this implies that the stela was originally displayed at Isthmia, not in urban Corinth, whence the lower fragment was relocated at some later date.

Even before Geagan's discovery (augmenting what he referred to as Stele B [= Corinth I-2194]), Broneer had already noted a connection between the initial find containing the proconsul's letter and another, nearly complete stela honoring Priscus (*IG* 4.203; subsequently referred to by Geagan as Stele A). This second stele, seen and drawn by archaeological travelers at Isthmia in the late seventeenth century, is now located in the Museo Lapidario in Verona.[66] After juxtaposing the pair, Geagan concluded,

> The two steles, which must have been set up in proximity to one another, appear to be part of a single dossier recording the benefactions of P. Licinius Priscus Juventianus to the Isthmian sanctuary. It is possible that a third stele containing documents once intervened between Stele A and Stele B, but its existence has not been demonstrated.[67]

These observations are relevant to our investigation for two reasons. First, they indicate decisively that the dating of the monument is linked to the

---

65. See Oscar Broneer, "An Official Rescript from Corinth," *Hesperia* 8 (1939): 186–90; IKorinthKent, 120–21; Geagan, "Isthmian Dossier," 357–60; Rizakis, Zoumbaki, and Kantirea, *Roman Peloponnese I*, Corinthia 378. See also, in addition to *AE* 2002.1320; *AE* 2004.1354, the dossier gathered by F. Camia, "IG IV 203: La cronologia di P. Licinius Priscus Iuventianus, Archiereus della lega achea," *Annuario della scuola archeologica di atene* 80 (2002): 361–78.

66. See also *SEG* 52.299, 53.283.

67. Geagan, "Isthmian Dossier," 349–50.

benefactions and building activity of Priscus. Second, they begin to suggest a context of display that informs our interpretation of the mixed-language nature of the stela. We will return to the latter point shortly. Unfortunately, with regard to the first observation, the inscription has proven difficult to date with precision. Scholars have opted broadly, on the basis of the earthquakes and structures mentioned in the Priscus dossier, to date the stelae sometime between the reigns of Vespasian and the Antonines. Considerations of archaeology are more helpful than letter forms or orthography in this particular instance, and most would now date the stelae to circa 150–175 CE.[68] Mary E. H. Walbank has recently emphasized the numismatic evidence, arguing that the coins help in establishing a *terminus ante quem* of 161–163 CE or soon after.[69] F. Camia, after reviewing the epigraphic dossier of Iuventianus, embraces a minority view and inclines, largely for reasons prosopographical, toward a pre- rather than post-Hadrianic date.[70]

From the perspective of this study, the dating of the Priscus stela is of interest because of the usual tendency to see Hadrian's reign as more or less a watershed between the use of Latin (pre-Hadrian) and Greek (post-Hadrian) in Roman Corinthian epigraphy. For many reasons—not least the close relationship of language choice to epigraphic genre, context of display, and the unreliability of dating by letter forms (all noted by Millis)[71]—this is a division that should be seriously questioned, even abandoned. This is so not least because it often prejudices (as seen above in §5.1 with the artist's signature from the Theater) the dating of fragments and potentially impedes the kind of sociolinguistic study of the epigraphical material outlined in this essay. One senses in those who have commented on the Priscus stela a tension generated by these prejudices: there is at once a mild surprise that the Latin postscript could possibly postdate

---

68. Geagan, "Isthmian Dossier," 359. Cf. Broneer, "An Official Rescript from Corinth," 190; Camia, "IG IV 203," 361–62.

69. Mary E. Hoskins Walbank, "Image and Cult: The Coinage of Roman Corinth," in Friesen, Schowalter, and Walters, *Corinth in Context*, 179–80. Walbank notes that the Palaimonion, one of the structures attributed to Priscus in *IG* 4.203, first appears on coins of this date. It is likely, however, that the building activity of Priscus, and the erection of these *stelae*, predates the coins.

70. Camia, "IG IV 203," 367–68. It is notable that *AE* 2004.1354 reports an inscription to Priscus cut in Greek beneath Poseidon astride a dolphin (part of the Prado collection in Madrid), the entire piece dated to Hadrian's reign on stylistic grounds.

71. Millis, "Social and Ethnic Origins," 23–5. Cf. Bitner, *Paul's Political Strategy*, 91–99.

Hadrian and a propensity to date the stone later because the bulk of the text is in Greek.[72] Yet, as becomes evident from a survey of the epigraphical material related to Priscus, the same figure was honored in both languages in different contexts—and in this case with both Greek and Latin on the same stone—within the Corinthian *territorium*.[73]

5.1.2.4. Convention, Language Use, and Performative Function

Although both Broneer and Geagan have commented on linguistic and orthographic features of this inscription, it is Robert who most closely linked its lexical choices and formulas with other rescripts in the Greek East.[74] Statements of acceptance and approval by the unnamed proconsul (ἀποδέχομαι, lines 9, 22) associate this stela with the genre of official testimonial or *matyria* described by Kokkinia.[75] In a subsequent study, Kokkinia has shown how such *martyriai* employ official Roman magisterial documents (often cleverly edited or "accommodated") to focus honor on local elites by means of multiple inscriptions integrated as a monumental complex.[76] This would seem to be precisely the case with the Priscus stelae. On Geagan's hypothesis that both were displayed in conjunction at

---

72. Cf. Concannon, *When You Were Gentiles*, 66: "To think of Latin not as a default [particularly in pre-Hadrianic Roman Corinthian epigraphy] but as an option in elite self-presentation is to think beyond assumptions about Corinth as either a Greek or Roman space."

73. See Camia, "IG IV 203," 370–78. It is striking that many of the inscriptions honoring Priscus in Greek are traceable to Isthmia, whereas one suspects that IKorinthKent §199, although its find spot is unrecorded (see IKorinthKent, 89) is in Latin because it was likely displayed in or near the Corinthian forum. Our focal inscription is a reminder, however, that even very large inscriptions could apparently be moved in later years from Isthmia to Corinth. Cf. IKorinthKent §§200 and 201. Ben Millis has confirmed to me, in conversation, that, perhaps unsurprisingly, the Isthmian epigraphy (much of it pre-Hadrianic) is overwhelmingly in Greek, whereas those inscriptions displayed in or near the forum were largely in Latin. I thank him for his helpful interaction.

74. Broneer, "An Official Rescript from Corinth," 183–85; Robert, "Un edifice du sanctuaire," 44–49; Geagan, "Isthmian Dossier," 358.

75. Christina Kokkinia, "Letters of Roman Authorities on Local Dignitaries: The Case of Vedius Antoninus," *ZPE* 142 (2003): 197–213.

76. Christina Kokkinia, "The Role of Individuals in Inscribing Roman State Documents," in *Selbstdarstellung und Kommunikation: Die Veröffentlichung staatlicher Urkunden auf Stein und Bronze in der römischen Welt*, ed. Rudolf Haensch (Munich: Beck, 2009), 191–206, Priscus at 200–201.

Isthmia (he speculated about the possibility of a third stela), the associated texts and monuments, within the vicinity of Priscus's Isthmian benefactions, would certainly function to elevate his name in the esteem of those attending the Isthmian Games.

Furthermore, assuming such a locus of display we are not able fully to answer the questions posed at the outset of this essay. In light of the possibilities of code-switching and contextualizing, the evidence as it stands is open to varied interpretations. Certainly the force of the Latin concluding postscript draws attention not only to the fact that Priscus was esteemed by the official sanction of a Roman magistrate; it also tells us that something quite similar to this decree was actually read out from the rostra (*bema*) in the Corinthian forum. It does not specify, however, whether the initial document or the version read out were in Latin or Greek. It is quite possible, if Priscus had a hand in shaping his own honorific monument at Isthmia, that he, as a regional elite playing to a regional audience, may have been behind the translation of an originally Latin text into Greek. Although the Greek is good[77] and representative of official translation Greek in similar documents of the Greek East,[78] there is no way of telling when, in the process of drafting, proclamation, and inscribing, the document was put into Greek. In any case, the juxtaposition of Greek text reminding passers-by of Priscus's generosity with many of the edifices they could see nearby works well with the official Latin imprimatur of the concluding line: the whole serves to honor the man in a *hybrid* cultural and *accommodated* sociolinguistic context.[79]

5.2. Language Contact in Monolingual Inscriptions[80]

Inscriptions in one language (i.e., script) may still evince language contact as described above. At Roman Corinth the following are representative instances of linguistic interference of various types.

---

77. "Athenian orthography," according to Geagan ("Isthmian Dossier," 358), yet without "strong influence of Latin epigraphic style which characterizes much of the Greek lettering at Corinth itself."

78. Cf. Bradley J. Bitner, "Augustan Procedure and Legal Documents in RDGE 70," *GRBS* 54 (2014): 639–64.

79. Concannon, *When You Were Gentiles*, 72–74.

80. In this and the following subsections I merely lay out data that, according to the typology introduced above, suggests further avenues for study.

- πενταετηρικὸν στρατηγόν for IIVIR QVINQ[81]
- εὐθηνίας ἐπιμελητήν for CVRATOR ANNONAE[82]
- φιλόκαισαρ for AMICVS CAESARIS[83]
- GENS AVGVSTA for γένος Σεβαστοῦ[84]
- AGONOTHETES for ἀγωνοθέτης[85]
- ISAGOGEVS for εἰσαγωγεύς[86]
- PRIMVS for πρῶτος[87]
- ARGYROTAMIAS for ἀργυροταμίας[88]
- Greek filiation expressed in Latin[89]

5.3. Language Contact in Graffiti and Minor Objects

Millis has noted the utter lack of a systematic study of Corinthian graffiti *dipinti* and crafstmen's marks or stamps, pointing to a few examples worthy of further investigation.[90] The following indicate the types of evidence that might contribute to our understanding of language contact and language use in Roman Corinth.

IKorinthKent §361 preserves a Greek graffito, apparently inscribed by workmen laboring on the rostra (*bema*) in the Roman Corinthian forum on a surface that may have been covered once construction was complete. This may be juxtaposed with the several Latin inscriptions associated with the rostra and its *scholae*.[91]

A Latin-Greek graffito on a Roman pan tile drain was found behind Room VI of the South Stoa.[92]

---

81. IKorinthMeritt §§76, 80, 81; IKorinthWest §§71, 72; cf. *IG* 4.795.
82. IKorinthMeritt §§74, 76; IKorinthWest §§83, 86–91.
83. IKorinthWest §15.
84. IKorinthWest §17.
85. IKorinthWest §§67, 71, 81; IKorinthKent §§150, 154, 156, [159], 170, [171], 173, [203], [208], 212, [213], [217].
86. IKorinthWest §§82–85; IKorinthKent §§[156], [173], *208, 209, *212, 213, [214]. Cf. Louis Robert, "Inscriptions de l'antiquité et du bas-empire à Corinthe." *REG* 79 (1966): 754–56.
87. IKorinthWest §68.
88. IKorinthWest §104ᵃ.
89. IKorinthWest §67.
90. Millis, "Social and Ethnic Origins," 26–30.
91. E.g., IKorinthKent §322.
92. Oscar Broneer, *The South Stoa and Its Roman Successors*, vol. 1.4 of *Corinth:*

Latin and Greek mason's marks and roof tile stamps exist in fair numbers.[93]

5.4. Language Contact in Dual-Perspective Inscriptions

In addition to Priscus (§5.1.2 above), there are several elite figures who are honored in both Latin and Greek at Corinth (although not in both languages at once, i.e., on the same stone). Gaius Iulius Spartiaticus is one well-known example (e.g., Greek: IKorinthMeritt §70; Latin: IKorinthWest §68).[94]

5.5. Language Contact in Multiple-Use Inscriptions

Some inscriptions show evidence of multiple use, with one language being inscribed either over the other (the first text usually partially effaced) or on another surface of the same stone. These offer fascinating material for considering linguistic and cultural contact and identity in Roman Corinth. Some indicative examples are the following.

- IKorinthMeritt §31 (traces of a Greek inscription, dated to the fourth century BCE) and IKorinthWest §1 (a Latin elegiac inscribed on a different surface, dated to the first century BCE)
- IKorinthMeritt §102 (Greek elegiac inscribed over partially erased Latin) and IKorinthWest §117 (the original four partially erased lines of Latin)
- IKorinthMeritt §106 (Greek dedication to a Roman magistrate with traces of Latin visible beneath).
- IKorinthWest §193 (Latin NER cut into the base of an earlier Greek tripod base).

Results of Excavations Conducted by the American School of Classical Studies at Athens (Cambridge: American School of Classical Studies at Athens, 1954), 65, pl. 16$_1$.

93. Oscar Broneer, *The Odeum*, vol. 10 of *Corinth: Results of Excavations Conducted by the American School of Classical Studies at Athens* (Cambridge: American School of Classical Studies at Athens, 1932), 135–39. See also Millis, "Social and Ethnic Origins," 26 nn. 43–44.

94. For full data, see Rizakis, Zoumbaki, and Kantirea, *Roman Peloponnese I*, Corinthia 353.

6. Conclusion[95]

In summary, mixed-language inscriptions and other inscribed instances of language contact at Roman Corinth are an area deserving increased study and attention. The results of a thorough investigation of the available material promises to contribute to our understanding of the linguistic and cultural identity of the early Roman colony and those who passed through its inscribed spaces and handled or even had a hand in manufacturing goods that were stamped or inscribed. Bringing sociolinguistic categories such as linguistic interference, code-switching (accommodation, contextualization), linguistic domain, and epigraphic community may help to augment historical studies of Roman Corinth that have employed categories of hybridity from cultural studies. One way forward would be to adopt something like the fivefold typology suggested above in order to gather and analyze all Roman Corinthian inscriptions that demonstrate language contact.

Appendix: Selection of Mixed-Language Inscriptions from Roman Corinth

The following is an annotated list of inscriptions with two scripts attested in the same text. Most would be categorized as "dual language" in the typology suggested above.

1.	IKorinthMeritt §71 + IKorinthKent §41 See §5.1.1 above	Latin-Greek	theater, artist's signature
2.	IKorinthMeritt §130	Latin-Greek	funerary

---

95. Earlier research for this project was funded by Macquarie University's Postgraduate Research Fund (2012–2013) as well as the Society for the Study of Early Christianity, associated with the Macquarie University Department of Ancient History. I remain very grateful for this support. An initial version of this essay was presented to the American Society of Greek and Latin Epigraphy panel at the 2012 meeting of the American Philological Association in Philadelphia. I thank those present for their interaction.

Epitaph with Latin names above Greek elegiac couplets. Dated second century CE by Meritt on letter forms, but Millis suggests it should be "probably much earlier" (Millis, "Social and Ethnic Origins," 25 n. 39).

3. IKorinthWest §65   Latin-Greek* funerary?
Epitaph in Latin but with mistakenly inserted Greek characters (line 5: BENE ΛΕ SE MIΛITO), possibly reflecting the stonecutter's language patterns and/or linguistic competency.

4. IKorinthKent §116   Greek-Latin* statue base
Honorific inscription in Greek but with a mistakenly inserted a Latin L (line 4) rather than a Οὐ (=Latin V) at the start of the name [Οὐ]ίβιον.

5. IKorinthKent §276   Latin-Greek testamentary dedication?
Latin text more or less directly translated by Greek below.

6. IKorinthKent §305   Greek-Latin* funerary
Greek with mistaken Latin letter (line 2: PR instead of ΠΡ).

7. IKorinthKent §306   Greek-Latin rescript on stela
See §5.1.2 above.

8. IKorinthKent §310   Latin-Greek* ?
Latin text with mistakenly inscribed Greek character (line 4: Φ instead of F).

9. IKorinthKent §342   Latin-Greek funerary?
A fragmentary line of Latin above an incomplete line of Greek. Includes a loan-word ([φα]μιλίαι = *familiae*).

10. *CIL* 3.536   Latin-Greek honorific decree
Latin text with concluding Ψ(ηφίσματι) Β(ουλῆς) instead of Latin *D(ecurionum) D(ecreto)*.

11. *Hesperia* 69 (2000): 335–42   Latin-Greek dedication? on stela
Editio princeps by Michael D. Dixon of a fragment with parts of four Latin lines followed by two in Greek, dated tentatively to the second century CE.

Works Cited

Adams, James N. *Bilingualism and the Latin Language*. Cambridge: Cambridge University Press, 2003.

———. "Bilingualism at Delos." Pages 103–27 in *Bilingualism in Ancient Society: Language Contact and the Written Text*. Edited by James N. Adams, Mark Janse, and Simon Swain. Oxford: Oxford University Press, 2002.

Adams, James N., Mark Janse, and Simon Swain, eds. *Bilingualism in Ancient Society: Language Contact and the Written Text*. Oxford: Oxford University Press, 2002.

Adams, James N., and Simon Swain. "Introduction." Pages 1–20 in *Bilingualism in Ancient Society: Language Contact and the Written Text*. Edited by James N. Adams, Mark Janse, and Simon Swain. Oxford: Oxford University Press, 2002.

Auer, Peter. *Bilingual Conversation*. Pragmatics and Beyond 8. Philadelphia: Benjamins, 1984.

Balzat, Jean-Sébastien, and Benjamin M. Millis. "M. Antonius Aristocrates: Provincial Involvement with Roman Power in the Late 1st Century B.C." *Hesperia* 82 (2013): 651–72.

Bitner, Bradley J. "Augustan Procedure and Legal Documents in RDGE 70." *GRBS* 54 (2014): 639–64.

———. "Coinage and Colonial Identity: Corinthian Numismatics and the Corinthian Correspondence." Pages 151–87 in *The First Urban Churches 1: Methodological Foundations*. Edited by James R. Harrison and L. L. Welborn. WGRWSup 7. Atlanta: SBL Press, 2015.

———. *Paul's Political Strategy in 1 Corinthians 1–4: Constitution and Covenant*. SNTSMS 163. Cambridge: Cambridge University Press, 2015.

Bookidis, Nancy, and Elizabeth G. Pemberton. *The Sanctuary of Demeter and Kore: The Greek Lamps and the Offering Trays*. Vol. 18.7 of *Corinth: Results of Excavations Conducted by the American School of Classical Studies at Athens*. Princeton: American School of Classical Studies, 2016.

Broneer, Oscar. *The Odeum*. Vol. 10 of *Corinth: Results of Excavations Conducted by the American School of Classical Studies at Athens*. Cambridge: American School of Classical Studies at Athens, 1932.

———. "An Official Rescript from Corinth." *Hesperia* 8 (1939): 181–90.

———. *The South Stoa and Its Roman Successors*. Vol. 1.4 of *Corinth: Results of Excavations Conducted by the American School of Classical Studies at Athens*. Cambridge: American School of Classical Studies at Athens, 1954.

Camia, F. "IG IV 203: La cronologia di P. Licinius Priscus Iuventianus, Archiereus della lega achea." *Annuario della scuola archeologica di atene* 80 (2002): 361–78.

Concannon, Cavan W. *"When You Were Gentiles": Specters of Ethnicity in Roman Corinth and Paul's Corinthian Correspondence*. New Haven: Yale University Press, 2014.
D'Hautcourt, A. "Corinthe: Financement d'une colonization et d'une reconstruction." Pages 427–38 in *Constructions publiques et programmes édilitaires en Grèce entre le IIe siècle av. J.-C. et le Ier siècle ap. J.-C.: Actes du colloque organisé par l'École française d'Athènes et le CNRS, Athènes, 14–17 mai 1995*. Edited by J.-Y. Marc and J.-C. Moretti. BCHSup 39. Athens: École française d'Athènes; de Boccard, 2001.
Dittenberger, Wilhelm, and Karl Purgold. *Die Inschriften von Olympia*. Berlin: Asher, 1896.
Donderer, Michael. *Die Architekten der späten römischen Republik und der Kaiserzeit: Epigraphische Zeugnisse*. Erlangen: Universitätsbund Erlangen-Nürnberg, 1996.
Fraser, P. M., and E. Matthews, eds. *The Peloponnese, Western Greece, Sicily, and Magna Graecia*. Vol. 3A of *Lexicon of Greek Personal Names*. Oxford: Clarendon, 1997.
Geagan, Daniel J. "The Isthmian Dossier of P. Licinius Priscus Iuventianus." *Hesperia* 58 (1989): 349–60.
Guarducci, Margherita. *Epigrafi di carattere private*. Vol. 3 of *Epigrafia Greca*. Rome: Instituto Poligrafico, 1974.
Hellmann, Marie-Christine. "Les signatures d'architectes en langue grecque: Essai de mise au point." *ZPE* 104 (1994): 151–78.
Hock, Hans Henrich, and Brian D. Joseph. *Language History, Language Change, and Language Relationship: An Introduction to Historical and Comparative Linguistics*. Trends in Linguistics: Studies and Monographs 93. Berlin: de Gruyter, 1996.
Horsley, G. H. R. "The Fiction of 'Jewish Greek.'" *NewDocs* 5:1–40.
James, Sarah A. "The Last of the Corinthians? Society and Settlement from 146 to 44 BCE." Pages 17–37 in *Corinth in Contrast: Studies in Inequality*. Edited by Steven J. Friesen, Sarah A. James, and Daniel N. Schowalter. NovTSup 155. Leiden: Brill, 2014.
Kaimio, Jorma. *The Romans and the Greek Language*. CHL 64. Helsinki: Societas Scientiarum Fennica, 1979.
Kalinka, Ernst. *Tituli Lyciae linguis Graeca et Latina conscripti*. Vol. 2 of *Tituli Asiae Minoris*. 3 fasc. Vienna: Hölder, 1920–1944.
Kearsley, Rosalinde, with Trevor V. Evans. *Greeks and Romans in Imperial Asia: Mixed Language Inscriptions and Linguistic Evidence for Cultural Interaction until the End of AD III*. IGSK 59. Köln: Habelt, 2001.

Keegan, Peter. "Texting Rome: Graffiti as Speech-Act and Cultural Discourse." Pages 165–90 in *Ancient Graffiti in Context*. Edited by Jennifer A. Baird and Claire Taylor. London: Routledge, 2010.

Kent, John Harvey, ed. *The Inscriptions, 1926–1950*. Vol. 8.3 of *Corinth: Results of Excavations Conducted by the American School of Classical Studies at Athens*. Princeton: American School of Classical Studies at Athens, 1966.

Kokkinia, Christina. "Letters of Roman Authorities on Local Dignitaries: The Case of Vedius Antoninus." *ZNW* 142 (2003): 197–213.

———. *Die Opramoas-Inschrift von Rhodiapolis: Euergetismus und soziale Eliten in Lykien*. Bonn: Habelt, 2000.

———. "The Role of Individuals in Inscribing Roman State Documents." Pages 191–206 in *Selbstdarstellung und Kommunikation: Die Veröffentlichung staatlicher Urkunden auf Stein und Bronze in der römischen Welt*. Edited by Rudolf Haensch. Munich: Beck, 2009.

Larson, Jennifer. "Bilingual Inscriptions and Translation in the Ancient Mediterranean World." Pages in 50–74 in *Complicating the History of Western Translation: The Ancient Mediterranean in Perspective*. Edited by Siobhán McElduff and Enrica Scarrino. New York: Routledge, 2011.

Leiwo, Martti. "From Contact to Mixture: Bilingual Inscriptions from Italy." Pages 168–95 in *Bilingualism in Ancient Society: Language Contact and The Written Text*. Edited by James N. Adams, Mark Janse, and Simon Swain Oxford: Oxford University Press, 2002.

———. "The Mixed Languages in Roman Inscriptions." Pages 293–301 in *Acta Colloquii Epigraphici Latini, Helsingiae 3–6 September* 1991. Edited by Heikki Solin, Olli Salomies, and Uta-Maria Liertz. CHL 104. Helsinki: Societas Scientiarum Fennica, 1995.

L'Institut Fernand-Courby. *Nouveau choix d'inscriptions grecques*. Paris: Belles lettres, 1971.

Loewy, Emanuel. *Inschriften Griechischer Bildhauer*. 1885. Repr., Chicago: Ares, 1976.

Ma, John. "Seleukids and Speech-Acts: Performative Utterances, Legitimacy and Negotiation in the World of the Maccabees." *Scripta Israelica Classica* 19 (2000): 71–112.

McLean, Bradley M. *An Introduction to Greek Epigraphy of the Hellenistic and Roman Periods from Alexander the Great down to the Reign of Constantine (323 BC–AD 337)*. Ann Arbor: University of Michigan Press, 2002.

Meritt, Benjamin Dean, ed. *Greek Inscriptions, 1896–1927*. Vol. 8.1 of *Corinth: Results of Excavations Conducted by the American School of Classical Studies at Athens*. Cambridge: American School of Classical Studies at Athens, 1931.

Millis, Benjamin M. "The Social and Ethnic Origins of the Colonists in Early Roman Corinth." Pages 13–35 in *Corinth in Context: Comparative Studies on Religion and Society*. Edited by Steven J. Friesen, Daniel N. Schowalter, and James C. Walters. NovTSup 134. Leiden: Brill, 2010.

Price, Jonathan J. and Shlomo Naeh. "On the Margins of Culture: The Practice of Transcription in the Ancient World." Pages 257–88 in *From Hellenism to Islam: Cultural and Linguistic Change in the Ancient Near East*. Edited by Hannah Cotton. Cambridge: Cambridge University Press, 2009.

Reynolds, Joyce. *Aphrodisias and Rome*. Journal of Roman Studies Monographs 1. London: Society for the Promotion of Roman Studies, 1982.

Rizakis, Athanasios D., Sophia B. Zoumbaki, and Maria Kantirea. *Roman Peloponnese I: Roman Personal Names in Their Social Context*. Paris: de Boccard, 2001.

Robert, Louis. "Un edifice du sanctuaire de l'Isthme dans une inscription de Corinthe." *Hell* 1 (1940): 43–53.

———. *Hellenica: Recueil d'épigraphie de numasmatique et d'antiquités grecques*. Vols. 11–12. Paris: Librairie d'amérique et d'orient, Adrien-Maisoneuve, 1960.

———. "Inscriptions de l'antiquité et du bas-empire à Corinthe." *REG* 79 (1966): 754–56. Repr. as pages 572–74 in Robert, *Épigraphie et antiquités grecques*. Vol. 6 of *Opera Minora Selecta*. Amsterdam: Hakkert, 1989.

Robinson, Betsey A. "Fountains and the Formation of Cultural Identity at Roman Corinth." Pages 111–140 in *Urban Religion in Roman Corinth*. Edited Daniel N. Schowalter and Steven J. Friesen. HTS 53. Cambridge: Harvard University Press, 2005.

Sanders, G. D. R. "Urban Corinth: An Introduction." Pages 11–24 in *Urban Religion in Roman Corinth*. Edited Daniel N. Schowalter and Steven J. Friesen. HTS 53. Cambridge: Harvard University Press, 2005.

Smith, K. K. "Greek Inscriptions from Corinth II." *AJA* 23 (1919): 331–93.

Spawforth, Antony J. S. *Greece and the Augustan Cultural Revolution*. Cambridge: Cambridge University Press, 2012.

———. "Roman Corinth: The Formation of a Colonial Elite." Pages 167–82 in *Roman Onomastics in the Greek East: Social and Political Aspects; Proceedings of the International Colloquium on Roman Onomastics, Athens, 7-9 September 1993*. Edited by A. D. Rizakis. Μελητήματα 21. Athens: Κέντρος Ἑλληνικῆς καὶ Ῥωμαϊκῆς Ἀρχαιότητος τοῦ Ἐθνικοῦ Ἱδρύματος Ἐρευνῶν, 1996.

Stroud, Ronald S. *The Sanctuary of Demeter and Kore: The Inscriptions*. Vol. 18.6 of *Corinth: Results of Excavations Conducted by the American School of Classical Studies at Athens*. Princeton: American School of Classical Studies at Athens, 2013.

Sturgeon, Mary C. "Dedications of Roman Theaters." Pages 411–29 in *ΧΑΡΙΣ: Essays in Honor of Sara A. Immerwahr*. Edited by Anne P. Chapin. Hesperia Supplements 33. Princeton: American School of Classical Studies at Athens, 2004.

———. "Roman Sculptures from Corinth and Isthmia: The Case for a Local 'Workshop.'" Pages 114–21 in *The Greek Renaissance in the Roman Empire: Papers from the Tenth British Museum Classical Colloquium*. Edited by Susan Walker and Averil Cameron. BICSSup 55. London: University of London, Institute of Classical Studies, 1989.

———. *Sculpture: The Assemblage from the Theater*. Vol. 9.3 of *Corinth: Results of Excavations Conducted by the American School of Classical Studies at Athens*. Athens: American School of Classical Studies at Athens, 2004.

Thomas, Christine M. "Greek Heritage in Roman Corinth and Ephesos: Hybrid Identities and Strategies of Display in the Material Record of Traditional Mediterranean Religions." Pages 117–47 in *Corinth in Context: Comparative Studies on Religion and Society*. Edited by Steven J. Friesen, Daniel N. Schowalter, and James C. Walters. NovTSup 134. Leiden: Brill, 2010.

Touloumakos, Johannes. "Bilingue [Grieschisch-Lateinische] Weihinschriften der römischen Zeit," Τεκμήρια 1 (1995): 79–129.

Walbank, Mary E. Hoskins. "Image and Cult: The Coinage of Roman Corinth." Pages 151–97 in *Corinth in Context: Comparative Studies on Religion and Society*. Edited by Steven J. Friesen, Daniel N. Schowalter, and James C. Walters. NovTSup 134. Leiden: Brill, 2010.

West, Allen Brown, ed. *Latin Inscriptions, 1896–1926*. Vol. 8.2 of *Corinth: Results of Excavations Conducted by the American School of Classical Studies at Athens*. Cambridge: American School of Classical Studies at Athens, 1931.

"The God of This Age" (2 Cor 4:4) and Paul's Empire-Resisting Gospel at Corinth*

Fredrick J. Long

Introduction

The interpretation of "the god of this age" in 2 Cor 4:4 was more puzzling to ancient interpreters than for modern ones. Among commentators today, Paul simply makes reference to Satan,[1] who deludes potential converts and

---

* Some of this research was initially presented in the Intertextuality in the New Testament Session at the Annual SBL Meeting in San Francisco, 19 November 2011, but subsequently substantially revised. Many thanks are due to Vernon K. Robbins and Roy R. Jeal for their helpful comments on my research.

1. So Carl F. G. Heinrici, *Der zweite Brief an die Korinther, mit einem Anhang: Zum Hellenismus des Paulus*, 8th ed., KEK (Göttingen: Vandenhoeck & Ruprecht, 1900), 147; Hans Windisch, *Der zweite Korintherbrief*, 9th ed., KEK (Göttingen: Vandenhoeck & Ruprecht, 1970), 135–36; Rudolf Karl Bultmann, *The Second Letter to the Corinthians*, trans. Roy A. Harrisville (Minneapolis: Augsburg, 1985), 103; against a Qumran background, see Gerhard Dautzenberg, "Überlegungen zur Exegese und Theologie von 2 Kor 4,1–6," *Bib* 82 (2001): 325–44. Philip E. Hughes states, "It is plain that by 'the god of this age' Satan is meant" (*Paul's Second Epistle to the Corinthians: The English Text with Introduction, Exposition and Notes*, NICNT [Grand Rapids: Eerdmans, 1962], 126); Paul Barnett simply states, "the god of this age, Satan, has blinded their eyes" (*The Second Epistle to the Corinthians*, NICNT (Grand Rapids: Eerdmans, 1997], 211). Cf. Murray J. Harris, *The Second Epistle to the Corinthians: A Commentary on the Greek Text*, NIGTC (Grand Rapids: Eerdmans, 2005), 327.

In this regard, interpreters are often right to associate "the god of this age" with "the rulers of this age" in 1 Cor 2:6–8; Eph 2:2; John 12:31; 14:30; 16:11 (e.g., Windisch, Bultmann, Hughes, and Dautzenberg) but fail to understand how these passages refer to human rulers; see note 16 below. Bultmann relegated Paul's notion to the gnostic concept of the aeon's or world's power in opposition to God as evil, not just imperfect, before then demythologizing it (*Second Letter to the Corinthians*, 203–4). A Jewish

afflicts Paul with suffering.[2] However, in the early church the difficulty of the passage was seen clearly by Tertullian, who mused over three interpretive possibilities.[3] First, Tertullian rejected Marcion's "two-god" gnostic theory (*Marc.* 5.11, *ANF* 3:454).[4] Second, Tertullian proposed an interpretation eventually held by Irenaeus (*Haer.* 4.48), Origen, Chrysostom, Oecumenius, Theodoret, and Theophylact in which "of this age" is taken not with "God" but with "unbelievers" at the end of the verse, so that the verse speaks of God blinding the minds of "the unbelievers of this age."[5] Third, Tertullian favored the more common view held today that "the god of this age" is none other than the devil, and he immediately quoted Isa 14:14 in support, "I will be like the Most High; I will exalt my throne in the clouds," as if this were Isaiah's report on the devil's own egoistical statement (*Marc.* 5.11, *ANF* 3:454). But, Tertullian was himself blinded in that Isaiah was not reporting Satan's speech but the speech of the arrogant king of Babylon, as a taunt against the king:[6] "How you have fallen from heaven, O star of the morning [MT: הֵילֵל; LXX: ὁ ἑωσφόρος; Vulgate: *Lucifer*], son of the dawn [MT: בֶּן־שָׁחַר; LXX: ὁ πρωὶ ἀνατέλλων]! You have been cut down to the earth, You who have weakened the nations!" (Isa 14:12 NASB).[7]

---

gnostic dualistic background using Qumran documents (esp. 1QS 3–4) for interpreting the passage is found in Dautzenberg ("Überlegungen zur Exegese und Theologie," 340).

2. For the delusion of potential converts, see, e.g., Victor B. Cole, "The Message and Messenger of the Gospel," *Evangelical Review of Theology* 29 (2005): 178–84. for afflicting Paul with suffering, see, e.g., Susan R. Garrett, "The God of This World and the Affliction of Paul: 2 Cor 4:1–12," in *Greeks, Romans, and Christians: Essays in Honor of Abraham J. Malherbe*, ed. David L. Balch, Everett Ferguson, and Wayne A. Meeks (Minneapolis: Fortress, 1990), 99–117.

3. For discussion, see Norbert Brox, "Non Huius Aevi Deus: Zu Tertullian, *Adv Marc* V 11, 10," *ZNW* 59 (1968): 259–61; and Margaret E. Thrall, *2 Corinthians 1–7: A Critical and Exegetical Commentary*, ICC (London: T&T Clark, 1994) 305–10.

4. See, e.g., Hans Conzelmann, "φῶς, φωτίζω, κτλ.," *TDNT* 9:346 n. 291: "The expression ὁ θεὸς τοῦ αἰῶνος τούτου is dualistic, cf. 1 C. 2:8; Eph. 2:2; Jn. 12:31."

5. Instead of Satan, James M. Scott gives "a slight preference" to viewing God as the referent (*2 Corinthians*, NIBCNT 8 [Peabody, MA: Hendrickson, 1998], 85–86).

6. Typical is John D. W. Watts: "Whatever the myth might have said, the text in Isaiah tells of a tyrant king who is overcome, not by the resistance of a god, but by his own ambition to be as high as a god, to *ascend to heaven*, to reign *above the stars*, to sit in *the mountain assembly*, and to be *like the Most High*" (*Isaiah 1–33*, WBC 24 [Dallas: Word, 2002], 210–11, emphasis original).

7. Unless otherwise noted, biblical translations are mine.

Akin to the referent in Isaiah, I will argue that "the god of this age" in 2 Cor 4:4 should be understood as a counterimperial statement against the profusion of iconography and ideology propounding the Roman emperors as godlike and self-proclaimed gods. The expression "the god of this age" would have been readily so-identified, since there had been a long-established tradition of praising Mediterranean kings as gods[8] and, more recently, the emperor and the imperial family were acclaimed as a god (θεός) or gods (θεοί) in the Greek-speaking world, dead or alive.[9] But more specifically, the deified Augustus was featured prominently in statuary on a lavish podium in the center of the Corinthian forum dating to Tiberius's reign. The dedicatory inscription began with [DIVO A]VGVS[TO] SACRVM / ... / [AV]GVSTALES "Holy to the Divine Augustus / ... / the Augustans."[10] Several other statues of imperial gods were also manifest at Corinth.[11] Margaret L. Laird comments on the importance of the central statue: "This is a dedication that was commissioned to participate in a developing civic program of emperor worship focusing in various forms in Corinth's Forum. As positioned, the *Augustales* statue and base were

---

8. For a review of the Hellenistic notion of deified human rulers, see Hermann Kleinknecht, "θεός, θεότης, κτλ.," *TDNT* 3:69–70; cf. LSJ, 1569, s.v., σεβαστός.

9. E.g., G. Adolf Deissmann, *Light from the Ancient East: The New Testament Illustrated by Recently Discovered Texts of the Graeco-Roman World*, trans. L. R. M. Strachan, 4th ed. (New York: Doran, 1927), 347–53. Augustus was further identified as the god Mercury, the ἄγγελος τοῦ Διός "the angel of Zeus" (A. D. Nock, "Notes on Ruler-Cult I–IV," *JHS* 48 [1928]: 33). Nero was considered a νέος Κάβειρος "a new Cabeirian divinity," Ἀπόλλων κτίστης "Apollo Founder," and Ζεύς Ἐλευθέριος "Zeus the Deliverer" (Nock, "Notes on Ruler-Cult," 34; references are provided in nn. 57, 65, and 68). Augustus and successive emperors identified themselves with and were identified as Jupiter/Zeus; see J. Rufus Fears, "The Cult of Jupiter and Roman Imperial Ideology," *ANRW* 17.1:3–141.

10. John Harvey Kent, ed., *The Inscriptions, 1926–1950*, vol. 8.3 of *Corinth: Results of Excavations Conducted by the American School of Classical Studies at Athens* (Princeton: American School of Classical Studies at Athens, 1966), §53 (= IKorinthKent).

11. Other inscriptions praising deified members of the Julian-Claudian household include DIVO IUL[IO] [SACRUM] (IKorinthKent §50) and then two others for Julia: IULIA DIVA AVGVSTA referring to a poetry contest at imperial games for Livia ca. 25 CE (IKorinthKent §153) and THEA IOULIA SEBASTE dated either before her death (29 CE) or at her deification (42 CE) (Benjamin Dean Meritt, ed., *Greek Inscriptions, 1896–1927*, vol. 8.1 of *Corinth: Results of Excavations Conducted by the American School of Classical Studies at Athens* [Cambridge: American School of Classical Studies at Athens, 1931], §19).

nestled among several loci of emperor worship, each celebrating a different aspect of imperial power."[12] Additional social-historical data from the mid-first century at Corinth (summarized in the first section below) would indicate that a prevailing influence of the imperial cult existed as a tempting influence on the early Christian believers there.[13]

To suppose that the audience at Roman Corinth or the broader environs of Achaia would hear the statement as referring directly to the devil or Satan is unlikely. Margaret Thrall, like so many commentators, accepts Satan as the referent, "even though such a designation appears to have no parallels."[14] Indeed, no Jewish background accounts for the expression, as Craig S. Keener summarizes, "Other Jewish teachers did not explicitly speak of Satan as the 'god of this age.'"[15] Additionally, when Paul elsewhere speaks of Satan, the devil, or the evil one, he does so rather directly,

---

12. Margaret L. Laird, "The Emperor in a Roman Town: The Base of the *Augustales* in the Forum at Corinth," in *Corinth in Context: Comparative Studies on Religion and Society*, ed. Steven J. Friesen, Daniel N. Schowalter, and James C. Walters, NovTSup 134 (Leiden: Brill, 2010), 89.

13. More generally, for the pervasiveness of the imperial cult and the deification of Augustus, see S. R. F. Price, *Rituals and Power: The Roman Imperial Cult in Asia Minor* (Cambridge: Cambridge University Press, 1984); and the excellent essays in Alastair Small, ed., *Subject and Ruler: The Cult of the Ruling Power in Classical Antiquity; Papers Presented at a Conference Held in the University of Alberta on April 13–15, 1994, to Celebrate the 65th Anniversary of Duncan Fishwick*, JRASup 17 (Ann Arbor: Journal of Roman Archaeology, 1996); more recently, see Rebecca Edwards, "Divus Augustus Pater: Tiberius and the Charisma of Augustus" (PhD diss., Indiana University, 2003); and P. J. J. Botha, "Assessing Representations of the Imperial Cult in New Testament Studies," *Verbum et Ecclesia* 25 (2004): 14–45.

14. Thrall, *2 Corinthians 1–7*, 308. So, too, e.g., Frank G. Carver: "The expression the god of this age (*aiōnos*) is without parallel in the NT" (*2 Corinthians: A Commentary in the Wesleyan Tradition*, New Beacon Bible Commentary [Kansas City: Beacon Hill, 2009], 146).

15. The quotation continues, "but most of them recognized that the nations (everyone but themselves) were ruled by spiritual powers under Satan's command" (Craig S. Keener, *The IVP Bible Background Commentary: New Testament*, 2nd ed. (Downers Grove, IL: IVP Academic, 2014), 505. Dautzenberg agrees: "Die Qualifikation der dämonischen Gegenmacht als 'Gott dieses Äons' ist vor dem Hintergrund der exklusiven jüdischen Gottesaussage einmalig und mehr als ungewöhnlich. In frühjüdischen Texten und Überlieferungen begegnet die Bezeichnung אל (Gott, Gottheit) zwar für Engel, die als Mittlergestalten fungieren, aber nicht für den Satan" ("Überlegungen zur Exegese und Theologie," 339).

as a review of his usage clearly demonstrates.[16] The Pauline Epistles evince a broader recognition of rulers and authorities under and/or in opposition to God, but typically in the plural.[17] One notable exception is "the ruler of the authority of the air, the spirit now working among the sons of disobedience" (Eph 2:2); however, considerable evidence exists that "the ruler" here is the emperor (accusative case), and "the authority of the air, the spirit" (genitive case) refers to Jupiter-Zeus, the god identified in pagan commentaries with air (ἀήρ) and well-known as controlling the air (storms, lightning, rain, hail, etc.).[18] Moreover, in the Pauline Epistles, whenever the word "god" (θεός) is used and not referring to the One God, it refers to the "so-called (pagan) gods" or human stand-ins for God (Gal 4:8; 1 Cor 8:5; 2 Thess 2:4; cf. Phil 3:19). Thus, a preliminary review of "god" (θεός) in Paul and of other references to opposing forces, such as rulers and authorities) in the Pauline Epistles would initially indicate that

---

16. "Satan" (Rom 16:20; 1 Cor 5:5; 7:5; 2 Cor 2:11; 11:14; 12:7; 1 Thess 2:18; 2 Thess 2:9; 1 Tim 1:20; 5:15); "devil" (Eph 4:27; 6:11; 1 Tim 3:6-7; 2 Tim 2:26) and "the evil one" (Eph 6:16; 2 Thess 3:3). Outside of Paul, reference is made to "the ruler of this world" in John 12:31; 14:30; 16:11; however, Warren Carter has argued, and I agree and supply further evidence (see essay in n. 19 below), that these references are to "Pilate, agent of Roman power," who was also an active promoter of the imperial cult; see Carter, *John and Empire: Initial Explorations* (New York: T&T Clark, 2008), 182; Carter, *Pontius Pilate: Portraits of a Roman Governor* (Collegeville, MN: Liturgical Press, 2003); Joan E. Taylor, "Pontius Pilate and the Imperial Cult in Roman Judaea," *NTS* 52 (2006): 555-82.

17. A list of evil forces occurs in Eph 6:12, beginning with ἀρχή with ἐξουσία in the plural, as is found elsewhere in the Pauline Epistles as "rulers and authorities" (Rom 8:38; 1 Cor 15:24; Eph 1:21; 3:10; 6:12; Col 1:16; 2:10, 15; Titus 3:1; cf. the ἡ ἐξουσία τοῦ σκότους in Col 1:13). As closest analogies to 2 Cor 4:4, often interpreters will offer 1 Cor 2:6, 8 ("the rulers of this age"), Eph 2:2 ("the ruler of the authority of the air, the spirit"), and Phil 3:19 ("their god is their belly"), but Phil 3:19 is probably metaphorical or perhaps debunks some paganism at Philippi influenced by Epicureanism; 1 Cor 2:6, 8 refers to earthly, human rulers (see, decisively, Gordon D. Fee, *New Testament Exegesis: A Handbook for Students and Pastors*, 3rd ed. [Louisville: Westminster, 2002], 84-89); for Eph 2:2, see the following note.

18. Regarding this interpretation of Eph 2:2, see my "Roman Imperial Rule under the Authority of Jupiter-Zeus: Political-Religious Contexts and the Interpretation of 'the Ruler of the Authority of the Air' in Ephesians 2:2," in *The Language of the New Testament: Context, History and Development*, ed. Stanley E. Porter and Andrew W. Pitts, Linguistic Biblical Studies 6, Early Christianity in Its Hellenistic Environment 3 (Leiden: Brill, 2013), 113-54.

in 2 Cor 4:4 Paul had a pagan deity and/or human referent in view when he spoke of "the god of this age."

I have found only one proponent holding a similar view, George Wesley Buchanan.[19] While walking through Paul's argument in 2 Cor 3:1–4:6, Buchanan describes broadly the Jewish conception of *ages* under foreign domination. The period 586–146 BCE featured the god of "the Greek age, the evil age, the age of slavery, the beasts, and the Gentiles," Antiochus Epiphanes. That age was followed by the Hasmonean age, and "the god of that age was the Jewish God, incarnate in the various Hasmonean leaders." Finally, the next age, "this age" in Paul's thought, was dominated by the Romans: "It was also thought of as the evil age and the captivity. Another early Jew called Beliar the 'ruler of this world' (Asc. of Isa. 4:2). ... The god of this age, then, was the god of the Romans, and it was incarnate in Caesar. There was probably no doubt at all in the minds of Jews and Christians about what Paul meant when he used this expression." Buchanan provides no further explanation or evidence. More specifically than Buchanan, I argue that "the god of this age" would have found referent in the deified emperor Augustus, whose iconography on coins, statues, reliefs, gems, temples, and other realia truly provided a counter-brightness so as to blind the minds of unbelievers.

In what follows I will present four lines of investigation to support this interpretation. First, I will briefly summarize the populace of Corinth's participation in and devotion to local and regional imperial cults and closely allied activities. Second, brief consideration will be given to the ideological significance of the pervasive triumphal processional theme in 2 Cor 2:14–7:2 that corresponds to events impacting Roman Corinth as Paul was composing his epistles. Third, an investigation of the Roman imperial topics in 4:1–6 will be seen to strongly imply a restricted referent to "the god of this age" in 4:4. Fourth and last, a study of the discursive development and parallels between 4:1–6 and 6:14–7:1 will show a thematic and referential link between "the god of this age" and Paul's warnings to the Corinthians not to have accord (συμφώνησις) with the mysterious Beliar (6:15), which was a code name for the leader of the Romans (e.g., the Qumran War Scroll, etc.), thus implicitly referring to the new emperor Nero.

---

19. George Wesley Buchanan, "Paul and the Jews (II Cor 3:4–4:6 and Rom 11:7–10)," in *When Jews and Christians Meet*, ed. Jakob Josef Petuchowski (Albany: State University of New York Press, 1988), 156.

Imperial Devotion at Corinth and Achaia

Archeological and exegetical studies have rightfully drawn our attention to the active presence and influence of the imperial cult at Roman Corinth.[20] The director of US Archeologists in Corinth, Charles Williams II, has stated, "Paul's greatest enemy in Corinth was the Imperial Cult."[21] The Corinthian converts to Christ appear to have struggled with imperial cultic participation, which is not surprising, since Corinth from its refoundation as the *Colonia Laus Iulia Corinthiensis* maintained active connections with the imperial family and cult. Many additional historical considerations support this view.[22] First, several imperial temples and buildings were constructed in Corinth.[23] Second, at least four cult groups at Corinth were committed to honoring the imperial family and participating in the imperial cult during Paul's preaching there: the *Lares Augusti* (constituted by minor municipal officials), the subsidiary cults of *Providentia Augusti* and *Salus Publica* (probably during Tiberius's reign), the Claudian cult of *Victoria Britannica* commemorating his victory,[24] and the influential association in Corinth of the *Augustales*, made up of freedmen

---

20. Mary E. Hoskins Walbank, "Evidence for the Imperial Cult in Julio-Claudian Corinth," in Small, *Subject and Ruler*, 201-13; Laird, "Emperor in a Roman Town," 67-116; Bruce W. Winter, *After Paul Left Corinth: The Influence of Secular Ethics and Social Change* (Grand Rapids: Eerdmans, 2001), 269-86; and Mark T. Finney, "Christ Crucified and the Inversion of Roman Imperial Ideology in 1 Corinthians," *BTB* 35 (2005): 20-33, esp. 26-27.

21. As related by Ross Saunders, "Paul and the Imperial Cult," in *Paul and His Opponents*, ed. Stanley E. Porter, Pauline Studies 2 (Leiden: Brill, 2005), 227.

22. A more extensive elaboration of these is found in Fredrick J. Long, "Roman Imperial Analogues and Referents in 2 Corinthians," a paper presented at the Midwest Region of the Society of Biblical Literature, Bourbonnais, IL, 8 February 2015.

23. Details are summarized from Walbank, "Evidence for the Imperial Cult," 209-10; and Laird, "Emperor in a Roman Town," 89-91.

24. Giles Standing, "The Claudian Invasion of Britain and the Cult of *Victoria Britannica*," *Britannia* 34 (2003): 281-88. Although Claudius's victory over Britannia is celebrated elsewhere (e.g., Aphrodisias with the imperial cult), dedicatory inscriptions for the cult of Victoria Britannica have been found at Narbonne, Pisidian Antioch, Rome (Palatine, Julia Basilica), Roselle (Tuscany), and Lyon. At Corinth, Standing indicates, "The true focus of the cult, however, was the emperor Claudius himself, for it was his victory which was personified and venerated at Corinth" (286).

and freeborn, responsible for the statue of the deified Augustus.[25] Third, at least three deceased members of the imperial family held an established cult: Julius, Augustus, and Livia.[26] The deceased heirs of Augustus, Gaius and Lucius, should probably be included as well, since they "were portrayed as gods located together with a dedication to the imperial family living and deceased."[27] However, the most prominent statue was that of the deified Augustus sponsored by the Augustales in the center of the forum. Fourth, the Corinthian coinage reflects intimate and ongoing interest to the details of the broader imperial family.[28] Fifth, the official establishment of the provincial imperial cult in Achaia remarkably only occurred in 54 CE in coordination with Nero's accession to the throne.[29] Sixth, Achaia hosted various games (*ludi*), animal spectacles (*venationes*), and gladiatorial contests (*munera*).[30] With the institution of the Achaian imperial cult in 54 CE, imperial games were held yearly commemorating the birth of the current emperor, Nero, probably commencing in the spring of 55 CE; at these events were *venationes* and probably *munera*, organized by the senior magistrates.[31] The apostle Paul was visiting and sending letters to the Corinthian Christ followers at the ascension of Nero and the institution of the provincial Achaian imperial cult.

---

25. See esp. Walbank, "Evidence for the Imperial Cult," 210–11; and Laird, "Emperor in a Roman Town," 72–75.

26. Discussed in Walbank, "Evidence for the Imperial Cult."

27. Bruce W. Winter, "The Enigma of Imperial Cultic Activities and Paul in Corinth," in *Greco-Roman Culture and the New Testament Studies Commemorating the Centennial of the Pontifical Biblical Institute*, ed. David E. Aune and Frederick E. Brenk, NovTSup 143 (Leiden: Brill, 2012), 66. Winter cites in support Paul D. Scotton, "A New Fragment of an Inscription from the Julian Basilica at Roman Corinth," *Hesperia* 74 (2005): 99–100.

28. Walbank, "Evidence for the Imperial Cult," 202.

29. See Antony J. S. Spawforth, "The Achaean Federal Cult Part I: Pseudo-Julian, Letters 198," *TynBul* 46 (1995): 151–68; and Bruce W. Winter, "The Achaean Federal Imperial Cult II: The Corinthian Church," *TynBul* 46 (1995): 169–78.

30. Summarized from Walbank, "Evidence for the Imperial Cult," 211; Spawforth, "Achaean Federal Cult," 161–64; and Winter, *After Paul Left Corinth*, 269–78.

31. Michael J. D. Carter summarizes the standard procedure: "The presentation of gladiatorial combats and wild beast hunts was especially the responsibility of senior magistrates, *aediles* and *duoviri*, in the Roman colonies" ("The Presentation of Gladiatorial Spectacles in the Greek East: Roman Culture and Greek Identity" [PhD diss., McMaster University, 1999] 168–72, here 171).

All in all, then, we should consider what evidence exists that might show that the Corinthian Christ followers were affected by these historical developments. From 1 Cor 8–10, it becomes clear that, in fact, they struggled with idolatrous affiliations associated with feasting at temples. More specifically, Bruce W. Winter has argued that behind Paul's admonitions here lies the imperial cult.[32] Specifically, "the cup of demons" (ποτήριον δαιμονίων) of 10:21 refers to libation offerings poured out to the genii of the imperial family, who are in 8:5 described as the "so-called gods whether in heaven or on earth."[33] This is more than plausible, since in nearby Athens not just the emperors but a significant number of imperial family members were acknowledged as gods.[34] Importantly, the "associative language" of 1 Cor 10, namely, μετέχω (10:17, 21), κοινωνία (10:16), and κοινωνός (10:18, 20) was strategically redeployed by Paul in 2 Cor 6:14 with μετοχή and κοινωνία, thus indicating continuity of the rhetorical exigency between the two Corinthian letter.[35] Discursively, in 2:14–7:2 Paul uses Roman triumphal processional themes and builds them climactically to address the Christ followers as Corinthians (Κορίνθιοι 6:11), a name that highlights their civic identity, precisely when he confronts their idolatrous relationships (6:14–16).

---

32. Winter, "Achaean Federal Imperial Cult II." Winter summarizes: "There are good reasons then for suggesting that when Paul speaks of 'gods on the earth' he included the emperor and his family. In fact, the imperial cult may well have been specifically in his mind when he made that statement and could account for the dichotomy of 'in heaven' and 'on earth'" (175).

33. Bruce W. Winter, "Identifying the Offering, the Cup and the Table of the 'Demons' in 1 Cor 10:20–21," in *Saint Paul and Corinth: International Scientific Conference Proceedings, Corinth, 23-25 September, 2007*, ed. C. Belezos, S. Despotis, and C. Karakolis (Athens: Psychogios, 2009), 847–68.

34. Fernando Lozano, "*Divi Augusti* and *Theoi Sebastoi*: Roman Initiatives and Greek Answers," *CQ* 57 (2007): 139–52.

35. I accept the view that 2 Cor 6:14–7:1 is not an interpolation; for a review of the evidence, see Harris, *Second Epistle*, 14–25. However, for a recent exposition of the arguments for 2 Corinthians consisting of five letters and letter fragments, including a suggestion regarding their sequence, see L. L. Welborn, *An End to Enmity: Paul and the "Wrongdoer" of Second Corinthians*, BZNW 185 (Berlin: de Gruyter, 2011), xix–xxviii; and Hans Dieter Betz, "2 Cor 6:14–7:1: An Anti-Pauline Fragment?" *JBL* 92 (1973): 88–108.

God's Triumphal Procession in Christ

God's triumphal procession in Christ in 2:14–15 is a clear analogue to Roman imperial realia.[36] David Aus has outlined ten technical procedural elements across 2 Corinthians.[37] However, no one more than Paul Brooks Duff has explored this imagery in 2 Cor 2:14–7:2 in relation not only to Roman triumphs but also cultic epiphany processions.[38] This unit begins and ends dramatically with processional reference: "Thanks be to God who always leads us in triumphal procession in Christ [θριαμβεύω] in every way" (2:14); and "Make room for us!" (Χωρήσατε ἡμᾶς)—a command of heralds for spectators to make room for the coming procession (7:2).[39] However, a close examination of the primary texts utilized by Duff and the surveys of Roman triumphs by H. S. Versnel, Mary Beard, Ida Östenberg, and Aus reveals more than forty processional-cultic and military triumphant themes in 2:14–7:2.[40]

---

36. A large majority of interpreters find allusion to Roman triumph at 2 Cor 2:14; see the excellent recent review by Kar Yong Lim, *"The Sufferings of Christ Are Abundant in Us" (2 Corinthians 1.5): A Narrative Dynamics Investigation of Paul's Sufferings in 2 Corinthians*, LNTS 399 (London: T&T Clark, 2009), 68–79.

37. Roger David Aus, *Imagery of Triumph and Rebellion in 2 Corinthians 2:4–17 and Elsewhere in the Epistle: An Example of the Combination Greco-Roman and Judaic Traditions in the Apostle Paul* (Lanham, MD: University Press of America, 2005), 3–4, 7–39.

38. Paul Brooks Duff, "The Transformation of the Spectator: Power, Perception, and the Day of Salvation," in *Society of Biblical Literature 1987 Seminar Papers*, SBLSP 26 (Missoula, MT: Scholars Press, 1987), 233–43; Duff, "Metaphor, Motif, and Meaning: The Rhetorical Strategy behind the Image 'Led in Triumph' in 2 Corinthians 2:14," *CBQ* 53 (1991): 79–92; Duff, "Apostolic Suffering and the Language of Processions in 2 Corinthians 4:7–10," *BTB* 21 (1991): 158–65; Duff, "Processions," *ABD* 5.469–73.

39. Duff, "Apostolic Suffering," 159–60; Duff later added "Widen up" (πλατύνθητε) in 6:13 ("Metaphor, Motif, and Meaning," 88).

40. See H. S. Versnel, *Triumphus: An Inquiry into the Origin, Development and Meaning of the Roman Triumph* (Leiden: Brill, 1970); Mary Beard, *The Roman Triumph* (Cambridge: Harvard University Press, 2007); Ida Östenberg, *Staging the World: Spoils, Captives, and Representations in the Roman Triumphal Procession*, Oxford Studies in Ancient Culture and Representation (Oxford: Oxford University Press, 2009). I presented these themes at the 2011 Society of Biblical Literature Annual Meeting Intertextuality session with the same title as this essay. I am preparing to publish a paper enumerating these triumphal-processional themes titled "Paul in Triumphal Procession in 2 Corinthians." Paul's travel plans as led in God's triumph in Christ frame the entire discourse (1:15–16; 12:12–21; 13:1–2, 10). Duff also provides a help-

Interpreters have pondered Paul's role in the triumphal march: Is he a captive, a soldier, an incense bearer, or a devotee?[41] A more important question, however, is why Paul invoked the triumphal-processional theme. Here Duff correctly considers the social-ideological use of the triumphal or epiphanic-cultic processional imagery. The Roman triumphal parade was the most prominent kind of epiphanic procession: the celebration of a god's powerful presence vanquishing enemies.[42] Literary and sarcophagal depictions of cultic epiphanic processions were cast as triumphs, thus co-opting them for the promotion of their cult.[43] The apostle Paul, too, co-opted the triumphal-processional theme, even while trumping it by adding important modifiers in 2:14: "always" (πάντοτε) and "in every place" (ἐν παντὶ τόπῳ). Simply put, Paul presented a thoroughgoing countertriumphal and imperial reality: God in Christ provides the ultimate triumph against all other competing religio-political claims, and this reality should affect how Christ-followers viewed and lived in the world, specifically in Corinth in Achaia.[44] Duff correctly concludes: what Paul presents with God in Christ is "a triumphant deity and a triumphal/epiphany pro-

---

ful summary of processional themes from his prior research ("Metaphor, Motif, and Meaning," 87–91).

41. Paul is portrayed as a captured prisoner of shame (BDAG, s.v.; Cilliers Breytenbach, "Paul's Proclamation and God's 'Thriambos' (Notes on 2 Corinthians 2:14-16b)," *Neot* 24 [1990]: 257–71), an accompanying soldier (Aus, *Imagery of Triumph*), an incense bearer or legate (Breytenbach, "Paul's Proclamation," 266–68), or a religious devotee (Duff, "Metaphor, Motif, and Meaning"). Aus argues well that Paul describes "himself and co-workers metaphorically as soldiers participating in their general's, the Lord God of hosts', triumphal procession" (*Imagery of Triumph*, 17). However, Paul's deployment of the triumphal imagery allows him to occupy multiple roles. Additionally, Paul may think of himself as a former enemy taken captive, either remaining a slave or liberated into citizenship mercifully (see "received mercy" in 4:1). Alternatively, he may regard himself as a recaptured citizen showcased in the triumphal march, now freed, who is in debt to God because of the conquering actions of the Lord Messiah Emperor.

42. That the Roman triumph communicated such a dominating worldview, see Östenberg, *Staging the World*, 272–92.

43. See esp. Duff, "Metaphor, Motif, and Meaning," 84–86. Thus, Duff concludes, "an epiphany procession of a deity could be metaphorically portrayed as a triumphal procession. This metaphorical usage … probably came about because many deities in the ancient world were considered victors" (83).

44. Later in his writings, in Col 2:15 (cf. Eph 4:8–11), Paul will more concisely deploy the triumphal theme explicating this subversion.

cession" that was strategically presented for the promotion of the cult of Christ.[45] Moreover, we must consider how God's triumph in Christ pertains to "the god of this age" at 4:4.

What made this co-option of triumphal imagery so attractive and necessary for the Corinthian converts was the sheer number of triumphal processions observed by Romans and non-Romans alike: 320 by the time of Vespasian's reign.[46] Augustus had erected the *Fasti Triumphatores*, or list of *Triumphators*, on a larger monumental inscription called the *Fasti Capitolini*, beginning with Romulus and ending in 19 BCE with the last nonimperial family general awarded a full triumph, Cornelius Balbus. Triumphal motifs were depicted virtually everywhere on "arches, reliefs, statues, columns, coins, cups, cameos, medallions, and in paintings and the theatre."[47] Additionally, emperors and their family members increasingly controlled and co-opted the triumphal marching. Germanicus, of the imperial household, was the last "general" under Tiberius allowed an independent major triumph in 17 CE (Tacitus, *Ann.* 2.41),[48] possibly because Tiberius himself had celebrated one earlier in 12 CE under the auspices of the emperor Augustus (Suetonius, *Tib.* 20). After Germanicus, minor triumphs (ovations) were celebrated by Caligula in 40 CE (Suetonius, *Cal.* 49.2), Claudius in 44 CE (Suetonius, *Claud.* 17; Pliny the Elder, *Nat.* 33.54), the general Aulus Plautius in 47 CE, who was accompanied by the emperor Claudius the whole time,[49] and Nero in 55 CE, very near to the writing of 2 Corinthians (Suetonius, *Nero* 25; Tacitus, *Ann.* 13.8).

Ideologically, recognizing the pervasiveness of triumphal/epiphanic processional imagery is critical for properly interpreting 2:14–7:2, because "as processions in the Greco-Roman world came to be used more and more as an instrument for the propagation of a particular cult, they began to emphasize in a particularly dramatic way the power of the deity

---

45. To use the words of Duff, who is summarizing evidence that indicates epiphany processions looked like triumphal processions ("Metaphor, Motif, and Meaning," 86).

46. Aus, *Imagery of Triumph*, 2; one will find reference to 350 for all the recorded triumphs (e.g., Peter Marshall, "A Metaphor of Social Shame: *Thriambeuein* in 2 Cor 2:14," *NovT* 25 [1983]: 302–17).

47. Marshall, "Metaphor," 304.

48. The following references to triumphs and ovations are from Aus, *Imagery of Triumph*, 1–2, 11, 37.

49. Described in Dio Cassius, *Hist. rom.* 60.30.2; Suetonius, *Claud.* 24.3; see Aus, *The Image of Triumph*, 37.

whose cult they were proclaiming."[50] Quoting Ramsay MacMullen, Duff aptly reflects on this social-religious significance: "Driving all competition from the field head-on was crucial. The world, after all, had many dozens and hundreds of gods. Choice was open to everybody. It could thus be only a most exceptional force that would actually displace alternatives and compel allegiance; it could be only the most probative demonstrations that would work."[51] The most pertinent question for interpreters of this central portion of 2 Corinthians, then, is: Against which deities was Paul set in competition to employ Roman triumphal and epiphanic processional imagery so thoroughly?

The elephants are standing in the room. Nero's inaugural coins minted in Rome (55 CE) sported four elephants pulling the triumphal chariot consisting of two thrones upon which were seated the divine Augustus and the newly divine Claudius at his right hand.[52] Indeed, the elephant *quadriga* indicated deification[53] and was used in representation of mystery-cult gods in their processions on sarcophagi.[54] An earlier coin of *Divus Augustus* in Tiberius's reign is similar.[55] Such propaganda legitimated the heir and new emperor Nero as *divi filius*, "son of the deified one." The practice was as old as Augustus, who with Julius's apotheosis (*consecratio*) indicated by a comet became *divi filius*. Augustus's triumphs in 40 and 36 BCE (both ovations) describe him as *Imp. Caesar Divi f.* in the *Fasti Triumphales* (12 BCE).[56]

---

50. Duff, "Transformation of the Spectator," 241.

51. Ramsay MacMullen, *Christianizing the Roman Empire: A.D. 100-400* (New Haven: Yale University Press, 1984), 27, as quoted by Duff, "Transformation of the Spectator," 242.

52. James M. Scott, "The Triumph of God in 2 Cor 2:14: Additional Evidence of Merkabah Mysticism in Paul," *NTS* 42 (1996): 272 n. 60. Image of the coin is from Harold Mattingly, *Augustus to Vitellius*, vol. 1 of *Coins of the Roman Empire* (London: British Museum, 1965), 201 and pl. 38.4, 5.

53. Michael Pfanner, *Der Titusbogen*, Beiträge zur Erforschung hellenistischer und kaiserzeitlicher Skulptur und Architektur 2 (Mainz am Rhein: von Zabern, 1983), 99, which is cited by Scott, "Triumph of God," 272 n. 60.

54. See sources and discussions in Duff, "Metaphor, Motif, and Meaning," 85-86.

55. See Mattingly, *Augustus to Vitellius*, 134 and pl. 24.9.

56. For reconstruction, see Attilio Degrassi, *Fasti Capitolini* (Turin: G. B. Paravia, 1954).

Imperial Topoi Surrounding "the God of this Age" in 2 Cor 4:4 and Paul's Message of the Gospel

At this point I will continue to work out the implications of Paul's ideological use of the triumphal processional imagery in his confrontation of the Corinthians' idolatry, which, I argue, involves especially the provincial imperial cult centered at Corinth for the whole of Achaia.[57] Evidence for identifying "the god of this age" as an imperial referent comes from the imperial themes in 4:1–6.

In 4:1–3 Paul continues the imperial triumphal theme in two ways. First, Paul affirms, "we received [God's] mercy" (ἠλεήθημεν). Pardoning and the granting of mercy was the imperial strategy for handling and pacifying subjected peoples.[58] Mercy was visibly seen in triumphal marches, since most captured enemies were granted slavery or citizenship, instead of death; thus the Roman triumph was a rite of passage into Roman life.[59] Mercy scenes depict conquered foes bowing with arms outstretched to the conquering emperor (Augustus on Boscoreale Cup 1, Trajan's Column, etc.). Seneca wrote *De clementia* for the young emperor Nero, in which he

---

57. For an excellent summary of the imperial cults generally, see Finney, "Christ Crucified," 21–26.

58. The offering of mercy served political ends. Andrew Wallace-Hadrill explains: "The victorious Caesar [Augustus] had discovered that the most effective technique for disarming political opposition was to 'forgive' his opponents, just as Roman generals had often 'forgiven' their barbarian enemies. Henceforth *clementia* plays a cardinal role in Roman politics" ("The Golden Age and Sin in Augustan Ideology," *Past and Present* 95 [1982]: 29). It is no wonder that Seneca expounds upon Augustus's example of extending mercy (*Clem.* 1.9–10). This understanding was represented in various forms, such as a silver cup of Boscoreale dated ca. 12 CE depicting Augustus godlike and encouraged by the gods extending a right hand in mercy to a bowing conquered leader; for descriptions and discussions, see Salomon Reinach, *Répertoire de Reliefs Grecs et Romains*, 3 vols. (Paris: Leroux, 1909–1912), 1:92–97; Cornelius C. Vermeule, *Roman Imperial Art in Greece and Asia Minor* (Cambridge: Harvard University Press, 1968), 133–34, 140; Eugénie S. Strong, *Apotheosis and After Life: Three Lectures on Certain Phases of Art and Religion in the Roman Empire* (Freeport, NY: Books for Libraries Press, 1969), 73–75; and Paul Zanker, *The Power of Images in the Age of Augustus*, trans. Alan Shapiro, Jerome Lectures 16 (Ann Arbor: University of Michigan Press, 1988), 229–30.

59. For striking examples and jibes against Caesar for allowing Gauls to enter the senate, see Beard, *The Roman Triumph*, 140–41; cf. examples described in Östenberg, *Staging the World*, 160–63.

espoused the ideology of imperial mercy. Second, Paul recalled 2 Cor 2:15 by referring again to those adversely impacted in God's triumph, "among the ones that are perishing" (ἐν τοῖς ἀπολλυμένοις).

Jan Lambrecht argues that "the god of this age" is the defeated foe in God's triumphal procession in Christ.[60] However, what foe in the context has God defeated in Christ? Duff tentatively suggests that "the god of this age" is "the hands of Fate" overcome by the gospel of Christ.[61] But no exegetical support is provided, except for the more general cultic processional parallels that Duff provides from the Isis cult. A much more obvious answer was standing in the center of the Corinthian forum, the prominence of which is still evident today by the massive statue base that once held an 8-foot-tall bronze statue of the Jupiter-like man-god Augustus. Margaret Laird's reconstruction captures the grandeur of this statuary.[62] The triumphal parade was an epiphany procession that featured the general/emperor representing Jupiter. The procedure of Roman triumph began with an epistle of request, an offering of thanksgiving to the gods for the victory, and the procession proper (spending the night at Isis's temple), then ending the next day at Jupiter's Capitoline Temple.[63] What I am positing is that Paul strategically designed

---

60. Jan Lambrecht, "The Defeated Paul, Aroma of Christ: An Exegetical Study of 2 Corinthians 2:14-16b," *LS* 20 (1995): 185.

61. Duff, "Transformation of the Spectator," 234.

62. Laird, "Emperor in a Roman Town," 96, fig. 4.10: "Reconstruction drawing of the monument of the Augustales. Illustration by author." Used here by permission of the author. The nakedness of Augustus reflected his status as deity; cf. 2 Cor 5:3–4. It seems quite plausible that Paul's description of being naked or clothed reflects common depictions of afterlife/deification in Greco-Roman statuary in afterlife by way of nakedness.

63. This temple's establishment, argues Fears, indicated "Jupiter's election of

the argumentative flow of 2 Cor 2:14–7:2, beginning with epistles and thanksgiving (2:14–3:1) and culminating with a picture of God's people as God's temple (6:16) with numerous triumphal-processional themes throughout, to mimic and undercut the pagan Roman imperial ideology by presenting a counternarrative of God's triumphing in Christ always and in every place.

At the start of the Roman triumph, the emperor was given the divine paraphernalia of Jupiter's statue—*corona, toga, tunica, sceptrum*— described as the *ornatus Jovis* or *insignia Iovis*, which was returned at the end; the *corona triumphalis*—Jupiter's crown—was a heavy golden crown held over the *triumphator*'s head by a slave.[64] He rode in the *quadriga* (four-horsed chariot), as did Jupiter atop his Capitoline Temple; he wore red lead-based rouge on his cheeks, as was applied concurrently to the statue of Jupiter. Germane, too, is Tertullian's recorded statement, fictional or not, that an appointed slave stood behind the *triumphator* repeatedly saying, "Look behind thee; remember thou are but a man" (*Respice te, hominem te memento*, Tertullian, *Apol.* 33.4). The second Boscoreale Cup vividly portrays Tiberius riding the triumphal chariot, holding a staff topped with Jupiter's eagle.[65]

The emperor and those around him exploited his identification with Jupiter, as is seen in literature and artifact.[66] Virgil and Horace secured Augustus's identification with Jupiter; additionally, "Ovid and Manilius celebrated Augustus as the earthly counterpart of Jupiter."[67] Such imagery spread across other visual media (coins, statuary, reliefs, food implements [e.g. Boscoreale Cup 1], jewelry [e.g., *Gemma Augustea*], etc.). J. Rufus Fears argues, "The significance of the association of *princeps* and Jupiter in Augustan writers ... contained the seeds of theocratic monarchy ...

Rome for world rule," as indeed Jupiter says to Venus in the *Aeneid* (1.279): "I gave rule without end" (*imperium sine fine dedi*) (Fears, "Cult of Jupiter," 41).

64. Versnel, *Triumphus*, 72–74.

65. For the striking example of the Boscoreale Cups, see Ann L. Kuttner, *Dynasty and Empire in the Age of Augustus: The Case of the Boscoreale Cups* (Berkeley: University of California Press, 1995); and Fred S. Kleiner, "The Boscoreale Cups: Copies of a Lost Monument?" *JRA* 10 (1997): 377–80.

66. It is true that Augustus's own religious policies invited devotion to other deities in addition to Jupiter (like Apollo, Mars Ultor, Divus Julius). For the nuanced discussion and many examples, see Fears, "Cult of Jupiter," 56–66.

67. Ibid. References to ancient authorities in what follow on this topic are found in Fears.

the eternal image of the emperor as the divinely chosen vice-regent of the supreme king of gods and men."[68] This ideology derived from the widespread Greek notion that "Kings are from Zeus" (Hesiod, *Theog.* 94–96), reflecting a Mediterranean divine election motif, a theme also surveyed by Fears.[69] Indeed, the identification of Augustus with Jupiter has been well documented.[70]

What was begun with Augustus was rearticulated under Caligula, who, according to Suetonius (*Gaius* 22), adopted the title *Optimus Maximus Caesar*, attempted to have his head replace Zeus's head on the statue at Olympia, and wanted visitors to worship and hail him as *Jupiter Latiaris*.[71] Dio Cassius also reported that Caligula was called *Jupiter* and *Olympius* (*Hist. rom.* 28.8, 59.26). Philo (*Legat.* 29.188, 43.346) and Josephus (*Ant.* 19.4, 19.11) record his being hailed in the east as *Zeus Epiphanes Neos Gaios*.[72] Once again, the emperor-Jupiter association is found with Nero, as seen poignantly in Seneca's *De clementia*, written for the young emperor circa 55 CE, who expressed that Nero was vice-regent of the gods (*Clem.* 1.1) and comparable to Jupiter (*Clem.* 1.7.2, 1.19.8).[73] The poet Calpurnius Siculus (*Ecl.* 4.92–94, 142–144) identified Nero with Jupiter and speculated that Nero was Jupiter on earth.[74] The poet Lucan, a client of Nero's and Seneca's nephew, associated Nero with Jupiter. A. D. Nock in a short article helpfully describes Lucan's *Proem* that praised Nero.

---

68. Ibid., 69.

69. J. Rufus Fears, *Princeps a Diis Electus: The Divine Electio of the Emperor as a Political Concept at Rome*, Papers and Monographs of the American Academy in Rome 26 (Rome: American Academy, 1977).

70. Margaret M. Ward, "The Association of Augustus with Jupiter," *SMSr* 9 (1933): 203–24; and Ward, *The Association of Augustus with Jupiter* (Bologna: Zanichelli, 1933).

71. Fears, "Cult of Jupiter," 71.

72. Ibid., 72.

73. In 52 CE, Paul ascended the judgment seat (τὸ βῆμα) of Seneca's brother, Gallio, proconsul of Corinth (Acts 18:12–16), contributing to the view that Paul knew Seneca, who "would become an adviser to the emperor Nero and perhaps influence the favorable outcome of Paul's first arrest in Rome" (J. R. McRay, "Corinth," in *Dictionary of New Testament Background: A Compendium of Contemporary Biblical Scholarship*, ed. Craig A. Evans and Stanley E. Porter [Downers Grove, IL: InterVarsity Press, 2000], 230).

74. We must be cautious here, since significant arguments against a Neronian dating have been put forth by Edward Champlin, "The Life and Times of Calpurnius Siculus," *JRS* 68 (1978): 95–110.

As here [in the *Proem*] Lucan reflects Imperial plans and aspirations, so later in his apotheosis of Nero (1.45 ff.) does he reproduce ideas current at the time, while adapting a Virgilian model, the beginning of the first Georgic. Nero has two choices offered, *sceptra tenere*, to be Jupiter, or to mount the car of Phoebus and be the Sun. Now as Ζεὺς Ἐλευθέριος he was hailed by the grateful Greeks in 67 [CE]. He may well have been so regarded even earlier, as were Theophanes of Mytilene and Augustus. Calpurnius Siculus, *Ecl.* 4.142, holds that he may be Jupiter in disguise, and coins of Dioshieron in Lydia have as their obverse-type busts of Nero and Zeus, with the inscription ΖΕΥΣ ΝΕΡΩΝ ΚΑΙΣΑΡ. As νέος ἥλιος ["new sun"] Nero received homage at most times: that he liked the part is shown by the fact that he set up a colossus of the Sun with his own features in front of the Golden House. We must recognize in Lucan ... that in what seems to us extravagant flattery he is speaking the conventional language of the age, and expressing notions widely held.[75]

It is tantalizing to consider what relation these imperial and the later divine attributions of "Zeus deliverer" (Ζεὺς Ἐλευθέριος) might have with the somewhat unexpected and climactic move Paul introduces in 2 Cor 3:17, when he affirms "The Lord is the Spirit, and where the Spirit of the Lord is, there is deliverance" (ὁ δὲ κύριος τὸ πνεῦμά ἐστιν· οὗ δὲ τὸ πνεῦμα κυρίου, ἐλευθερία).[76] Deliverance, Lordship, and Spirit were imperial attributes identified in Nero, who at his inauguration was called the "new good spirit" (νέος ἀγαθὸς δαίμων). Obviously, it is anachronistic to correlate 2 Cor 3:17 with Achaia's later hailing Nero as Ζεὺς Ἐλευθέριος, when Nero freed them from taxation in 67 CE upon his visit there; however, one wonders what earlier policies and propaganda circulated prior to this decisive moment that might have encouraged Paul preemptively to lay claim to Christ's "deliverance" for the Corinthian Christ-followers.

Deliverance (ἐλευθερία) in Jewish Second Temple literature spoke to political realities. In 1 Esd 4:49, 53 (NRSV), King Darius "wrote in behalf of all the Jews who were going up from his kingdom to Judea, in the interest of their freedom [ἐλευθερία], that no officer or satrap or governor or treasurer should forcibly enter their doors ... that all who came from Babylonia to build the city should have their freedom [ἐλευθερία]." On either side of the Maccabean war, Simon and his followers as well as Antiochus

---

75. A. D. Nock, "The Proem of Lucan," *The Classical Review* 40 (1926): 18.

76. The Vulgate reads "Dominus autem Spiritus est ubi autem Spiritus Domini ibi libertas."

VII offered "freedom" to Israel. In response to Simon's having "established freedom for Israel [ἔστησαν αὐτῷ ἐλευθερία]" (1 Macc 14:26), the people erected on pillars at Mount Zion bronze tablets as an honorific inscription praising Simon's "justice and faithfulness" (τὴν δικαιοσύνην καὶ τὴν πίστιν) (1 Macc 14:27–45). In response, Antiochus wrote a letter before waging war with the new regime, saying, "I grant freedom [ἐλεύθερα] to Jerusalem and the sanctuary" (1 Macc 15:3). In Egypt, King Ptolemy Philopator in a letter proscribing persecution against the Jews in Alexandria promised any informant exposing those assisting the Jews, that they will receive property, remuneration, and "will be crowned with freedom [τῇ ἐλευθερίᾳ στεφανωθήσεται]" (3 Macc 3:28). In subsequent literature, the term is used likewise (e.g., Sib. Or. 11.74, 14.309).[77] Philo provides a rich understanding of deliverance/freedom, subordinating it ultimately to God, yet also elevating it as the ultimate expression of devotion to God instead of to oppressive rulers and idolatry.[78] In *Legat.* 116, Philo explicitly refers to the Italians adulterating "the native disposition of Roman freedom" (τὸ εὐγενὲς τῆς Ῥωμαϊκῆς ἐλευθερίας) when they bowed before Gaius as if he were a god. For Philo, Augustus was the far better example, "who gave freedom [ἐλευθερία] to every city, who brought disorder into order, who civilized and made obedient and harmonious, nations which before his time were unsociable, hostile, and brutal" (*Legat.* 147; cf. 287).

---

77. However, for an instance of moral formative freedom, see Apos. Con. 7.39.4 (= Hel. Syn. Pr. 8.5).

78. E.g., *Cher.* 107: "And the purified intellect rejoices in nothing more than in confessing that it has for its master him who is the Lord of all; for to be the servant of God is the greatest boast, and is more honourable, not only than freedom [ἐλευθερίας], but even than riches or dominion, or than anything which the race of mankind is eager for"; *Sacr.* 117: "If therefore nature hinders one's improvement for the better, let us not strive against her in an unprofitable way, but if she co-operates with us then let us honour the Deity with the first fruits and honours, which are the ransom of our soul, emancipating it from subjection to cruel masters, and elevating it to freedom"; and *Conf.* 93–94: "And what man in his senses is there who, if he saw the tasks of the generality of men, and the exceeding earnestness with which they labour at the pursuits to which they are accustomed to devote themselves, whether it be the acquisition of money, or glory, or the enjoyment of pleasure, would not be greatly concerned and cry out to God, the only Saviour, that he would lighten their labours, and pay a ransom and price for the salvation of the soul, so as to emancipate [εἰς ἐλευθερίαν] and deliver it? (94) What, then, is the surest freedom? The service of the only wise God." Cf. *Spec.* 1.57. Translations from Charles D. Yonge, *The Works of Philo: Complete and Unabridged* (Peabody, MA: Hendrickson, 1995).

But not all viewed imperial rule so favorably. The word *freedom* (Latin *libertas*) expressed Roman resistance to tyrannical imperial rule, as was reflected in Julius Caesar's slayer, Brutus, who was influenced by his father-in-law Marcus Cato. Cato had supported Pompey rather than Julius Caesar, yet Seneca later reflected on the reasoning behind Cato's choice, concluding that Cato must have reasoned, "It is not liberty [*libertas*] that is at stake now; that has long since perished. The question is whether the state shall belong to Caesar or Pompey.... A tyrant [*dominus*] is being selected" (Seneca, *Ep.* 14.13).[79] Lucan, in his poem *Pharsalia*, or *On the Civil War* (ca. 61–65 CE), concerning the struggle between Caesar and Pompey, also described Cato's "guilt" of choosing one ruler and the demise of freedom (*libertas*) to reside only in one man, Julius Caesar.[80] But Cato's ideal of freedom from tyranny influenced Brutus to follow "Freedom's Name ... even to the grave" (*Phars.* 2.343–344).[81] Lucan was referring to Cato's suicide "for freedom," which Julius Caesar displayed in cartoon mockery in his triumphal parade (46 BCE) along with the suicides of his other detractors, Lucius Scipio and Petreius; the mockery backfired terribly, resulting in the crowds' aversion to Caesar and the circulation of competing propaganda.[82]

---

79. Quoted and discussed in Ramsay MacMullen, *Enemies of the Roman Order: Treason, Unrest, and Alienation in the Empire* (Cambridge; Harvard University Press, 1966), 4.

80. The verse of Lucan, *Phars.* 2.312–322 is particularly striking; Magnus is Pompey's cognomen (translation is from Sir Edward Ridley, *The Pharsalia of Lucan* [London: Longmans, Green, 1896]):

> For Cato's conduct shall approve his own.
> Pompeius, with the Consul in his ranks,
> And half the Senate and the other chiefs,
> Vexes my spirit; and should Cato too
> Bend to a master's yoke, in all the world
> The one man free is Caesar. But if thou
> For freedom and thy country's laws alone
> Be pleased to raise the sword, nor Magnus then
> Nor Caesar shall in Brutus find a foe.
> Not till the fight is fought shall Brutus strike,
> Then strike the victor.

81. The eulogizing of Brutus's choice to follow Freedom to the grave is found in *Phars.* 2.262–394

82. MacMullen, *Enemies of the Roman Order*, 5. Immediately, Cicero and Brutus each wrote treatises on behalf of Cato, while Caesar and Hirtius did the opposite; these later were then rebuffed in works written by Fadius Gallus and Munatius Rufus.

Such resistance, even to the point of death, continued throughout the Julian-Claudian reign. Dying at the command of Nero for their alleged opposition, Seneca and Thrasea Paetus, says Rufus Fears, "offered their blood as a libation to Jupiter Liberator. They perished, they would say, as sacrifices for the concept of *libertas*."[83] Fears describes such resistance succinctly: "In the later Julio-Claudian period, specifically under Gaius and Nero, there is evidence that Jupiter became a figure of partisan conflict between supporters of *principatus* with its absolutist implications and the senatorial opposition to the principate. The former sought to associate Jupiter with the emperor as the earthly image of the god. The senatorial opposition took *libertas* as its battle cry and looked back to Cicero, Cato the Younger, and those Optimates who had revered Jupiter as the preserver of the free *res publica*."[84] So, we must understand that the concept of freedom as *libertas* was an actively discussed topic in the early principate that signified anti-imperial sentiment and opposition to tyranny.[85]

So, in 2 Cor 3:17, Paul's proclamation of the Lord Jesus bringing *freedom* is oxymoronic yet climactically strategic. It represents the culmination of a series of progressive statements concerning the nature of Paul's ministry. As enumerated, this ministry begins first with Paul's participation in God's triumph in Christ (2:14–15); second, Paul speaks with integrity before God in Christ (2:16–17); third, his confidence rests in the Corinthians' being his letter of recommendation, indeed Christ's epistle (3:1–4); fourth, Paul's sufficiency (ἱκανότης) as a minister of the new covenant comes from the Lord (3:5-12a; cf. 2:16b);[86] fifth, Paul's exercising "much

---

83. Fears cites Tacitus, *Ann*. 15.64; 16.35 ("Cult of Jupiter," 72). Among the nine definitions for *libertas*, the *OLD* begins with (1) "The civil status of a free man" and (2) "The political status of a sovereign people"; the word can also denote (6) "Freedom as a mark of character, independence" and (7) "Frankness of speech, outspokenness, plain speaking." In 2 Corinthians, one wonders whether Paul would have both the political and moral sense relating to frankness of speech simultaneously.

84. Fears, "Cult of Jupiter," 73.

85. For overviews of the opposition, see MacMullen, *Enemies of the Roman* Order, 1–94; Chaim Wirszubski, *Libertas as a Political Idea at Rome during the Late Republic and Early Principate*, Cambridge Classical Studies (Cambridge: Cambridge University Press, 1950), 124–71; cf. C. D. Gordon, "Review of *Libertas as a Political Idea at Rome during the Late Republic and Early Principate* by C. Wirszubski," *Phoenix* 6 (1952): 27–29.

86. The intertextual connection with Moses's insufficient (ἱκανός) speech at Exod 4:10 (LXX) is well made by Scott, "Triumph of God," 274.

boldness of speech" (πολλῇ παρρησίᾳ χρώμεθα) (3:12b–16) is exemplified in identifying the Lord with the Spirit, who brings freedom (3:17–18); finally, throughout 2:16b–3:18 Paul implicitly and explicitly compares himself to Moses by *synkrisis*, emphasizing Paul's boldness and freedom to proclaim the gospel of the Lord Jesus.[87]

Although many commentators observe *synkrisis* in 2 Cor 3, in which Moses's poor speech is compared with Paul's poor speaking ability, what has been neglected is the comparison of Moses's confrontation of the idolatry of the Israelites with Paul's confrontation of the Corinthians' idolatry in association with pagan unbelievers and the implications this has for interpreting 2:14–7:2.[88] In 1 Cor 8–10 (esp. 10:14, 19–21, 27–28), Paul uses the Moses and Israelite tradition from Exodus and Numbers precisely to confront the Corinthian Christ-followers' flirting with idolatry. Paul's argument there integrally concerns a proper exercise of "freedom" (ἐλευθερία, 10:29; cf. ἐλεύθερος in 9:1, 19). So, in 2 Cor 3 Paul's reference to Moses's interaction with the Israelites in Exod 33–34 and to freedom recalls his earlier treatment in 1 Cor 10, thus indicating that the Corinthians were still struggling with idolatry. As was already noted above, the "associative" language of 1 Cor 10:16–21 (μετέχω, κοινωνία, κοινωνός) converges in 2 Cor 6:14 (μετοχή, κοινωνία). Putting this together, then, if 6:14–7:1 is genuinely from Paul belonging in this literary context—and strong support exists for this view[89]—then it is evident that Paul was confronting the Corinthians' idolatry and, moreover, that he chose to subsume this bold and freedom-based confrontation under the metaphor of God's "always and in every place triumphing in Christ." Paul is bold to proclaim such a gospel.

Thus 4:1–6 continues previous themes, even as this pericope marks a distinct movement in Paul's argument.[90] Strategically, these verses con-

---

87. In particular, see the conclusions of Robert B. Sloan, "2 Corinthians 2:14–4:6 and 'New Covenant Hermeneutics': A Response to Richard Hays," *BBR* 5 (1995): 129–54, esp. 142.

88. Aus is unique here, but his proposal to understand Paul as alluding to the rebellion in Num 16 is highly unlikely (*Imagery of Triumph*, 47–79 at 49 n. 6).

89. For recent reviews of the issues and determinants in favor of its inclusion, see William J. Webb, *Returning Home: New Covenant and Second Exodus as the Context for 2 Corinthians 6.14–7.1*, JSNTSup 85 (Sheffield: JSOT Press, 1993); James M. Scott, "The Use of Scripture in 2 Corinthians 6.16c–18 and Paul's Restoration Theology," *JSNT* 17 (1995): 73–99; Thrall, *2 Corinthians 1–7*, 25–36; and Barnett, *Second Epistle*, 338–41.

90. E.g., Stephen B. Heiny is correct to observe that "there is an obvious break

tinue the triumphal imagery of 2:14–17 by repeating the phrase "among those who are perishing [ἐν τοῖς ἀπολλυμένοις]" again at 4:3.[91] By extension, Lambrecht concludes effortlessly, and without any precise identity, that "the god of this age" is God's conquered foe, the defeated leader, in the triumphal procession. However, this god "blinded" (ἐτύφλωσεν) unbelievers yet continues in direct competition with God in Christ by providing a counter-brightness "to the gospel of the glory of Christ, who is the image of God" (4:4). This alternative "god" does not match with descriptions of death or the hands of fate, as Duff proposed. But what god could have blinded unbelievers with the purpose of continuing to shine so brightly against all ruling competitors? Augustus so intended to outshine others. So much can be gathered by his Res gestae divi Augusti, which also states near the end (34): "After that time [27 BCE, the end of the civil war], I surpassed all in honorable rank" (praestiti omnibus dignitate; ἀξιώματι πάντων διήνεγκα). Augustus also allowed others to praise him with such claims, as seen in the "Letter of Paulus Fabius Maximus and Decrees by Asians

---

in sense between 3:18 and 4:1. Paul has stitched together two separate discussions of δόξα here" ("The Motive for Metaphor: 2 Corinthians 2:14–4:6," in *Society of Biblical Literature 1987 Seminar Papers*, SBLSP 26 [Missoula, MT: Scholars Press, 1987], 11); Thrall, *2 Corinthians 1–7*, 297–98; David Hellholm, "Moses as διάκονος of the παλαιὰ διαθήκη—Paul as διάκονος of the καινὴ διαθήκη: Argumenta Amplificationis in 2 Cor 2,14–4,6," ZNW 99 (2008): 247–89. For the discernment of distinct "adversaries" to Paul in 3:1–18 (Judiazers) and 4:1–6 (*Pneumatikoi*), even if misidentified, see Jerome Murphy-O'Connor, "Pneumatikoi and Judaizers in 2 Cor 2:14–4:6," ABR 34 (1986): 42–58.

91. Often it is understood that 4:1–6 recapitulates 3:1–18 and forms a ring-composition with 2:14–17 around the themes of "among those perishing" (ἐν τοῖς ἀπολλυμένοις [2:15; 4:3]), "before God" (κατέναντι θεοῦ [2:17] // ἐνώπιον τοῦ θεοῦ [4:2]), "the knowledge of [the glory of] God" (τῆς γνώσεως αὐτοῦ [2:14] // τῆς γνώσεως τῆς δόξης τοῦ θεοῦ [4:5]), and "the word of God" (τὸν λόγον τοῦ θεοῦ [2:17; 4:2]). See e.g., Ralph P. Martin, *2 Corinthians*, WBC 40 (Waco, TX: Word, 1985), 75–76; he is followed by Barnett, *Second Epistle*, 210. However, it is better to understand 4:1–5:10 as initiating the next stage of Paul's self-commendation, following 2:14–3:18, which is then followed by a final section in 5:11–7:1, each section beginning with commendation language, an acknowledgment of God's "oversight," Paul's attributes distancing him from rivals, and the Corinthians' own evaluation of Paul; see a description of these movements as the *probatio* of 2 Corinthians in Fredrick J. Long, *Ancient Rhetoric and Paul's Apology: The Compositional Unity of 2 Corinthians* SNTSMS 131 (Cambridge: Cambridge University Press, 2004), 162–72.

concerning the Provincial Calendar" (9 BCE).[92] Here Augustus was said to have "surpassed" (ὑπερβαλόμενος) previous benefactors, "but neither among future ones leaving a hope of surpassing [him]" (ἀλλ' οὐδ' ἐν τοῖς ἐσομένοις ἐλπίδα ὑπολιπὼν ὑπερβολῆς).[93]

Conceived within this context of totalizing imperial claims, Paul's ideological use of the triumphal metaphor functions to articulate the counter "mega-narrative" of God's triumph in Christ "always in every place."[94] One may construct a chart to show the polemical parallelism of Paul's meganarrative to that of the god of this age:[95]

Identity	4:4: "The god of this age" (ὁ θεὸς τοῦ αἰῶνος τούτου)	4:4: "The glory of the Messiah, who is the image [εἰκών] of God"
		4:5: "Jesus Messiah is Lord [κύριον]"
		4:6: Face of Messiah reveals God's glory
Actions of "god"	4:4: "the god of this age blinds" (ἐτύφλωσεν)	4:6: "God speaks" (ὁ θεὸς ὁ εἰπών)
		4:6: "God shines light" (φῶς λάμψει)
Purpose	4:4: "in order that they not see the illumination of the gospel of the glory of the Messiah" (εἰς τὸ μὴ αὐγάσαι τὸν φωτισμὸν τοῦ εὐαγγελίου τῆς δόξης τοῦ Χριστοῦ)	4:6: "for the illumination of the knowledge of the glory of God in the person/face of Jesus Messiah" (πρὸς φωτισμὸν τῆς γνώσεως τῆς δόξης τοῦ θεοῦ ἐν προσώπῳ [Ἰησοῦ] Χριστοῦ.)

---

92. This title and the treatment of this honorific inscription are from Frederick W. Danker, *Benefactor: Epigraphic Study of a Graeco-Roman and New Testament Semantic Field* (St. Louis: Clayton, 1982), 215–22.

93. Robert K. Sherk, *Roman Documents from the Greek East: Senatus Consulta and Epistulae to the Age of Augustus* (Baltimore: Johns Hopkins University Press, 1969), §65D.37–39. See also the parallel Donald F. McCabe, *Priene Inscriptions: Texts and List* (Princeton: Princeton Institute for Advanced Study, 1987), §6.37–39.

94. I first learned of this term from my colleague David Bauer; it communicates the complete claim over against other "meta-" narratives.

95. Cf. the parallel presentation of 4:4 and 4:6 as depicted in Hellholm, "Moses as διάκονος," 261.

Human Proclamation	4:5: [proclaims himself as Lord?? (cf. Οὐ ἑαυτοὺς κηρύσσομεν)]	4:5: Paul proclaims "Jesus as Lord" [κηρύσσομεν...Ἰησοῦν Χριστὸν κύριον]
Interior Human Space	4:4: "The minds of unbelievers" (τὰ νοήματα τῶν ἀπίστων)	4:6: "in our hearts" (ἐν ταῖς καρδίαις ἡμῶν)
Metaphorical Realm	4:6: "from darkness" (ἐκ σκότους)	4:6: "light" (φῶς)

The parallelism allows us to see precisely the places of greatest opposition around identity, actions, purpose, proclamation, contested interior human space, and metaphorical realms: the shining (λάμπω) of light (φῶς) in the gospel (τὸ εὐαγγέλιον) of the glory of the Messiah (ὁ Χριστός), who is the image of God (εἰκὼν τοῦ θεοῦ) and proclaimed Lord (κύριος). These acclamations for Jesus were counterimperial and would have been recognizable as such in Roman Corinth; thus, we should not solely consider Jewish materials to explain Paul's language.[96] Deissmann rightly identified Paul's language a "polemical parallelism" to the imperial cult.[97]

The space it would require to work through the available data for each key word—*shining, light, blinding, image, Lord, God, gospel, Messiah*—is not available in this context. Although these words are used diversely, one must consider their convergence together as critical and mutually informing. Also, the commentary interpretive tradition has understood this passage against Paul's own religious experiences and Jewish wisdom/creation theology. However, such an interpretive approach diminishes or ignores the ideological weight of these terms within their original social-political context; more specifically, such an interpretive stance fails to consider how

---

96. On the precise point of opposition between "the god of this age" and Christ's bearing God's image and glory, Dautzenberg is correct, even if he is mistaken to consider only and extensively Qumran (e.g., 1QS 3–4) and Jewish backgrounds (e.g., Wisd 7:25-26) to Paul's argument ("Überlegungen zur Exegese und Theologie," 333–41); such an approach is common (e.g. Scott, *2 Corinthians*, 85–86).

97. Deissmann repeatedly referred to the early New Testament writers' intended "polemical parallelism" and "(silent) protests" against the cult of the Caesar; moreover, he specifically maintained that Paul's insistence on calling Jesus "Lord" amounted to a "protest" to the imperial cult (*Light from the Ancient East*, 247, 342, 346–47, 350, 352–53, 359–60, 363, 366–67, 395).

the terms and ideas would speak to recent converts of Christ in Roman Corinth.

To begin, *Christ* or *Messiah* as the center of devotion hardly needs comment, except a reminder of its inherent political meaning identifying the Jewish king. That Paul never lost this basic understanding is evidenced in how easily he attaches *Christ* to *Lord* in distinction from other "lords" (see below) and the position of ultimate mimesis and authority in relation to God's kingdom for believers within the church (e.g., Rom 4:24; 5:17, 21; 6:23; 7:25; 8:39; 1 Cor 11:1; 15:25; Col 2:10, 15; Eph 1:19–23; 4:5, 13, 20–22; 5:5). Recently N. T. Wright has demonstrated how thoroughly Jesus as Messiah/Christ informed Paul's narrative theology in Galatians: the term *Christ* is not a proper name but is set within God's covenantal and eschatological expectation of supplying a ruler for God's people, the Messiah.[98]

The noun *gospel* (εὐαγγέλιον) is rare but carries imperial import.[99] It is found twice in the famous imperial inscription at Priene celebrating the birth of Augustus as "good news" (*OGI* 458, l. 40) and then in the third century of the accession of the emperor G. Julius Verus Maximus.[100]

God occurs six times in 2 Cor 4:2–6, including the odd expression "the god of this age." It is well-known that *god* (θεός) was used for the reigning emperor and apotheosized emperors and imperial family members, who were more generously celebrated as deified, even while still living, in the Greek East than at Rome.[101] Hermann Kleinknecht summarizes, "In the

---

98. N. T. Wright, "Messiahship in Galatians?" in *Galatians and Christian Theology: Justification, the Gospel, and Ethics in Paul's Letter*, ed. Mark W. Elliot et al. (Grand Rapids: Baker, 2014), 3–23.

99. See also discussion in Finney, "Christ Crucified," 29.

100. See Deissmann, *Light from the Ancient East*, 370–72; James Hope Moulton and George Milligan, *The Vocabulary of the Greek Testament Illustrated from the Papyri and Other Non-literary Sources* (Grand Rapids: Eerdmans, 1930), 259.

101. In the Julio-Claudian period, at Rome seven members of the imperial family are divinized: Julius Caesar, Augustus, Drusilla, Livia, Claudius, Claudia Augusta, Poppaea Augusta. At Athens sixteen members were celebrated as divine, and "they were commonly termed gods and *Sebastoi* in the East during their reign, and priests were appointed to their cults": Augustus, Livia, Julia (Augustus's daughter), Gaius Caesar (son of Julia and M. Agrippa), Tiberius, Drusus Nero (Tiberius's brother), Drusus Tiberius (Tiberius's son), Julia Livilla (Germanicus's daughter), Drusilla (Germanicus's daughter), Germanicus, Caligula, Claudius, Messalina, Agrippina, Nero, Antonia Minor; see chart and discussion in Lozano, "*Divi Augusti*," 142–44.

Hellenistic period an outstanding ruler may be called a θεός as the creator of a new political order.... In the Hell.[enistic] cult of the ruler and the Roman cult of the emperor θεός becomes a designation of office."[102] A few examples will illustrate this belief. In 48 BCE, at Ephesus, Julius Caesar was hailed as "the god manifest from Ares and Aphrodite and common savior of human life" (τὸν ἀπὸ Ἄρεως καὶ Ἀφροδε[ί]της θεὸν ἐπιφανῆ καὶ κοινὸν τοῦ ἀνθρωπίνου βίου σωτῆρα) (*SIG* 760.7). Strabo repeatedly referred to Julius as "the god Caesar" (ὁ θεὸς Καῖσαρ) (*Geogr.* 4.1.1, 5.1.6, 5.3.8, 17.1.6). Augustus received a building dedication "for Caesar Emperor god from god" (ὑπὲρ Καίσαρος Αὐτοκράτορος θεοῦ ἐκ θεοῦ) (*OGI* 655.1–2). At Erythrai, a coastal Ionian city of Asia Minor, the *demos* of Erythrai praised the deceased Caesar, "The Demos to Gaius Julius Augustus Caesar Heavenly God" (ὁ δῆμος Γαίωι Ἰουλίωι Σεβαστῶι Καίσαρι θεῶι ἐπουρανίωι).[103] Dating from 45–54 CE is another bilingual inscription from Pontus and Paphlagonia (northern Asia Minor) that begins by acknowledging the peace (εἰρήνη) of Augustus and offering honor to Caesar Claudius before turning to speak of Gaius Aquila as "the high priest of the heavenly god Augustus" (ὁ τοῦ ἐπουρανίου θεοῦ Σεβαστοῦ ἀρχιερεύς).[104] The Latin inscription makes no reference to "heavenly" and simply has *divi Augusti* "divine Augustus."[105] In Pisidia, Claudius was also hailed a "god manifest" (θεὸν ἐπιφανῆ) (*IGRR* 3.328) and also at Lycia (*TAM* 2.760). In Pisidia, Nero was hailed "Emperor new Sun god manifest" (Αὐτοκράτορα νέ]ον Ἥλιον θ[εὸν ἐπιφανῆ]) (*SEG* 18.566). The emperors are also deemed lord and god together, as described below.

Lord is repeated four-times in 2 Cor 3:16–18, preparing for 4:5. The wording of 4:5 also has puzzled interpreters: What situation lies behind Paul's distancing himself from the title "Lord" when saying "We do not preach ourselves but Jesus Messiah as Lord"? Thrall's review of the options and her conclusion reads far too much into the statement: Paul was

---

102. Hermann Kleinknecht, "θεός, θεότης, κτλ.," *TDNT* 3:69.
103. Donald F. McCabe, *Erythrai Inscriptions: Texts and List* (Princeton: Princeton Institute for Advanced Study, 1986), §63.
104. Christian Marek, *Stadt: Ära und Territorium in Pontus-Bithynia und Nord-Galatia*, Istanbuler Forschungen 39 (Tübingen: Wasmuth, 1993), §1,c; cf. 1,a.
105. The association of the deified Caesars in the "heavenly realms," using an appellation for the gods in the heavens or the ἐπουράνιοι, has tremendous implications for interpreting the Christ hymn at 2:10 and Ephesians that emphasizes Christ's heavenly position above all other rule (Eph 1:3, 20; 2:6; cf. 3:10; 6:12).

responding to Judaizers who were critiquing as fantasy Paul's Damascus road visionary experience and his "egotistical concern to achieve power over people" (as an overcompensation for his poor apostolic backing).[106] Moreover, such an interpretation fails to account for the positive affirmation of Jesus as Lord within this context.[107] A simpler and better solution comes from philological data of the religious-political term *lord* (κύριος) used for the reigning emperor.[108] Werner Foerster provides numerous examples prior to the empire to justify saying, "For the ruler κύριος βασιλεύς is often used in Egypt between 64 and 50 B.C."[109] For the imperial period, Deissmann's review is still helpful: in Egypt and Syria, the use of *Lord* as a title for rulers is well-documented "in numerous Greek inscriptions, papyri, and ostraca of the earliest Imperial period."[110] Unknown to Deissmann were the following two inscriptions: In *BGU* 1197.I.15 dated to 12 BCE, Augustus is called "god and lord Emperor Caesar" (θεὸς καὶ κύριος Καῖσαρ Αὐτοκράτωρ). In P.Oxy. 1143.4–5 dated to 1 CE sacrifices are offered "on behalf of the god and lord Emperor Caesar" (ὑπὲρ τοῦ θεοῦ καὶ κυρίου Αὐτοκράτορος [Καίσαρος...]). In *OGI* 606, "The salvation of the Augustan Lords" (ὑπὲρ τῆς τῶν κυρίων Σε[βαστῶν] σωτηρίας) possibly describes Tiberius and Livia. Caligula demanded to be called Lord (Aurelius Victor, *Caes.* 3), and Claudius in an ostracon is ascribed "Lord" in 54 CE (O.Wilck. 1038). Moreover, "For Nero 'the lord,' i.e. in the time of the most important of St. Paul's letters, the number of examples suddenly rushes up tremendously."[111] Based upon such evidence, Deissmann rightly

---

106. Thrall, *2 Corinthians 1–7*, 312–13.

107. See also a discussion of the counterimperial significance of Paul's use of κύριος presented in Finney, "Christ Crucified," 28–29.

108. See Joseph D. Fantin, *The Lord of the Entire World: Lord Jesus, a Challenge to Lord Caesar?* New Testament Monographs 31 (Sheffield: Sheffield Phoenix, 2011).

109. Werner Foerster, "κύριος, κύρια, κτλ.," *TDNT* 3:1049–50.

110. Deissmann, *Light from the Ancient East*, 357–58.

111. Deissmann, *Light from the Ancient East*, 357, and previous references. Searching the Duke Databank of Documentary Papyri, one finds dozens of references to "the Lord Nero" (all but one are articular) in letters dating from 54 to 68 CE: Chrest. Wilck. 312 (55 CE); P.Mert. 12 (58 CE); SB 9572 (61 CE), 12008 (56/70 CE), 13279 (61 CE); O.Stras. 75 (54/68 CE), 84 (60 CE), 85 (63 CE), 88 (68 CE), 265 (56 CE), 266 (58 CE), 267 (63 CE), 269 (65/66 CE); O.Deiss. 36A (62 CE), 39 (62 CE); P. Lond. 1215 (65–66 CE); O.Elkab 34 (68 CE); P.Oxy. 246 (66 CE); O.Petr. 84 (65 CE), 85 (66 CE), 86 (68 CE); O.Wilck. 418 (67 CE), 419 (67 CE), 420 (68 CE), 422 (68 CE), 1040 (58 CE); O.Erem. 1 (63 CE), 8 (68 CE); P.Gen. 95 (65 CE); P.Heid. 257 (57 CE), 258 (63

concluded: "the Christians of the East who heard St. Paul preach in the style of Phil. 2:9, 11 and 1 Cor. 8:5, 6 must have found in the solemn confession that Jesus Christ is 'the Lord' a silent protest against other 'lords,' and against 'the lord,' as people were beginning to call the Roman Caesar. And St. Paul himself must have felt and intended this silent protest—as well as Jude, when he calls Jesus Christ "our *only* master and Lord."[112] In Acts 25:26 "the Lord" (ὁ κύριος) is used quite simply and naturally by Festus, the procurator of Judea, to refer to the reigning emperor Nero. Thus, within the interpretive context established in this essay for 2 Cor 4:5, Paul would be countering the imperial claim to the status of emperor as Lord.

Paul's use of *image* (εἰκών) in 2 Cor 3:18 and 4:4 has not readily been accounted for, since it appears to be "self-explanatory" for the Corinthian audience.[113] Although interpreters have sought to interpret Paul's usage against wisdom and creation motifs, this does not explain Paul's particular reconfiguration of the biblical texts nor his rhetorical-ideological purposes here.[114] The Corinthian Christians could have readily understood that Paul's affirmation of the Lord Christ as God's image (εἰκών τοῦ θεοῦ) was counterimperial, since imperial εἰκόνες were protected, projected, and pervasive in society.[115] The first definition of εἰκών in BDAG is "likeness,

---

CE); O.Camb. 30 (62 CE) (for abbreviations, see http://papyri.info/browse/ddbdp/). Moreover, the Latin *dominus* for "a supreme ruler, sovereign, lord, despot" (*OLD*, s.v.) had been in use for some time for a political ruler and the emperor in particular (e.g. Cicero, *Rep.* 1.69.12; 2.47.1–3; *Leg.* 3.28.3; Seneca, *Ep.* 14.13; Tacitus, *Hist.* 4.42.31).

112. Deissmann, *Light from the Ancient East*, 359.

113. Thrall, *2 Corinthians 1–7*, 309. In the end, Thrall favors a Jewish wisdom background in which the "image of God" is restored from creation (Wisd 7:25–26).

114. See the problem associated with identifying strictly the source for Paul's scriptural allusions in Thrall, *2 Corinthians 1–7*, 310 and 315. In the end, Paul's creative employment rather should point interpreters to consider the ideological benefit for the Corinthian Christians, which must then lead one to consider the movement of Paul's argument to confront the Corinthians' idolatry.

115. On the powerfully pervasive influence of images related to the emperor, see generally Zanker, *Power of Images*. On the valuation of the emperor's images on coins in social practice, see Andrew Wallace-Hadrill, "Image and Authority in the Coinage of Augustus," *JRS* 76 (1986): 66–87; on the prints of Nero, see Ulrich W. Hiesinger, "The Portraits of Nero," *AJA* 79 (1975): 113–24; in Asia Minor, see Price, *Rituals and Power*; on the use of precious metals to signify divine honors beginning with Caligula, Nero, and Domitian et al., see Kenneth Scott, "The Significance of Statues in Precious Metals in Emperor Worship," *TAPA* 62 (1931): 101–23. For a study illustrating the canonization of such portraits, see Lee Ann Riccardi, "Uncanonical Imperial Portraits

portrait ... of the emperor's head on a coin ... of an emperor's image ... Of the image of a god." Numerous examples are there provided. The precedent for a human ruler to reflect deity is an ancient idea and lies behind the biblical affirmation that humans were made in God's image (Gen 1:26-27).[116] In Egypt, Ptolemy Epiphanes was the "living image of Zeus" (εἰκόνος ζώσης τοῦ Διός).[117] Eugénie Strong and Paul Zanker have argued independently that portrait types and images on various media—coins, cups, reliefs, statuary, architectural planning and design, house paintings, table sideboards, and so on—communicated effectively and pervasively the greatness of Rome's emperor.[118] Paul Zanker, reciting a German proverb, has said, "If the emperor grew a beard, the citizens of the whole empire grew one too."[119] Caroline Vout aptly summarizes: "For the major-

---

in the Eastern Roman Provinces: The Case of the Kanellopoulos Emperor," *Hesperia* 69 (2000): 105-32. On the public conveyance of the emperor's virtues from Vespasian to Severus Alexander (69-235 CE) (some of which applies earlier), see Carlos F. Noreña, "The Communication of the Emperor's Virtues," *JRS* 91 (2001): 146-68.

116. Gordon Wenham writes, "That man is made in the divine image and is thus God's representative on earth was a common oriental view of the king. Both Egyptian and Assyrian texts describe the king as the image of God.... that man is a divine representative on earth arises from the very idea of an image. Images of gods or kings were viewed as representatives of the deity or king. The divine spirit was often thought of as indwelling an idol, thereby creating a close unity between the god and his image." Wenham concludes, "The strongest case has been made for the view that the divine image makes man God's vice-regent on earth." (*Genesis 1-15*, WBC 1 [Dallas: Word, 2002], 30-32).

117. *OGI* 90, l. 3, of Ptolemy Epiphanes, cited in Moulton and Milligan. *Vocabulary of the Greek Testament*, s.v.

118. Strong argues: "To students of the Augustan period, it is clear that Augustus called in the service of art to help his religious schemes to an extent as great or even than that of poetry.... whether representing the actual deification, or merely showing the Emperor in the majestic pose which his exalted state demanded—seen in every public place, at every street corner, repeated, we may add, in miniature for the sideboard and the dining table, must have gone far to fill the popular imagination with the Imperial idea.... The opening of the First Georgic, the Sixth Aeneid, the Imperial lyrics of Horace were possibly less potent factors in the establishment of the Empire than the pictures of the Imperial 'might, majesty, and dominion,' of which cameos and coins and silver cups have preserved us the copies" (*Apotheosis and After Life*, 75-76).

119. Paul Zanker, "Bürgerliche Selbstdarstellung am Grab im romischen Kaiserreich," in *Die römische Stadt in 2. Jahrhundert n.Chr.: Der Funktionswandel des offentlichen Raumes, Kolloquium Xanten 2. bis 4. Mai 1990*, ed. Hans-Joachim Schalles, Henner von Hesberg, and Paul Zanker (Köln: Rheinland-Verlag, 1992), 348.

ity of people across the empire, the emperor was his image. These images and the presence of emperors past and present were everywhere."[120] Much later, Menander Rhetor can safely say of the emperor: "Full of his images [πλήρεις εἰκόνων] are the cities, some of painted tablets, some maybe of more precious material."[121]

The New Testament usage of the term reflects this prevalent meaning, as over half of the New Testament uses have explicit reference to an imperial εἰκών: (1) Caesar's image on a coin (Matt 22:20 // Mark 12:16 // Luke 20:24); (2) the image of the Beast, often worshiped, that is, the emperor's εἰκών (Rev 13:14, 15 [3x]; 14:9, 11; 15:2; 16:2; 19:20; 20:4); (3) an image of human idol forms, inclusive of the emperor (Rom 1:23); (4) the image of Christ (Rom 8:29; 1 Cor 15:49 [2x]; 2 Cor 3:18; 4:4; Col 3:10); (5) the image of God that Christ is (Col 1:15) or humans bear (1 Cor 11:7; cf. Col 3:10); and (6) the true reality/image that the law cannot reflect (Heb 10:1). In addition to this, arguably the references to εἰκών in Romans, 1 and 2 Corinthians, and Colossians contest the alternative (imperial) εἰκόνες.[122]

Returning to 2 Cor 4:4, the god of this age deceives by *blinding* (τυφλόω) the minds of unbelievers from perceiving the true εἰκών of God, namely, Jesus the Lord Messiah. Such blinding is clearly metaphorical, yet it may be grounded in a tyrant's prerogative to gouge out eyes (among other atrocities), as the king of Babylon did (2 Kgs 25:5, ἐκτυφλόω), or as acknowledged by Eleazer before the tyrant Antiochus IV (4 Macc 5:30), or as recalled by Plutarch regarding the Sicilian tyrant Agathocles (*Reg. imp. apophth.* 3 [176F], προσεκτυφλόω).[123] Such mutilation of captives "supplies a visible inscribed monument or document of the king's power, equivalent to the herms, pillars, or statues that chart the imperialist's tri-

---

120. Caroline Vout, "Representing the Emperor," in *The Cambridge Companion to the Roman Historians*, ed. Andrew Feldherr, Cambridge Companions to Literature (Cambridge: Cambridge University Press, 2009), 263. Similarly, James B. Rives says, "Images of the emperor ... like those of the gods, were omnipresent, ranging from larger-than-life statues in public spaces to small figures in private residences to images on coins. And like the images of the gods, their constant presence helped to shape people's sense of who they were" (*Religion in the Roman Empire* [Malden, MA: Blackwell, 2007], 152).

121. Menander Rhetor, *Epitr.* 2.1-2 (Spengel 377,26-28). I am indebted to my colleague Craig Keener for this reference.

122. It is possible that Paul used εἰκών in Rom 1:23 negatively and then positively in Rom 8:39, 2 Cor 4:4 (cf. 3:18), and Col 1:15 with this imperial background in mind.

123. I am indebted to Jon Ensor for this suggestion.

umphal progress and record his victories."¹²⁴ Understood differently, the blinding may be accomplished by covering up God's εἰκών in Jesus or by proliferating an alternatively bright substitute brilliant image. For example, Josephus in *C. Ap.* 2.132 indicated, "Sesostris, the famed king of the Egyptians, has blinded [ἐτύφλωσεν] him [Apion]," although Josephus restrains from boasting about the Jewish kings David and Solomon, who conquered many nations. This usage—to be so beguiled by the brilliance of a king—corresponds well with Paul's emphasis on the *light* and *shining* in relation to the gospel.¹²⁵ What ruler would have been so blinding for the minds of unbelievers? It is Augustus. Estimates are that as many as twenty-five to fifty thousand portraits (not including coin images!) of Augustus were spread across the empire, one per one to two thousand persons; thus, Michael Peppard ventures, "it does not seem an exaggeration to call the emperor—especially Augustus—the only Empire-wide god in the Roman pantheon."¹²⁶

When the imperial topoi of *god*, *lord*, *image*, and *gospel* are connected with *illumination* (ὁ φωτισμός), *glory* (ἡ δόξη), *light* (φῶς) and *shining* (λάμπω), a counter religious motif comparable to mystery-cult practices seems quite possible.¹²⁷ Key words associated with the mystery cults include *light* contrasted with *darkness* and the verb ἐλλάμπω, which is a technical term in Iamblichus, *De mysteriis*.¹²⁸ Light and illumination of the mind were associated with mystery cults symbolically, represented commonly by lamps and torches in worship.¹²⁹ Such lamps

---

124. Deborah Tarn Steiner, *The Tyrant's Writ: Myths and Images of Writing in Ancient Greece*, Princeton Legacy Library (Princeton: Princeton University Press, 2015), 155.

125. The Greek lawgiver Solon, in verse, warned against Pisistratus's tyranny as like "lightning's blinding flash" that "enslaves unwary people" (David Mulroy, *Early Greek Lyric Poetry* [Ann Arbor: University of Michigan Press, 1999], 73).

126. Michael Peppard, *The Son of God in the Roman World: Divine Sonship in Its Social and Political Context* (New York: Oxford University Press, 2011), 91.

127. Contrast the exegesis and theology of Dautzenberg ("Überlegungen zur Exegese und Theologie"), who interprets this language against Jewish wisdom and creation accounts.

128. As described in the section "Light in the Cultus" by Conzelmann ("φῶς, φωτίζω, κτλ.," 315–16).

129. See Martin P. Nilsson, "Lampen und Kerzen im Kult der Antike," *Opuscula Archaeologica* 6 (1950): 96–111, cited in H. W. Pleket, "An Aspect of the Emperor Cult: Imperial Mysteries," *HTR* 58 (1965): 343.

were used to illuminate the mystery's deity image (ἄγαλμα), but in imperial mysteries the lamps' illumination was on the image (εἰκών) of the emperor.[130] One mutilated text from Ephesus may describe that "Dionysius and the emperor, together with many other gods and goddesses, were the objects of μυστήρια."[131] Under Hadrian, one inscription (IPergamon 374) describes the use of "sacrificial cakes, frankincense, and lamps for the Sebastoi" (πόπανον καὶ λίβανον καὶ λύχνους τῶι Σεβαστῶι) (face B, 19-20) and "the appointed uninitiated choral singers will offer [missing] ... to the images of the Sebastoi for good fortune" (δώσουσιν δὲ οἱ καθιστάμενοι ἐξωτικοὶ ὑμνῳδοὶ εἰς εἰκόνας τῶν Σεβαστῶν ... ἀγαθῆι τύχη[ι]) (face C, 13).[132]

H. W. Pleket and Philip A. Harland have argued against the assumption that participation in the imperial cults was merely perfunctory with no true religious feeling.[133] Instead one finds enthusiastic use of mystery-cult practices and titles with functionary equivalents for the imperial cults. Pleket summarizes, "the εἰκόνες of the emperor are on a par with the ἀγάλματα of the gods: both were object of the devotion of the people."[134] James B. Rives remarks, "The initiates of Demeter performed their mysteries for the emperors along with their goddess. Officially deified emperors were in all cases treated the same as other gods."[135] So socially powerful among the masses were the mystery cults that the emperors themselves were initiated into them (e.g., Augustus at Eleusis).[136] At the same time, devotion was offered by the masses to the emperors in the provinces in the imperial cults, even Asia Minor, which included elements of mysteries.[137] Equally significant is Harland's conclusion:

---

130. Pleket, "Aspect of the Emperor Cult," 343-45; it is important to remember that the term εἰκών is used for humans, whereas ἄγαλμα is used for deities (LSJ, ἄγαλμα, def. 3).

131. Pleket, "Aspect of the Emperor Cult," 337.

132. Roy Jeal identified this source discussed in Philip A. Harland, *Associations, Synagogues, and Congregations: Claiming a Place in Ancient Mediterranean Society* (Minneapolis: Fortress, 2003), 131.

133. E.g., Harland, *Associations, Synagogues, and Congregations*, 132. He rightly critiques Martin P. Nilsson, *Geschichte der griechischen Religion: Die hellenistische und römische Zeit*, 2nd ed. (Münich: Beck, 1961), 370.

134. Pleket, "Aspect of the Emperor Cult," 341.

135. Rives, *Religion in the Roman Empire*, 152.

136. Mary Beard, John North, and S. R. F. Price, *Religions of Rome: A History* (Cambridge: Cambridge University Press, 1998), 1:223.

137. Pleket, "Aspect of the Emperor Cult"; also, in a brief note on the presence

imperial gods were an important component within the self-understanding or identity of many associations. The performance of sacrifices, mysteries, or other rituals for emperors in the group setting was not simply an outward and meaningless statement of political loyalty. This was a symbolic expression of a worldview held in common by those participating. Within this cosmic framework, the *Sebastoi*, were placed at the height of power alongside other gods in a realm separate from, though in interaction with, humans and human communities.... Overall, the evidence from Asia suggests that religious rites for imperial gods, which paralleled the sacrifices, mysteries, and other rituals directed at traditional deities, were a significant component within numerous associations.[138]

Even more specifically, imperial mysteries were conducted with functionaries called *sebastophants* (cf. *hierophants*), who were "revealers of the *Sebastoi*."[139] Harland again summarizes the social significance for participants at even this smallest scale: "Through participating in similar religious practices in a small-group setting the members of an association could feel a sense of belonging not only within the group, but also

---

of royal mystery cult in Egypt, Nilsson concludes, "It ought not to be surprising that the Ptolemaic kings were celebrated in a mystery cult. The mysteries devoted to the emperors are well known. The cult of the emperors is a continuation of Hellenistic ruler cult, and so too the ruler mysteries. In a time which was fond of mystery cults, as was the Hellenistic age, it was natural to enlarge the ruler cult with mysteries" (Nilsson, "Royal Mysteries," 66).

138. Harland, *Associations, Synagogues, and Congregations*, 135–36.

139. See ibid., 128–32; see also the literature discussed there, esp. Pleket, "Aspect of the Emperor Cult." From the online PHI database, we have in a text from Sardis (second century?): "the sebastophant and hierophant of the mysteries" (σε[βαστοφάντην καὶ] [τῶν] μυστη[ρίων ἱεροφάντην]) (William Hepburn Buckler and David Moore Robinson, *Greek and Latin Inscriptions*, vol. 7.1 of *Sardis* [Leiden: Brill, 1932], §62); in Bithynia, an inscription speaks of "the hierophant and sebastophant of the common temple" (τοῦ κοινοῦ νάου τῶν μυστηρίων [ἱ]εροφάντην καὶ σεβαστοφάντην) (Walter Ameling, *Die Inschriften von Prusias ad Hypium*, Inschriften griechischer Städte aus Kleinasien 27 [Bonn: Habelt, 1985], §17); cf., in Bithynia, Ameling, *Die Inschriften von Prusias ad Hypium*, §47; in Galatia, Johan H. M. Strubbe, "Descriptive Catalogue and Bibliography of the Inscribed Monuments of Pessinus," in *Les Fouilles de la Rijksuniversiteit te Gent à Pessinonte*, ed. John Devreker and Marc Waelkens, Dissertationes Archaeologicae Gandenses 22 (Brugge: De Tempel, 1984), §§17 and 18 (both perhaps from the late first or second century).

within this broader civic or imperial context."[140] Harland summarizes the presence of imperial elements more specifically within the Demetriasts of Ephesus: "Also significant here is the incorporation of the imperial gods within the ritual life of this group. Alongside the central ritual of sacrifice, mysteries were among the most respected and revered acts of piety in the Greco-Roman world. Few human actions so effectively maintained fitting relations between the realm of humans and that of the gods, ensuring benefaction and protection for the individual, group or community in question."[141]

If Paul's language of *seeing* (αὐγάζω), *light* (φῶς), and *shining* (λάμπω) in 2 Cor 4:4–6 was not reflective of imperial mystery-cult language, then he simply may have been describing the gospel of Christ using the language of "solar monarchy" (see further below). A striking parallel occurs in one inscription for Gaius Caligula from Mysia dated 37 CE that hails Gaius Caesar Sebastos Germanicus as "the new Sun" (ὁ νέος Ἥλιος) who is willing "to co-illuminate with his own sun beams" (συναναλάμψαι ταῖς ἰδίαις αὐγαῖς) satelite kingdoms. Intriguing in this regard is Paul's use of αὐγάζω, a *hapax legomena* and cognate to αὐγή "sun beam" used in this inscription in relation to Gaius.[142] Moreover, Paul used the aorist infinitive form αὐγάσαι. Is it coincidental that this form sounds like the adjective αὔγουστος, the equivalent to σεβαστός, also used to refer to Octavian Augustus? Although αὔγουστος occurs more commonly after the first century in imperial contexts, it is attested during Augustus's reign, as is the Latinized αὐγουστᾶλις (for *Augustales*) in 44 CE.[143]

If Paul has drawn upon the imperial mystery-cult or solar-monarchy background in 4:1–6, what might this mean for the identity of the "unbelievers" in 4:4? They are likely pagan unbelievers, distinguished from Jewish unbelievers yet awaiting the Messiah Jesus to remove the veil that lies over

---

140. Harland, *Associations, Synagogues, and Congregations*, 129.

141. Philip A. Harland, "Imperial Cults within Local Cultural Life: Associations in Roman Asia," *Ancient History Bulletin/Zeitschrift für Alte Geschichte* 17 (2003): 92.

142. Matthias Barth and Josef Stauber, eds., *Inschriften Mysia and Troas* (Munich: Leopold Wenger Institut, 1993), §1439.

143. For attestation during Augustus's reign, see Donald F. McCabe, *Aphrodisias Inscriptions: Texts and List* (Princeton: Princeton Institute for Advanced Study, 1991), §37; for 44 CE, see McCabe, *Ephesos Inscriptions: Texts and List*, 3 vols. (Princeton: Princeton Institute for Advanced Study, 1991), §§227–230.

their minds and hearts, described just prior in 3:14–16.[144] That ἄπιστοι in 4:4 refers to pagan unbelievers finds support in 1 Cor 10:27, where Paul instructs Corinthian Christ-followers how to respond to an unbeliever explicitly offering meat sacrificed to a god to them.[145] The majority view of the meaning of ἄπιστοι in 2 Cor 6:14 is that pagan unbelievers are meant;[146] the reasons supplied for the context of 6:14 are the same as for 4:4. If so, then Paul constructs his argumentation that has begun with the Roman triumphal and processional themes of 2:14 forward to the climactic covenantal call to faithful separation from paganism at Corinth in 6:14–7:2. Elsewhere in the his writings Paul explicitly maintains an ethnographic distinction between the Jewish response and Greek/pagan response to the gospel (1 Cor 1:22–24; 10:32; Rom 1–3; Eph 1:3–14; 2:1–3; cf. 1 Thess 2:14–16). Paul clearly was thinking in such categories. So, in 2 Cor 3:7–16 Paul addresses particularly a Jewish response of unbelief to the gospel despite their having the law and Moses as a leader; then, in 4:1–6 Paul describes the unbelief among the pagans because of the blinding caused by the Roman emperor Augustus, the god of this age.

Discursive Development and Parallels between 2 Cor 4:1–6 and 6:14–7:1

Much can be learned about the ideological confrontation that Paul was engaged in with the "Corinthians" (Κορίνθιοι 6:11), by considering 6:14–7:1, where Paul calls the Corinthian Christ-followers to separate them-

---

144. *Contra* the view that mainly Jewish unbelievers are in view, for which see, e.g., Thrall, *2 Corinthians 1–7*, 305; Dautzenberg, "Überlegungen zur Exegese und Theologie," 341.

145. I think it is highly likely that Paul envisions pagan unbelievers in every occurrence of the word, which is intriguingly found almost exclusively in the Corinthian correspondence: 1 Cor 6:6; 7:12, 13, 14 (2x), 15; 10:27; 14:22 (2x), 23, 24, but also in 1 Tim 5:8 and Titus 1:15.

146. See the review of the five options in appendix A of Webb, *Returning Home*, 184–99. The options are (1) untrustworthy persons as a backhanded slam against Paul; (2) gentile Christians who do not keep the law; (3) the immoral within the Christian community; (4) the false apostles, false teachers in the community; (5) non-Christian, pagans outside the community, which has been the majority view and comports with Pauline usage elsewhere. However, Webb views 4:4 as in reference to non-Christians in general (198 n. 3).

selves from the pagan unbelievers (ἄπιστοι). After doing so, Paul pointedly asks five questions while making key contrasts (6:14–16):

- What partnership (μετοχή) has righteousness and lawlessness?
- What fellowship (κοινωνία) has light with darkness?
- What harmony (συμφώνησις) has Christ with Belial?
- What portion (μερίς) for a believer exists with an unbeliever?
- What agreement (συγκατάθεσις) has the temple of God with idols?

These questions debar the Corinthians from certain incompatible allegiances and associations, while carrying forward critical themes from 4:1–6 and recalling Paul's exhortation to separate from idolatrous association from 1 Cor 10. The table below categorizes the type of association, the pairing of incompatible relationships, and the nature of the incompatible elements.

Type of Association	Pairing of Incompatibles		Nature of Incompatibles
partnership	righteousness	lawlessness	moral conduct
fellowship	light	darkness	common abstraction
harmony	Messiah	Beliar	Political-religious figure
part	believer	unbeliever	human relation to the gospel
agreement	God's temple	cultic image (idol)	sacred/cultic object

At this point we can construct the ideological polemical parallelism in Paul's co-opting of the Roman triumphal and epiphanic procession metaphor as initiated at 2:14 and culminating with 6:14–7:1 climactically.[147]

---

147. So also Barnett: "With this powerful appeal Paul now brings the apostolic excursus, begun at 2:14, to its climax" (*Second Epistle,* 337).

	2:14–17	Climactic Exhortation 6:14–7:1		4:1–6
[unstated referent]	God's "manifest" triumph			the god of this age's "blinding"
Deity:	God	temple of the living God, Father Almighty	idols	[Jupiter et al.]
Image:	Jesus Messiah	Messiah	Beliar = Nero	[emperor, Augustus]
Ethics:	righteousness; plain truth	righteousness	lawlessness	secret shame, trickery, falsifying
Metaphor:	light	light	darkness	darkness
Spectators:	"Those saved"	Believers	Unbelievers	Perishing unbelievers

At the human scale, believers are distinguished from unbelievers; their respective association with light/righteousness versus darkness/lawlessness achieves this. Additionally and more critically, their disassociation revolves around divine figures, literally in the middle position (Christ versus Beliar) and in the final, climactic position (the living God versus idols). God is opposed to idols, the chief of which would be Jupiter/Zeus, whose image was the most prominent of any god in the Mediterranean world, yet actively being co-opted by Roman emperors.[148] Likewise, Jesus Messiah is opposed to the mysterious and interpretively troubling Beliar.[149]

---

148. While no specific data for Achaia is given, for the Latin West and Asia Minor Jupiter/Zeus occurs two and a half times more frequently than other deities in the inscriptions (Ramsay MacMullen, *Paganism in the Roman Empire* [New Haven: Yale University Press, 1981], 6–8).

149. See, e.g., Thrall, *2 Corinthians 1–7*, 474–75. She holds the typical position that Beliar is "a personal name for Satan in the later Jewish writings," citing texts, some of which are discussed here, although admitting that "Paul's usual designation for the

This odd figure, however, can be readily explained and becomes mutually affirmative of the interpretation that "the god of this age" refers to a deified Roman emperor Augustus.

The significance of Paul's use of Beliar in 6:15 corresponds to its use as a term of Jewish imperial resistance.[150] The Qumran War Scroll described the battle of the Kittim led by their god, Belial, against the holy ones of the Jews. Who were the Kittim? Who was Belial? The Kittim are the Romans (see different recensions of Dan 11:30 LXX).[151] As for Belial, alternatively named Beliar, the spiritual figure is often identified as Satan but in the Jewish materials may be identified as a human. According to Sib. Or. 3.63, "Then Beliar will come from the *Sebastēnoi*," meaning the Augustan family line that ended with Nero.[152] Also, in these texts Nero is said to be born of Zeus and Hera (Sib. Or. 5.140), reflecting the imperial ideology of divine descent. Likewise, Ascen. Isa. 4.1–4 indicates that Beliar "will descend from his firmament in the form of a man, a king of iniquity, a murderer of his mother—this is the king of the world.... This angel, Beliar, will come in the form of that king.... he will act and speak like the Beloved, and will say, 'I am the Lord, and before me there was no one.'" The likely identity of this human figure is once again the emperor Nero, who was renowned for murdering his mother, Agrippina.[153] Paavo Tucker surveys and inter-

---

supreme demonic power is Satan." Rightly, Thrall co-identifies Beliar with "the god of this age" of 4:4. Although citing Hans Walter Huppenbauer, Thrall and others treat the Belial figure monolithically, even though the Huppenbauer survey indicates diversity of meaning and the allowance that individuals and diverse nations might be there signified, if even under the control of the "Feindsengel: Belial" (Hans Walter Huppenbauer "Belial in den Qumrantexten," *TZ* 15 [1959]: 81–89).

150. Cf. Dautzenberg, "Überlegungen zur Exegese und Theologie." My approach differs from Dautzenberg's mainly by my considering how Paul's argument and language would have been heard by Greeks at Corinth; otherwise, it is intriguing that Dautzenberg has identified a number of ideological parallels with 1QS 3–4. I would argue that a combined background—Roman imperial and Jewish apocalyptic *resistance literature*—will be most illuminating for interpreting both Paul's dependence on theological resources and his rhetorical, metaphorical, and ideological references to persuade the Corinthian Christians.

151. H. E. del Medico, "L'identification des Kittim Avec Les Romains," *VT* 10 (1960): 448–53.

152. John J. Collins, "The Sibylline Oracles, Book 3: Introduction," in *Old Testament Pseudepigrapha*, ed. James H. Charlesworth, 2 vols. (New York: Doubleday, 1983–1985), 1:360.

153. John J. Collins, *The Sibylline Oracles of Egyptian Judaism*, SBLDS 13 (Mis-

prets the growing association of political regimes and pagan rulers with the Hebrew בליעל in the Dead Sea Scrolls, LXX, and Second Temple literature, supporting my interpretation of 2 Cor 6:15 that Beliar refers to Nero. Tucker concludes: "These texts evince a complex notion of Beliar as denoting not only a demonic spirit such as Satan, but often also human referents controlled by Satan, such as foreign rulers who oppose God and his people.... Βελιάρ should be understood as a reference to Nero as the representative of the power of Satan in opposition to Christ."[154]

Regardless of the dating of the portions of these two documents, it is evident that in circulation in the later half of the first century Nero could be identified with Beliar/Belial. Part and parcel with such a Jewish apocalyptic view that Rome was under Satan's control. For the interpretation of "the god of this age" in 2 Cor 4:4, however, we must not miss the primary referent that Paul intended for the Corinthians to understand: opposed to the gospel of Jesus the Lord and Messiah as the image of God was the imperial ideology promoted in its localized cults that the Caesars (Augustus and Nero) were not merely human benefactors and mediators for the gods but gods themselves worthy of devotion and imitation; they must be identified and resisted.

Before concluding, it is instructive to consider the implications of Paul's statement in 2 Cor 11:14 that Satan "disguises himself as an angel of light" (μετασχηματίζεται εἰς ἄγγελον φωτός), since this passage is linked thematically to 4:4–6.[155] How would the Corinthians have understood Satan in this way? The referent "angel/messenger of light" is readily supplied from the Roman imperial political ideology: their rulers were thought of as angels/messengers/Mercury and were likened to the sun/stars/Apollo. Augustus identified himself as the messenger of the gods, Mercury-Hermes, such that ἄγγελος was applied to him: "Augustus might be Mercury, sent down as ἄγγελος τοῦ Δίος to do his father's work."[156] This is well

---

soula, MT: Society of Biblical Literature, 1974), 80–88. Although the accounts of Tacitus (*Ann.* 14.1–8), Dio Cassius (*Hist. rom.* 63.11–15), and Suetonius (*Nero* 32) disagree on details, all ascribe guilt to Nero.

154. Paavo Tucker, "Reconsidering Βελιάρ: 2 Corinthians 6:15 in Its Anti-imperial Jewish Apocalyptic Context," *Journal of Paul and His Letters* 4 (2014): 67.

155. Harris, *Second Epistle*, 774.

156. Nock, "Notes on Ruler Cult," 34. Nock also states: "Accordingly when Horace speaks of Augustus as Mercury in human form [*Odes* I 2, 41] ... he is not uttering the casual flattery of a Court poet, but rather what would in the Greek East be a commonplace" ("Studies in the Graeco-Roman Beliefs of the Empire," *JHS* 45 [1925]: 94 n. 84).

represented on coins.¹⁵⁷ Also, Philo records that Gaius Caligula, as well as wanting to look like Mercury and Mars, "would customarily metamorphosize and transform himself into Apollo [εἰς δὲ Ἀπόλλωνα μετεμορφοῦτο καὶ μετεσκευάζετο], crowning his head with radiate crowns" (*Legat.* 95). Stefan Weinstock has reviewed the development of this solar-monarchy theme in relation to Julius Caesar and subsequent Roman rulers.¹⁵⁸ Coinage and artifacts reflected this association, either by depicting the ruler crowned radiate looking like Helios or Sol or by physically placing a sun or star on the coin or artifact above the emperor, as in the Cameo of Nero and Agrippina. For Nero, Marianne Bermann summarizes, "The comparison of Nero with Apollo/Sol as the god of the Golden Age was, as Seneca's *Apocolocyntosis* demonstrates, propagated right from the beginning of Nero's reign."¹⁵⁹ Satan was disguised as the angel of light, the new emperor Nero hailed eventually as "the new sun shining upon the Greeks" (νέος Ἥλιος ἐπιλάμψας τοῖς Ἕλλησιν) (*IG* 7.2713.34, Akraiphia Boiotia, 67 CE).

Conclusion

By "the god of this age" in 2 Cor 4:4 Paul did not specifically have as his referent Satan but the deified emperor Augustus who everywhere in public, civic spaces was blinding and counter-shining the glorious gospel of the Messiah Jesus.¹⁶⁰ Although Paul's later statements in 11:14 that Satan is

---

157. Jacqueline Chittenden, "Hermes-Mercury, Dynasts, and Emperors," *The Numismatic Chronicle and Journal of the Royal Numismatic Society* 6/5 (1945): 41–57.

158. An excellent review of this developing ideology is found in Stefan Weinstock, *Divus Julius* (Oxford: Clarendon, 1971), 370–84.

159. Marianne Bergmann, "Portraits of an Emperor—Nero, the Sun, and Roman *Otium*," in *A Companion to the Neronian Age*, ed. Emma Buckley and Martin T. Dinter, Blackwell Companions to the Ancient World (Chichester, West Sussex, UK: Wiley-Blackwell, 2013), 342. Overall, I find Bergmann's distinction between official lack of support versus private and provincial support of Nero as Apollo/Sol to be more convincing than the view of Champlin ("Life and Times").

160. Similar, but not the same, is David Aune's position regarding Revelation: "Christ is the true king in contrast to the Roman emperor who is both a clone and tool of Satan" ("The Form and Function of the Proclamations to the Seven Churches (Revelation 2–3)," *NTS* 36 (1990): 204; quoted approvingly by Jan Willem van Henten, "Dragon Myth and Imperial Ideology in Revelation 12–13," in *The Reality of Apocalypse: Rhetoric and Politics in the Book of Revelation*, ed. David L. Barr, SBLSymS 39 (Atlanta: Society of Biblical Literature, 2006), 202.

disguised as an angel of light would have helped the Corinthian Christ-followers to understand how Satan worked through the reigning emperor Nero and hence Augustus, we ought not see Satan as the primary referent to "the god of this age." Paul was more than "demonizing" Augustus; he was critiquing the age present at Corinth that was reflecting the broader Mediterranean world, which was enamored with (all-)powerful earthly rulers. This is idolatry.

The pervasive Roman imperial triumphal and epiphanic processional imagery extending from 2:14 to 7:2 helps us to understand how Paul understood the gospel of Christ the Lord as a counterimperial movement. Critical imagery of freedom/deliverance (3:17) and mercy (4:1) powerfully prepare for 4:3–6, in order to place the god of this age in ideological contrast with and opposition to the glory of the gospel of Christ, who is the (true) image (εἰκών) of God. Paul's contrasting descriptions of God and the god of this age reveal their counteractivities on the critical question of who is "the image of God" and who is proclaimed "Lord." For Paul, the unequivocal answer is Jesus the Messiah. Although the emperor held sway over the pagan unbelievers (the ἄπιστοι), Paul urged the Corinthian converts to Christ to remain faithful and distinct from the ἄπιστοι. His urgent appeal continued and culminated in 6:14-16a with a command not to be yoked togehter with them followed by five striking contrasts posed in the form of rhetorical questions. The contrasts in 6:14-16a pick up themes from 4:1–6, while also revealing more about just who is to be contrasted with Christ, namely, Beliar. This appellation was understood within Jewish resistance literature to refer to the spiritual leader of the Kittim (the Romans), and this leader is sometimes identified with the emperor Nero, who was newly ascended to the throne as Paul wrote 2 Corinthians. The proposed interpretation of "the god of this age" in 4:4 as defied Augustus is consonant with the puzzling figure Beliar in 6:15 as Nero; they are mutually affirming. To this may be added the interpretation of 11:14, where Satan is said to disguise himself as "an angel of light." Roman imperial ideology included emperors identifying themselves as Hermes/Mercury and also Apollos, adopting at the same time the ubiquitous Mediterranean solar monarchy motif that identified the ruling emperor with the sun god Helios or Sol, a light for the world.

In modern translation, the phrase "the god of this age" in 4:4 may be placed within "scare quotes" and given a brief explanation in a footnote: "In Roman Corinth, a prominent bronze statue of deified Augustus was dedicated 'To the god/divine Augustus' and stood in the center of the forum." For the initial audience, however, neither scare quotes nor a footnote would have been necessary, since the Christ-followers at Corinth would have understood the brilliant glory of Paul's empire-resisting gospel of the Lord Jesus, the Son of God.

WORKS CITED

Ameling, Walter. *Die Inschriften von Prusias ad Hypium*. Inschriften griechischer Städte aus Kleinasien 27. Bonn: Habelt, 1985.
Aune, David. "The Form and Function of the Proclamations to the Seven Churches (Revelation 2–3)." *NTS* 36 (1990): 182–204.
Aus, Roger David. *Imagery of Triumph and Rebellion in 2 Corinthians 2:4–17 and Elsewhere in the Epistle: An Example of the Combination Greco-Roman and Judaic Traditions in the Apostle Paul*. Lanham, MD: University Press of America, 2005.
Barnett, Paul. *The Second Epistle to the Corinthians*. NICNT. Grand Rapids: Eerdmans, 1997.
Barth, Matthias, and Josef Stauber, eds. *Inschriften Mysia and Troas*. Munich: Leopold Wenger Institut, 1993.
Beard, Mary. *The Roman Triumph*. Cambridge: Harvard University Press, 2007.
Beard, Mary, John North, and S. R. F. Price. *Religions of Rome: A History*. Cambridge: Cambridge University Press, 1998.
Bergmann, Marianne. "Portraits of an Emperor—Nero, the Sun, and Roman *Otium*." Pages 332–62 in *A Companion to the Neronian Age*. Edited by Emma Buckley and Martin T. Dinter. Blackwell Companions to the Ancient World. Chichester, West Sussex, UK: Wiley-Blackwell, 2013.
Betz, Hans Dieter. "2 Cor 6:14–7:1: An Anti-Pauline Fragment?" *JBL* 92 (1973): 88–108.
Botha, P. J. J. "Assessing Representations of the Imperial Cult in New Testament Studies." *Verbum et Ecclesia* 25 (2004): 14–45.
Breytenbach, Cilliers. "Paul's Proclamation and God's 'Thriambos' (Notes on 2 Corinthians 2:14–16b)." *Neot* 24 (1990): 257–71.
Brox, Norbert. "Non Huius Aevi Deus: Zu Tertullian, *Adv Marc* V 11, 10." *ZNW* 59 (1968): 259–61.
Buchanan, George Wesley. "Paul and the Jews (II Cor 3:4–4:6 and Rom 11:7–10)." Pages 141–62 in *When Jews and Christians Meet*. Edited by

Jakob Josef Petuchowski. Albany: State University of New York Press, 1988.

Buckler, William Hepburn, and David Moore Robinson. *Greek and Latin Inscriptions*. Vol. 7.1 of *Sardis*. Leiden: Brill, 1932.

Bultmann, Rudolf Karl. *The Second Letter to the Corinthians*. Translated by Roy A. Harrisville. Minneapolis: Augsburg, 1985.

Carter, Michael J. D. "The Presentation of Gladiatorial Spectacles in the Greek East: Roman Culture and Greek Identity." PhD diss., McMaster University, 1999.

Carter, Warren. *John and Empire: Initial Explorations*. New York: T&T Clark, 2008.

———. *Pontius Pilate: Portraits of a Roman Governor*. Collegeville, MN: Liturgical Press, 2003.

Carver, Frank G. *2 Corinthians: A Commentary in the Wesleyan Tradition*. New Beacon Bible Commentary. Kansas City: Beacon Hill, 2009.

Champlin, Edward. "The Life and Times of Calpurnius Siculus." *JRS* 68 (1978): 95–110.

Chittenden, Jacqueline. "Hermes-Mercury, Dynasts, and Emperors." *The Numismatic Chronicle and Journal of the Royal Numismatic Society* 6/5 (1945): 41–57.

Cole, Victor B. "The Message and Messenger of the Gospel." *Evangelical Review of Theology* 29 (2005): 178–84.

Collins, John J. *The Sibylline Oracles of Egyptian Judaism*. SBLDS 13. Missoula, MT: Society of Biblical Literature, 1974.

———. "The Sibylline Oracles, Book 3: Introduction." Pages 354–61 in vol. 1 of *Old Testament Pseudepigrapha*. Edited by James H. Charlesworth. 2 vols. New York: Doubleday, 1983–1985.

Conzelmann, Hans. "φῶς, φωτίζω, κτλ." *TDNT* 9:310–58.

Danker, Frederick W. *Benefactor: Epigraphic Study of a Graeco-Roman and New Testament Semantic Field*. St. Louis: Clayton, 1982.

Dautzenberg, Gerhard. "Überlegungen zur Exegese und Theologie von 2 Kor 4,1–6." *Bib* 82 (2001): 325–44.

Degrassi, Attilio. *Fasti Capitolini*. Turin: Paravia, 1954.

Deissmann, G. Adolf. *Light from the Ancient East: The New Testament Illustrated by Recently Discovered Texts of the Graeco-Roman World*. Translated by L. R. M. Strachan. 4th ed. New York: Doran, 1927.

Duff, Paul Brooks. "Apostolic Suffering and the Language of Processions in 2 Corinthians 4:7–10." *BTB* 21 (1991): 158–65.

———. "Metaphor, Motif, and Meaning: The Rhetorical Strategy behind the Image 'Led in Triumph' in 2 Corinthians 2:14." *CBQ* 53 (1991): 79–92.

———. "Processions." *ABD* 5:469–73.

———. "The Transformation of the Spectator: Power, Perception, and the Day of Salvation." Pages 233–43 in *Society of Biblical Literature 1987 Seminar Papers*. SBLSP 26. Missoula, MT: Scholars Press, 1987.

Edwards, Rebecca. "Divus Augustus Pater: Tiberius and the Charisma of Augustus." PhD diss., Indiana University, 2003.

Fantin, Joseph D. *The Lord of the Entire World: Lord Jesus, a Challenge to Lord Caesar?* New Testament Monographs 31. Sheffield: Sheffield Phoenix, 2011.

Fears, J. Rufus. "The Cult of Jupiter and Roman Imperial Ideology." *ANRW* 17.1:3–141.

———. *Princeps a Diis Electus: The Divine Electio of the Emperor as a Political Concept at Rome*. Papers and Monographs of the American Academy in Rome 26. Rome: American Academy, 1977.

Fee, Gordon D. *New Testament Exegesis: A Handbook for Students and Pastors*, 3rd ed. Louisville: Westminster, 2002.

Finney, Mark T. "Christ Crucified and the Inversion of Roman Imperial Ideology in 1 Corinthians." *BTB* 35 (2005): 20–33.

Foerster, Werner. "κύριος, κύρια, κτλ." *TDNT* 3:1039–58.

Garrett, Susan R. "The God of This World and the Affliction of Paul: 2 Cor 4:1–12." Pages 99–117 in *Greeks, Romans, and Christians: Essays in Honor of Abraham J. Malherbe*. Edited by David L. Balch, Everett Ferguson, and Wayne A. Meeks. Minneapolis: Fortress, 1990.

Gordon, C. D. "Review of *Libertas as a Political Idea at Rome during the Late Republic and Early Principate* by C. Wirszubski." *Phoenix* 6 (1952): 27–29.

Harland, Philip A. *Associations, Synagogues, and Congregations: Claiming a Place in Ancient Mediterranean Society*. Minneapolis: Fortress, 2003.

———. "Imperial Cults within Local Cultural Life: Associations in Roman Asia." *Ancient History Bulletin/Zeitschrift für Alte Geschichte* 17 (2003): 85–107.

Harris, Murray J. *The Second Epistle to the Corinthians: A Commentary on the Greek Text*. NIGTC. Grand Rapids: Eerdmans, 2005.

Heinrici, Carl F. G. *Der zweite Brief an die Korinther, mit einem Anhang: Zum Hellenismus des Paulus*. 8th ed. KEK. Göttingen: Vandenhoeck & Ruprecht, 1900.

Heiny, Stephen B. "The Motive for Metaphor: 2 Corinthians 2:14–4:6." Pages 1–22 in *Society of Biblical Literature 1987 Seminar Papers*. SBLSP 26. Missoula, MT: Scholars Press, 1987.

Hellholm, David. "Moses as διάκονος of the παλαιὰ διαθήκη—Paul as διάκονος of the καινὴ διαθήκη: Argumenta Amplificationis in 2 Cor 2,14–4,6." *ZNW* 99 (2008): 247–89.

Henten, Jan Willem van. "Dragon Myth and Imperial Ideology in Revelation 12–13." Pages 181–203 in *The Reality of Apocalypse: Rhetoric and Politics in the Book of Revelation*. Edited by David L. Barr. SBLSymS 39. Atlanta: Society of Biblical Literature, 2006.

Hiesinger, Ulrich W. "The Portraits of Nero." *AJA* 79 (1975): 113–24.

Hughes, Philip E. *Paul's Second Epistle to the Corinthians: The English Text with Introduction, Exposition and Notes*. NICNT. Grand Rapids: Eerdmans, 1962.

Huppenbauer, Hans Walter. "Belial in den Qumrantexten.." *TZ* 15 (1959): 81–89.

Keener, Craig S. *The IVP Bible Background Commentary: New Testament*. 2nd ed. Downers Grove, IL: IVP Academic, 2014.

Kent, John Harvey, ed. *The Inscriptions, 1926–1950*. Vol. 8.3 of *Corinth: Results of Excavations Conducted by the American School of Classical Studies at Athens*. Princeton: American School of Classical Studies at Athens, 1966.

Kleiner, Fred S. "The Boscoreale Cups: Copies of a Lost Monument?" *JRA* 10 (1997): 377–80.

Kleinknecht, Hermann. "θεός, θεότης, κτλ." *TDNT* 3:122–123.

Kuttner, Ann L. *Dynasty and Empire in the Age of Augustus: The Case of the Boscoreale Cups*. Berkeley: University of California Press, 1995.

Laird, Margaret L. "The Emperor in a Roman Town: The Base of the *Augustales* in the Forum at Corinth." Pages 67–116 in *Corinth in Context: Comparative Studies on Religion and Society*. Edited by Steven J. Friesen, Daniel N. Schowalter, and James C. Walters. NovTSup 134. Leiden: Brill, 2010.

Lambrecht, Jan. "The Defeated Paul, Aroma of Christ: An Exegetical Study of 2 Corinthians 2:14-16b." *LS* 20 (1995): 170–86.

Lim, Kar Yong. *"The Sufferings of Christ Are Abundant in Us" (2 Corinthians 1.5): A Narrative Dynamics Investigation of Paul's Sufferings in 2 Corinthians*. LNTS 399. London: T&T Clark, 2009.

Long, Fredrick J. *Ancient Rhetoric and Paul's Apology: The Compositional*

Unity of 2 Corinthians. SNTSMS 131. Cambridge: Cambridge University Press, 2004.

———. "Roman Imperial Analogues and Referents in 2 Corinthians." Paper presented at the Midwest Region of the Society of Biblical Literature, Bourbonnais, IL, 8 February 2015.

———. "Roman Imperial Rule under the Authority of Jupiter-Zeus: Political-Religious Contexts and the Interpretation of 'the Ruler of the Authority of the Air' in Ephesians 2:2." Pages 113–54 in *The Language of the New Testament: Context, History and Development.* Edited by Stanly E. Porter and Andrew W. Pitts. Linguistic Biblical Studies 6, Early Christianity in Its Hellenistic Environment 3. Leiden: Brill, 2013.

Lozano, Fernando. "*Divi Augusti* and *Theoi Sebastoi*: Roman Initiatives and Greek Answers." *CQ* 57 (2007): 139–52.

MacMullen, Ramsay. *Christianizing the Roman Empire: A.D. 100–400.* New Haven: Yale University Press, 1984.

———. *Enemies of the Roman Order: Treason, Unrest, and Alienation in the Empire.* Cambridge: Harvard University Press, 1966.

———. *Paganism in the Roman Empire.* New Haven: Yale University Press, 1981.

Marek, Christian. *Stadt: Ära und Territorium in Pontus-Bithynia und Nord-Galatia.* Istanbuler Forschungen 39. Tübingen: Wasmuth, 1993.

Marshall, Peter. "A Metaphor of Social Shame: *Thriambeuein* in 2 Cor 2:14." *NovT* 25 (1983): 302–17.

Martin, Ralph P. *2 Corinthians.* WBC 40. Waco, TX: Word, 1985.

Mattingly, Harold. *Augustus to Vitellius.* Vol. 1 of *Coins of the Roman Empire.* London: British Museum, 1965.

McCabe, Donald F. *Aphrodisias Inscriptions: Texts and List.* Princeton: Princeton Institute for Advanced Study, 1991.

———. *Ephesos Inscriptions: Texts and List.* 3 vols. Princeton: Princeton Institute for Advanced Study, 1991.

———. *Erythrai Inscriptions: Texts and List.* Princeton: Princeton Institute for Advanced Study, 1986.

———. *Priene Inscriptions: Texts and List.* Princeton: Princeton Institute for Advanced Study, 1987.

McRay, J. R. "Corinth." Pages 227–31 in *Dictionary of New Testament Background: A Compendium of Contemporary Biblical Scholarship.* Edited by Craig A. Evans and Stanley E. Porter. Downers Grove, IL: InterVarsity Press, 2000.

Medico, H. E. del. "L'identification des Kittim Avec Les Romains." *VT* 10 (1960): 448–53.
Meritt, Benjamin Dean, ed. *Greek Inscriptions, 1896–1927*. Vol. 8.1 of *Corinth: Results of Excavations Conducted by the American School of Classical Studies at Athens*. Cambridge: American School of Classical Studies at Athens, 1931.
Moulton, James Hope, and George Milligan. *The Vocabulary of the Greek Testament Illustrated from the Papyri and Other Non-literary Sources*. Grand Rapids: Eerdmans, 1930.
Mulroy, David. *Early Greek Lyric Poetry*. Ann Arbor: University of Michigan Press, 1999.
Murphy-O'Connor, Jerome. "Pneumatikoi and Judaizers in 2 Cor 2:14–4:6." *ABR* 34 (1986): 42–58.
Nilsson, Martin P. *Geschichte der griechischen Religion: Die hellenistische und römische Zeit*. 2nd ed. München: Beck, 1961.
———. "Lampen und Kerzen im Kult der Antike." *Opuscula Archaeologica* 6 (1950): 96–111.
Nock, A. D. "Notes on Ruler-Cult I–IV." *JHS* 48 (1928): 21–43.
———. "The Proem of Lucan." *The Classical Review* 40 (1926): 17–18.
———. "Studies in the Graeco-Roman Beliefs of the Empire." *JHS* 45 (1925): 84–101.
Noreña, Carlos F. "The Communication of the Emperor's Virtues." *JRS* 91 (2001): 146–68.
Östenberg, Ida. *Staging the World: Spoils, Captives, and Representations in the Roman Triumphal Procession*. Oxford Studies in Ancient Culture and Representation. Oxford: Oxford University Press, 2009.
Peppard, Michael. *The Son of God in the Roman World: Divine Sonship in Its Social and Political Context*. New York: Oxford University Press, 2011.
Pfanner, Michael. *Der Titusbogen*. Beiträge zur Erforschung hellenistischer und kaiserzeitlicher Skulptur und Architektur 2. Mainz am Rhein: von Zabern, 1983.
Pleket, H. W. "An Aspect of the Emperor Cult: Imperial Mysteries." *HTR* 58 (1965): 331–47.
Price, S. R. F. *Rituals and Power: The Roman Imperial Cult in Asia Minor*. Cambridge: Cambridge University Press, 1984.
Reinach, Salomon. *Répertoire de Reliefs Grecs et Romains*. 3 vols. Paris: Leroux, 1909–1912.
Riccardi, Lee Ann. "Uncanonical Imperial Portraits in the Eastern Roman

Provinces: The Case of the Kanellopoulos Emperor." *Hesperia* 69 (2000): 105–32.
Ridley, Edward. *The Pharsalia of Lucan*. London: Longmans, Green, 1896.
Rives, James B. *Religion in the Roman Empire*. Malden, MA: Blackwell, 2007.
Saunders, Ross. "Paul and the Imperial Cult." Pages 227–37 in *Paul and His Opponents*. Edited by Stanley E. Porter. Pauline Studies 2. Leiden: Brill, 2005.
Scott, James M. *2 Corinthians*. NIBCNT 8. Peabody, MA: Hendrickson, 1998.
———. "The Triumph of God in 2 Cor 2:14: Additional Evidence of Merkabah Mysticism in Paul." *NTS* 42 (1996): 260–81.
———. "The Use of Scripture in 2 Corinthians 6.16c–18 and Paul's Restoration Theology." *JSNT* 17 (1995): 73–99.
Scott, Kenneth. "The Significance of Statues in Precious Metals in Emperor Worship." *TAPA* 62 (1931): 101–23.
Scotton, Paul D. "A New Fragment of an Inscription from the Julian Basilica at Roman Corinth." *Hesperia* 74 (2005): 95–100.
Sherk, Robert K. *Roman Documents from the Greek East: Senatus Consulta and Epistulae to the Age of Augustus*. Baltimore: Johns Hopkins University Press, 1969.
Sloan, Robert B. "2 Corinthians 2:14–4:6 and 'New Covenant Hermeneutics': A Response to Richard Hays." *BBR* 5 (1995): 129–54.
Small, Alastair, ed. *Subject and Ruler: The Cult of the Ruling Power in Classical Antiquity; Papers Presented at a Conference Held in the University of Alberta on April 13–15, 1994, to Celebrate the 65th Anniversary of Duncan Fishwick*. JRASup 17. Ann Arbor: Journal of Roman Archaeology, 1996.
Spawforth, Antony J. S. "The Achaean Federal Cult Part I: Pseudo-Julian, Letter 198." *TynBul* 46 (1995): 151–68.
Standing, Giles. "The Claudian Invasion of Britain and the Cult of *Victoria Britannica*." *Britannia* 34 (2003): 281–88.
Steiner, Deborah Tarn. *The Tyrant's Writ: Myths and Images of Writing in Ancient Greece*. Princeton Legacy Library. Princeton: Princeton University Press, 2015.
Strong, Eugénie S. *Apotheosis and After Life: Three Lectures on Certain Phases of Art and Religion in the Roman Empire*. Freeport, NY: Books for Libraries Press, 1969.
Strubbe, Johan H. M. "Descriptive Catalogue and Bibliography of the

Inscribed Monuments of Pessinus." Pages 216–44 in *Les Fouilles de la Rijksuniversiteit te Gent à Pessinonte*. Edited by John Devreker and Marc Waelkens. Dissertationes Archaeologicae Gandenses 22. Brugge: De Tempel, 1984.

Taylor, Joan E. "Pontius Pilate and the Imperial Cult in Roman Judaea." *NTS* 52 (2006): 555–82.

Thrall, Margaret E. *2 Corinthians 1–7: A Critical and Exegetical Commentary*. ICC. London: T&T Clark, 1994.

Tucker, Paavo. "Reconsidering Βελιάρ: 2 Corinthians 6:15 in Its Anti-imperial Jewish Apocalyptic Context." *Journal of Paul and His Letters* 4 (2014): 65–82.

Vermeule, Cornelius C. *Roman Imperial Art in Greece and Asia Minor*. Cambridge: Harvard University Press, 1968.

Versnel, H. S. *Triumphus: An Inquiry into the Origin, Development and Meaning of the Roman Triumph*. Leiden: Brill, 1970.

Vout, Caroline. "Representing the Emperor." Pages 261–75 in *The Cambridge Companion to the Roman Historians*. Edited by Andrew Feldherr. Cambridge Companions to Literature. Cambridge: Cambridge University Press, 2009.

Walbank, Mary E. Hoskins. "Evidence for the Imperial Cult in Julio-Claudian Corinth." Pages 201–13 in *Subject and Ruler: The Cult of the Ruling Power in Classical Antiquity; Papers Presented at a Conference Held in the University of Alberta on April 13–15, 1994, to Celebrate the 65th Anniversary of Duncan Fishwick*. Edited by Alastair Small. JRASup 17. Ann Arbor: Journal of Roman Archaeology, 1996.

Wallace-Hadrill, Andrew. "The Golden Age and Sin in Augustan Ideology." *Past and Present* 95 (1982): 19–36.

———. "Image and Authority in the Coinage of Augustus." *JRS* 76 (1986): 66–87.

Ward, Margaret M. "The Association of Augustus with Jupiter." *SMSR* 9 (1933): 203–24.

———. *The Association of Augustus with Jupiter*. Bologna: Zanichelli, 1933.

Webb, William J. *Returning Home: New Covenant and Second Exodus as the Context for 2 Corinthians 6.14–7.1*. JSNTSup 85. Sheffield: JSOT Press, 1993.

Welborn, L. L. *An End to Enmity: Paul and the "Wrongdoer" of Second Corinthians*. BZNW 185. Berlin: de Gruyter, 2011.

Wenham, Gordon. *Genesis 1–15*. WBC 1. Dallas: Word, 2002.

Windisch, Hans. *Der Zweite Korintherbrief.* 9th ed. KEK. Göttingen: Vandenhoeck & Ruprecht, 1970.
Winter, Bruce W. "The Achaean Federal Imperial Cult II: The Corinthian Church." *TynBul* 46 (1995): 169–78.
———. *After Paul Left Corinth: The Influence of Secular Ethics and Social Change.* Grand Rapids: Eerdmans, 2001.
———. "The Enigma of Imperial Cultic Activities and Paul in Corinth." Pages 49–72 in *Greco-Roman Culture and the New Testament Studies Commemorating the Centennial of the Pontifical Biblical Institute.* Edited by David E. Aune and Frederick E. Brenk. NovTSup 143. Leiden: Brill, 2012.
———. "Identifying the Offering, the Cup and the Table of the 'Demons' in 1 Cor 10:20–21." Pages 847–68 in *Saint Paul and Corinth: International Scientific Conference Proceedings, Corinth, 23–25 September, 2007.* Edited by C. Belezos, S. Despotis, and C. Karakolis. Athens: Psychogios, 2009.
Wirszubski, Chaim. *Libertas as a Political Idea at Rome during the Late Republic and Early Principate.* Cambridge Classical Studies. Cambridge: Cambridge University Press, 1950.
Wright, N. T. "Messiahship in Galatians?" Pages 3–23 in *Galatians and Christian Theology: Justification, the Gospel, and Ethics in Paul's Letter.* Edited by Mark W. Elliot et al. Grand Rapids: Baker, 2014.
Yonge, Charles D. *The Works of Philo: Complete and Unabridged.* Peabody, MA: Hendrickson, 1995.
Zanker, Paul. "Bürgerliche Selbstdarstellung am Grab im romischen Kaiserreich." Pages 339–58 in *Die römische Stadt in 2. Jahrhundert n.Chr.: Der Funktionswandel des offentlichen Raumes, Kolloquium Xanten 2. bis 4. Mai 1990.* Edited by Hans-Joachim Schalles, Henner von Hesberg, and Paul Zanker. Köln: Rheinland-Verlag, 1992.
———. *The Power of Images in the Age of Augustus.* Translated by Alan Shapiro. Jerome Lectures 16. Ann Arbor: University of Michigan Press, 1988.

PAUL AND THE *AGŌNOTHETAI* AT CORINTH: ENGAGING THE CIVIC VALUES OF ANTIQUITY

James R. Harrison

1. CORINTH AND THE SPREAD OF CIVIC VALUES FROM THE APEX TO THE BASE OF THE SOCIAL PYRAMID

The study of the role and influence of Greek and Roman civic officials in the Roman East and its relevance to New Testament studies is still in its infancy, though it has increasingly featured in discussion of the Corinthian epistles. There are several reasons for this muted response on the part of biblical scholars. First, the study of any civic official in antiquity requires comprehensive control of the epigraphic evidence in particular. However, close analysis of the civic inscriptions still remains a "sleeping giant" among the many methodologies employed by New Testament scholars these days in the study of Paul's epistles.[1] Second, in the case of the book of Acts, Paul's frequent encounters with civic officials are vital to its narrative flow and theological significance and therefore command scholarly attention. By contrast, Paul's use of the language of civic officialdom, in literal and metaphorical contexts, is more restrained, infrequent, and allusive in his epistles.[2] Third, because New Testament scholars are largely unfamiliar with the inscriptions of the civic officials from the Hellenistic and Roman East, they can easily overlook the significance of the

---

[1] On the eastern Mediterranean context of civic officialdom, see Sviatoslav Dmitriev, *City Government in Hellenistic and Roman Asia Minor* (Oxford: Oxford University Press, 2005). The ground-breaking work on the inscriptions in New Testament studies was Frederick W. Danker, *Benefactor: Epigraphic Study of a Graeco-Roman and New Testament Field* (St. Louis: Clayton, 1982).

[2] On Paul's "civic language," see Raymond F. Collins, *The Power of Images in Paul* (Collegeville, MN: Glazier, 2008), 53–56.

recurring motifs, rhetorical style, and civic conventions revealed in the inscriptions of local civic officials. Consequently, they miss the intriguing intersections of terminology and social discourse occurring between the polis and the *ekklēsia* of believers, and, in particular, the different understanding civic ideology and social conventions articulated between each group. Is Paul engaging with the civic ideals of Corinth in his epistles to the Corinthian believers in an affirming or critical way, or are such polarizations too simplistic a construct?

It is worth noting in this regard that the local associations aped the ethos of the civic inscriptions and the institutions to which they pointed. Danker argues that the local associations imitated the "bureaucratic" diction and syntax of the late Hellenistic city-state decrees, not only assigning honor to the socially elite benefactors of their clubs but also allocating honor to their nonelite members. Members of the associations were of diverse social status, including among their constituency the urban poor, slaves, and freedmen,[3] and all the members appropriated, by virtue of their membership, the honorific titles and rituals of the association decrees.[4] As Danker explains,

---

3. Stephen G. Wilson, "Voluntary Associations: An Overview," in *Voluntary Associations in the Graeco-Roman World*, ed. John S. Kloppenborg and Stephen G. Wilson (London: Routledge, 2003), 1–15, esp. 10–11. For a bibliography on the associations, see Richard S. Ascough, Philip A. Harland, and John S. Kloppenborg, eds., *Associations in the Greco-Roman World: A Sourcebook* (Waco, TX: Baylor University Press, 2012). Additionally, see John S. Kloppenborg and Richard S. Ascough, eds., *Attica, Central Greece, Macedonia, Thrace*, vol. 1 of *Greco-Roman Associations: Texts, Translations, and Commentary*, BZNW 181 (Berlin: de Gruyter 2011); Monique Dondin-Payre and Nicolas Tran, eds., *Collegia: Le phénomène associatif dans l'Occident romain* (Bordeaux: Ausonius, 2012); Pierre Fröhlich and Patrice Hamon, eds., *Groupes et associations dans cités grecques (IIIe siècle av. J.-C.–IIe siècle ap. J.-C.): Actes de la table ronde de Paris, INHA, 19–20 juin 2009* (Geneva: Droz, 2013); Philip A. Harland, *The North Coast of the Black Sea, Asia Minor*, vol. 2 of *Greco-Roman Associations: Texts, Translations, and Commentary*, BZNW 204 (Berlin: de Gruyter 2014).

4. Note the hierarchy of offices in the Bacchic Society (*SIG* 1109, ll. 1–10, 117–27; provenance: Athens [164/165 CE]). But hierarchy is restricted in the feasts: "All members are, however, eligible for the roles of the deities" (ll. 126–27). A democratization of honor occurs in the Society's recognition of the special honors and achievements of any member (127–28), including receipt of citizen status, athletic prizes, and civic honors (128–37). Elite association members could attain public honors within the polis, while experiencing through their Society "alternate" paths of honor (Koenraad

these clubs and associations affected the diction and syntax of the council chambers of city-states or of the chanceries of the Ptolemies or of the Seleucids. This diction and syntax brought to verbal expression deeply imbedded cultural values. For a brief moment, as is the case in a variety of deistic societies popular since the French Revolution, their members could play the role of esteemed civil service officials, of members of councils, and planning committees.[5]

Given the analogies between the Macedonian associations and the early house churches of Thessalonica and Philippi,[6] an investigation of the Corinthian inscriptions honoring local civic dignitaries could provide us rich insights into the self-promotion and self-sufficiency of the powerful (οὐ πολλοὶ δυνατοί) and well-born (οὐ πολλοὶ εὐγενεῖς), whether within the city or inside the *ekklēsia* of believers (1 Cor 1:26).[7] The boastful ethos of the civic elites had moved from the apex of the social pyramid to its base because of the influence of the local associations and their benefactors.[8] While the focus of many association inscriptions is the honorific recom-

---

Verboven, "The Associative Order, Status and Ethos of Roman Businessmen in Late Republic and Early Empire," *Athenaeum* 95 [2007]: 861–93, esp. 882–86).

5. Frederick W. Danker, "On Stones and Benefactors," *CurTM* 8 (1981): 352; Verboven, "The Associative Order," 869–71.

6. For analogies between the Macedonian Christian communities and the local voluntary associations, see Richard S. Ascough, *Paul's Macedonian Associations: The Social Context of Philippians and 1 Thessalonians*, WUNT 2/161 (Tübingen: Mohr Siebeck, 2003).

7. On the powerful in the Corinthian house churches, see L. L. Welborn, *An End to Enmity: Paul and the "Wrongdoer" of Second Corinthians*, BZNW 185 (Berlin: de Gruyter, 2011), 230–83.

8. In terms of the associations at Corinth, our extant evidence is not as extensive as that found for their operations in other eastern Mediterranean cities, though the associations undoubtedly flourished at Corinth. See the fragmentary inscription of a Corinthian society (*thiasos*) (Ascough, Harland, and Kloppenborg, *Associations*, §26) and a grave from Kenchreai (Ascough, Harland, and Kloppenborg, *Associations*, §25; cf. Rom 16:1–2) honoring a member from an association devoted to Dionysius. There is also the second-century CE monument erected by the association (*collegium*) of the Lares to honor the imperial house (John Harvey Kent, *The Inscriptions, 1926–1950*, vol. 8.3 of *Corinth: Results of Excavations Conducted by the American School of Classical Studies at Athens* [Princeton: American School of Classical Studies at Athens, 1966] [= IKorinthKent], §62). Last, in terms of the literary evidence, there is the *thiasos* of Kotys (Ada Adler, ed., *Suidae Lexicon*, vol. 1.2 [Leipzig: Teubner, 1967], θιασώτης Κότυος, §381).

pense of their powerful benefactors, even low-status members of an association were able to acquire personal kudos and social capital because of the self-congratulatory and eulogistic culture of the associations,[9] and an association itself could gain deflected honor because of its imperial connections.[10] These self-serving and self-promoting values had impacted deleteriously upon the leadership and body life of the Corinthian churches.[11] Because the believers at Corinth were so acculturated to the values and

---

9. Not only are the names alone of low-status association members listed in honorific decrees (e.g., Ascough, Harland, and Kloppenborg, *Associations*, §§90, 92, 109, 115, 117, 177, 185, 234, 235, 237, 242, 243, 257, 300, 313) and in burial lists (§§31, 155, 158, 245, 323), but also the roles of members in the association (§§84, 91, 212) or donations to its activities (ibid., §162) could be eulogized. A remarkable inscription is the membership list an association of banqueters in Sparta (§29) in which people of varying social and occupational status are mentioned. For the personal and family kudos acquired by virtue of the membership of an association of Isis-devotees, note this excerpt from a grave epitaph from Prusa near Olympos (late Hellenistic or early imperial period): "Honored by dead me, O stranger, I gained a remarkable reputation among the Isis-devotees (*Isiakoi*) as a testimony. For I have brought glory for my father Menesthes, leaving behind three children" (Ascough, Harland, and Kloppenborg, *Associations*, §98).

10. Deflected glory was acquired by virtue of an association's connection with the imperial ruler or his family members. The provincial assembly of Asia for hymn singers acquires deflected glory through its hymning of the Roman ruler: "the hymn singers from all Asia, coming together in Pergamon for the most sacred birthday of Augustus Tiberius Caesar, god, accomplish a magnificent work for the glory of the synod" (Ascough, Harland, and Kloppenborg, *Associations*, §160). Note, too, how the synod of Alexandria athletes situates itself imperially as an honor-conferring body: "The emperor-loving, Roman-loving, travelling, pious synod of Alexandrians honored T. Flavius Archibios of the Quirinia tribe" (§312). Note the grave site erected by association devoted to Marcus Agrippa, son-in-law of Augustus ("the friends-of-Agrippa companions," §187), as well as the altar erected to a priestess by the "friends of the Augusti" (§120). Jewish synagogues in Rome also made overtures to the Roman ruler and his relatives by virtue of the names chosen for the association: the synagogue of the "Augustesians" (*CIJ* 284, 301, 338, 368, 416, 496) and of the "Agrippesians" (*CIJ* 365, 425, 503). See Harry J. Leon, *The Jews of Ancient Rome* (Philadelphia: Jewish Publication Society of America, 1960), 140–142; Peter Richardson, "Augustan-Era Synagogues in Rome," in *Judaism and Christianity in First-Century Rome*, ed. Karl P. Donfried and Peter Richardson (Grand Rapids: Eerdmans, 1998), 17–29.

11. James R. Harrison, "Paul's House Churches and the Cultic Associations," *RTR* 58 (1999): 31–47, esp. 45–47; Harrison, "The Brothers as the 'Glory of Christ' (2 Cor 8:23): Paul's *Doxa* Terminology in Its Ancient Benefaction Context," *NovT* 52 (2010): 156–88, esp. 181–87.

ethics of the Greco-Roman honor system, only Paul's gospel of the "foolishness" and the "weakness" of the cross, culminating in the resurrection and ascension of its dishonored Lord, could dislodge the myopic quest for personal status occurring among many of the Corinthian believers.

The obvious candidates for discussion as far as the Corinthian civic officials are either the *duoviri* or the *agōnothetai*, though both magistracies feature in the *cursus honorum* of most powerful individuals in the city. Neither official is mentioned in the New Testament, so there is no terminological reason why we should prefer one to the other, although several commentators have argued that the figure of the *agōnothetēs* is alluded to in Paul's athletic imagery in Phil 3:14.[12] However, the investigation of local officials not named in the New Testament is nevertheless a valuable exercise for the indirect light that it throws on issues such as Paul's pastoral and ethical formation of his congregations, to cite the example of the gymnasiarch, which I have discussed elsewhere.[13] However, the *agōnothetēs* was chosen for this investigation because he, as the president and/or benefactor of the games, had intimate familiarity with the athletic ideal of antiquity with which Paul interacts in the Corinthian epistles.[14] The *agōnothetai*, many of whom would have belonged to the local athletic associations,[15] were committed to promoting their own civic profile and the fame of their households, thereby spawning intense rivalry

---

12. Jean-François Collange, *The Epistle of Saint Paul to the Philippians* (London: Epworth, 1979), 134; Gerald F. Hawthorne, *Philippians*, WBC 43 (Waco, TX: Word, 1983), 154–55; Peter T. O'Brien, *Commentary on Philippians: A Commentary on the Greek Text*, NIGTC (Grand Rapids: Eerdmans, 1991), 430–31. The upward call of God in Christ (Phil 3:14: τῆς ἄνω κλήσεως) alludes, it is argued, to the *agōnothetēs* calling the athlete up to the bema to receive his prize. See also the visual evidence below at §2.2.2.

13. James R. Harrison, "Paul and the Gymnasiarchs: Two Approaches to Pastoral Formation in Antiquity," in *Paul: Jew, Greek, and Roman*, ed. Stanley E. Porter, Pauline Studies 5 (Leiden, Brill, 2008), 141–78. See the marble statue of a gymnasiarch (Musei Capitoloni, Rome, inv. no. 196) wrapped in his cloak and staring at the (imaginary) ephebes before him with fixed eyes and a severe expression (D. Vanhove, ed., *Le sport dans la Grèce antique: Du jeu à la compétition* [Brussels: Palais des Beaux-Arts, 1992], 213, §72).

14. See James R. Harrison, "Paul and the Athletic Ideal in Antiquity: A Case Study in Wrestling with Word and Image," in *Paul's World*, ed. Stanley E. Porter, Pauline Studies 4 (Leiden, Brill, 2007), 81–109.

15. Note the mention of "the president of the games" (Ascough, Harland, and Kloppenborg, *Associations*, §303, ll. 58–59), named as a synod official in the 194 CE

and competition among their peers. Timothy B. Savage speaks insightfully regarding the significance of the *agōnothetai* and other similar Corinthian civic luminaries in the study of the Corinthian epistles:

> These men admittedly represented the upper crust of Corinthian society and thus not necessarily the typical convert in Paul's young congregation. Nevertheless they do serve to illustrate something dear to *all* Corinthians—that with a little ambition and application one could rise from level zero to social respectability and a measure of power.[16]

It is likely, therefore, that many of the "powerful" and "well-born" in the Corinthian house churches had imbibed the civic culture of *syncrisis* (comparison; see 2 Cor 10:12) and had unconsciously transferred its ethos to the operations of the body life of the *ekklēsia*. They measured the "inferior" credentials of their apostle (1 Cor 2:1–5; 2 Cor 10:2, 10; 11:6a; 12:11–18) against the more charismatically endowed "apostolic" interlopers (2 Cor 3:1; 11:12–15, 22–23; 12:11–13) and against the rhetorically superior Apollos (1 Cor 1:12; 3:5–9, 21; 4:6; cf. Acts 18:24), boasting in the wisdom of their attachment to leaders (1 Cor 1:12; 3:19–21; cf. 2 Cor 10:12b) other than their weak, discredited, and powerless apostle. However, it would be unwise to assume that this was a predilection of the powerful alone. The extension of the elitist boasting culture to the base of the social pyramid by means of the local associations should alert us to the likelihood that these views were also supported by some of the "weak" and "foolish in the Corinthian body of Christ as much as by the "strong" and "wise" (1 Cor 1:27; 4:8; cf. 2 Cor 11:19–21).

Furthermore, the inscriptions of the *agōnothetai*, I will argue, give clear rhetorical indications that the *agōnothetai* and their families were

---

papyrus diploma of Hermeios the boxer, a document that notified Hermeios of his admission into the athletic synod at Hermopolis Magna, Upper Egypt.

16. Timothy B. Savage, *Power through Weakness: Paul's Understanding of the Christian Ministry in 2 Corinthians*, SNTSMS 86 (Cambridge; Cambridge University Press, 1996), 40, emphasis original. The most studied Corinthian official is Paul's Erastus (Rom 16:23b) and his relation to the aedile of the Corinthian inscription (IKorinth-Kent §232). For the most recent discussion, see Welborn, *An End to Enmity*, 260–83; Alexander Weiss, "Keine Quästoren in Korinth: Zu Goodrichs (und Theißens) These über das Amt des Erastos (Röm 16:23)," *NTS* 56 (2011): 576–81; Timothy A. Brookins, "The (In)frequency of the Name 'Erastus' in Antiquity: A Literary, Papyrological, and Epigraphic Catalogue," *NTS* 59 (2013): 496–516.

conversant with the traditional boasting conventions of the Roman elites of republican and early imperial times.[17] They transferred the "grand style" of the Roman self-eulogy from the Latin West, which focused more on the *cursus honorum* (course of honors) than moral accolades, to their own rhetorical posturing for precedence among the local elites in the Roman colony of Corinth. We shall see that the honorific inscription of the *agōnothetēs* Nikias from Isthmia, a mere 13 km east of ancient Corinth, affords us unexpected insight into the oratorical quest for preeminence that the Corinthians so valued but that Paul so savagely debunked. The dynamics of honor and dishonor are especially potent here.

Finally, this study, it is hoped, will throw further light on a little-studied official from antiquity,[18] illustrating the riches that flow from an inscriptional study of the civic setting of the Corinthian epistles.[19] Where appropriate, I will refer to the inscriptional evidence of the *agōnothetai* of

---

17. See James R. Harrison, *Paul and the Imperial Authorities at Thessalonica and Rome: A Study in the Conflict of Ideology*, WUNT I 273 (Tübingen: Mohr Siebeck, 2011), 201–69.

18. See E. Reisch, "Ἀθλοθέτης," PW 2.2:2063–65; Daniel J. Geagan, "Notes on the Agonistic Institutions of Roman Corinth," *GRBS* 9 (1968): 69–80; Blaise Nagy, "The Athenian Athlothetai," *GRBS* 19 (1978): 307–13; Donald G. Kyle, *Athletics in Ancient Athens* (Leiden: Brill, 1993); F. Camia, "Spending on the Agones: The Financing of Festivals in the Cities of Roman Greece," *Tyche* 26 (2011): 41–76. More generally, see Benjamin W. Millis, "The Local Magistrates and Elite of Corinth," in *Corinth in Contrast: Studies in Inequality*, ed. Steven J. Friesen, Sarah A. James, and Daniel N. Schowalter, NovTSup 155 (Leiden: Brill, 2014), 38–53. On the *agōnothetēs* at Corinth, see John K. Chow, *Patronage and Power: A Study of Social Networks in Corinth*, JSNTSup 75 (Sheffield: JSOT Press, 1992), 61–64; Andrew D. Clarke, *Secular and Christian Leadership in Corinth: A Socio-historical and Exegetical Study of 1 Corinthians 1–6*, AGJU 18 (Leiden: Brill, 1993), 18–21; Cavan W. Concannon, *"When You Were Gentiles": Specters of Ethnicity in Roman Corinth and Paul's Corinthian Correspondence* (New Haven: Yale University Press, 2014), 201.

19. For studies of civic officials and their relation to Paul's ministry metaphors in the Corinthian epistles, see Anthony Bash, *Ambassadors for Christ: An Exploration of Ambassadorial Language in the New Testament*, WUNT 2/92 (Tübingen: Mohr Siebeck, 1992); John K. Goodrich, *Paul as an Administrator of God in 1 Corinthians*, SNTSMS 152 (Cambridge: Cambridge University Press, 2012). See also the discussion of the Corinthian official Tiberius Claudius Dinippus (IKorinthKent §§158–63, 393–94) in relation to 1 Cor 7:26: Bruce W. Winter, "Secular and Christian Responses to Corinthian Famines" *TynBul* 40 (1989): 86–106; James R. Harrison, "Times of Necessity," *New Docs* 9 (2002): 8–9; Barry N. Danylak, "Tiberius Claudius Dinippus and the Food Shortages in Corinth," *TynBul* 59 (2008): 231–70. For a fine discussion of Corin-

Ephesus for further background, a city in which Paul ministered for two to three years (Acts 19:8–10; 20:31) and whose inscriptional corpus is the most extensive of the eastern Mediterranean (over 3,600 inscriptions). The likelihood is that the apostle was quite familiar with the boastful public inscriptions of the *agōnothetai* at Corinth and Ephesus, as were the house churches in both cities.[20]

2. The Isthmian Games, Corinth, and the *Agōnothetai*

2.1. The Isthmian Games in the Early Julio-Claudian Period

The Isthmian games belonged to a "circuit" (*periodos*) of four panhellenic games celebrated under the patronage of a divinity: the Pythian games at Delphi (under the auspices of Apollo), the Isthmian games at Corinth (under the auspices of Poseidon), and the games at Nemea and Olympia (both under the auspices of Zeus).[21] It is likely that Paul sources his athletic imagery in his Corinthian epistles not only from philosophical commonplaces and the ubiquitous iconographic and numismatic athletic imagery of the Greco-Roman world[22] but also from his own experience as

---

thian inscriptional candidates for the "wrongdoer" of 2 Corinthians, see Welborn, *An End to Enmity*, 288–335.

20. In saying this, I recognize that, in terms of our knowledge of the Pauline congregations, "we have no prosopographic information from most of the cities" visited by Paul (Steven J. Friesen, "Prospects for a Demography of the Pauline Mission," in *Urban Religion in Roman Corinth: Interdisciplinary Approaches*, ed. Daniel Schowalter and Steven J. Friesen, HTS 53 [Cambridge: Harvard University Press, 2005], 355). However, the evidence is concentrated in Corinth and either Ephesus or Rome. So, the *agōnothetai* provide a convenient lens though which we can view the potential impact of civic values upon known members of the mid-50s house churches at Corinth. See Friesen's helpful diagram (354 fig. 13.1) of the cities where the apostle founded assemblies, was contacted by assemblies founded by others, or through which he passed without significant contact.

21. On the iconographic evidence, see Harrison, "Paul and the Athletic Ideal." On the popular philosophers and Paul's athletic imagery, see V. C. Pfitzner, *Paul and the Agon Motif: Traditional Athletic Imagery in the Pauline Literature*, NovTSup 16 (Leiden: Brill, 1967); Edgar Krentz, "Paul, Games and the Military," in *Paul and the Graeco-Roman World: A Handbook*, ed. J. Paul Sampley (Harrisburg, PA: Trinity Press International, 2003), 344–83; Martin Brändle, *Der Agon bei Paulus: Herkunft und Profil paulinischer Agonmetaphorik*, WUNT 2/222 (Tübingen: Mohr Siebeck, 2006).

22. Elizabeth R. Gebhard "The Sanctuary of Poseidon on the Isthmus of Corinth

a spectator of the Isthmian games, or, at the very least, his personal visit to the site of Isthmia in 51 CE.[23] As background to the Corinthian "runner" image (1 Cor 9:24, 26a; cf. Phil 3:12–14), for example, Paul may well have seen the starting point and finishing point of the racetrack (181.15 m long) at the *later* stadium at Isthmia.[24] This stadium, situated in a natural hollow a small distance (ca. 250 m) southeast of the sanctuary of Poseidon, was used during Hellenistic and Roman times.

But caution must be exercised here. We face a fundamental problem: Where were the Isthmian games actually held at the time of the apostle Paul's visit to Corinth? The sanctuary was abandoned in the late Hellenistic period, sometime after the Roman destruction of 146 BCE. The Isthmian games, however, continued under the supervision of Sicyon as long as Corinth lay deserted (Pausanias, *Descr.* 2.11.2). Elizabeth R. Gebhard argues on the basis of the archaeological, inscriptional, and numismatic evidence that control of the Isthmian games returned to Corinth in 40 BCE,[25] but they did not return permanently to the sanctuary of Poseidon until 50–60 CE, and they flourished once again when Nero enrolled as a competitor in the games in 67 CE. However, Mika Kajava asserts that the games recommenced at the Isthmus several years earlier.[26] This conclusion

---

and the Isthmian Games," in *Mind and Body: Athletic Contests in Ancient Greece*, ed. Olga Tzachou-Alexandri (Athens: Ministry of Culture, National Hellenic Committee I.C.O.M., 1989), 82–88; Gebhard, "The Isthmian Games and the Sanctuary of Poseidon in the Early Empire," in *The Corinthia in the Roman Period*, ed. Timothy E. Gregory, JRASup 8 (Ann Arbor: Journal of Roman Archaeology, 1993), 78–94. On Paul's attitude toward the idolatry associated with the Isthmian games, see Oscar Broneer, "Paul and the Pagan Cults of Isthmia," *HTR* 64 (1971): 169–87. For a general coverage, with excellent photographs and diagrams of site plans and buildings, of Isthmia, its sanctuary, and its games, see Panos Valavanis, *Games and Sanctuaries in Ancient Greece: Olympia, Delphi, Isthmia, Nemea, Athens* (Los Angeles: J. Paul Getty Museum, 2004), 269–304.

23. Jerome Murphy-O'Connor, "Corinth," *ABD* 1:1138.

24. On the *later* stadium, see Nicos Papahatzis, *Ancient Corinth: The Museums of Corinth, Isthmia and Sicyon* (Athens: Ekdotike Helados S.A., 1994), 36–37; Valavanis, *Games and Sanctuaries*, 292–301. On the earlier classical stadium (close to the Temple of Poseidon) and its sophisticated starting arrangements, see Oscar Broneer, *Topography and Architecture*, vol. 2 of *Isthmia* (Princeton: American School of Classical Studies at Athens, 1973), 46–66, 137–42; Valavanis, *Games and Sanctuaries*, 286–91.

25. Gebhard, "The Isthmian Games," 78–94.

26. Mika Kajava, "When Did the Isthmian Games Return to the Isthmus? Rereading Corinth 8.3.153," *CP* 97 (2002): 168–78.

is based upon Kajava's reediting of IKorinthKent §153. Kajava contends that (1) the *agōnothetēs* Cn. Cornelius Pulcher was its honorand and that (2) the inscription indicates that the Isthmian games were first celebrated by the Colonia Laus Iulia Corinthiensis in 43 CE. We see here the difficulties of historical reconstruction for interpreters of the New Testament when the inscriptions, our primary sources, are in a fragmentary state, with lacunae to be filled in with editorial restorations.

In conclusion, the location at which Paul may have seen the Isthmian and Caesarean games in 51 CE cannot be definitively determined. It was possibly still at Corinth or, more likely, at the Isthmian sanctuary itself. Three significant changes, however, occurred during the early Julio-Claudian period regarding the organization of the games.[27] First, when Corinth recovered management of the Isthmian games from Sicyon, the Kaisareia games were added to the Isthmia games ("Ἴσθμια καὶ Καισάρεια). However, as Camia and Kantiréa observe, the "Kaisareia and Isthmia, although celebrated in the context of the one and same festival (dedicated to Poseidon) and presided over by a single agonothetes, represented two independent series of competitions."[28] Second, under Tiberius a third set of competitions was introduced, always named after the current Roman ruler. Third, under the reign of Claudius the Isthmian games, which had been celebrated at Corinth, returned to Isthmia, although, as we have see, the exact date is disputed. Last, in addition to the Corinthian contests above was

---

27. F. Camia and Maria Kantiréa, "The Imperial Cult in the Peloponnese," in *Society, Economy and Culture under the Roman Empire: Continuity and Innovation*, vol. 3 of *Roman Peloponnese*, ed. Athanasios D. Rizakis and Claudia E. Lepenioti (Athens: National Hellenic Research Foundation, 2010), 375–406, esp. 385–86. On the basis of *SEG* 11.61 and Benjamin Dean Meritt, *Greek Inscriptions, 1896–1927*, vol. 8.1 of *Corinth: Results of Excavations Conducted by the American School of Classical Studies at Athens* (Cambridge: American School of Classical Studies at Athens, 1931) (= IKorinthMeritt]), §14, Camia and Kantiréa argue that this occurred in 3 CE ("The Imperial Cult," 386).

28. Camia and Kantiréa, "The Imperial Cult, " 386. James C. Walters ("Civic Identity in Roman Corinth and Its Impact on Early Christians," in Schowalter and Friesen, *Urban Religion in Roman Corinth*, 408) argues that, by celebrating the Caesarean games "in conjunction with the Isthmian games, the Romans guaranteed the status of the imperial games." Consequently, the heated competition for status among the Greek cities, fueled through their own local games, was supplanted by the "more vertical pattern" of status conferred through a client-patron relationship with Rome. This blurred the boundaries between Greek and Roman, facilitating the Roman hegemony in the Greek East.

the Asklepieia, an athletic and dramatic festival for which the *agōnothetai* were also the administrators.²⁹

What, then, was the role of the *agōnothetēs* in the Isthmian games? In the next section I discuss more generally the official's function and moral status before moving onto the Corinthian inscriptional evidence itself (§3 below).

2.2. A General Portrait of the *Agōnothetēs*

2.2.1. The Responsibilities of the *Agōnothetēs*

Generally speaking, the *agōnothetēs* was responsible for the administration of the games in the city and could hold the office many times. He was an elected official who, in the case of Corinth at least, was assisted by a board of ten *hellanodikai*,³⁰ and as a benefactor he shouldered the expenditure of the games.³¹ Administratively and financially, therefore, he checked the entries, classified the competitors into their age groups, organized the games' staffing, arranged the housing for the visiting athletes, provided the food and refreshments for the competitors, secured the awards and prizes/prize money, approved the honorific inscriptions and statues for the victors, and was the final arbiter of all disputes. However, in a Corinthian context, there is an interesting anomaly regarding the status of the *agōnothetēs*. In Corinth the *agōnothetēs* was more influential and honored than the *duovir quinquennalis*, who elsewhere was the chief official in the other Roman colonies. Donald W. Engels comments regarding the Corinthian situation, "The international character of the games meant that (the *agōnothetēs*) would receive the honor and esteem of the whole world."³² Last, the terminology for the *agōnothetēs* differed from state to

---

29. Geagan, "Notes on the Agonistic Institutions," 70, 75.
30. Donald W. Engels, *Roman Corinth: An Alternative Model for the Classical City* (Chicago: University of Chicago Press, 1990), 18.
31. Camia, "Spending on the Agones," passim. At Ephesus the *agōnothetēs* was responsible for the festival of the Dionysius: "[it be hereby resolved by the Council] to commend Lysicon for his merit and goodwill, and that he be crowned with [a crown] of gold by the president of the games ([ἀ]γωνοθέτην) at the festival of Dionysius" (Hermann Wankel et al., eds., *Die Inschriften von Ephesos*, 8 vols. [Bonn: Habelt, 1979–1984] [= IEph], 5.1457).
32. Engels, *Roman Corinth*, 97.

state (e.g., at Olympia, Nemea), as well as the manner in which the games were organized (e.g., at Athens).[33]

A question worth asking is whether the *archiereus* (high priest) was invariably the person responsible for the staging of *venationes* (animal fights) and the *munera gladiatora* (gladiator fights) in the Greek city-states.[34] Did the *agōnothetēs* ever fulfill the role? The vast majority of honorific inscriptions eulogizing the sponsors of gladiatorial games in Asia Minor are linked to the imperial cult, with the *archiereus* being the chief official overseeing its spectacles.[35] Nonetheless, there are a few rare occasions in the honorific inscriptions in which the *agōnothetēs* alone is mentioned as a sponsor of the gladiatorial games.[36]

We are perhaps grasping the proverbial horns of a false dilemma in this instance. We must remember that the high priest of the imperial cult belonged to the wealthy aristocratic houses of the local city-states. Consequently, it was expected that he, at a particular stage in his *cursus honoum*, would as the *agōnothetēs* underwrite the expenses of the athletic games while, at another stage of his *cursus honoum*, he would as the *archiereus* sponsor the imperial cult and the gladiatorial spectacles. For example, the inscriptional roll call of civic virtue of the powerful Vedii family of Ephesus recounts all the prestigious family positions from the Ephesian *cursus honorum*, including high priests, priestesses, and a "secretary and agonothete of the great world-wide Ephesia."[37] Everyday Ephesians would only have noticed that it was often the same individual from the Vedii who sponsored the imperial cult, gladiatorial contests, and athletic games over

---

33. For full details, see Wolfgang Decker, "Agonothetes," *BNP* 1:347–48.

34. On the sponsorship of gladiatorial spectacles and animal fights, see Michael J. D. Carter, *The Presentation of Gladiatorial Spectacles in the Greek East: Roman Culture and Greek Identity* (PhD diss., McMaster University, 1999), 144–241; Carter, "Archiereis and Asiarchs: A Gladiatorial Perspective," *GRBS* 44 (2004): 41–68.

35. In the inscriptions honoring the sponsors of gladiatorial contests, even where the honorand's magistracy of *agōnothetēs* is actually specified, it is invariably mentioned in conjunction with the prestigious position of *archiereus*. See Louis Robert, *Les gladiateurs dans l'orient grec* (Amsterdam: Hakkert, 1971), §6 (Apollonia of Iyyria), §97 (Sagalassos), §99 (Selge), §152 (Magnesia of Meandros); *SEG* 17.315 (Beroi).

36. In an inscription honoring a sponsor of a gladiatorial contest from Megara (Robert, *Les gladiateurs*, §59), the *agōnothetēs* eulogized is not an *archiereus* but rather holds the magistracies of *stratēgos* (general) and *agoranomos* (clerk of the market).

37. IEph 7.3072

a period of time. The precise career path was ultimately the concern of the aristocrats.

But what is the situation at Roman Corinth regarding the role of the *agōnothetēs* and the sponsorship of animal fights and gladiatorial contests in the city as part of the imperial cult? Was the magistracy associated with this type of benefaction? It is clear that Corinth hosted such spectacles. There is evidence that the theater had been modified for gladiatorial combats,[38] with paintings on a wall of *bestiarii* fighting against lions, leopards, and bulls.[39] The gladiators who fought wild animals in hunting spectacles (*venatores*) had erected a bronze statue with an honorific inscription to the doctor Trophimos in the amphitheater,[40] while there is also an important gladiator epitaph of the *retarius* Draukos from Corinth.[41] A vast array of pottery lamps from Corinth also shows various scenes from the gladiatorial games.[42] The literary evidence also confirms the presence of gladiato-

---

38. Benjamin Dean Meritt, " Excavations at Corinth, 1927," *AJA* 31 (1927): 450–61, esp. 457–58

39. Theodore Leslie Shear, "Excavations at Corinth in 1925," *AJA* 29 (1925): 381–97, esp. 383–85. On the southern wall opposite the center of the theater stage, we see on its eastern section the crimson-booted and purple-costumed director of games, who faces a charging lion, but with the protection of a gladiator standing behind him (384, fig. 3). Another painting in the same section shows a charging lion and a gladiator with his spear poised for attack (385, fig. 4). See also Shear, "Excavations in the Theatre District of Corinth in 1926," *AJA* 30 (1926): 444–63, esp. 451–52. Moving further to the west of the wall, we observe a see a box cage for beasts and a gladiator; this is followed by two gladiators and a bull pinioned on the spear of a crouching gladiator (451, fig. 6). Beyond this is another gladiator in violent action, accompanied by an acrobat leaping over a charging leopard (452, fig. 7). On the badly damaged western section of the wall is a striding gladiator who faces a rushing lion, with a graffito, "The lion recognizes the man under the bull as his savior and licks him," alluding to the story of Androcles and the lion (453). What is unusual regarding this painted wall is that the chief official of the Corinthian games is involved in the combat on this occasion, "in contrast to the quiet stationary attitude of the director of games painted on a similar wall surrounding the amphitheatre at Pompeii" (Shear, "Excavations at Corinth in 1925," 385). For a picture of the official, see Johannes Overbeck and August Mau, *Pompeii*, 4th ed. (Leipzig: Engelmann, 1884), 182 fig. 107. For a general description of the pictures on the podium wall at the amphitheater at Pompeii, see Luciana Jacobelli, *Gladiators at Pompeii* (Los Angeles: J. Paul Getty Museum, 2003), 59–62.

40. Robert, *Les gladiateurs*, §61.

41. Michael Carter, "A *Doctor Secutorum* and the *Retiarius* Draukos from Corinth," *ZPE* 12 (1999): 262–68.

42. Oscar Broneer, *Terracotta Lamps*, vol. 4.2 of *Corinth: Results of Excavations*

rial games at Corinth (Dio Chrysostom, *Rhod.* 121–122; Lucian, *Demon.* 57; Apuleius, *Metam.* 10.18). Moreover, if Pseudo-Julian, *Ep.* 198 is redated to the first century CE,[43] there is further proof for the establishment of the Achaian *koinon* at Corinth and elsewhere, with its imperial cult and gladiatorial games, under the reign of Nero. But, with the exception of the wall paintings at the theater of Corinth (n. 39 above), this does not throw any light on whether the *agōnothetēs* was the official responsible for the spectacles in the Roman colony. However, if we assume that Corinth as a colony was governed by a charter identical to the Julian charters in the Spanish Roman colony of Urso,[44] then the *Lex Colonia Genetiva Julia* from Urso (47–44 BCE) is unequivocally clear about who is responsible for spectacles in the colony: it is the *duoviri* and aediles who celebrate gladiatorial shows and dramatic spectacles to Jupiter, Juno, and Minerva, spending no less than 2,000 sesterces from their own money and no more than 2,000 sesterces from the public money.[45] Clearly, then, in the Julian charters for the Roman colonies throughout the empire, the *duovir* and aedile, not the *agōnothetēs*, were responsible for such spectacles.

2.2.2. Visual Evidence Relating to the *Agōnothetēs*

In addition to the inscriptional evidence for *agōnothetai*, there is numismatic and ceramic evidence for the officials in the Greek East. First, a difference exists in numismatic practice regarding the naming of civic officials between Roman Corinth and the Greek city-states. Whereas in some Greek cities (e.g., Aigai) the names of *agōnothetai* were stamped on the city coinage,[46] Roman Corinth eschewed this practice. Rather, the money-

---

Conducted by the American School of Classical Studies at Athens (Cambridge: Harvard University Press, 1930), §§427, 460–61, 492, 534, 634–53, 1192–97.

43. Antony J. S. Spawforth, "Corinth, Argos and the Imperial Cult: Pseudo-Julian, Letters 198," *Hesperia* 63 (1994): 211–32; Camia and Kantiréa, "The Imperial Cult in the Peloponnese," 388–89.

44. On the Spanish colonial charter in relation to Corinth's constitution, cultural ethos, and city design and its exegetical consequences for 1 Corinthians, see Bradley J. Bitner, *Paul's Political Strategy in 1 Corinthians 1–4: Constitution and Covenant*, SNTSMS 163 (Cambridge: Cambridge University Press, 2015).

45. Alan Chester Johnson, Paul Robinson Coleman-Norton, and Frank Card Bourne, *Ancient Roman Statutes* (Austin: University of Texas Press, 1961), §114, sections 70–71.

46. A rare and unpublished copper coin from Aigai, struck during the time of

ers of Roman Corinth struck bronze coins with Latin legends, LAVS IVLI CORINT, CORINT, or COR, which up to Galba's death usually bore the names of the *duoviri*.[47] Second, in terms of the ceramic evidence, there are examples of the names of the *agōnothetai* of the Panathenaia appearing on Hellenistic and Roman amphorae.[48]

A further example of ceramic ware, a red-figured calyx-krater (wine bowl) from the British Museum, shows a bearded and laurel-wreathed kitharest who wears a long chiton and holds his kithara (an eight-stringed lyre) in his left hand, mounting the two-stepped *bema* in victory from the left.[49] Toward him flies a very large Nike (Victory), possibly holding out a victory wreath. On the extreme right sits a bearded man on a chair, the *agōnothetēs*, wrapped in a mantle and wreathed; to the extreme left in the corresponding position a chiton-clad female figure is seated on raised ground, with a spear resting on her right hand and shoulder. Above the female figure another smaller figure of Nike swoops down from the heights toward the kitharest holding two *phialae* (wide, flat bowls). In sum, the prestige of this particular kitharest's victory is not only underlined by two Nike figures (one large, one small) presenting him with honorific awards but is also further emphasized by the presence of the high-status official of the *agōnothetēs* at the ceremony.

Last, at the South Stoa of Corinth in the (presumed) office of the *agōnothetēs*, a Severan mosaic portrays a nude male athlete after his triumph, rendered by the symbols of the wreath and palm, standing before a seated, semidraped goddess with "Good Luck" inscribed upon her shield (Εὐτυχία).[50] Betsey Ann Robinson has recently argued that the goddess is

---

Hadrian (117–138 CE), shows on the obverse the draped bust of the laureate Senate with the legend ΙΕΡΑ - CVNKΛΗΤΟC, whereas the reverse displays the front-standing cult-statue of Apollo Chresterios with hands outstretched, holding a branch (?) in the left and an unidentifiable object in the right. The legend, ΕΠΙ.ΑΓΩ.ΟVΛ - [...], indicates that it was struck under the *agonothete* Ovl. [Pol.?]). For the coin, see http://www.asiaminorcoins.com/gallery/displayimage.php?pid=5852.

47. See Michel Amandry, *Le monnayage des duovirs Corinthiens*, BCHSup 15 (Athens: École française d' Athènes; Paris: de Boccard, 1988).

48. G. Roger Edwards, "Panathenaics of Hellenistic and Roman Times," *Hesperia* 26 (1957): 320–49; see plates 12, 14, 39.

49. The krater comes from the British Museum Hamilton Collection (1772,0320.26 [Vase E460]) and may be seen at http://tinyurl.com/SBL4208i.

50. Helmut Koester, ed., *Cities of Paul: Images and Interpretations from the Harvard New Testament Archaeology Project* (Minneapolis: Fortress, 2005), s.v. "Corinth"

Corinth herself, though depicted with the attributes of the goddess Aphrodite of the Acrocorinth and with the nymph beside her left leg symbolizing the nymph Peirene of Corinth's fresh-water spring.[51] Not only is Good Luck extended to the original athlete, but it is also extended to the viewer of the mosaic. More important, if Robinson has correctly interpreted the mosaic, the games represent a fusion of the Roman civic gods (represented by the goddess of the Julian colony) with the traditional indigenous Greek deities of the city (represented by Aphrodite and Peirene). The *agōnothetēs* would have been intimately familiar with this ideology and would have promoted its rich intersection of indigenous and Roman elements in his activities at the Isthmian games. The mosaic, if correctly identified as located in the office of the *agōnothetēs*, is a revealing portrait of how the local aristocracies of the Greek East, by seeking status through the magistracies of the *cursus honorum*, worked seamlessly with the Romans in fostering the welfare of the city, its institutions, and its values.

2.2.3. The Ancestral and Moral Status of the *Agōnothetēs* as Coordinator and Dispenser of Beneficence: Case Studies from Ephesus

This section will briefly discuss several inscriptions from Isthmia and Ephesus to gain a sense of the ancestral and moral status accorded to the *agōnothetēs* in his role of providing and coordinating beneficence for the games in the city. First, two stelae—Stela A (originally at Isthmia, now at located Verona) and Stela B (a fragment at Isthmia, with another at fragment at Corinth)—have been suggested to make up a single dossier registering gratitude for the benefactions of P. Licinius Priscus Juventianus to the Isthmian sanctuary. Both stelae were probably set up at Poseidon's shrine at Isthmia, with large fragment of Stela B being later relocated to Corinth for reuse in building projects.[52] The date of the dossier is uncer-

---

(Forum: go to "South Stoa: Wreath Monument"). In the area encompassed by the South Stoa, the mosaic is found in room C, the *agōnotheteion* (the presumed Corinthian office of the *agōnothetēs* for the Isthmian games). For a map of the site, see Murphy-O'Connor, "Corinth," 1137.

51. Betsey Ann Robinson, "'Good Luck' from Corinth: A Mosaic of Allegory, Athletics, and City Identity," *AJA* 116 (2012): 105–32. On Peirene, see Robinson, *Histories of Peirene: A Corinthian Fountain in Three Millenia* (Princeton: American School of Classical Studies at Athens, 2011).

52. For the finds of the stelae, their fragments, and various locations, see D. J.

tain, having been assigned either to the reign of Vespasian or to circa 170 CE. There also exists a highly fragmentary inscription in honor of Priscus at Corinth (IKorinthWest §70).

Stela A catalogs Priscus's many gifts to the sanctuary at Isthmia, but we confine our attention to the introduction of the stela, where Priscus's beneficence to the Isthmian games is enunciated (*IG* 4.203, ll. 1–7):

> To the ancestral gods
> and the fatherland
> P(ublius) Licinius, P(ublius's) s(on), (of the) Aem(ilian tribe), Priscus
> Juventianus, lifelong high priest
> He furnished
> the quarters for the athletes from the *oikoumene* who were present for the Isthmia.

Stela B is a rescript from the Roman proconsul of Achaia, who acknowledges publicly the generosity of Priscus and makes arrangements for the running of the Isthmian games in light of Priscus's beneficence (IKorinth-Kent §306, ll. 17–33). The gifts donated by the Isthmian benefactor, who held the magistracy of *agoranomos* (clerk of the market), had already been exhaustively outlined in Stela A for all to see. Therefore the proconsul deliberates about the administrative details in his rescript:

> Therefore since also in this
> Pri[s]c[u]s generously comports himself so as, as a price
> for the aforementioned locale, to give to the citizens
> each a denarius, not only do I assent to the proposal of the [s]enate
>   and *populus*,
> but also I congratulate the man so generously
> comporting himself in all matters. And I permit
> the aforesaid locale to be made over to him
> under the following conditions, that in perpetuity the resulting
> *oikoi* be available to the athletes free of charge on the occasion
> of the games and that the *agōnothetēs* have the authority
> on each occasion to allot

Geagan, "The Isthmian Dossier of P. Licinius Priscus Juventianus," *Hesperia* 58 (1989): 349–60, esp. 349–50.

guest chambers to them. If perchance anyone should object to this
he shall be free to instruct me before the Kalends
of January next. It is my prayer that you prosper.
Given four days before the Kalends of December and read from the
    rostra
the day before the Kalends
of December.

For our purposes, the two stelae are important for the light they throw on benefaction culture and the relation between the Romans, the *agōnothetēs*, and his civic rivals. First, the *oikoi* that the benefactor Priscus built at Isthmia for visiting athletes may have been dwellings, as Robert suggests,[53] which functioned as units for athlete housing during the festivals and as shops in the interim periods. The dwellings are offered free of charge for athletes during the festival in perpetuity. It is clear that the massive range of benefactions outlined in lines 1–30 of Stela A reveals a rapidly rising civic luminary of Isthmia who, by achieving posts additional to those he currently possessed (i.e., *archiereus*, *agoranomos*), would become a candidate for the office of *duovir* or *agōnothetēs*. In these gambits for civic status through benefactions and magistracies,[54] we gain insight into the competitive social world of "the well-born" and "powerful" in the Corinthian house churches (1 Cor 1:26). Second, there is no doubt in the Roman proconsul's mind who the chief official regarding the operation of the games actually is: only the *agōnothetēs* has the authority (ἐξουσίαν) to allot guest chambers in the dwellings to the athletes. The strongly hierarchic nature of eastern Mediterranean urban culture is exposed for all to see in the interactions of Greek aristocratic elites with the Roman authorities.

Second, several Ephesian inscriptions gives us insight into the ancestral and moral status of the *agōnothetēs*. First, in IEph 3.730, we read:

Good luck. The council and people of the city of the
Ephesians, the first and greatest metropolis of Asia
and twice temple-warden of the emperors honored

---

53. See Louis Robert, *Hellenica: Recueil d'épigraphie, de numismatique et d'antiquités grecques*, 13 vols. (Limoges: Bontemps, 1940–65), 1:43–53, cited in Geagan, "The Isthmian Dossier," 356.

54. Stela 2 had already euologized Priscus thus: "who has served his polis in a most generous fashion" ([πε]πολειτευμένον φιλοτειμότατα, l. 10).

Pop(lius) Vedius Papianus Antoninus, senator,
the *kratistos* and agonothete for life and by hereditary right
of the great Hadrianeia,
the benefactor descended from ancestors and a family
(of benefactors), and *ktises* of our native-land.
The statue was set up by the Koresseians,
those from the gate to the stadium.

This inscription emphasizes family honor, underscoring Antoninus's descent from ancestors and a family of benefactors. Inherited wealth, generation by generation, ensured the ability of powerful elites not only to dominate civic politics but also to accumulate moral status and ancestral fame by their beneficence to the city. It is interesting in this regard that there is no mention of Antoninus being given the privilege of being called *aleitourgētos* (free from the public burden), as was the case with some other Ephesian benefactors (IEph 3.946, 956A).[55] This was where benefactors, because of their generosity to their city, were given exemption from further beneficence for a period of time in order that they might replenish their reserves. By contrast, Antoninus was called an agonothete for life because presumably he had, in contrast to less-wealthy Ephesian benefactors, inexhaustible reserves.

Third, an inscription (IEph 1.24A, B, C: 162–164 CE) deals with a decree from the Ephesian assembly relating to the administration of the festivals and sacrifices to Artemis during the Artemesia and the maintenance of the sanctity of the month Artemision. The inscription comprises three parts: the edict of the Roman proconsul ratifying the Ephesian decree (A, ll. 1–21), the original Ephesian decree itself (B, ll. 1–34), and, last, an honorific decree eulogizing the role of the *agōnothetēs* Titus Aelius Marcianus Priscus (C, ll. 1–17). The honorific decree eulogizes Priscus thus:

His own city honors
Titus Aelius Marcianus Priscu[s], son of Titus,
of the Cl(audian tribe),
the president of the games [ἀγωνοθετήν] and the leader of the festival
 [πα(νηγυριάρχην)]

---

55. On the status of ἀλειτούργητος, see James R. Harrison, *Paul's Language of Grace in Its Graeco-Roman Context*, WUNT 2/172 (Tübingen: Mohr Siebeck, 2003), 254.

of the great Artemesia, (because)
he was first [πρῶτον] to conduct the
festival in its entiret[y [κατὰ τέλειο(ν)]]
and obtained festal holidays for the entire
month [εἰς ὅλον μῆνα] named after the goddess and
established the Artemesiac
contest and increased
the prizes for the contestants
and erected statues
for the ones who won.
L. Faenius Faustus,
his relative,
erected this in his honor.

While Priscus's "devotional and moral character" is "couched in terms entirely typical for such texts," as Richard Oster rightly notes,[56] there are interesting features in this honorific inscription that elevate it from the merely formulaic. The rhetorical use of the word πρῶτος, although frequent, locates Priscus's boasting in the eulogistic tradition of the Roman elites in the Latin West.[57] The routine mention of his father ensures that his achievements enhance his family honor, whereas the deflected honor also accorded the Claudian tribe ensures its prominence in the hiearchy of Ephesian tribal organization.[58] The emphasis on the entire completion of the Artemesia and the provision of festal holidays for the whole of Artemision underscores the faithfulness of Priscus to his responsibilities as an official. As Oster observes, "Apparently, the fidelity and scrupulousness with which the sacred time and accompanying festivals of Artemis had been kept were waning."[59] Last, Priscus's faithfulness to his word and office is matched by his readiness to increase beneficence to the Artemesiac contest. In other words, in an era of declining commitment to the Artemesia

---

56. Richard Oster, "Holy Days in Honour of Artemis," *NewDocs* 4:77.
57. Harrison, *Paul and the Imperial Authorities*, 223–34.
58. Note the alternative suggestion of Rick Strelan (*Paul, Artemis and the Jews in Ephesus*, BZNW 80 [Berlin: de Gruyter, 1996], 67 n. 106) regarding Priscus and the Claudian tribe: "Interestingly, he is identified as being of the Claudian tribe (*I. Eph* Ia.24). Was that tribe, in that year, responsible for the festival?"
59. Oster, "Holy Days," 77.

among some in the city, Priscus evinces costly piety toward the goddess of Ephesus.[60]

Having established the role and moral status of the *agōnothetēs* from the visual and inscriptional evidence, we are now ready to investigate the Corinthian inscriptions of the *agōnothetai*. What picture of the official emerges from their evidence, and what light does the ethos and rhetoric of the inscriptions throw on the Corinthian epistles?

3. The Corinthian *Agōnothetai*

This section will concentrate only on Corinthian *agōnothetai* inscriptions from the Julio-Claudian period.[61] Each *agōnothetēs* inscription is honorific, erected either by members of his family, by his tribe or fellow religious officials, or by powerful individuals from other cities indebted to him. Nevertheless, there are other Corinthian inscriptional contexts in which a name of an *agōnothetēs* can appear, such as the 3 CE list of victors in the Isthmia Caesarea, inscribed on the three sides of a headless marble herm near the gymnasium (IKorinthMeritt §14, l. 5). Three of our four honorands below are from the Fabian tribe (IKorinthWest §§67, 68, 86), with the exception of one from the Collinan tribe (IKorinthWest §81). Interestingly, two of the *agōnothetai* inscriptions, though Fabian, are honored by the Atian (IKorinthWest §86) and the Calpurnian (IKorinthWest §68) tribes. From this we can deduce that the Fabian tribe had precedence in the hierarchy of municipal tribes, presumably by numbers and social status. What follows does not provide a detailed exposition of the inscription, for which the commentaries accompanying each inscription in IKorinthWest may be consulted, but primarily enunciate the civic and imperial ethos contained therein and, where appropriate, note its relevance for its intersection with the Corinthian epistles.

---

60. See the discussion of Guy M. Rogers (*The Mysteries of Artemis of Ephesos: Cult, Polis and Change in the Graeco-Roman World* [New Haven: Yale University Press, 2012], 275–85) on the decline of the Artemis cult from the late second CE onward due to her failure to protect the polis and herself.

61. For second-century CE Corinthian *agōnothetai*, see IKorinthMeritt §80 (reign of Hadrian); IKorinthWest §71 (reign of Trajan and Hadrian: word *agōnothetēs* restored); §72 (reign of Trajan); §93 (second century CE). For indeterminate date, see IKorinthWest §105.

3.1. Latin Inscriptions Mentioning *Agōnothetai* from Tiberius to Nero

3.1.1 Father and Son *Agōnothetai*: Laco and Spartiaticus

IKorinthWest §67: Reigns of Caligula and Claudius

(This monument is dedicated) to the procurator
of Tiberius Claudius Caesar
Augustus Germanicus,
C. Julius Laco, son of C., of the Fabian tribe,
augur, president
of the Isthmian and Caesarean (games),
duovir quinquennalis, curio, flamen of the deified Augustus:
Cydichus Simonis
(from) Thisbeus (erected the statue). Well deserved.

C. Julius Laco was the son of the Spartan dynast C. Julius Eurycles. The father, because he had assisted Augustus at Actium with a small naval contingent from Sparta, was honored as hegemon of Sparta and made a citizen of Rome but experienced exile under Augustus in 2 BCE due to attacks on his character by the descendants of the old Spartan aristocracy.[62] However, Laco, the son of this famous benefactor of Greek cities, also experienced disgrace under the reign of Tiberius in 33 CE when he was deprived by exile of the power that his father had formerly held (Strabo, *Geogr.* 8.5.5; Tacitus, *Ann.* 6.18).[63] Thus Laco and his son subsequently settled in Corinth. But his significant setback was reversed under Caligula, with Laco and his family being honored throughout the province of Achaia (*IG* 5.1.1243; 5.2.541–42; cf. *SIG* 787 n. 2, 789) and his career continuing to flourish at Corinth.[64]

In the case of our inscription, as Allen Brown West notes, it is difficult to determine whether Laco's offices in the *cursus honorum* are "in ascending or descending order": Was he *duovir* before he became *agōnothetēs* or vice versa?[65] I suspect that they are in descending order, given that his

---

62. For Eurycles's meteoric career and his eventual exile, see Welborn, *An End to Enmity*, 312–15.
63. For details, see ibid., 315–16.
64. IKorinthWest, 48.
65. Ibid.

procuratorship heads the list, a sure sign that he is now thoroughly incorporated into the imperial system again,[66] with the title being an honorific for a client of Rome in the same way that the Romans rewarded the king of the Cottian Alps, Domnus, with the title prefect.[67] Analogously, therefore, Laco is now an *amicus* (friend) of Caligula and Claudius, having put behind him the earlier debacle under Tiberius.[68]

Important for our purposes are the offices relating to Laco's involvement in the imperial cult: *flamen augustalis* (a priest of the deified Augustus) and *agōnothetēs* (director of the Caesarean games on the Isthmus). His other offices are also prestigious. He held the municipal office, *duovir quinquennalis*, which was elected every five years for one year, performing the role of censor in the city. The office of *curio* provided Laco with priestly oversight of the tribes, which were the basis for local municipal administration.[69] As an augur, he was responsible for taking the auspices and interpreting the will of the gods in relation to the cult, commerce, and intercity relations. Clearly, the unknown figure of Cydichus Simonis is indebted to Laco in some way. He does not come from Corinth, but he may have been an influential figure in the city somehow, or, alternatively, he decided somewhat pretentiously and provocatively to highlight the city of his birth in the inscription, even though he had also become a Corinthian citizen.

Last, the intriguing rhetorical flourish ending the inscription (BM = *bene meritus*, "well deserved") is unusual in the Latin inscriptions of Corinth, occurring elsewhere only once in the corpus.[70] It not only highlights how posterity was to view the worthiness of Laco for the honors and offices he had received but also emphasizes the justness of the Roman reciprocity system in rewarding such men of excellence. More important, it is a political comment on how decisively and gloriously Laco had overcome his fall from grace under Tiberius, having been subsequently restored to even greater honors at Corinth and Achaia more widely.

---

66. IKorinthWest, 49. Welborn (*An End to Enmity*, 311 n. 140) suggests that "Laco and Spartiaticus held a procuratorship of imperial estates in the province of Achaia."

67. IKorinthWest, 49.

68. James R. Harrison, "'More Than Conquerors' (Rom 8:37): Paul's Gospel and the Augustan Triumphal Arches of the Greek and Latin West," *BurH* 47 (2011): 11.

69. IKorinthWest, 49.

70. The only other place in the Latin Corinthian inscriptions where the abbreviation appears is IKorinthWest §110 (*bene meritae*).

IKorinthWest §68 (cf. IKorinthMeritt §70): Reign of Claudius (54/55 CE)

> (This monument is dedicated) to C. Iulius Spartiaticus, son
> of Laco, grandson of Eurycles, of the Fabian tribe,
> procurator of Caesar and of Augusta
> Agrippina, military tribune, with the public horse
> decorated by deified Claudius, *flamen*
> of the deified Julius, *pontifex, duovir quinquennalis* twice,
> president of the Isthmian and Caesarean-
> Sebastean (games), high priest [*archierus*] of the Augustan house
> for life, the first [*primo*] of the Achaians
>   (to hold this office) on account of his virtue [*virtutem*] and unspar-
>   ing [*animosam*]
>   and most lavish liberality [*fusissiamque munificientiam*] both to the
>   divine
> family [*domum divinam*] and to our colony: the tribesmen
> of the Calpurnian tribe (erected the statue)
> to (their) patron.

The inscription of Spartiaticus underscores at the outset his ancestral fame, with the Corinthian readers of the inscription being well aware of the glory attached to his famous forebears who had been rehabilitated under Caligula,[71] notwithstanding their setbacks in Sparta under Augustus and Tiberius. Spartiaticus is conspicuously setting the record straight. Like his father, he was appointed the procurator of the imperial estates in the province of Achaia under Claudius and Augusta Agrippina, that is, before the time that Agrippina's brief co-regency with Nero came an end (55 CE) but after the divinization of Claudius (54 CE).[72] Whereas I argued that Laco's offices in the *cursus honorum* are in descending order, Welborn rightly concludes that Laco's offices in the *cursus honorum* are in ascending order.[73] In other words, Spartiaticus demonstrates in the rhetorical style of the Roman Scipionic *elogia* how he surpassed the highpoints of his

---

71. Welborn, *An End to Enmity*, 316.
72. Ibid., 310.
73. Ibid., 311. See the 90 CE inscription of the priest Lucius Papius Venereus "(who served as isagogeus to the agonothete Tiberius Claudius Anaxilaus" (IKorinthKent §212, ll. 2–3). West (IKorinthWest, 92) notes that "the text is a sort of priestly *cursus honorum* given in the ascending order."

ancestral fame. In Laco's case, the highpoint was ultimately the reacquisition of his procuratorship through the *amicitia* (friendship) of Julio-Claudian rulers, thereby reversing the shame of his exile. However, in the case of Spartiaticus, with the procuratorship as the foundation of his power, the ensuing *cursus honorum* demonstrates how Spartiaticus consistently exceeded the achievements of his father, Laco.

This is rhetorically achieved in several ways in the inscription. Spartiaticus highlights the increasing novelty of the positions he held under the imperial and municipal *cursus honorum*, climaxing in the most prestigious magistracy, itself a vignette of unparalleled status; he employs numbers to illustrate high points in his achievements and how he surpassed his father in the same post; he catalogs the posts under displays of excellence in particular areas that again demonstrate how he exceeded his father.

First, in terms of novelty of achievement, absent from the *cursus honorum* of Laco is any mention of admission to equestrian rank. But Spartiaticus was enrolled as an *equus publicus* by Claudius himself (Dio Cassius, *Hist. rom.* 59.9; Suetonius, *Claud.* 16) and therefore serves as a military tribune (i.e., a senior staff officer). Like his father, he was the *agōnothetēs* of the imperial games at the Isthmus but presided over the games named after Claudius (i.e., the Caesarean-Sebastean games), who, unlike his two predecessors, Tiberius and Caligula, had been deified.

Second, in terms of the rhetorical use of numbers, like his father he had held the same municipal censorial position (*duovir quinquennalis*), but "twice," unlike his father. He was the "first" (*primus*; cf. πρῶτος) of the Achaians to hold the high priesthood of the house of Augustus.[74]

Third, the catalog of the priesthoods of Spartiaticus are revealing in the way that they demonstrate his superior status. He is an unspecified *pontifex*, but, in contrast to his father, he was a *flamen* of the deified Julius as opposed to a *flamen* of the deified Augustus. West underlines the rarity of the phrase *flamen Divi Iuli*, observing that he found no other reference to such a priest at Corinth.[75] While it might seem at first blush that an Augustan priesthood trumps a Julian priesthood in prestige, we would do

---

74. The same rhetorical use of numbers appears in the Corinthian duoviri inscriptions: IKorinthKent §150 ("*duovir* twice … serving in place of *duovir* (once) … a second time by order of [the emperor Augustus]), §158 ("curator of the grain supply three times"), §272 ("in Corinth he won the contest of the Caesarea twice in succession").

75. IKorinthWest, 53.

well to remember who was the founder of the Julio-Claudian house, who was its first deified member, and who established the colony of Corinth: Julius Caesar. The importance of this "Julian" detail in Spartiaticus's *cursus honorum* is reinforced by the fact that it is the Calpurnian tribe that honored him, the tribe named after Julius Caesar's wife Calpurnia. The unusualness of Spartiaticus's Julian priesthood highlights his precedence in priestly lineage over his father.

Last, Spartiaticus's priesthood of Augustus in the province of Achaia is, as Welborn reminds us,[76] "the highest office in the province," enhanced by the fact that his office was linearly the first and held in perpetuum.[77] In this implicit paralleling and surpassing of his father's *cursus honorum*, we see how Spartiaticus increased the family glory in ways that the republican nobles of Rome would have recognized and approved.[78] As a sidelight to our discussion, in an intriguing piece of scholarship Welborn speculates whether this Corinthian Gaius, after his conversion, was the Gaius who, in his view, opposed Paul as the "wrongdoer." Upon surveying the similarities and differences, Welborn shies away from the identification, although he makes the valid point that the Corinthian Gaius of the house church would have come from a similar social background.[79]

In conclusion, this remarkable roll call of honor, achieved through Spartiaticus's acquisition of magistracies in the *cursus honorum*, calls forth moral accolades, rarely a feature of the Corinthian inscriptions: his virtue is unsparing and most lavish in its liberality.

3.1.2 The *Agōnothetēs* T. Manlius Juvencus

IKorinthWest §81 (cf. IKorinthKent §154): Reign of Tiberius or Before

(This monument is dedicated) to T. Manlius Juvencus,

---

76. Welborn, *An End to Enmity*, 312.

77. See also the Athenian inscription honoring Spartiaticus for the same imperial priesthood: *SIG* 790 (διὰ βίου πρῶτον).

78. For discussion, see James R. Harrison, "The Imitation of the Great Man in Antiquity: Paul's Inversion of a Cultural Icon," in *Christian Origins and Classical Culture: Social and Literary Contexts for the New Testament*, ed. Stanley E. Porter and Andrew W. Pitts, Early Christianity in Its Hellenistic Context 1, TENTS 9 (Leiden: Brill, 2013), 223–25.

79. Welborn, *An End to Enmity*, 317–19. On the final exile of Spartiaticus, see 317.

son of T., of the Collinan tribe,
aedilis, praefectus iure dicundo,
duovir, pontifex,
president of the Isthmian
and Caesarean (games)
who first conducted the Caesarea before the Isthmia:
the Hieromnemones (erected the inscription).

T. Manlius Juvencus comes from a tribe (Collina) different from the other Fabian *agōnothetai*. He is honored by the otherwise unknown Hieromnemones in the Corinthian inscriptions, whom, West proposes, "were priests of Poseidon second to none in dignity and importance" (Plutarch, *Quaest. conv.* 8.8.4 [730D–E]).[80] Most of the magistracies are conventional enough (*aedilis, duovir, pontifex*), but the fact that T. Manlius Juvencus holds the office of *duovir* could mean, as we have argued above, that he was responsible for the imperial gladiator and wild beast spectacles, as specified in the colonial charters. It is difficult to determine when these spectacles penetrated the Greek East and the province of Achaia in particular: a Tiberian date for these at Corinth is certainly early. Nevertheless, four of the Galatian priests of the deified Augustus mentioned in an inscription from the reign of Tiberius on the left anta in the Augusteum at Ancyra in Northern Galatia[81] stage spectacles and gladiator and bull fights for the citizens. Consequently, a Tiberian date for Corinthian spectacles coordinated by a *duovir*, although early, is not without precedent and so remains a possibility.

Additionally, Juvencus was the *agōnothetēs* of the Isthmian and Caesarean games of Tiberius.[82] The inscription mentions that he gave the

---

80. IKorinthWest, 66.

81. *OGI* 533; Robert, *Les gladiateurs*, §86. For a translation and discussion, see Stephen Mitchell and David French, *From Augustus to the End of the Third Century AD*, vol. 1 of *The Greek and Latin Inscriptions of Ankara (Ancyra)*, Vestigia 62 (Munich: Beck, 2012), §2, 138–50.

82. For another prestigious *agōnothetēs* in the reigns of Augustus and Tiberius, see the career of Lucius Castricius Regulus (ca. 10 BCE–23 CE), who was "[the first] to preside over the Isthmian games at the Isthmus under the sponsorship of Colonia Laus Julia Corinthiensis" (IKorinthKent §153, ll. 7–8). His role as a powerful benefactor at the Isthmian sanctuary and involvement in the imperial cult is emphasized in the inscription: "He introduced [poetry contests in honor of] the divine Julia Augusta,

Caesarian games precedence in their celebration ("first ... before"). This clearly demonstrates that "the imperial cult was being emphasized in Achaia" at that time.[83] Juvencus's post of *praefectus iure dicundo* confirms this impression, because in this office he acted as an honorary *duovir* on behalf of the Julio-Claudian ruler (or a member of his household).[84] In sum, the Romanization of the Greek institution of the *agōnothesia* is pronounced even at this early period of the Julio-Claudian principate.

3.1.3. Tiberius Claudius Dinippus: Benefactor in the "Pressing Times"

IKorinthWest §86 (cf. §§87–90; IKorinthKent §§158–63): Reign of Nero

(This inscription is dedicated)
to Tiberius Claudius Denippus, son of P(ublius), of the Fabian tribe,
duovir, duovir quinquennalis, augur, priest
of Victoria
Britannica, *tribunus militum* of Legion VI,
curator annonae,
president of the Neronian
Isthmian and Caesarean games: the tribesmen
of the Atian tribe (erected the inscription).

This inscription has been extensively discussed by classical and New Testament scholars,[85] so I will only highlight what is unusually prestigious about Dinippus's status and what is germane for the Corinthian epistles. I will not retrace the scholarly work done on the food shortages at Corinth 51 to 54 CE, while Dinippus was *curator annonae* (curator of grain) on three occasions (IKorinthKent §158),[86] though I note the relevance of

---

and [a contest for] girls, and after all the buildings of the Caesarea were renovated, he [quickly (?)] completed [the construction of (?) – – –], and gave a banquet for all the inhabitants of the colony" (IKorinthKent §153, ll. 9–13).

83. IKorinthWest, 64.
84. IKorinthWest, 65–66.
85. See Winter, "Secular and Christian Responses"; Danylak, "Tiberius Claudius Dinippus."
86. See the fragmentary Claudian inscription of an unnamed *agōnothetēs* and *curator annonae* in IKorinthWest §83.

this background to the "present distress" of 1 Cor 7:26.[87] We have already noted several of the magistracies in the *cursus honorum*: *duovir*, *duovir quinquennalis*, *augur*, and *tribunus militum*. As was the case with the other *agōnothetai* under previous Julio-Claudian rulers, Dinippus conducted the imperial games of Nero. Dinippus's acquisition of the prestigious position of imperial priest of Victoria Britannica was a career coup. The post commemorated Claudius's victory in Britain (43 CE), one of the greatest Roman military exploits in decades of Julio-Claudian rule, to which provincials reacted with rapturous responses in inscriptions, cultic celebration, and iconographic representation.[88] In sum, the Roman priests of the imperial cult basked in Claudius's military glory, and the momentum of this appointment continued with Dinippus's post of *agōnothetēs* under Nero.

In what ways do these intensely rich portraits of the Corinthian *agōnothetai* throw light on the Corinthian epistles?

4. Honor and Paul's Rhetorical Response to the Corinthian Boasting Culture: Insights from the *Agōnothetai* Inscriptions

4.1. The Reframing of the Honor System within the Body of Christ

At the outset, it should be underscored that Paul does not disassemble the Greco-Roman honor system.[89] Certainly, he extends the scope of its allocation to the base of the social pyramid through the honoring of the least gifted within the body of Christ in ways unimaginable to the self-aggrandizing Corinthian elite (1 Cor 12:22–25). He argues that this radical social upending in social relations was God's intention (12:24b). Moreover, this was based on God's divine election (1 Cor 1:26a, 26b, 28b: ἐξελέξατο) of the "foolish" and "weak" in the body of Christ so that the "wise" and the "strong" would be shamed (1:27a: ἵνα καταισχύνῃ τοὺς σοφούς; 1:27b: ἵνα καταισχύνῃ τὰ ἰσχυρά) and be brought to nothing (1:28b:

---

87. Winter, "Secular and Christian Responses"; Danylak, "Tiberius Claudius Dinippus"; Harrison, "Times of Necessity."

88. For full discussion, see Josiah Osgood, *Claudius Caesar: Image and Power in the Early Roman Empire* (Cambridge: Cambridge University Press, 2011), 101–5.

89. See James R. Harrison, "Paul and Ancient Civic Ethics: Redefining the Canon of Honour in the Graeco-Roman World," in *Paul's Graeco-Roman Context*, ed. Cilliers Breytenbach, BETL 277 (Leuven: Peeters; Leuven University Press, 2015), 75–118.

ἵνα τὰ ὄντα καταργήσῃ).⁹⁰ Consequently, the apostle will not tolerate the Corinthian elite in the house churches humiliating the poor (1 Cor 11:22b: καταισχύνετε τοὺς μὴ ἔχοντας;) by not waiting to eat with them at the Lord's Supper (1 Cor 11:22b, 33b). Little doubt, in an honorific culture where the wealthy benefactors were publicly awarded front seats at the theater and the privilege of eating in the public festivals (e.g., *SEG* 11.948, n. 129 below), eating ahead of the nonelites would be assumed by the majority to be an innate right of the powerful. Given that the *agōnothetai* hosted public feasts (n. 82 above) and, most likely, funded the meals of local associations at Corinth, the preferential treatment of the wealthy elites (cf. Jas 2:1–7; cf. 1:9–10, 27) would be, in the view of the socially influential, a cultural practice transferrable to the banqueting rituals of the house churches. Paul undermines that expectation.

Nevertheless, Paul emphasizes the importance of according honor to Phoebe, who was the patron of Corinthian believers and visitors from other cities to her house church, living as she did at Corinth's western harbor port, Kenchreai (Rom 16:2: προστάτις πολλῶν).⁹¹ Paul affirms the operations of the Greco-Roman reciprocity system in this instance. Moreover, Paul's insistence that Phoebe be welcomed in the Lord (ἐν κυρίῳ) in a way "worthily of the saints" (ἀξίως τῶν ἁγίων) should seen as recognition of her meritorious service of the body of Christ. Indeed, it might be posited that this is a Christian equivalent of the honorific *bene meritus* (well deserved) in the inscription of the *agōnothetēs* C. Julius Laco discussed above.

However, the underlying dynamic is somewhat different in this instance. First, such public affirmation is an expression of the brotherly love, mutual honoring, and acceptance that characterized social relations in the body of the Christ (see 1 Cor 12:26b: εἴτε δοξάζεται [ἐν] μέλος, συγχαίρει πάντα τὰ μέλη; Rom 16:2a: ἐν κυρίῳ: cf. Rom 12:10b; 13:7b; 15:7). Second, the unusual phrase "worthily of the saints" poses the question whether Paul is thinking along the lines of some type of meritorious recompense. I would suggest that there is certainly a "debt" being recompensed in this social transaction, but it is the "debt of love" (Rom 13:8–10) that all believers owe each other, no matter their status, family origins, or economic

---

90. For discussion, see L. L. Welborn, *Paul, the Fool of Christ: A Study of 1 Corinthians 1–4 in the Comic-Philosophic Tradition*, JSNTSup 293 (London: T&T Clark, 2005), 117–247.

91. On Phoebe, see Joan Cecelia Campbell, *Phoebe: Patron and Emissary* (Collegeville, MN: Liturgical Press, 2009).

situation. It is precisely for this reason that Paul suggests the socially unthinkable in antiquity: the Corinthian believers should, in recompense, extend help to their benefactor as required (Rom 16:2: παραστῆτε αὐτῇ ἐν ᾧ ἂν ἡμῶν χρῄζῃ πράγματι). The open-endedness of this request seems to involve more than just the cultural practice of the *salutatio*, the morning greeting of the Roman patron by his clients at Rome. More shockingly, Paul expects that the impoverished should act as benefactors themselves, thereby bringing the social ideal of equality to a paradoxical fulfillment (2 Cor 6:10; 8:1–6, 9, 13–15; cf. Mark 12:42–44).[92] In sum, Paul strips the benefactor of a prized social accolade in the transaction: the suppliant position of recipients before the benefactor, which, depending on the size of the benefaction, reduces them to a never-ending round of reciprocity rituals and the continuous expression of gratitude. Instead, Paul calls the recipients of grace to engage in ministry themselves in the body of Christ, recompensing not only their benefactor but also benefiting other believers through the exercise of their Spirit-allocated gifts (1 Cor 12:4–11). Ministry to others calls forth ministry from the recipients of grace as the body of Christ suffers and rejoices together in its experience of dishonor and honor (1 Cor 12:28; 2 Cor 6:8a, 10a).

Furthermore, the dynamic of benefaction and recompense is reconfigured socially in terms of the "brotherhood" of believers (1 Cor 16:15a). Thus *diakonia* in the family of God is gladly received and publicly acknowledged without the fear that the debt imposed might never be able to be adequately reciprocated (1 Cor 16:15b, 18b).[93] However, those who have accepted this ministry must nevertheless demonstrate submission—the characteristic of all relationships in the body of Christ (1 Cor 16:16a: ἵνα καὶ ὑμεῖς ὑποτάσσησθε τοῖς τοιούτοις; cf. Eph 5:21: Ὑποτασσόμενοι ἀλλήλοις)— toward the agents of ministry, their coworkers and colaborers (1 Cor 16:16b). Consequently, those who minister and those who are recipients of their ministry experience mutual rejoicing and spiritual refreshment together (16:17a, 18a). In conclusion, we must be alert to Paul's endorsement of Greco-Roman reciprocity ethics in various instances,[94] but we

---

92. See L. L. Welborn, "'That There May Be Equality': The Contexts and Consequences of a Pauline Ideal," *NTS* 59 (2013): 73–90.

93. On the pressure of not being able to reciprocate debts, real or promised, see, respectively, P.Oxy. 42.3057 and Dio Chrysostom, *Conc. Apam.* 3–4. See Harrison, *Paul's Language of Grace*, 81–83, 312.

94. Harrison, *Paul's Language of Grace*, 324–32.

must also look for the distinctive elements of Paul's approach that transform and revolutionize its dynamic within the body of Christ.

4.2. Paul and the Boasting Corinthians: The Rhetorical Subtleties of *Syncrisis*

The "fool's discourse" in 2 Cor 11:1–12:18 is relentlessly punctuated by a litany of "boasting" references (2 Cor 11:10, 12, 16, 17, 18, 30; 12:1, 5, 6, 9; cf. 10:8, 13, 15, 16, 17).[95] The apostle responds to the threat posed by the interloping apostles at Corinth with invective and—to the shock of contemporary auditors—a self-denigrating *syncrisis* (comparison).[96] The attack of the so-called super-apostles (2 Cor 11:5; cf. 11:13; 12:11) against Paul is easily enough reconstructed. In a stylized *syncrisis*, the opponents had claimed that they had superior *charismata* to Paul. They asserted that he was deficient in rhetorical skill (2 Cor 10:10; 11:6), personal presence and integrity (10:1, 2b, 9–11; 11:6; 12:1, 16–18), Jewish pedigree (10:2b; 11:22–23), and the requisite apostolic signs, whether miracles (12:12) or visionary revelations (12:1–5). How does Paul combat this invidious comparison employed by the intruders and their supporters?

In 2 Cor 11:16–29 Paul adopts a wide variety of rhetorical tactics to expose the foolishness of his opponents' self-commendation (2 Cor 10:12). We will confine our discussion to those that have resonance with the Corinthian *agōnothetai* inscriptions. First, Edwin A. Judge argues regarding 2 Cor 11:21b–29 that "the numerical and patterned way of his sufferings corresponds to the way in which great men summed up their achievements in a brief verbal diagram, designed to serve a mnemonic."[97] While this convention was widespread in antiquity, it particularly featured

---

95. For a brief discussion of the theme of foolishness in 2 Cor 11:1–12:18, see Jerry W. McCant, *2 Corinthians*, Readings (Sheffield: Sheffield Academic, 1999), 114–16. On foolishness within the context of ancient mime and its impact upon Paul's "fool's discourse," see L. L. Welborn, "The Runaway Paul," *HTR* 92 (1999): 115–63.

96. On Paul's invective, see Peter Marshall, "Invective: Paul and His Enemies in Corinth," in *Perspectives on Language and Text: Essays and Poems in Honor of Francis I. Andersen's Sixtieth Birthday July 29 1985*, ed. Edgar W. Conrad and Edward G. Newing (Winona Lake, IN: Eisenbrauns, 1987), 359–73.

97. Edwin A. Judge, "The Conflict of Educational Aims in the New Testament," in Judge, *The First Christians in the Roman World: Augustan and New Testament Essays*, ed. James R. Harrison, WUNT 229 (Tübingen: Mohr Siebeck, 2008), 707. The following draws upon my discussion of the fool's discourse in James R. Harrison, "In

in the honorific inscriptions of the great republican noble families, with their famous generals, and appeared in their funeral *elogia*.[98] Paul ruthlessly parodies all Greco-Roman inscriptional conventions of boasting, whether they are modeled on the benefaction, military, athletic, gladiatorial, charioteer, pantomime, or imperial forms of eulogy.[99] Each genre of boasting had catalogs of achievement, with numerical highlights drawing attention to singular attainments beyond the conventional in the *cursus honorum*. Paul's rhetoric would have registered with Corinthian audiences familiar with one or several of these eulogistic types.

We have seen that the same convention underlies the civic inscriptions of the *agōnothetai* at Corinth. The use of numbers in the *agōnothetai* inscriptions, along with those of the *duoviri* inscriptions (n. 74 above), emphasize the distinctiveness of the attainment reached: "the first of the Achaians (to hold this office)" (IKorinthWest §68); "*duovir quinquennalis* twice" (IKorinthWest §68); "[the first] to preside over the Isthmian games at the Isthmus" (IKorinthWest §153). Furthermore, detailed catalogs of magistracies occur within particular inscriptions and across the genre more generally: priesthoods, civic posts, president of the various games (Isthmian, Caesarean), military posts (military tribune), and, last, Roman appointments (procurator).[100] While a strict sequential order is not always present or expected, the appointments are usually given in ascending or descending status, as the rhetoric requires.[101] Clearly in the case of Roman

---

Quest of the Third Heaven: Paul and His Apocalyptic Imitators," *VC* 58 (2004): 24–55, esp. 46–55.

98. See, Harrison, *Paul and the Imperial Authorities*, 219–25.

99. For the ancient source examples for each genre, see Harrison, "In Quest of the Third Heaven," 47–48 nn. 71, 74–78. For several inscriptions in honor of a pantomime, including ones at Corinth and Ephesus, using catalog patterns, see William J. Slater, "The Pantomime Tiberius Iulius Apolaustus," *GRBS* 36 (1995): 263–92.

100. Priesthoods mentioned: *augur, pontifex, flamen* of *divus Julius, flamen* of *divus Julius*, priest of Victoria Britannica, high priest (*archierus*) of the Augustan house for life. Civic posts mentioned: *aedilis, praefectus iure dicundo, duovir, duovir quinquennalis*.

101. I argued above (§3.1.1) that the *cursus honorum* of the *agōnothetai* inscriptions of the father Laco and his son Spartiaticus are respectively descending and ascending in status, with Spartiaticus demonstrating how he had equaled and surpassed his father's glory. The priest Lucius Papius Vareneus (IKorinthKent §212: last half of first century CE), "co-agonothete with Lucius Vibullius Pius of the Isthmian games," sets out his priestly *cursus honorum* in ascending order.

colonies of the Greek East, the boasting conventions belonging to the *cursus honorum* of the Roman *nobiles* (nobles) and the Julio-Claudian house had been transferred to a colonial context; we also see the same meticulous accounting of the military magistracies in the Roman colony of Philippi. However Paul replaces the carefully tabulated honors of the eulogistic tradition (2 Cor 11:22–23a) with an equally carefully tabulated catalog of his own humiliations and sufferings (11:23b–29). By means of his self-derision, Paul underscores his weakness (2 Cor 11:21, 29, 30), the very issue for which he is criticized by his opponents (2 Cor 10:10: "his bodily presence is weak"). By inverting the content of his opponents' claims, Paul exposes the hollowness of their pretensions as "servants of Christ" (2 Cor 11:23).

Second, the *agōnothetai* inscriptions often climax with a career vignette that sums up the excellence and virtue of the *agōnothetēs*, such as president of the Neronian Isthmian and Caesarean games (IKorinthWest §86) or the "high priest (*archierus*) of the Augustan house for life, the first [*primo*] of the Achaians (to hold this office)" (IKorinthWest §68). By contrast, in the rhetorical climax to Paul's boasting in his own weaknesses and his identification with the weak (2 Cor 11:29a), Paul offers the countercultural vignette of his humiliating escape down the Damascus city wall in a basket (2 Cor 11:30–33; cf. Acts 9:23–25). Whether we interpret this as a spoof of the military *corona muralis* award or as an allusion to the "runaway fool" of Greek and Roman mimic drama or to the "cowardly benefactor" who (like the famous Demosthenes) fled from the city, Paul savagely debunks the entire boasting enterprise.[102]

But just when we think that Paul has plumbed the depths of self-derision in 2 Cor 11:30–33, he lifts our hopes with the even more graphic vignette of his (visionary? bodily?) trip to the third heaven (2 Cor 12:1–4). Surely this is where Paul's apostolic *cursus honorum* finally ascends out of the depths of shame to the unassailable heights of the highest heaven itself. We have seen from the *agōnothetai* inscriptions that magisterial status could be arranged in descending or ascending order. The Corinthians, listening for the first time to the letter being read out aloud in the house churches, would have expected the full unveiling of the "apocalyptic" Paul, superior in revelation and pneumatic power to his rivals, transcending the

---

102. See Judge, "The Conflict of Educational Aims," 706–8; Welborn, "The Runaway Paul," passim; Harrison, *Paul's Language of Grace*, 335–40; Harrison, "In Quest of the Third Heaven," 50–51.

weak and suffering apostle he had just depicted in his *cursus honorum*, whom his rivals at Corinth despised. But again their hopes are dashed. God intervenes and physically humbles his apostle (2 Cor 12:7), cutting off any opportunity to boast over his opponents (12:6), stripping him of self-reliance (12:5b), consigning him to the oblivion of being a "visionless visionary" who cannot articulate his superior revelation (12:4), and opening up to him the paradoxical experience of divine power accessed in abject weakness (12:8–9).[103] All opportunity of human boasting has been denied for the sake of Christ (12:10). In sum, the smugness of the Corinthian civic elites and the superiority of the interloping apostles has been pinpricked by the paradigm of Christ's resurrection power experienced in cruciform weakness (13:4a).

5. Nikias the *Agōnothetēs* of Isthmia

Inscribed on a statue base of white marble was the honorific epigram accorded to Nikias, an *agōnothetēs*, by his fellow officials. It was found in front of a semicircular foundation at the northern edge of the Palaimonion area at Isthmia. The marble base and the bronze statue of Nikias had been moved there later from its original location in the forechamber of the Temple of Poseidon (ll. 4, 8), some 13 km east of ancient Corinth. Although the inscription is undated, it is probably roughly contemporary with the early Roman period when the Palaimonion shrine was built (i.e., mid-first century–mid-second century). The inscription is set out below:

> First [τὸν πρῶτον] among orators, preeminent [ἄριστον] as *agōnothetēs*
> Having acquired glory [κῦδος] in every public office—
> For these achievements your colleagues in the office of *agōnothetēs*,
> Erected a statue of you, Nikias, in the forechamber of Poseidon.
> BY VOTE OF THE COUNCIL   5
> He verily pours forth words like streams
> At the mouths of ever-flowing rivers.
> He stands, a portrait of bronze, before the temple,
> In the midst of pure hands, by purifying streams (of water);
> And as a reward for his merit ('Ἀντ' ἀρετῆς) he received [a gold
>   crown(?)] by which they honored [ἔτεισαν] him.   10

---

103. See Harrison, "In Quest of the Third Heaven," 51–54.

Readily, unfalteringly the *athlothetai* knew (your worth),
O Nikias, a great delight to the city; and to the young—
Citizens and strangers alike—how great a blessing nature [ἔφυς]
has made you.[104]   15

Broneer argues that the two honors were conveyed on separate occasions. The first (a bronze statue) was awarded for Nikias's role as *agōnothetēs* (ll. 1–4), whereas the second (a gold crown?), the lettering of which has been deliberately erased from the stone, was awarded for his oratorical ability (ll. 6–7, 10–11). Broneer speculates what circumstances may have provoked this official censure,[105] but, more important, the erasure shows how quickly honor rituals were supplanted by dishonor when the honorand fell out of favor. This coheres with the recycling of inscriptions against which Dio Chrysostom railed (*Rhodiaca*), violating thereby the honor of the original honorand.[106] In a Corinthian context, too, the peripatetic philosopher Favorinus, who had visited Corinth three times (Dio Chrysostom, [*Cor.*] 1, 8, 9), experienced an unjust toppling of his statue by detractors in Corinth. This represented another version of *damnatio memoriae* through the disfiguring of an honorific monument, similar to the public dishonor experienced by the orator Nikias at Isthmia.[107]

The conventional language of preeminence (πρῶτος, ἄριστος) and glory (κῦδος) is attached to the first honor (l. 1). Significantly, ceremonial hand washing occurred in a basin at the entrance of the temple (l. 9), located just before the *pronaos* (an open vestibule) where Nikias's statue had originally been erected (ll. 4, 8). Nikias's reputation before posterity was thereby invested with an aura of cultic purity by virtue of its association with the sacred space and activities of the temple. Moreover, the distinction that Nikias has achieved in an array of public offices (l. 2), including the role of *agōnothetēs*, the official who instituted the games and defrayed their expenses (ll. 1, 3). This marks Nikias out as a socially powerful individual

---

104. Oscar Broneer, "Excavations at Isthmia: Fourth Campaign, 1957–1958," *Hesperia* 28 (1959): 298–43, esp. 324–26 (§5). The line numbers used here correspond to Broneer's English translation, as opposed to the slightly different line numbers of the Greek.

105. Ibid., 325–26.

106. See Harrison, "The Brothers," 170–74.

107. See the discussion of V. Henry T. Nguyen, *Christian Identity: A Comparative Study of 2 Corinthians*, WUNT 2/243 (Tübingen; Mohr Siebeck, 2008), 127–29.

with (undoubtedly) inherited wealth and property, casting him thereby in the estimation of the ancients as a man of conspicuous virtue.

In the case of the second (coronal?) honor (ll. 10–11), Nikias's oratorical power and personal worth ("a great delight to the city") is portrayed in such "exaggerated terms" that his civic virtue (ἀρετή) demands the reciprocation of honor.[108] His natural virtue (ἔφυς) is apparent to all generations: citizens and noncitizens of the city, the mature *athlothetai* and the aspiring young (ll. 13–15). We are witnessing the inflated moral language that dominated honor discourse in the early empire.[109]

In sum, we have highlighted the erasure of honor on public statues and their dedications. The rarity of these occurrences needs to be underscored. The reciprocation of worthy citizens for their civic contribution had to operate with finesse in order to ensure social cohesion and the smooth operation of the honor system. In the case of Roman Corinth, for example, orators are similarly honored in the public inscriptions: Publius Aelius Sospinus, grandson of an *agōnothetēs* (three times) like Nikias, for his "upright character and general excellence";[110] the "good orator" Maecius Faustinus for "his upright character";[111] and Poseidonius for his primacy as an orator (πρῶτός τε ῥήτο[ρ]).[112] While these moral accolades are entirely conventional, setting the remarkable Isthmian inscription of Nikias in even stronger relief by virtue of its florid and overstated accolades, nevertheless the Corinthian inscriptions underscore the city's obsession with rhetoric because of the precedence and moral reputation it con-

---

108. Broneer, "Excavations at Isthmia," 325.

109. See Arjan Zuiderhoek, *The Politics of Munificence in the Roman Empire: Citizens, Elites and Benefactors in Asia Minor* (Cambridge: Cambridge University Press, 2009), 122–28. Additionally, see the inflated metaphorical language used of Kallimachos (*OGI* 39, ll. 14–23 [provenance: Thebes, March 39 CE]). Translated by Stanley M. Burstein, *The Hellenistic Age from the Battle of Ipsos to the Death of Kleopatra VII* (Cambridge: Cambridge University Press, 1985), §111.

110. IKorinthKent §226 (third quarter of second century CE).

111. IKorinthKent §264 (mid-second century CE). Similarly, IKorinthKent §268: "[The city] by vote of the city council (erected this monument to) Marcus Valerius Taurinus, son of Marcus, [a – – – philosopher (and) a good orator] because of [his fine character]"; IKorinthKent §268: "Peducaeus Cestianus the Apollonian orator."

112. IKorinthKent §307 (end of second century CE). For other "orator" inscriptions asserting the precedence of the honorand, see *IG* 7.106, ll. 10–11 (Megaris): καί πρῶτον Πανέλληνα, ῥήτορα; *MAMA* 6, list 149, 162, ll. 5–6 (Phrygia): [ῥήτ]ορα καὶ πρῶτον [ἐν] τῇ πόλει.

veyed for its practitioners, as well as the deflected glory it accrued for the sponsors of particular orators. What light do these Corinthian inscriptions eulogizing orators and the Isthmian inscription of Nikias throw on rhetoric and honorific culture in the Corinthian epistles?

6. Rhetoric, the *Agōnothetae* of the Isthmian Games, and Paul's Gospel of Christ Crucified

The Corinthian believers had been boasting in their leaders (1 Cor 1:12; 3:4–6; 4:6, 21), with some preferring those luminaries at Corinth who were, in their view, more gifted orators than Paul (2 Cor 10:10b: ὁ λόγος ἐξουθενημένος).[113] In particular, some Corinthians preferred Apollos, who was professionally trained in rhetoric (Acts 18:24–28: ἀνὴρ λόγιος, v. 24), unlike Paul (ἰδιώτης τῷ λόγῳ: 2 Cor 11:7), to their apostle (4:6b).[114] Indeed, the apostle's lack of ability was exhibited for all to see in his poor oratorical performances at Corinth (1 Cor 2:1–5; 2 Cor 10:1b, 10). The devotees of eloquence in the Corinthian house churches considered skill in rhetoric to be a sign of great wisdom and personal power,[115] with the result that

---

113. On Greco-Roman rhetoric and the Corinthian Epistles, see A. Duane Litfin, *St. Paul's Theology of Proclamation: 1 Corinthians 1–4 and Greco-Roman Rhetoric*, SNTSMS 79 (Cambridge: Cambridge University Press, 1994); Bruce W. Winter, *Philo and Paul among the Sophists*, SNTSMS 96 (Cambridge: Cambridge University Press, 1996); Brian K. Peterson, *Eloquence and the Proclamation of the Gospel in Corinth*, SBLDS 163 (Atlanta: Scholars Press, 1998); Corin Mihaila, *The Paul-Apollos Relationship and Paul's Stance toward Graeco-Roman Rhetoric*, LNTS 402 (London: T&T Clark, 2009). On Greco-Roman education as a contributing factor to the Corinthian factionalism in 1 Cor 1–4, see Robert S. Dutch, *The Educated Elite in 1 Corinthians: Education and Community Conflict in Graeco-Roman Context*, JSNTSup 271 (Edinburgh: T&T Clark, 2005); Adam G. White, *Where Is the Wise Man? Graeco-Roman Education as Background to the Divisions in 1 Corinthians 1–4*, LNTS 536 (London: Bloomsbury T&T Clark, 2015). On Stoic philosophy, wisdom, and the divisions in 1 Cor 1–4, see Timothy A. Brookins, *Corinthian Wisdom, Stoic Philosophy and the Ancient Economy*, SNTSMS 159 (Cambridge: Cambridge University Press, 2014).

114. See Patrick J. Hartin, *Apollos: Paul's Partner or Rival?* (Collegeville, MN: Liturgical Press, 2009); Mihaila, *The Paul-Apollos Relationship*. However, Paul's claim to being ἰδιώτης τῷ λόγῳ (2 Cor 11:7) is a well-known oratorical motif and has to be assessed with caution as far as being an accurate indicator of Paul's rhetorical training or lack thereof. See Dale B. Martin, *The Corinthian Body* (New Haven: Yale University Press, 1995), 48–49.

115. Isocrates (*Ad. Nic.* 5–9) and Cicero (*De or.* 3.53) make explicit the connec-

they had become increasingly arrogant (1 Cor 4:18–20), boastful (1 Cor 3:7, 21; 4:7b), self-satisfied (1 Cor 3:8), and, in their own estimation, wise (1 Cor 3:18; 4:10b), because of their attachment to and financial support of the leading figures in the local rhetorical celebrity circuit (1 Cor 9:3–18; 2 Cor 12:14–18).

We have already noted the "baroque" exuberance with which the preeminence and oratorical skills of Nikias are vaunted in his honorific decree. Dio Chrysostom also speaks about the extravagant enthusiasm of the great cities for traveling rhetoricians in the same baroque style as our inscription:

> again, if I really like foreign travel, I should ... visit the greatest cities, escorted with much enthusiasm and éclat, the recipients of my visits being grateful for my presence and begging me to address them and advise them and flocking about my doors from early dawn, all without my having incurred any expense or having made any contribution, with the result that all would admire me and perhaps some would exclaim, "Ye gods! how dear and honored is this man to whatsoever town and folk he comes." (*Cont.* 22 [Cohoon])

What is fascinating is the fawning response of the recipients to Dio Chrysostom's visits, basking in the afterglow of the glorious advent of the great orator, as well as their financial support of him. In the responses of the eastern Mediterranean cities to Dio Chrysostom and of Isthmia to Nikias, we gain insight into the excitement that must have been generated in some of the Corinthian house churches when the rhetorically gifted Apollos arrived in the city and began his teaching ministry.

Furthermore, Dio Chrysostom, in his imaginative reconstruction of what the old Greek city of Corinth was like before its 146 BCE destruction by Rome, emphasizes the Corinthian love of rhetoric in its varied expressions:

> This was the time when one could hear crowds of wretched sophists around Poseidon's temple shouting and reviling one another, and their

---

tion between rhetoric and wisdom. See also the inscription from Iasos on a statue base honoring Aulus Mussius Asper: "on account of (his) most manifold and incomparable nobleness of nature in rhetoric and poetry and (in) all remaining wisdom [τῇ λοιπῇ πάσῃ σοφίᾳ]" (Wolfgang Blümel, *Die Inschriften von Iasos*, 2 vols., IGSK 28.1–2 [Bonn: Habelt, 1985], §94).

disciples, as they were called, fighting with one another, many writers reading aloud their stupid works, many poets reciting their poems while others applauded them, many jugglers showing their tricks, many fortune-tellers interpreting fortunes, lawyers innumerable perverting judgement, and peddlers not a few peddling [οὐκ ὀλίγων δὲ καπήλων διακαπηλευόντων] whatever they happened to have. (*Virt.* 9 [Cohoon, LCL])[116]

Significantly, Dio Chrysostom's language of "peddling" is employed by Paul in 2 Cor 2:17 (οἱ πολλοὶ καπηλεύοντες τὸν λόγον τοῦ θεοῦ) to differentiate his apostolic credentials and his gospel of Christ crucified from the message of his interloping rivals, who had recently arrived in the Corinthian house churches with their letters of recommendation (3:1–3). However, the Corinthian admiration of wisdom, *paideia* (education) and rhetoric at Corinth is not entirely explained by their encounters with peripatetic philosophers and orators such as Favorinus (85–162 CE)[117] or by the temporary presence of prestigious orators and benefactors such as Herodes Atticus in the city (101–177 CE)[118] or by the activity of teachers of rhetoric

---

116. Bruce W. Winter (*After Paul Left Corinth: The Influence of Secular Ethics and Social Change* [Grand Rapids: Eerdmans, 2001], 32) argues that the speech accurately reflects the situation of Corinth when Dio Chrysostom visited the games during his exile in 89–96 CE.

117. On Favorinus (Dio Chrysostom, *Corinthiaca*; Philostratus, *Vit. soph.* 489–492), see Litfin, *St. Paul's Theology of Proclamation*, 144–46; Winter, *Philo and Paul*, 132–36; Winter, "The Toppling of Favorinus and Paul by the Corinthians," in *Early Christianity and Classical Culture: Comparative Studies in Honour of Abraham J. Malherbe*, ed. John T. Fitzgerald, Thomas H. Olbright, and L. Michael White, NovTSup 110 (Leiden; Brill, 2003), 291–306; Jason König, "Favorinus' Corinthian Oration in Its Corinthian Context," *CJ* 47 (2001): 141–71; L. Michael White, "Favorinus's 'Corinthian Oration': A Piqued Panorama of the Hadrianic Forum," in Schowalter and Friesen, *Urban Religion in Roman Corinth*, 61–110; Concannon, *When You Were Gentiles*, 36–43.

118. For Corinthian inscriptions honoring the wife of Herodes Atticus, Regilla, and possibly himself, see IKorinthKent §§128–29. For a herm set up in honor of Herodes Atticus at Isthmia, see *SEG* 11.187. For a list of the inscriptions detailing the activities of Herodes Atticus and Regilla at Corinth, including evidence from portrait sculpture and architecture (e.g., Odeon, Peirene fountain), see Jennifer Tobin, *Patronage and Conflict under the Antonines* (Amsterdam: Gieben, 1997), 296–302. Additionally, see Alexandre Philadelpheus, "Un Hermès d'Hérode Atticus," *BCH* 44 (1920): 170–80; Walter Ameling, *Herodes Atticus*, 2 vols. (Hildesheim: Olms, 1983); Daniel N. Schowalter, "Regilla Standing By: Reconstructed Statuary and Re-inscribed Bases

and philosophy in the local gymnasium. Significantly, our Nikias inscription reveals that some of the Isthmian *agōnothetai* themselves were trained in rhetoric, having gained accolades for their rhetorical performance as much as their beneficence. We have already noted the inscription of Publius Aelius Sospinus, the grandson of a famous *agōnothetēs* from Corinth, set out fully below:

> The council and the citizens
> set up (this monument to honor)
> Publius Aelius Sospinus,
> an orator, the grandson
> of Antonius Sospis,
> the three times *agōnothetēs*,
> son of Publius Aelius Apol-
> lodotus and Antonia Sosipatra,
> on account of his upright character
> and all of his other
> excellence,
> by vote of the city council.[119]

The moral character (ἀνδραγαθία, ἀρετῇ) and prestigious ancestry of Publius are vaunted as much as his rhetorical reputation in the inscription. Plutarch (40–ca. 112 CE) comments on his own encounter with Publius's grandfather, the "three times" *agōnothetēs* Sospis, during the Isthmian games at a banquet:

> During the Isthmian Games, the second time Sospis was exhibitor [ἀγωνοθεσιῶν], I avoided the other banquets, at which he entertained a great many foreign visitors at once, and several times entertained all the citizens. Once, however, when he entertained in his home his closest friends [τοὺς μάλιστα φίλους], all the men of learning [φιλολόγους], I was present too. At the clearing away of the first course, someone came in to present Herodes the professor of rhetoric, as a special honour, with a palm-frond and a plaited wreath sent by a pupil who had won a con-

---

in Fourth-Century Corinth," in Friesen, James, and Schowalter, *Corinth in Contrast*, 166–86.

119. IKorinthKent §226 (reign of Hadrian). West (IKorinthWest, 97) argues that the phrase τῆς ἄλλης ἀρετῆς [ἁπάσης] (ll. 10–11) refers to Sospis's "general excellence (i.e. not only his excellence in speaking)."

test with an encomiastic oration. (*Quaest. conv.* 8.4.1 [723 A–B] [Minar, Sandbach, and Helmbold, LCL])

The pomposity and social superiority of Plutarch shines through in his revelation that he avoided the pedestrian banquets that Sospis hosted in which the plebs (i.e., foreign visitors and the citizens) were the guests. Rather, Plutarch attended those banquets where the "the men of learning" and Sospis's powerful *amici* (closest friends) were invited. Especially significant in this regard is the presence of Herodes Atticus at the banquet, the famous rhetorician and benefactor from Athens, who had spent time in Corinth and had financially underwritten various Corinthian civic projects. We are witnessing here how the Isthmian games, along with the other games throughout Greece,[120] attracted the philosophical and rhetorical glitterati of the eastern Mediterranean basin. As Nathan J. Barnes observes, "The games were attractive to many intellectuals and philosophers because they served as a platform for orations and debate."[121]

In sum, the upwardly mobile Corinthian believers craved leaders with oratorical reputation, maintained exclusivity within their self-congratulatory circles, and boasted in their discernment of what an accurate rhetorical evaluation of a leader really involved (2 Cor 10:10). The wise, powerful, and well-born of the Corinthian house churches would have been beguiled at an aspirational level by the boastful and self-sufficient values of the Corinthian elite, even though they personally fell short of the prestigious social rank of the *agōnothetai* at Corinth. Further, these self-serving and self-promoting values were also played out in the local associations, which mimicked the honorific system by means of its various accolades, pretentious-sounding offices, and banqueting culture sponsored by their benefactors. Last, as we have seen, the Isthmian games themselves had become a hotbed for philosophical debate and rhetorical posturing among the *agōnothetai*, visiting philosophers, and orators. The intense excitement generated by these "performances" would have trickled down throughout the congregation. Although Paul strategically sourced his athletic imagery (1 Cor 9:24–27) from the Isthmian games in order to depict the personal self-discipline required to live the other-centered life of being "all things

---

120. For evidence from the ancient sources charting the widespread philosophical discussion occurring during the games, see Nathan J. Barnes, *Reading 1 Corinthians with Philosophically Educated Women* (Eugene, OR: Pickwick, 2014), 135.

121. Ibid.

to all people" within a divided Corinthian body (9:19-23),[122] the potential downside conceptually for Paul was the value system sponsored by the rhetorical, philosophical, athletic, and civic celebrity circuit at Isthmia and Corinth.

As I have argued elsewhere, a wealthy and socially pretentious minority in the Corinthian hosted their Christian *collegia* and competed among themselves for status and pedigrees in the same way as the interloping intruders later did (1 Cor 1:11-12; 3:3-4, 18-20; 4:6b, 19-20; cf. 2 Cor 10:12). There is little doubt that the highly competitive rhetorical and intellectual culture associated with the Isthmian games, as well as the self-promoting behavior of the civic elites in Corinth, contributed to the hybristic behavior and values infecting the Corinthian house churches. This is the privileged social background from which, as L. L. Welborn has correctly argued,[123] the wrongdoer of 2 Corinthians originated. Was he a powerful and wealthy figure who hosted one of the house churches, used to inviting—as was Sospis—visiting orators and philosophers to his house for a soirée with the city's elite, thereby accruing deflected glory and increased social status? Presumably he would have been profoundly disappointed by the rhetorically incompetent, unpresentable, and impoverished apostle of Corinth (1 Cor 4:11; 2 Cor 6:10; 10:10b; 11:6a). Welborn suggests that the candidate in question was Gaius (Rom 16:23; 1 Cor 1:16).[124] While this is certainly possible, the wrongdoer may have been a more recent Corinthian convert than Gaius and, therefore, unidentifiable to us. As a new convert, this individual had flourished under the rhetorically powerful ministry of Apollos, having had his expectations aroused by the imminent arrival of the founding apostle, reputedly weighty in his epistolary word (2 Cor 10:10a) and pneumatically empowered (12:12)—only to have his hopes dashed by the unimpressive, weak, and rhetorical nothing who eventually arrived at Corinth (10:1, 10b; 11:20-21). Furthermore, the gospel of the apostle articulated a social policy at variance with his elitist presumptions regarding the order of the status quo. It is little wonder that the wrongdoer so vigorously opposed Paul in public (2 Cor 2:5-11; 7:12).

---

122. See Stephen C. Barton, "Was Paul a Relativist?" *Interchange* 19 (1976): 164-192; Barton, "'All Things to All People': Paul and the Law in the Light of 1 Corinthians 9.19-23," in *Paul and the Mosaic Law*, ed. James D. G. Dunn, WUNT 89 (Tübingen: Mohr Siebeck, 1996), 271-85.

123. Welborn, *An End to Enmity*, 301-53.

124. Ibid., 288-481.

In response, Paul dismantles the Corinthian boasting in rhetorical accomplishment by reference to the core values of the gospel of the crucified Christ. The ignominy and shame of the crucified Christ rendered obsolete the "wise man" (ποῦ σοφός;) and "debater of this age" (1 Cor 1:20a: ποῦ συζητητής;) because God's weakness and foolishness had overturned the power and wisdom of the world (1:17-18, 20b-25, 27; 2:6-7a; 4:20). The inversion of the world's values in Christ's cross (1 Cor 2:6-8) meant that Paul unleashed the power of the gospel by depending upon the Spirit in his preaching (2:4b, 5b, 13b),[125] rather than relying upon, as was the case with the orators of the world, human eloquence (2:1: καθ' ὑπεροχὴν λόγου) and human wisdom (1:17b: ἐν σοφίᾳ λόγου; 2:1: ἢ σοφίας; 2:4b: ἐν πειθοῖ[ς] σοφίας [λόγοις]; 2:5b: ἐν σοφίᾳ ἀνθρώπων; cf. 2:6b, 13a; 3:18-19).[126] The heavy emphasis on wisdom terminology is particularly revealing, especially since Paul sees Christ as the culmination of divine wisdom (1 Cor 1:30: ἐγενέθη σοφία ἡμῖν ἀπὸ θεοῦ). Not only is Paul pivoting here the wisdom of the world, exemplified in rhetoric, over against the gospel traditions about the wisdom of Christ (Matt 11:19; 11:28 [Sir 6:24-30]; 12:42; 13:54; Mark 6:2; Luke 2:40, 52; 7:35; 11:31, 49; 21:15), but the apostle is also summing up the entire Old Testament sapiental tradition in him.[127]

Boasting, therefore, in rhetorically gifted men is illegitimate (1 Cor 1:29, 31b; 3:21). In responding to the preference of some Corinthians for Apollos as an orator, Paul emphasizes that he and Apollos were united in the evangelistic and pastoral mission of the gospel (1 Cor 3:5-15). Paul's stance is that, while he has primacy as the church's founding apostle (1 Cor 3:6; 4:14-20), both he and Apollos are merely God's servants (3:5), with God and Christ having absolute primacy (3:6-9, 11). More generally, the apostles are consigned to being "last of all" (ἐσχάτους), sentenced to death as one of the worthless criminals condemned to fight wild animals in the last show of the day at the amphitheater (1 Cor 4:9a).[128]

---

125. See Timothy H. Lim, "'Not in Persuasive Words Of Wisdom, but in the Demonstration of the Spirit and Power,'" *NovT* 29 (1987): 137-49.

126. See Stephen M. Pogoloff, *Logos and Sophia: The Rhetorical Situation of 1 Corinthians*, SBLDS 134 (Atlanta: Scholars Press, 1992).

127. See Ben Witherington III, *Jesus the Sage: The Pilgrimage of Wisdom* (Minneapolis: Fortress, 1994).

128. See Cavan W. Concannon, "'Not for an Olive Wreath, but Our Lives': Gladiators, Athletes, and Early Christian Bodies," *JBL* 133 (2014): 193-214; James R. Unwin,

It is worth remembering in this regard that many of our self-important Corinthian *agōnothetai* had held the magistracy of *douvir* and thus probably had, as part of their official responsibilities under the Julian colonial charter, organized the gladiatorial and wild beast spectacles for the city. It is with deep irony, therefore, that Paul depicts himself, from an elite Corinthian perspective, as the dispensable and disposable human trash of the arena (4:9b, 13b). The relation of honorific culture to the ancient theater is worth considering here. The wealthy elites such as the *agōnothetai* and other dignitaries were given reserved front-row seats of honor in the theater,[129] the archaeological remains of which are still present in the theaters of Priene, Aphrodisias, and Hierapolis.[130]

The dishonored apostles, by contrast, shuffle last of all into the theater, appointed to die or perform there for the entertainment of the highly honored, including the celestial audience (4:9b). In sum, it was precisely the *elite* view of the spectacle that the *powerful* within the Corinthian churches had adopted in assessing and dismissing the ministry of their weak and suffering apostle (1 Cor 4:10). Yet the spectacle of the cross, where another condemned criminal was executed, had inverted the elite values of the world with a new wisdom and unprecedented power (1 Cor 1:23–25, 28–30). Paul's radical abdication of status pinpricks the pretentious claims of rhetoricians such as Nikias ("first [τὸν πρῶτον] among orators") and Poseidonius (πρῶτός τε ῥήτο[ρ]) at Isthmia and Corinth, respectively. Rather than boasting in Apollos or Paul, the Corinthians should realize that diversity of gifting is what makes God's church rich and vibrant in its ministry: it is an expression of the fact that all things are ours in Christ and God (1 Cor 3:21–23).

Last, we turn to the issue of the erasure of coronal honor (?) in the inscription of Nikias. Assuming that Broneer's restoration is correct, we

---

"'Thrown Down but Not Destroyed': Paul's Use of a Spectacle Metaphor in 2 Corinthians 4:7–15," *NovT*, forthcoming.

129. The benefactor Poseidippos is honored with "the front seats at the theater and the first place in a procession and (the privilege of) eating in the public festivals" (*SEG* 11.948; provenance: Cardamylae).

130. For Priene, see Ekrem Akurgl, *Ancient Civilizations and Ruins of Turkey*, 10th ed. (Istanbul: Net Turistik Yatinlar, 2007), 198, pl. 67 (top). For Aphrodisias, see Kenan T. Erin, *Aphrodisias: City of Venus Aphrodite* (London, Muller, Blond & White, 1986), 83 (lower picture). On inscriptions reserving seats at the theater of Ephesus for socially important civic groups, see Peter Scherrer, ed., *Ephesus: The New Guide*, rev. ed. (Turkey: Ege Yyinlari, 2000), 160.

see the force of Paul's assertion that coronal awards of honorific culture are "perishable" (1 Cor 9:25: φθαρτὸν στέφανον), even if Paul's imagery in this instance is drawn from the Isthmian games as opposed to the civic arena. Coronal awards belong to the world that is "passing away" (1 Cor 7:31), therefore Paul delays the award of an "imperishable crown" until the eschaton (1 Cor 9:25b: ἄφθαρτον).[131] But the believer's distinction—founded on Christ's imputed "righteousness" (2 Cor 5:21 [cf. 1 Cor 1:30]; Phil 3:9)[132]—will not be erased: God will come to their eschatological defense (cf. Rom 8:33) and allocate their crown (1 Cor 9:25b; cf. Phil 4:1; 1 Thess 2:19; cf. 2 Tim 4:8). In the present, however, while honorific culture has its legitimate place (1 Cor 12:21-25; cf. Rom 13:7b), Paul inverts the social hierarchy of honorific accolades, extending them from the most respectable to, in God's vast social reordering, the least respectable, weakest, and inferior within the body of Christ (1 Cor 12:22-25). Finally, in contrast to the intense fear of the erasure of honor in the ancient world, for Paul the experience of honor and dishonor are simply two different experiences of legitimate and praiseworthy service of Christ (2 Cor 6:8). The difference between the social worlds of Nikias and Paul could not be further apart.

7. Conclusion

We have investigated the little-studied figure of the *agōnothetēs*, concentrating on the inscriptional evidence of Ephesus, Isthmia, and Corinth for our study, as well as (where available) visual and numismatic evidence. Initially, such a study may have been presumed to have had little exegetical relevance for our understanding of the Corinthian epistles, given that that official is not mentioned in the New Testament, apart from the possible allusion to his role in awarding victorious athletes in Phil 3:14. However, we have seen that an examination of the *agōnothetai* inscriptions reveals in miniature many of the elitist civic values of the Roman colony of Corinth. These values not only impacted upon the socially influential in the Corinthian house churches but also reached to the very base of the social pyra-

---

131. See James R. Harrison, "'The Fading Crown': Divine Honour and the Early Christians," *JTS* 54 (2003): 493–529; Harrison, "Paul and the Athletic Ideal," 81–109.

132. Contra N. T. Wright, *Justification: God's Plan and Paul's Vision* (Downers Grove, IL: InterVarsity Press, 2009).

mid through the local associations, their benefactors, and socially diverse constituency.

Not only were the motifs of honor, triumph over dishonor, and boasting in the Corinthian epistles thereby illuminated—values characteristic of the *agōnothetai* inscriptions at Corinth—but also the divisive issues of rhetoric and wisdom within the house churches. New Testament scholars have underestimated the powerful influence that an *agōnothetēs* such as Nikias would have wielded as an orator in the city while serving as its most prestigious magistrate. Furthermore, the Isthmian games, like the other games of antiquity, had become a celebrated venue for philosophers and rhetoricians under the sponsorship of the *agōnothetai*.

The upwardly mobile would have been easily seduced by these values, coveting the prestigious pathways opened up to them through imperial priesthoods and the presidency of the Caesarean games. The gospel of Christ crucified set forth a radically different narrative of power and wisdom: service of the weak, foolish, and poor initiated though a compassionate and sacrificial identification with them.[133] It called believers away from the idolatry of the imperial and indigenous cults (1 Cor 8:10; 10:7–8, 14–22), with their allure of civic status, to the unprecedented Spirit-initiated experience of God in the body of Christ (1 Cor 3:16–17; 14:24–25). Thus the civic elites, who were dependent on inherited wealth and the sponsorship of the Roman ruler (cf. 1 Cor 2:8; 8:5–6), belonged to the passing age (7:31), whereas the "end of the ages" had dawned upon believers (10:11).

Works Cited

Akurgl, Ekrem. *Ancient Civilizations and Ruins of Turkey*. 10th ed. Istanbul: Net Turistik Yatinlar, 2007.
Amandry, Michel. *Le monnayage des duovirs Corinthiens*. BCHSup 15. Athens: École française d' Athènes; Paris: de Boccard, 1988.
Ameling, Walter. *Herodes Atticus*. 2 vols. Hildesheim: Olms, 1983.
Ascough, Richard S. *Paul's Macedonian Associations: The Social Context of Philippians and 1 Thessalonians*. WUNT 2/161. Tübingen: Mohr Siebeck, 2003.

---

133. 1 Cor 1:26–28; 8:11–12; 9:27; 11:22; 13:3; 2 Cor 6:10; 8:1–5, 9, 13–15; 11:16–12:10; 13:4.

Ascough, Richard S., Philip A. Harland, and John S. Kloppenborg, *Associations in the Greco-Roman World: A Sourcebook*. Waco, TX: Baylor University Press, 2012.

Barnes, Nathan J. *Reading 1 Corinthians with Philosophically Educated Women*. Eugene, OR: Pickwick, 2014.

Barton, Stephen C. "'All Things to All People': Paul and the Law in the Light of 1 Corinthians 9.19–23." Pages 271–85 in *Paul and the Mosaic Law*. Edited by James D. G. Dunn. WUNT 89. Tübingen: Mohr Siebeck, 1996.

———. "Was Paul a Relativist?" *Interchange* 19 (1976): 164–92.

Bash, Anthony. *Ambassadors for Christ: An Exploration of Ambassadorial Language in the New Testament*. WUNT 2/92. Tübingen: Mohr Siebeck, 1992.

Bitner, Bradley J. *Paul's Political Strategy in 1 Corinthians 1–4: Constitution and Covenant*. SNTSMS 163. Cambridge: Cambridge University Press, 2015.

Blümel, Wolfgang. *Die Inschriften von Iasos*. 2 vols. IGSK 28.1-2. Bonn: Habelt, 1985.

Brändle, Martin. *Der Agon bei Paulus: Herkunft und Profil paulinischer Agonmetaphorik*. WUNT 2/222. Tübingen: Mohr Siebeck, 2006.

Brookins, Timothy A. *Corinthian Wisdom, Stoic Philosophy and the Ancient Economy*. SNTSMS 159. Cambridge: Cambridge University Press, 2014.

———. "The (In)frequency of the Name 'Erastus' in Antiquity: A Literary, Papyrological, and Epigraphic Catalogue." *NTS* 59 (2013): 496–516.

Broneer, Oscar. "Excavations at Isthmia: Fourth Campaign, 1957–1958." *Hesperia* 28.4 (1959): 298–43.

———. *Terracotta Lamps*. Vol. 4.2 of *Corinth: Results of Excavations Conducted by the American School of Classical Studies at Athens*. Cambridge: Harvard University Press, 1930.

———. *Topography and Architecture*. Vol. 2 of *Isthmia*. Princeton: American School of Classical Studies at Athens, 1973.

Burstein, Stanley M. *The Hellenistic Age from the Battle of Ipsos to the Death of Kleopatra VII*. Cambridge: Cambridge University Press, 1985.

Camia, F. "Spending on the Agones: The Financing of Festivals in the Cities of Roman Greece." *Tyche* 26 (2011): 41–76.

Camia, F., and Maria Kantiréa. "The Imperial Cult in the Peloponnese." Pages 375–406 in *Society, Economy and Culture under the Roman*

Empire: Continuity and Innovation. Vol. 3 of *Roman Peloponnese*. Edited by Athanasios D. Rizakis and Claudia E. Lepenioti. Athens: National Hellenic Research Foundation, 2010.
Campbell, Joan Cecelia. *Phoebe: Patron and Emissary*. Collegeville, MN: Liturgical Press, 2009.
Carter, Michael. "A *Doctor Secutorum* and the *Retiarius* Draukos from Corinth." *ZPE* 12 (1999): 262–68.
Carter, Michael J. D. "Archiereis and Asiarchs: A Gladiatorial Perspective." *GRBS* 44 (2004): 41–68.
———. "The Presentation of Gladiatorial Spectacles in the Greek East: Roman Culture and Greek Identity." PhD diss., McMaster University, 1999.
Chow, John K. *Patronage and Power: A Study of Social Networks in Corinth*. JSNTSup 75. Sheffield: JSOT Press, 1992.
Clarke, Andrew D. *Secular and Christian Leadership in Corinth: A Sociohistorical and Exegetical Study of 1 Corinthians 1–6*. AGJU 18. Leiden: Brill, 1993.
Collange, Jean-François. *The Epistle of Saint Paul to the Philippians*. London: Epworth, 1979.
Collins, Raymond F. *The Power of Images in Paul*. Collegeville, MN: Glazier, 2008.
Concannon, Cavan W. "'Not for an Olive Wreath, but Our Lives': Gladiators, Athletes, and Early Christian Bodies." *JBL* 133 (2014): 193–214.
———. *"When You Were Gentiles": Specters of Ethnicity in Roman Corinth and Paul's Corinthian Correspondence*. New Haven: Yale University Press, 2014.
Danker, Frederick W. *Benefactor: Epigraphic Study of a Graeco-Roman and New Testament Field*. St. Louis: Clayton, 1982.
———. "On Stones and Benefactors." *CurTM* 8 (1981): 351–56.
Danylak, Barry N. "Tiberius Claudius Dinippus and the Food Shortages in Corinth." *TynBul* 59 (2008): 231–70.
Decker, Wolfgang. "Agonothetes." *BNP* 1:347–48.
Dio Chrysostom. *Discourses I–XI*. Translated by J. W. Cohoon. LCL. Cambridge: Harvard University Press, 1971.
Dmitriev, Sviatoslav. *City Government in Hellenistic and Roman Asia Minor*. Oxford: Oxford University Press, 2005.
Dondin-Payre, Monique, and Nicolas Tran, eds. *Collegia: Le phénomène associatif dans l'Occident romain*. Bordeaux: Ausonius, 2012.

Dutch, Robert S. *The Educated Elite in 1 Corinthians: Education and Community Conflict in Graeco-Roman Context.* JSNTSup 271. London: T&T Clark, 2005.
Edwards, G. Roger. "Panathenaics of Hellenistic and Roman Times." *Hesperia* 26 (1957): 320–49.
Engels, Donald W. *Roman Corinth: An Alternative Model for the Classical City.* Chicago: University of Chicago Press, 1990.
Erin, Kenan T. *Aphrodisias: City of Venus Aphrodite.* London, Muller, Blond & White, 1986.
Friesen, Steven J. "Prospects for a Demography of the Pauline Mission." Pages 351–70 in *Urban Religion in Roman Corinth: Interdisciplinary Approaches.* Edited by Daniel Schowalter and Steven J. Friesen. HTS 53. Cambridge: Harvard University Press, 2005.
———. "The Wrong Erastus: Ideology, Archaeology, and Exegesis." Pages 231–56 in *Corinth in Context: Comparative Studies on Religion and Society.* Edited by Steven J. Friesen, Daniel N. Schowalter, and James C. Walters. NovTSup 134. Leiden: Brill, 2010.
Fröhlich, Pierre, and Patrice Hamon, eds. *Groupes et associations dans cités grecques (IIIe siècle av. J.-C.–IIe siècle ap. J.-C.): Actes de la table ronde de Paris, INHA, 19–20 juin 2009.* Geneva: Droz, 2013.
Geagan, Daniel J. "The Isthmian Dossier of P. Licinius Priscus Juventianus." *Hesperia* 58 (1989): 349–60.
———. "Notes on the Agonistic Institutions of Roman Corinth." *GRBS* 9 (1968): 69–80.
Gebhard, Elizabeth R. "The Isthmian Games and the Sanctuary of Poseidon in the Early Empire." Pages 78–94 in *The Corinthia in the Roman Period: Including the Papers Given at a Symposium Held at The Ohio State University on 7–9 March, 1991.* Edited by Timothy E. Gregory. JRASup 8. Ann Arbor: Journal of Roman Archaeology, 1993.
———. "The Sanctuary of Poseidon on the Isthmus of Corinth and the Isthmian Games." Pages 82–88 in *Mind and Body: Athletic Contests in Ancient Greece.* Edited by Olga Alexandri. Athens: Ministry of Culture, National Hellenic Committee I.C.O.M., 1989.
Gill, D. W. J. "Erastus the Aedile," *TynBull* 40 (1989): 293–301.
Goodrich, John J. "Erastus, Quaestor of Corinth: The Administrative Rank of ὁ οἰκονόμος τῆς πόλεως (Rom 16:23) in an Achaean Colony." *NTS* 56 (2010): 90–115.
———. "Erastus of Corinth (Romans 16.23): Responding to Recent Proposals on His Rank, Status, and Faith." *NTS* 57 (2011): 583–86.

———. *Paul as an Administrator of God in 1 Corinthians*. SNTSMS 152. Cambridge: Cambridge University Press, 2012.
Harland, Philip A. *The North Coast of the Black Sea, Asia Minor*. Vol. 2 of *Greco-Roman Associations: Texts, Translations, and Commentary*. BZNW 204. Berlin: de Gruyter 2014.
Harrison, James R. "The Brothers as the 'Glory of Christ' (2 Cor 8:23): Paul's *Doxa* Terminology in Its Ancient Benefaction Context." *NovT* 52 (2010): 156–88.
———. "'The Fading Crown': Divine Honour and the Early Christians." *JTS* 54 (2003): 493–529.
———. "The Imitation of the Great Man in Antiquity: Paul's Inversion of a Cultural Icon." Pages 213–254 in *Christian Origins and Classical Culture: Social and Literary Contexts for the New Testament*. Edited by Stanley E. Porter and Andrew W. Pitts. Early Christianity in Its Hellenistic Context 1. TENTS 9. Leiden: Brill, 2013.
———. "In Quest of the Third Heaven: Paul and His Apocalyptic Imitators." *VC* 58 (2004): 24–55.
———. "Paul and Ancient Civic Ethics: Redefining the Canon of Honour in the Graeco-Roman World." Pages 75–118 in *Paul's Graeco-Roman Context*. Edited by Cilliers Breytenbach. BETL 277. Leuven: Peeters; Leuven University Press, 2015.
———. "Paul and the Athletic Ideal in Antiquity: A Case Study in Wrestling with Word and Image." Pages 81–109 in *Paul's World*. Edited by Stanley E. Porter. Pauline Studies 4. Leiden: Brill, 2007.
———. "Paul and the Gymnasiarchs: Two Approaches to Pastoral Formation in Antiquity." Pages 141–78 in *Paul: Jew, Greek, and Roman*. Edited by Stanley E. Porter. Pauline Studies 5. Leiden: Brill, 2008.
———. *Paul and the Imperial Authorities at Thessalonica and Rome: A Study in the Conflict of Ideology*. WUNT 273. Tübingen: Mohr Siebeck, 2011.
———. "Paul's House Churches and the Cultic Associations." *RTR* 58 (1999): 31–47.
———. *Paul's Language of Grace in Its Graeco-Roman Context*. WUNT 2/172. Tübingen: Mohr Siebeck, 2003.
———. "Times of Necessity." *NewDocs* 9:8–9.
Hartin, Patrick J. *Apollos: Paul's Partner or Rival?* Collegeville, MN: Liturgical Press, 2009.
Hawthorne, Gerald F. *Philippians*. WBC 43. Waco, TX: Word, 1983.
Jacobelli, Luciana. *Gladiators at Pompeii*. Los Angeles: J. Paul Getty Museum, 2003.

Johnson, Alan Chester, Paul Robinson Coleman-Norton, and Frank Card Bourne. *Ancient Roman Statutes*. Austin: University of Texas Press, 1961.

Judge, Edwin A. "The Conflict of Educational Aims in the New Testament." Pages 693–708 in Judge, *The First Christians in the Roman World: Augustan and New Testament Essays*. Edited by James R. Harrison. WUNT 229. Tübingen: Mohr Siebeck, 2008.

Kajava, Mika. "When Did the Isthmian Games Return to the Isthmus? Rereading Corinth 8.3.153." *CP* 97 (2002): 168–78.

Kent, John Harvey, ed. *The Inscriptions, 1926–1950*. Vol. 8.3 of *Corinth: Results of Excavations Conducted by the American School of Classical Studies at Athens*. Princeton: American School of Classical Studies at Athens, 1966.

Kloppenborg, John S., and Richard S. Ascough, eds. *Attica, Central Greece, Macedonia, Thrace*. Vol. 1 of *Greco-Roman Associations: Texts, Translations, and Commentary*. BZNW 181. Berlin: de Gruyter 2011.

Koester, Helmut, ed. *Cities of Paul: Images and Interpretations from the Harvard New Testament Archaeology Project*. Minneapolis: Fortress, 2005.

König, Jason. "Favorinus' Corinthian Oration in Its Corinthian Context." *CJ* 47 (2001): 141–71.

Krentz, Edgar. "Paul, Games and the Military." Pages 344–83 in *Paul and the Graeco-Roman World: A Handbook*. Edited by J. Paul Sampley. Harrisburg, PA: Trinity Press International, 2003.

Kyle, Donald G. *Athletics in Ancient Athens*. Leiden: Brill, 1993.

Leon, Harry J. *The Jews of Ancient Rome*. Philadelphia: Jewish Publication Society of America, 1960.

Lim, Timothy H. "'Not in Persuasive Words Of Wisdom, but in the Demonstration of the Spirit and Power.'" *NovT* 29 (1987): 137–49.

Litfin, A. Duane. *St. Paul's Theology of Proclamation: 1 Corinthians 1–4 and Greco-Roman Rhetoric*. SNTSMS 79. Cambridge: Cambridge University Press, 1994.

Marshall, Peter. "Invective: Paul and His Enemies in Corinth." Pages 359–73 in *Perspectives on Language and Text: Essays and Poems in Honor of Francis I. Andersen's Sixtieth Birthday July 29 1985*. Edited by Edgar W. Conrad and Edward G. Newing. Winona Lake, IN: Eisenbrauns, 1987.

Martin, Dale B. *The Corinthian Body*. New Haven: Yale University Press, 1995.

McCant, Jerry W. *2 Corinthians*, Readings. Sheffield: Sheffield Academic, 1999.
Meggitt, Justin J. "The Social Status of Erastus (Rom 16:23)." *NovT* 38 (1996): 218–23.
Meritt, Benjamin Dean. "Excavations at Corinth, 1927." *AJA* 31 (1927): 450–61.
———, ed. *Greek Inscriptions, 1896–1927*. Vol. 8.1 of *Corinth: Results of Excavations Conducted by the American School of Classical Studies at Athens*. Cambridge: American School of Classical Studies at Athens, 1931.
Mihaila, Corin. *The Paul-Apollos Relationship and Paul's Stance toward Graeco-Roman Rhetoric*. LNTS 402. London: T&T Clark, 2009.
Millis, Benjamin W. "The Local Magistrates and Elite of Roman Corinth." Pages 38–53 in *Corinth in Contrast: Studies in Inequality*. Edited by Steven J. Friesen, Sarah A. James, and Daniel N. Schowalter. NovTSup 155. Leiden: Brill, 2014.
Mitchell, Stephen, and David French. *From Augustus to the End of the Third Century AD*. Vol. 1 of *The Greek and Latin Inscriptions of Ankara (Ancyra)*. Vestigia 62. Munich: Beck, 2012.
Murphy-O'Connor, Jerome. "Corinth." *ABD* 1:1134–39.
Nagy, Blaise. "The Athenian Athlothetai." *GRBS* 19 (1978): 307–13.
Nguyen, V. Henry T. *Christian Identity: A Comparative Study of 2 Corinthians*. WUNT 2/243. Tübingen; Mohr Siebeck, 2008.
O'Brien, Peter T. *Commentary on Philippians: A Commentary on the Greek Text*. NIGTC. Grand Rapids: Eerdmans, 1991.
Osgood, Josiah. *Claudius Caesar: Image and Power in the Early Roman Empire*. Cambridge: Cambridge University Press, 2011.
Oster, Richard. "Holy Days in Honour of Artemis." *NewDocs* 4:74–82.
Overbeck, Johannes, and August Mau. *Pompeii*. 4th ed. Leipzig: Engelmann, 1884.
Papahatzis, Nicos. *Ancient Corinth: The Museums of Corinth, Isthmia and Sicyon*. Athens: Ekdotike Helados S.A., 1994.
Peterson, Brian K. *Eloquence and the Proclamation of the Gospel in Corinth*. SBLDS 163. Atlanta: Scholars Press, 1998.
Pfitzner, V. C. *Paul and the Agon Motif: Traditional Athletic Imagery in the Pauline Literature*. NovTSup 16. Leiden: Brill, 1967.
Philadelpheus, Alexandre. "Un Hermès d'Hérode Atticus." *BCH* 44 (1920): 170–80.

Plutarch. *Plutarch's Moralia*. Vol. 9. Translated by Edwin L. Minar Jr., F. H. Sandbach, and W. C. Helmbold. LCL. Cambridge: Harvard University Press, 1961.

Pogoloff, Stephen M. *Logos and Sophia: The Rhetorical Situation of 1 Corinthians*. SBLDS 134. Atlanta: Scholars Press, 1992.

Reisch, E. "Ἀθλοθέτης." PW 2.2:2063–65.

Richardson, Peter. "Augustan-Era Synagogues in Rome." Pages 17–29 in *Judaism and Christianity in First-Century Rome*. Edited by Karl P. Donfried and Peter Richardson. Grand Rapids: Eerdmans, 1998.

Robert, Louis. *Les gladiateurs dans l'orient grec*. Amsterdam: Hakkert, 1971.

———. *Hellenica: Recueil d'épigraphie, de numismatique et d'antiquités grecques*. 13 vols. Limoges: Bontemps, 1940–65.

Robinson, Betsey Ann. "'Good Luck' from Corinth: A Mosaic of Allegory, Athletics, and City Identity." *AJA* 116 (2012): 105–32.

———. *Histories of Peirene: A Corinthian Fountain in Three Millenia*. Princeton: American School of Classical Studies at Athens, 2011.

Rogers, Guy M. *The Mysteries of Artemis of Ephesos: Cult, Polis and Change in the Graeco-Roman World*. New Haven: Yale University Press, 2012.

Savage, Timothy B. *Power through Weakness: Paul's Understanding of the Christian Ministry in 2 Corinthians*. SNTSMS 86. Cambridge: Cambridge University Press, 1996.

Scherrer, Peter, ed. *Ephesus: The New Guide*. Rev. ed. Turkey: Ege Yyinlari, 2000.

Schowalter, Daniel N. "Regilla Standing By: Reconstructed Statuary and Re-inscribed Bases in Fourth-Century Corinth." Pages 166–86 in *Corinth in Contrast: Studies in Inequality*. Edited by Steven J. Friesen, Sarah A. James, and Daniel N. Schowalter. NovTSup 155. Leiden: Brill, 2014.

Shear, Theodore Leslie. "Excavations at Corinth in 1925." *AJA* 29 (1925): 381–97.

———. "Excavations in the Theatre District of Corinth in 1926." *AJA* 30 (1926): 444–63.

Slater, William J. "The Pantomime Tiberius Iulius Apolaustus." *GRBS* 36 (1995): 263–92.

Spawforth, Antony J. S. "Corinth, Argos and the Imperial Cult: Pseudo-Julian, Letters 198." *Hesperia* 63 (1994): 211–32.

Strelan, Rick. *Paul, Artemis and the Jews in Ephesus*. BZNW 80. Berlin: de Gruyter, 1996.

Tobin, Jennifer. *Patronage and Conflict under the Antonines.* Amsterdam: Gieben, 1997.
Unwin, James R. "'Thrown Down but Not Destroyed': Paul's Use of a Spectacle Metaphor in 2 Corinthians 4:7–15." *NovT*, forthcoming.
Valavanis, Panos. *Games and Sanctuaries in Ancient Greece: Olympia, Delphi, Isthmia, Nemea, Athens.* Los Angeles: J. Paul Getty Museum, 2004.
Vanhove, D. ed. *Le sport dans la Grèce antique: Du jeu à la compétition.* Brussels: Palais des Beaux-Arts, 1992.
Verboven, Koenraad. "The Associative Order, Status and Ethos of Roman Businessmen in Late Republic and Early Empire." *Athenaeum* 95 (2007): 861–93.
Walters, James C. "Civic Identity in Roman Corinth and Its Impact on Early Christians." Pages 319–418 in *Urban Religion in Roman Corinth: Interdisciplinary Approaches.* Edited by Daniel Schowalter and Steven J. Friesen. HTS 53. Cambridge; Harvard University Press, 2005.
Wankel, Hermann, et al., eds. *Die Inschriften von Ephesos.* 8 vols. Bonn: Habelt, 1979–1984
Welborn, L. L. *An End to Enmity: Paul and the "Wrongdoer" of Second Corinthians.* BZNW 185. Berlin: de Gruyter, 2011.
———. *Paul, the Fool of Christ: A Study of 1 Corinthians 1–4 in the Comic-Philosophic Tradition.* JSNTSup 293. London: T&T Clark, 2005.
———. "The Runaway Paul." *HTR* 92 (1999): 115–63.
———. "'That There May Be Equality': The Contexts and Consequences of a Pauline Ideal." *NTS* 59 (2013): 73–90.
Weiss, Alexander. "Keine Quästoren in Korinth: Zu Goodrichs (und Theißens) These über das Amt des Erastos (Röm 16:23)." *NTS* 56 (2011): 576–81.
White, Adam G. *Where Is the Wise Man? Graeco-Roman Education as Background to the Divisions in 1 Corinthians 1–4.* LNTS 536. London: Bloomsbury T&T Clark, 2015.
White, L. Michael. "Favorinus's 'Corinthian Oration': A Piqued Panorama of the Hadrianic Forum." Pages 61–110 in *Urban Religion in Roman Corinth: Interdisciplinary Approaches.* Edited by Daniel Schowalter and Steven J. Friesen. HTS 53. Cambridge: Harvard University Press, 2005.
Wilson, Stephen G. "Voluntary Associations: An Overview." Pages 1–15 in *Voluntary Associations in the Graeco-Roman World.* Edited by John S. Kloppenborg and Stephen G. Wilson. London: Routledge, 2003.

Winter, Bruce W. *After Paul Left Corinth: The Influence of Secular Ethics and Social Change*. Grand Rapids: Eerdmans, 2001.

———. *Philo and Paul among the Sophists*. SNTSMS 96. Cambridge: Cambridge University Press, 1996.

———. "Secular and Christian Responses to Corinthian Famines." *TynBull* 40 (1989): 86–106.

———. "The Toppling of Favorinus and Paul by the Corinthians." Pages 291–306 in *Early Christianity and Classical Culture: Comparative Studies in Honour of Abraham J. Malherbe*. Edited by John T. Fitzgerald, Thomas H. Olbright, and L. Michael White. NovTSup 110. Leiden: Brill, 2003.

Witherington, Ben, III. *Jesus the Sage: The Pilgrimage of Wisdom*. Minneapolis: Fortress, 1994.

Wright, N. T. *Justification: God's Plan and Paul's Vision*. Downers Grove, IL: InterVarsity Press, 2009.

Zuiderhoek, Arjan. *The Politics of Munificence in the Roman Empire: Citizens, Elites and Benefactors in Asia Minor*. Cambridge: Cambridge University Press, 2009.

Contributors

Bradley J. Bitner (PhD, 2013, Macquarie University, Sydney) is currently Tutor in New Testament and Greek at Oak Hill College, London. Recent publications include *Paul's Political Strategy in 1 Corinthians 1–4: Constitution and Covenant* (Cambridge: Cambridge University Press, 2015).

Cavan Concannon (PhD, 2010) is Assistant Professor of Religion at the University of Southern California. He is the author of *'When You Were Gentiles': Specters of Ethnicity in Roman Corinth and Paul's Corinthian Correspondence* (Yale University Press, 2014), *Assembling Early Christianity: Trade, Networks, and the Letters of Dionysios of Corinth* (Cambridge University Press, 2017), and editor (with Lindsey Mazurek) of *Across the Corrupting Sea: Post-Braudelian Approaches to the Ancient Eastern Mediterranean* (Routledge, 2016).

Kathy Ehrensperger (PhD, 2002) is Research Professor of the New Testament in Jewish Context, at the Abraham Geiger College, University of Potsdam. Recent publications include *Paul and the Dynamics of Power* (T&T Clark, 2008) and *Paul at the Crossroads of Cultures* (T&T Clark, 2013).

James R. Harrison studied Ancient History at Macquarie University and graduated from the doctoral program in 1997. Professor Harrison is the Research Director at the Sydney College of Divinity and an Honorary Associate of Macquarie University Ancient History Department. His recent publications include *Paul's Language of Grace in Its Graeco-Roman Context* (Mohr Siebeck, 2003) and *Paul and the Imperial Authorities at Thessalonica and Rome* (Mohr Siebeck, 2011).

Fredrick J. Long (PhD, 1999) is Professor of New Testament and Director of Greek Instruction at Asbury Theological Seminary. Recent publications include *Koine Greek Grammar* (GlossaHouse, 2015) and *2 Corinthians: A Handbook on the Greek Text* (Baylor University Press, 2015).

Michael Peppard is Associate Professor of Theology at Fordham University in New York. His most recent book is *The World's Oldest Church: Bible, Art, and Ritual at Dura-Europos, Syria* (Yale University Press, 2016).

David K. Pettegrew (PhD, 2006) is Associate Professor of History at Messiah College. His recent publications include *The Isthmus of Corinth: Crossroads of the Mediterranean World* (University of Michigan Press, 2016) and (with W. R. Caraher and R. S. Moore) *Pyla-Koutsopetria I: Archaeological Survey of an Ancient Coastal Town* (American Schools of Oriental Research, 2014).

L. L. Welborn (PhD, 1992) studied New Testament and Early Christianity at Vanderbilt University and the University of Chicago and is currently Professor of New Testament and Early Christianity at Fordham University. Recent publications include *Paul, the Fool of Christ: A Study of 1 Corinthians 1–4 in the Comic-Philosophic Tradition* (T&T Clark, 2005) and *An End to Enmity: Paul and the "Wrongdoer" of Second Corinthians* (de Gruyter, 2011).

Primary Sources Index

Old Testament

Genesis
  1–3   92
  1:26–27   248

Exodus
  4:10 (LXX   239
  33–34   240

Numbers
  16   240

2 Kings
  2:15–16   124
  25:5   249

Psalms
  133:1   149

Isaiah
  11:1–5   124
  14:12   220
  14:14   220
  61:1   124

Daniel
  11:30 LXX   257

Joel
  2:28   124

Deuterocanonical Books

Wisdom of Solomon
  7:25–26   243, 247

Sirach
  6:24–30   314

1 Maccabees
  14:26   237
  14:27–45   237
  15:3   237

1 Esdras
  4:49   236
  4:53   236

3 Maccabees
  3:28   237

4 Maccabees
  5:30   249

Pseudepigrapha

Ascension of Isaiah
  4.1–4   257
  4:2   224

Testament of Job
  49.1–50.3   127

Sibylline Oracles
  3.63   257
  5.140   257

Sibylline Oracles (cont.)
11.74	237
14.309	237

Dead Sea Scrolls

1QS	
3–4	220, 243, 257
War Scroll	224

Ancient Jewish Writers

Josephus, *Antiquitates judaicae*
4.213	118
19.4	235
19.11	235

Josephus, *Bellum judaicum*
3.540	171

Josephus, *Contra Apionem*
2.132	250

Philo, *De cherubim*
107	237

Philo, *De confusione linguarum*
93–94	237

Philo, *Legatio ad Gaium*
29.188	235
43.346	235
116	237
147	237
287	237

Philo, *De sacrificiis Abelis et Caini*
117	237

Philo, *De specialibus legibus*
1.57	237
4.137–139	118

New Testament

Matthew
11:19	314
11:28	314
12:42	314
13:54	314
22:20	249

Mark
6:2	314
10:13–31	145
12:16	249
12:42–44	301
13:11	147

Luke
2:40	314
2:52	314
7:35	314
11:31	314
11:49	314
20:24	249
21:15	314

John
3:5	145
12:31	219, 223
14:30	219, 223
16:11	219, 223

Acts
9:23–25	304
18:8	69
18:11	7
18:12	50
18:12–16	235
18:12–17	10, 21
18:24	86, 276
18:24–28	308
19:8–10	278
20:31	278
25:26	247

PRIMARY SOURCES INDEX

Romans	
1–3	254
1:14	27
1:21	117
1:23	249
1:25	117
4:24	244
5:17	244
5:21	244
6:3–4	98
6:23	244
7:25	244
8:1–30	144
8:29	249
8:33	316
8:38	223
8:39	244, 249
12:10	300
12:18	129
13:7	300, 316
13:8–10	300
13:8–19	27
14:15–21	144
15:7	300
15:27	105
16	67
16:1–2	26, 273
16:2	300–301
16:20	223
16:22	67, 68
16:23	16, 67, 70–71, 313

1 Corinthians	
1:10	148
1:10–12	75
1:11	68, 89
1:11–12	313
1:12	86, 276, 308
1:13	96
1:14	69, 70
1:14–16	75
1:16	68, 120, 313
1:17	314
1:17–18	314
1:18–2:2	121

1:18–2:5	125
1:20	314
1:20–25	314
1:22–24	254
1:23–25	315
1:26	66, 273, 288, 299
1:26–28	65, 317
1:26–30	17
1:27	12, 276, 299, 314
1:28	27, 299
1:28–30	315
1:29	12, 314
1:30	12, 92, 314, 316
1:31	314
2:1	92, 314
2:1–5	276, 308
2:4	314
2:5	314
2:6	11, 223, 314
2:6–7	92, 314
2:6–8	121, 219, 314
2:8	11, 223, 317
2:9–16	121
2:13	105, 314
3:1	105
3:3–4	313
3:4–6	86, 308
3:5	314
3:5–9	276
3:5–15	314
3:5–4:5	17
3:6	314
3:6–9	314
3:7	309
3:8	309
3:9	17
3:11	314
3:13	92
3:15–5:1	144
3:16	93
3:16–17	317
3:18	309
3:18–19	314
3:18–20	313
3:19–21	276

1 Corinthians (cont.)

3:21	276, 309, 314	7:13	120, 254
3:21–23	315	7:14	254
3:22	86	7:15	254
4	73, 141	7:18	92
4:1–25	144	7:21	66, 120
4:6	86, 276, 308, 313	7:22	66
4:7	309	7:26	277, 299
4:8	73, 276	7:31	12, 316, 317
4:9	314, 315	8	135
4:10	309, 315	8–10	87, 112, 227, 240
4:11	16, 313	8–11	119, 128
4:13	315	8:1	12
4:14	146	8:1–11:1	96
4:14–5:13	147	8:5	107, 223, 227, 247
4:14–15	147	8:5–6	11, 20, 317
4:14–20	314	8:6	92, 247
4:16	147	8:7	107
4:18–20	309	8:7–13	12
4:19–20	313	8:10	12, 317
4:20	144	8:11	135
4:21	308	8:11–12	135, 317
5	96, 135, 143	8:13	92
5:1	92	9:1	240
5:1–13	147	9:3–18	309
5:3–4	96, 147	9:5	86
5:5	223	9:11	105
5:7–8	92	9:19	13
5:13	141	9:19–23	313
6	143, 144	9:20	13
6:1–8	20, 134, 148	9:21	13
6:1–11, pp. 133-51	133	9:22	13
6:5	146	9:24	279
6:5–8	134	9:24–27	12, 28, 312
6:6	146, 254	9:25	13, 316
6:8	149	9:26	279
6:9	133, 145, 148	9:27	12, 317
6:9–10	147	10	85, 92, 227, 240
6:9–11	134, 144	10:1–10	92
6:11	147	10:2	96
6:12	107	10:3	95, 100
6:19	17, 93	10:7	28
6:20	66	10:7–8	317
7:5	223	10:11	12, 317
7:12	254	10:14	107, 240
		10:14–22	12, 28, 317

10:16	227	13	125, 127
10:16–21	240	13:3	317
10:17	227	14	106, 126, 127
10:18	227	14:22	254
10:19–21	240	14:23	254
10:20	107, 227	14:24	254
10:21	227	14:24–25	17, 317
10:23	12, 107	14:34	92
10:24	13	14:37	105
10:27	254	15:3–4	92
10:27–28	240	15:5	86
10:28–29	12	15:21–22	92
10:32	12, 254	15:24	223
10:33	13	15:24–25	144
11	67	15:25	244
11:1	13, 244	15:27	92
11:7	249	15:29	33, 87, 96
11:8–9	92	15:44–45	92
11:12	92	15:49	249
11:17–24	19	15:50	144
11:17–34	19, 66	16:1–4	73
11:18	74, 148	16:7	89
11:21	66	16:8	92
11:22	17, 67, 73, 300, 317	16:12	86
11:29–30	67	16:15	68–69, 301
11:33	300	16:16	301
12–14	106	16:17	68, 301
12:1–11	105–32	16:18	301
12:2	28, 106–21		
12:3	28, 121–22	2 Corinthians	
12:3–11	105	1:15–16	228
12:4–5	122	2:5–11	313
12:4–11	122–27, 301	2:11	223
12:8–10	125	2:12–13	89
12:9	105, 126	2:14	228–29, 241, 254–55, 260
12:10	126	2:14–15	228, 239
12:12–13	96	2:14–16	89
12:12–27	93	2:14–17	241, 256
12:13	27, 96	2:14–3:1	234
12:21–25	316	2:14–3:18	241
12:22–25	299, 316	2:14–7:2	224, 227–28, 230, 234, 240
12:24	299	2:15	233, 241
12:25	148	2:16	239
12:26	300	2:16–17	239
12:28	301	2:16–3:18	240

2 Corinthians (cont.)

Reference	Pages	Reference	Pages
2:17	241, 310	8:1–6	301
3	85, 92, 240	8:9	17, 301, 317
3:1	276	8:13–15	301, 317
3:1–3	310	8:14	74
3:1–4	239	8:20	74
3:1–18	241	10:1	302, 308, 313
3:1–4:6	224	10:2	276, 302
3:3–18	92	10:8	302
3:5-12	239	10:9–11	302
3:6	92	10:10	146, 276, 302, 304, 308, 312–13
3:7–16	254	10:12	276, 302, 313
3:12–16	240	10:13	302
3:14	92	10:15	302
3:14–16	254	10:16	302
3:16–18	245	10:17	302
3:17	236, 239, 260	11:1–12:18	302
3:17–18	240	11:3	92
3:18	241, 247, 249	11:4	94
4:1	229, 241, 260	11:5	302
4:1–3	232	11:6	276, 302, 313
4:1–6	224, 232, 240–41, 254–59, 260	11:7	308
4:1–5:10	241	11:10	302
4:2	241	11:12	302
4:2–6	244	11:12–15	276
4:3	241	11:13	302
4:3–6	260	11:14	223, 258, 259, 260
4:4	223, 219–69	11:16	302
4:4–6	253	11:16–29	302
4:5	241–43, 245, 247	11:16–12:10	317
4:6	92, 242, 243	11:17	302
5:3–4	233	11:18	302
5:11–7:1	241	11:19–21	276
5:21	13, 92, 316	11:20–21	313
6:8	301, 316	11:21	304
6:10	17, 301, 313, 317	11:21–29	302
6:11	227, 254	11:22	86
6:14	227, 240, 254	11:22–23	276, 304
6:14-16	227, 255, 260	11:23	304
6:14–7:1	224, 227, 240, 254–59	11:23–29	304
6:15	224, 257, 258, 260	11:27	17
6:16	234	11:29	304
7:2	228, 260	11:30	302, 304
7:12	313	11:30–33	304
8:1–5	17, 317	12:1	302
		12:1–4	304

12:4	305	4:27	223
12:5	302, 305	5:5	145, 244
12:6	302, 305	5:21	301
12:7	223, 305	6:11	223
12:8–9	305	6:12	105, 223, 245
12:9	302	6:16	223
12:10	305		
12:11	302	Philippians	
12:11–13	276	2:9	247
12:12	302, 313	2:11	247
12:12–21	228	3:9	316
12:14–18	309	3:12–14	279
12:16–18	302	3:14	275, 316
13:1–2	228	3:19	223
13:4	305, 317	4:1	316
13:10	228		
		Colossians	
Galatians		1:13	223
3–4	144	1:15	249
3:15–5:1	136	1:16	223
3:23–4:7	144	2:10	223, 244
4:8	223	2:15	223, 229, 244
5	144	3:10	249
5:13	144	3:11	27
5:16–26	144	3:18–25	145
5:21	144, 145	3:24	145
5:22–6:1	145	3:24–25	145
6:1	105		
		1 Thessalonians	
Ephesians		2:11–12	144
1:3	245	2:14–16	254
1:3–14	254	2:18	223
1:13–14	145	2:19	316
1:17–18	145	4:3–8	148
1:19–23	244	4:9	148
1:20	245	5:21	125
1:21	223		
2:1–3	254	2 Thessalonians	
2:2	219, 223	2:4	223
2:6	245	2:9	223
3:10	223, 245	3:3	223
4:5	244		
4:8–11	229	1 Timothy	
4:13	244	1:20	223
4:20–22	244	3:6–7	223

336   PRIMARY SOURCES INDEX

1 Timothy (cont.)
5:8 — 254
5:15 — 223

2 Timothy
2:26 — 223
4:8 — 316

Titus
1:15 — 254
3:1 — 223

Hebrews
10:1 — 249

James
1:9–10 — 300
1:27 — 300
2:1–7 — 300

Revelation
13:14 — 249
13:15 — 249
14:9 — 249
14:11 — 249
15:2 — 249
16:2 — 249
19:20 — 249
20:4 — 249

Early Christian Literature

Apostolic Constitutions and Canons
7.39.4 — 237

Didache
7.1 — 145

Ignatius, *To the Ephesians*
10.3 — 148
16.1 — 148

Ignatius, *To the Philadelphians*
3.3 — 148
5.1 — 148

Ignatius, *To the Romans*
6.1 — 148
6.2 — 148

Irenaeus, *Adversus haereses*
4.48 — 220

Tertullian, *Apologeticus*
33.4 — 234

Tertullian, *Adversus Marcionem*
5.11 — 220

Greco-Roman Literature

Aelius Aristides, *Orationes*
47.23 — 108

Alciphron, *Letters of Parasites*
24 [3.60.1] — 52
24 [3.60.2] — 52
24 [3.60.3] — 53

Anthologia Graeca
7.297 — 8
7.493 — 9
9.151 — 9
9.284 — 8

Appian, *Bella civilia*
136.4–6 — 10

Appian, *Punica*
136 — 70

Apuleius, *Metamorphoses*
10.18 — 56
10.18–35 — 51

Aristophanes, *Thesmophoriazusae*
647–648 — 163

Athenaeus, *Deipnosophistae*
12.29.525c — 4

PRIMARY SOURCES INDEX

Aurelius Victor, *De Caesaribus*		43.50.3–5	70
3	246	59.9	295
		59.26	235
Calpurnius Flaccus, *Declamations*	140	60.24	10
		60.30.2	230
Calpurnius Siculus, *Eclogae*		63.11.1	10
4.92–94	235	63.11–15	258
4.142	236	63.16.1	168
4.142–144	235		
		Dio Chrysostom, *De concordia cum*	
Cicero, *De oratore*		*Apamensibus*	
3.53	308	3–4	301
Cicero, *De divinatione*		Dio Chrysostom, *Contio*	
1.128	123	22	309
Cicero, *De legibus*		Dio Chrysostom, *Corinthiaca*	49, 310
2.19.5	115	8	49
2.27	115	36	50
3.28.3	247		
		Dio Chrysostom, *De virtute*	
Cicero, *De natura deorum*		9	310
1.55–56	123		
2.166–167	110	Diodorus Siculus, *Bibliotheca historica*	
3.2.5	109	27.1	8
		32.4.5	8
Cicero, *De republica*		fr. 7.9.2–6	2
1.69.12	247		
2.47.1–3	247	Herodotus, *Histories*	
		3.48–53	4
Cicero, *Tusculanae disputations*		3.52	3
3.22	10	5.92	2, 4
3.53	9		
		Hesiod, *Theogonia*	
Codex justinianus		94–96	235
8.46.6	140		
		Homer, *Iliad*	
Columella, *Res rustica*		2.570	2, 48
11.1.19	116	6.152–153	2
		13.664	2
Democritus of Ephesus			
FGrHist 267 F 1	4	Homer, *Odyssey*	
		11.734	2
Dio Cassius, *Historia romana*			
28.8	235	Iamblichus, *De mysteriis*	250

338 PRIMARY SOURCES INDEX

Isocrates, *Ad Nicoclem*
5–9   308

Livy, *Ab urbe condita*
42.16   164

Lucan, *Pharsalia*
2.312–322   238
2.343–344   238

Menander Rhetor, *Epitrepontes*
2.1–2   249

Nicolaus of Damascus
FGrHist 90 F 59   3

Pausanias, *Graeciae descriptio*
2.1.2   7, 8, 190
2.1.5   173
2.2.8   94
2.3.1   20
2.3.3   3
2.3.5   97
2.3.6   3, 15
2.3.8   3
2.4.6   90
2.11.2   279
7.16.8   7, 190
7.17.2   10
7.17.4   10
8.22.3   97

Philostratus, *Nero*
3–4   171

Philostratus, *Vita Apollonii*
5.19   171

Philostratus, *Vitae sophistarum*
489–492   310

Plato, *Euthydemus*
302C   114

Plato, *Respublica*
2.371C   69

Pliny the Elder, *Naturalis historia*
4.6.22   10
4.9–10   163
33.54   230

Pliny the Younger, *Epistulae*
10.65.3   141
10.66.2   141

Plutarch, *Aratus*
40   3

Plutarch, *Caesar*
57.5   10
57.5   70

Plutarch, *De defectu oraculorum*
13.52–53 [416F]   113

Plutarch, *Titus Flamininus*
12.13   10

Plutarch, *De fraterno amore*
8 (482E)   142
9, 11 (482D)   143
11 (483E–F)   142–43
17 (488B–C)   141

Plutarch, *Praecepta gerendae rei publicae*
20 (816D)   50

Plutarch, *Quaestionum convivialium libri IX*
8.4.1 (723 A–B)   312
8.8.4 (730D–E)   297
9.2 (737A)   7

Plutarch, *Regum et imperatorum apophthegmata*
Agothocles 3 (176F)   249

PRIMARY SOURCES INDEX 339

Plutarch, *De vitando aere alieno*
   7 (830D–831B)   50–51

Polybius, *Histories*
   4.19.7–9   164
   5.101   163
   5.101.4   164
   8.3–11   7
   18.46   190
   39.7–17   7

Quintilian, *Institutio oratoria*
   7.4.10–12   140

Res gestae divi Augusti   241

Seneca the Elder, *Controversiae*
   1.1   139–40
   1.1.3   140
   1.1.6   140
   1.1.7   140
   1.1.10   140
   1.1.23   140
   1.4   140
   1.6   140
   1.7   140
   1.8   140
   2.1   140
   2.2   140
   2.4   140, 142
   2.4.13   142
   2.7   140
   3.3   140
   3.3.1   141
   3.4   140
   4.3   140
   4.5   140
   4.6   140
   5.2   140
   5.3   140
   5.4   140
   6.1   140
   6.2   140
   6.3   140, 143
   6.7   143
   7.1   140
   7.1.25   140
   7.3   140
   7.5   140
   7.5.1   141
   8.3   140
   8.5   140
   9.3   140
   9.4   140
   9.5   140
   9.5.6   141
   10.2   140

Seneca the Younger, *De clementia*
   1.1   235
   1.7.2   235
   1.9–10   232
   1.19.8   235

Seneca the Younger, *De superstitione*
   Ep. 95.47   118

Seneca the Younger, *Epistulae morales*
   14.13   238, 247

Strabo, *Geographica*
   4.1.1   245
   5.1.6   245
   5.3.8   245
   6.2.4   3
   7.5.8   3
   8.2.1   160, 163
   8.5.5   292
   8.6.4   160
   8.6.20   48–49, 156
   8.6.22   160
   8.6.23   7, 10, 49, 70, 190
   10.2.8   3
   17.1.6   245

Suetonius, *Gaius Caligula*
   49.2   230

Suetonius, *Divus Claudius*
   16   295

Suetonius, Divus Claudius (cont.)		3.8–16	164
17	230	6.3.2	3
24.3	230	8.1–10	164
25	10	8.7–10	163
25.3	10, 50		

Timaeus
    FGrHist 566 F 80   3

Suetonius, Gaius		Valerius Maximus, *Facta et dicta*	
22	235	*memorabilia*	
Suetonius, Nero		1.1a–b	109
16.2	177		
19.2	171	**INSCRIPTIONS AND PAPYRI**	
24.2	10		
25	230	*L'Année épigraphique*	
32	258	2004.1354	207
Suetonius, Tiberius		Ascough, Harland, and Kloppenborg,	
20	230	*Associations*	
		25	273
Suetonius, Vespasianus		26	273
8.4	10	31	274
		90	274
Tacitus, Annales		92	274
1.76.4	10, 50	98	274
1.80.1	10	109	274
2.41	230	115	274
6.18	292	117	274
13.8	230	120	274
14.1–8	258	155	274
15.42	168	158	274
15.54	177	160	274
15.64	239	162	274
16.35	239	177	274
		185	274
Tacitus, Historiae		187	274
4.42.31	247	234	274
		235	274
Theophrastus, Characteres		237	274
11	52	242	274
		243	274
Thucydides, History of the Peloponnesian		245	274
War		257	274
1.13.2–5	5	300	274
1.24.2	3	303	275
1.56.2	3		

312	274	IEph	
313	274	1.24A, B, C	289
323	274	3.730	288
		3.946	289
Bulletin épigraphique		3.956A	289
1990.103	201	5.1457	281
		7.3072	282
BGU			
1197.I.15	246	*Inscriptiones Graecae*	
		2.4313	198
Chrest.Wilck.		4.1.431	198
312	246	4.203	206, 287
		4.698	198
Corpus des inscriptions de Delphes		4.795	210
4.143.2–3	141	5.1.1243	292
		5.2.541–42	292
Corpus Inscriptionum Graecarum		7.106	307
3.6174	198	7.2713.34	259
		11.4.1173	198
Corpus Inscriptionum Judaicarum		14.1264	198
284	274		
301	274	*Inscriptiones graecae ad res romanas*	
338	274	*pertinentes*	
365	274	3.328	245
368	274	4.813	72
416	274	4.1435	72
425	274	4.1630	72
496	274	40	9
503	274	41	194, 197, 212
		44	197
Corpus Inscriptionum Latinarum		50	221
3.536	213		
5.1305	56	IKorinthKent	
6.1.857	198	53	60, 221
6.3956	56	57	91
6.4454	56	62	273
6.11541	56	82	11
		116	213
Iasos		125	16
94	309	128–29	310
		130	15
IDelos		137	13
5.2342	197	139	197
		149–51	13
		150	13, 210, 295

IKorinthKent (cont.)		322	15, 210
150–51	58	323	15, 59
152	56, 188	327	15
153	15, 21, 221, 280, 297, 298	333	15
154	210	334	15
155	22, 59	336	199
156	15, 210	342	213
158	295, 298	361	90
158–63	60, 64, 277, 298	393–94	277
159	210	433	199
170	210	724	17
171	210	728	17
173	210		
176	59	IKorinthMeritt	
170	15	14	280, 291
200	208	19	221
201	208	31	211
203	210	70	211
208	210	71	194, 195, 212
208–30	13	74	210
209	210	76	210
212	210, 294, 303	80	210, 291
213	210	81	210
214	210	102	211
217	210	106	211
224	13	130	212
226	307, 311		
231–38	13	IKorinthStroud	
232	16, 276	14	33
233	13	28	33
241	22	127	28
251	55		
259	59	IKorinthWest	
264	307	1	5, 211
268	307	2–3	22
272	295	15	188, 210
276	13, 213	17	210
303	87	65	213
305	213	67	58, 63–64, 210, 291–93
306	14, 185, 201–2, 213, 287	68	58, 63, 64, 65, 210, 211, 291, 294–96, 303–4
307	307		
310	213	70	287
311	15	71	210, 291
314	15	72	210, 291
321	14	77	60

81	210, 291, 296–98
82	55
82–85	210
83	298
84	55
120	55
83	
86	291, 298–99, 304
86–90	60, 64
86–91	210
87–90	298
93	291
98–99	22
100–101	22
104^a	210
105	291
110	293
117	211
120	15, 55
122	15
124–25	14
125	14
130	15
131	22
132	59
153	303
193	211

Inscriptiones latinae selectae

1514	68

IPergamon

374	251

Isthmia

I-261	201, 202

MAMA

6, list 149, 162, ll. 5–6	307

O.Camb.

30	247

O.Deiss.

36A	246

39	246

O.Elkab

34	246

O.Erem.

1	246
8	246

Orientis Graeci Inscriptiones Selectae

90	248
458	244
533	297
606	246
655.1–2	245

O.Petr.

84	246
85	246
86	246

O.Stras.

75	246
84	246
85	246
88	246
265	246
266	246
267	246
269	246

O.Wilck.

418	246
419	246
420	246
422	246
1038	246
1040	246

P.Cair.

10575	136

P.Gen.

95	246

P.Heid.
  257   246
  258   246

P. Lond.
  1215   246

P.Mert.
  12   246

P.Oxy.
  42.3057   301
  246   246
  1143.4–5   246

P.Turner
  34   143

Robert, *Les gladiateurs*
  6   282
  59   282
  61   283
  86   297
  97   282
  99   282
  152   282

Sammelbuch griechischer Urkunden aus Aegypten
  13301   136
  9572   246
  12008   246
  13279   246

Supplementum epigraphicum graecum
  11.187   310
  11.948   300
  17.315   282
  18.566   245
  23.170   26
  37.263   201
  38.293   201
  39.340   201
  52.299   206
  53.283   201, 206
  57.332   28

Sylloge inscriptionum graecarum
  787   292
  790   296
  814   10, 22
  1109   272

Tituli Asiae Minoris
  2.760   245

COINS

RPC 1
  1117   23
  1118   23
  1119   23
  1121   23
  1122   23
  1124   92
  1125   23
  1127–28   23, 58
  1129–31   58
  1132   58
  1133   23, 58
  1134–35   58
  1135   23
  1136–37   58
  1137   23
  1139–42   58
  1145   23
  1146   25
  1147   23
  1148   25
  1153   25
  1155–56   25
  1159   25
  1160–61   25
  1162   23
  1164   23
  1168   23
  1172   23
  1185   23
  1186–88   23
  1189   25

1192	23	170–72	23
1195	23	173	23
1197	23	174–77	23
1200	23	178–81	23
1201	23	183–93	23
1207	23, 25	200–203	23
1212	23	204	25
1213	23, 25	207	23
1214	25	207–19	23
1222	23	208–17	23
1223	23	218	23
1225	23		
1227	23		
1234	23		
1235–36	23		

TERRACOTTA LAMPS

Broneer, *Terracotta Lamps*

427	284
460–61	284
492	284
534	284
634–53	284
1192–97	284
2529–30	29
2532–33	29

RPC 2

101	23
105	11
107	11
108–9	11
109	11, 25
110	25
113	11, 23
114	23
114–16	23
119	11
122	25
124	25
125	23
126	11, 23
129	11
131	11
133–35	11, 23
137–38	11
137–39	23
139–45	11
141–43	23
145–46	25
147–52	11
148–50	23
152	25
153–54	23
154–57	11
156	23

Modern Authors Index

Adams, Edward 17, 19, 34, 38
Adams, James N. 88, 101, 186–87, 189, 213–14
Adamsheck, Beverley 26, 35
Ajootian, Aileen 21, 26–27, 35
Akurgl, Ekrem 315, 317
Alcock, Susan E. 168, 173, 178
Amandry, Michel 11, 13, 18, 23, 35–36, 54–55, 58, 75, 76, 285, 317
Ameling, Walter 252, 261, 311, 318
Anderson, J. G. C. 48, 75
Andrews, Antony 4, 35
Arafat, K. W. 9, 35
Arzt-Grabner, Peter 69, 75
Ascough, Richard S. 272–75, 318, 322
Auer, Peter 189, 214
Aune, David 259, 261
Aus, Roger David 228–30, 240, 261
Badian, Ernst 31, 35
Balzat, Jean-Sébastien 191, 214
Baranowski, Donald Walter 8, 35
Barigazzi, Adelmo 49, 76
Barnes, Nathan J. 312, 318
Barnett, Paul 219, 240–41, 255, 261
Barrett, C. K. 167, 178
Bartchy, S. Scott 56, 76
Barth, Matthias 253, 261
Barton, Stephen C. 71, 76, 313, 318
Bash, Anthony 277, 318
Beard, Mary 109–10, 120, 130, 137–38, 149, 228, 232, 251, 261
Bergmann, Marianne 18, 44, 50, 84, 259, 261
Berry, D. H. 136, 149
Bettini, Mauruzio 123, 130

Betz, Hans Dieter 74, 76, 142, 149, 227, 261
Bhabha, Homi K. 21, 35
Biers, Jane C. 21, 35, 97, 102
Biers, William R. 28, 35, 49
Bingen, Jean 137, 149
Bitner, Bradley J. 17, 19, 22, 29–30, 35, 190, 193, 207, 209, 214, 284
Blümel, Wolfgang 309, 318
Bodel, John 115–16, 130
Boedeker, Deborah 113–14, 130
Bonner, Stanley F. 136, 138–40, 143, 150
Bookidis, Nancy 3, 35, 109, 111, 130, 187, 214
Bornkamm, Günther 67, 76
Botha, P. J. J. 222, 261
Bourdieu, Pierre 138, 150
Bourne, Frank Card 19, 38, 284, 322
Bove, Lucio 69, 76
Bowersock, Glen W. 58, 76
Bradley, K. R. 173, 178
Brändle, Martin 278, 318
Breytenbach, Cilliers 229, 261
Broneer, Oscar 5, 18, 20, 29, 33–35, 54, 76, 90, 102, 201, 204, 206–8, 210–11, 214, 279, 283, 306–7, 316, 318
Brookins, Timothy A. 276, 308, 318
Brox, Norbert 220, 262
Bruneau, Philippe 18, 36
Buchanan, George Wesley 224, 262
Buckler, William Hepburn 48, 75, 252, 262
Bultmann, Rudolf Karl 219, 262
Burnett, Andrew 11, 23, 36, 58, 76
Burstein, Stanley M. 307, 318

-347-

MODERN AUTHORS INDEX

Cadbury, Henry J. 72, 76
Cameron, Ron 85, 102
Camia, F. 20, 36, 206–8, 214, 277, 280–81, 284, 319
Campbell, Joan Cecelia 300, 319
Carradice, Ian 11, 36
Carter, Michael 18, 36, 283, 319
Carter, Michael J. D. 226, 262, 282, 319
Carter, Warren 223, 262
Cartledge, Paul 64, 76
Carver, Frank G. 222, 262
Champlin, Edward 169, 178, 235, 259, 262
Chittenden, Jacqueline 259, 262
Chow, John K. 20, 36, 277, 319
Chrimes, K. M. T. 64, 76
Ciampa, Roy E. 121, 126, 130, 156, 167, 178
Clarke, Adam 155, 178
Clarke, Andrew D. 20, 30, 36, 59, 76, 135, 150, 277, 319
Cole, Victor B. 220, 262
Coleman-Norton, Paul Robinson 19, 38, 284, 322
Collange, Jean-François 275, 319
Collins, John J. 257, 258, 262
Collins, Raymond F. 134, 145, 150, 271, 319
Concannon, Cavan W. 18, 21, 24–25, 36, 85, 87, 91–92, 97, 102, 192–93, 208–9, 215, 277, 310, 315, 319
Conybeare, W. J. 155, 178
Conzelmann, Hans 49, 76, 145, 150, 156, 178, 220, 250, 262
Cook, R. M. 163–64, 178
Cox, Sherry C. 57, 76
Cramer, J. A. 160, 178
Danker, Frederick W. 242, 262, 271–73, 319
Danylak, Barry N. 61, 64, 67, 76, 277, 298–99, 319
Dautzenberg, Gerhard 219–20, 222, 243, 250, 254, 257, 262
De Vos, Craig Steven 71, 74, 77
Decker, Wolfgang 282, 319

Degrassi, Attilio 231, 262
Deissmann, G. Adolf 221, 243–44, 246–47, 263
DeMaris, Richard E. 33, 36, 96–100, 102
Derrett, J. Duncan M. 135, 150
Devijver, Hubert 60, 77
D'Hautcourt, A. 215
Dickie, Matthew W. 5, 9, 37
Dittenberger, Wilhelm 198, 215
Dixon, Michael D. 6–7, 31–32, 36, 213
Dmitriev, Sviatoslav 271, 320
Donderer, Michael 198, 215
Dondin-Payre, Monique 272, 320
Duff, Paul Brooks 228–31, 233, 241, 263
Duncan-Jones, Richard P. 63, 77
Dutch, Robert S. 24, 30, 36, 308, 320
Edwards, Charles M. 26–27, 37
Edwards, G. Roger 285, 320
Edwards, Katherine N. 58, 77
Edwards, Rebecca 222, 263
Ehrensperger, Kathy 28, 130
Eliot, C. W. J. 26, 37
Eliot, Mary 26, 37
Elliott, John H. 135, 148, 150
Engels, Donald W. 6, 10, 23–25, 37, 59, 77, 154, 155, 169, 178, 281, 320
Erin, Kenan T. 315, 320
Evans, Trevor V. 186, 216
Fantin, Joseph D. 12, 37, 246, 263
Faraone, Christopher A. 26, 28, 37, 113–14, 130
Fears, J. Rufus 221, 233–35, 239, 263
Fee, Gordon 70, 77, 223, 263
Finlay, George 161, 179
Finney, Mark T. 225, 232, 244, 246, 263
Fitzmyer, Joseph A. 70, 77
Fobes, Francis H. 52, 77
Foerster, Werner 246, 263
Foss, Peter 112, 131
Fotopoulos, John 12, 37
Fowler, Harold N. 55, 77
Fox, Sherry C. 98–99, 102
Frankfurter, David 88, 102
Fraser, P. M. 56, 77, 195, 197, 201, 215
Freeman, Sarah Elizabeth 54, 82

MODERN AUTHORS INDEX 349

French, David 297, 323
Frend, William H. C. 154, 179
Frier, Bruce 61, 77
Friesen, Steven J. 48, 53, 65–67, 70–72, 77–78, 81, 278, 320
Fröhlich, Pierre 272, 320
Garnsey, Peter 173, 179
Garrett, Susan R. 220, 263
Garroway, Joshua D. 144, 150
Geagan, Daniel J. 28, 32–33, 35, 37, 63–64, 78, 201, 203–9, 215, 277, 281, 287–88, 320
Gebhard, Elizabeth R. 5, 9, 21, 23, 37, 174, 179, 278–79, 320
Georgi, Dieter 86, 102
Gerster, Béla 169–72, 179
Gill, D. W. J. 14, 38, 320
Goodrich, John J. 277, 321
Gordon, C. D. 239, 263
Gordon, Mary L. 57, 70, 78
Grant, Robert M. 17, 38, 143, 150
Gregory, Timothy E. 27, 38, 174, 179
Grewe, Klaus 171–72, 179
Griffin, Miriam T. 173, 179
Groag, Edmund 141, 150
Guarducci, Margherita 198, 215
Gunderson, Erik 137–38, 150
Hafemann, Scott J. 156, 179
Hahn, Scott 156, 179
Hammond, N. G. L. 3, 38
Hamon, Patrice 272, 320
Hansen, Mogens Herman 153, 179
Harland, Philip A. 89, 93, 102, 251–53, 263, 272–75, 318
Harrill, J. Albert 57, 66, 78
Harris, Murray J. 219, 227, 258, 264
Harrison, James R. 12, 27–28, 38, 133, 274–75, 277–78, 289–90, 293, 296, 299, 301–6, 316, 321
Hartin, Patrick J. 308, 322
Haufe, Günter 145, 150
Hawthorne, Gerald F. 275, 322
Hawthorne, John G. 26, 38
Hayes, John W. 166, 174, 179–80
Hays, Richard B. 134, 150, 240, 267
Heath, Malcolm 136, 149
Heinrici, Carl F. G. 219, 264
Heiny, Stephen B. 240, 264
Hellholm, David 241–42, 264
Hellmann, Marie-Christine 197, 215
Hemans, Frederick P. 174, 179
Henten, Jan Willem van 259, 264
Hiesinger, Ulrich W. 247, 264
Higgins, Michael D. 180
Higgins, Reynold A. 180
Highet, Gilbert 73, 78
Hill, Bert Hodge 97, 103
Hill, Herbert 180
Hock, Hans Henrich 188, 215
Hodge, A. Trevor 171–72, 180
Hodge, Caroline E. Johnson 133, 150
Hohlfelder, Robert L. 26, 38
Hopkins, Keith 65, 78
Hopper, Robert John 1, 4, 38
Horden, Peregrine 88, 97, 103
Horrell, David G. 17, 20, 38, 135, 150, 156, 180
Horsley, G. H. R. 68, 78, 189, 215
Horsley, Richard A. 135, 150
Howson, J. S. 155, 178
Hughes, Philip E. 219, 264
Huppenbauer, Hans Walter 257, 264
Ibrahim, Leila 26, 38, 42
Jacobelli, Luciana 283, 322
James, Sarah A. 48, 53, 78, 190, 215
Janowitz, Naomi 112, 131
Janse, Mark 88, 101, 186–89, 214, 216
Jewett, Robert 67, 78
Johannowsky, Werner 173, 180
Johnson, Allan Chester 19, 38, 284, 322
Johnson, F. P. 20, 38
Jones, C. P. 91, 103
Jongman, Willem M. 61, 62, 65, 78
Jordan, David R. 29, 39
Joseph, Brian D. 188, 215
Judge, Edwin A. 66, 68–69, 79, 302, 304, 322
Kaimio, Jorma 189, 215
Kajava, Mika 21, 39, 279–80, 322
Kalinka, Ernst 205, 215

Kantiréa, Maria 12, 20, 36, 39, 280, 284, 319
Kardara, Chrysoula 4, 39
Kearsley, Rosalinde 186, 216
Keegan, Peter 189, 216
Keener, Craig S. 156, 180, 222, 249, 264
Kent, John Harvey 9, 13, 15, 39, 55, 72, 79, 87, 90, 103, 193, 196–97, 201, 204, 206, 216, 221, 264, 273, 322. *See also* IKorinthKent in the primary sources index.
Kirner, Guido O. 73, 79
Klauck, Hans-Josef 66, 79
Kleiner, Fred S. 234, 264
Kleinknecht, Hermann 221, 244–45, 264
Kloppenborg, John S 272–75, 318, 322
Koeppen, A. L. 160–61, 180
Koester, Helmut 285, 322
Kokkinia, Christina 204, 208, 216
König, Jason 310, 322
Korka, Elena 177, 180
Koutsoumba, Despina 160–64, 180
Kraay, Colin M. 4, 39
Krentz, Edgar 278, 322
Kuttner, Ann L. 234, 264
Kyle, Donald G. 56, 79, 277, 322
Laird, Margaret L. 60, 79, 221–22, 225–26, 233, 264
Lambrecht, Jan 233, 241, 264
Lampe, Peter 66–67, 71, 79
Landvogt, Peter 71–72, 79
Larson, Jennifer 186, 216
Lavezzi, John C. 1, 39
Lawall, Mark L. 166, 180
Leaf, Walter 1, 39
Leiwo, Martti 188–89, 216
Leon, Harry J. 274, 322
Lightstone, Jack 117–18, 131
Lim, Kar Yong 228, 265
Lim, Timothy H. 314, 322
Lindemann, Andreas 69, 80
Litfin, A. Duane 308, 310, 322
Loewy, Emanuel 198, 216
Lohmann, Hans 160–62, 164, 181
Long, Fredrick J. 25, 225, 241, 265
Losch, Richard R. 2, 39
Lozano, Fernando 227, 244, 265
Ma, John 189, 216
MacDonald, Brian R. 164, 181
Mack, Burton 95, 101, 103
MacMullen, Ramsay 231, 238–39, 256, 265
Madsen, Jesper Majbom 22, 39
Malherbe, Abraham J. 69–71, 80
Malitz, Jürgen 169, 181
Marek, Christian 245, 265
Marquis, Timothy L. 89, 103
Marshall, Peter 230, 265, 302, 322
Martin, Dale B. 66, 72, 73, 80, 93, 103, 124, 127, 129, 131, 133, 135, 150, 308, 323
Martin, Ralph P. 241, 265
Mason, Hugh J. 51–53, 56, 72, 80
Matthews, E. 56, 77, 195, 197, 201, 215
Mattingly, Harold 231, 265
Mau, August 283, 323
McCabe, Donald F. 242, 245, 253, 265
McCant, Jerry W. 302, 323
McGlew, James F. 4, 39
McLean, Bradley M. 198, 216
McRay, J. R. 235, 266
Medico, H. E. del 257, 266
Meeks, Wayne A. 59, 67–71, 80, 154, 156, 181
Meggitt, Justin J. 47, 70, 72, 80, 83, 323
Meiggs, R. 181
Meijer, Fik 6, 39
Meritt, Benjamin Dean 19, 39, 196, 213, 217, 221, 266, 280, 283, 323. *See also* IKorinthMeritt in the primary sources index.
Mihaila, Corin 308, 323
Miller, Merrill P. 85, 102
Milligan, Georg 244, 248, 266
Millis, Benjamin W. 9, 22, 39, 58–60, 63, 80, 88, 103, 191–93, 197, 207–8, 210–11, 213–14, 217, 277, 323
Mills, Harrianne 27, 38, 174, 179
Minor, Mitzi L. 156, 181
Mitch, Curtis 156, 179

Mitchell, Alan C.   20, 40, 133, 135–36, 149–50
Mitchell, Stephen   297, 323
Montague, George T.   156, 181
Mott, Valentine   160, 181
Moulton, James Hope   244, 248, 266
Mouritsen, Henrik   60, 80
Muir, Steven   88, 103
Mulroy, David   250, 266
Murphy-O'Connor, Jerome   4, 8–9, 19, 21, 30–31, 40, 48–49, 51, 53, 70–71, 80, 154, 167, 173, 181, 241, 266, 279, 286, 323
Nabers, Ned   14, 40
Naeh, Shlomo   186, 217
Nagy, Blaise   277, 323
Nakas, Yannis   160–64, 180
Nanos, Mark D.   120, 125, 131
Nash, Robert Scott   156, 181
Nasrallah, Laura Salah   57, 66, 80
Nguyen, V. Henry T.   306, 323
Nielsen, Thomas Heine   153, 179
Nilsson, Martin P.   250–52, 266
Nock, A. D.   221, 235–36, 258, 266
Noreña, Carlos F.   248, 266
North, John   109–10, 120, 130, 251, 261
Noy, David   70, 81, 89, 103
O'Brien, Peter T.   275, 323
Öhler, Markus   108, 112, 119, 131
Økland, Jorunn   30, 40, 111, 131
Oost, Stewart Irvin   3, 40
Orelli, Johann Kaspar von   15, 40
Osgood, Josiah   299, 323
Östenberg, Ida   228–29, 232, 266
Oster, Richard   290, 323
Overbeck, Johannes   283, 323
Pais, Ettore   48, 80
Papageorgiadou-Bani, Harikleia   29, 40
Papahatzis, Nicos   2, 27, 29, 40, 279, 323
Pawlak, Marcin L.   22, 40
Pemberton, Elizabeth G.   4, 40, 187, 214
Peppard, Michael   20, 138, 142, 147, 151, 250, 266
Petersen, Leiva   63, 82
Peterson, Brian K.   308, 323

Pettegrew, David K.   5, 16, 19, 26, 40, 157–58, 160–67, 170–71, 174, 177, 181
Pfanner, Michael   231, 266
Pfitzner, V. C.   278, 324
Philadelpheus, Alexandre   311, 324
Pleket, H. W.   59, 62, 80, 250–52, 266
Pogoloff, Stephen M.   314, 324
Pomeroy, Sarah B.   5, 40
Price, Jonathan J.   186, 217
Price, S. R. F.   109, 110, 120, 130, 222, 247, 251, 261
Purcell, Nicholas   88, 97, 103
Purgold, Karl   198, 215
Quass, Friedemann   59, 80
Rajak, Tessa   70, 81
Ramage, Edwin S.   26, 42
Reinach, Salomon   232, 267
Reisch, E.   277, 324
Reynolds, Joyce   205, 217
Riccardi, Lee Ann   247, 267
Rice, Joshua   20, 40
Richardson, Peter   135, 143, 151, 274, 324
Rickman, Geoffrey   181
Ridgway, Brunilde Sismonde   54, 81
Ridley, Edward   238, 267
Rife, Joseph L.   26, 28, 37, 98–99, 103, 177, 180–81
Ripollés, Pere Pau   23, 36, 58, 76
Risser, Martha K.   4, 40
Rives, James B.   249, 251, 267
Rix, Helmut   70, 81
Rizakis, Athanasios D.   20, 22–23, 36, 42–43, 55, 58, 61–62, 81–82, 191, 199, 206, 211, 217–18, 280, 319
Robert, Louis   18, 28, 41, 196, 201, 204–5, 208, 210, 217, 282–83, 288, 297, 324
Robertson, Edwin H.   167, 182
Robertson, Noel   2, 41
Robinson, Betsey A.   23, 41, 91, 97, 103, 193, 217, 285, 286, 324
Robinson, David Moore   252, 262
Robinson, Henry S.   20, 41
Roebuck, Mary Campbell   4, 41

Rogers, Guy M. 291, 324
Romano, David Gilman 16, 18–20, 41, 55, 81, 157, 174, 182
Romano, Irene B. 8, 41
Rosner, Brian S. 121, 126, 130, 134–35, 151, 156, 167, 178
Rothaus, Richard M. 26, 41, 97, 104
Rowlandson, Jane 137, 151
Rüpke, Jörg 108, 131
Russell, D. A. 136, 151
Rutter, Jeremy 1, 41
Salmeri, Giovanni 75, 81
Salmon, Edward T. 70, 81, 153, 182
Salmon, J. B. 3, 41
Salomies, Olli 70, 81
Sanders, G. D. R. 190, 217
Šašel Kos, Marjeta 18, 41
Saunders, Ross 225, 267
Savage, Timothy B. 276, 324
Scheidel, Walter 61, 65, 81
Scherrer, Peter 315, 324
Schmeller, Thomas 67, 82
Schowalter, Daniel N. 48, 53, 78, 311, 324
Schrage, Wolfgang 70, 82, 134, 151
Schüssler Fiorenza, Elisabeth 85, 104
Scott, James M. 220, 231, 239–40, 243, 267
Scott, Kenneth 247, 267
Scotton, Paul D. 20, 42, 226, 267
Scranton, Robert L. 26, 42, 53–54, 56, 59–60, 81–82
Scroggs, Robin 135, 151
Sealey, Raphael 3, 42
Sears, Joshua M., Jr. 26, 42
Shaw, Joseph W. 26, 42
Shear, Theodore Leslie 18, 42, 283, 324
Sherk, Robert K. 68, 82, 242, 267
Shewan, A. 1, 42
Shotter, David C. A. 169, 182
Shuckburgh, Evelyn S. 5, 42
Slane, Kathleen W. 166, 182
Slater, William J. 303, 324
Sloan, Robert B. 240, 267
Small, Alastair 222, 267
Smith, Dennis Edwin 90, 104
Smith, Jonathan Z. 93–95, 104
Smith, K. K. 195–96, 217
Solin, Heikki 68, 70, 82
Souza, Philip de 6, 42
Spawforth, Antony J. S. 18, 22, 29, 39, 42, 55, 58, 60, 63–64, 72, 76, 82, 191–92, 217, 226–67, 284, 325
Spitzer, Doreen C. 21, 42
Standing, Giles 225, 267
Stanley, Christopher D. 87, 92, 104
Stansbury, Harry A. 14, 42, 48, 50, 53, 55–63, 70–71, 82
Stauber, Josef 253, 261
Stegemann, Ekkehard 71, 82
Stegemann, Wolfgang 71, 82
Stein, Arthur 63, 82
Steiner, Deborah Tarn 250, 268
Stern, Wilma Olch 26, 42
Stickler, Timo 3, 43
Stillwell, Agnes N. 2, 43
Stillwell, Richard 50, 54, 55, 82, 77
Stowers, Stanley K. 95, 100, 104, 108, 112, 125, 131
Strelan, Rick 290, 325
Strong, Eugénie S. 232, 248, 268
Stroud, Ronald S. 3, 19, 33, 35, 43, 187, 192, 218. See also IKorinthStroud in the primary sources index.
Strubbe, Johan H. M. 252, 268
Sturgeon, Mary C. 194–200, 218
Sumney, Jerry L. 86, 104
Sussman, Lewis A. 140–41, 151
Swain, Simon 186–87, 189, 214
Swift, Emerson Howland 20, 43
Takahashi, Ryosuke 137, 151
Taylor, Joan E. 223, 268
Taylor, Lily Ross 58, 63–64, 68
Theissen, Gerd 47–49, 66–72, 82
Thiselton, Anthony C. 18, 43, 124, 131
Thomas, Christine M. 17, 97, 104, 193, 218
Thrall, Margaret E. 220, 222, 240–41, 245–47, 254, 256–57, 268
Tobin, Jennifer 311, 325

MODERN AUTHORS INDEX

Touloumakos, Johannes 186, 218
Tran, Nicolas 272, 320
Trebilco, Paul 16, 43
Treggiari, Susan 60, 83
Tucker, J. Brian 10–11, 14, 18–20, 25, 43
Tucker, Paavo 258, 268
Tumolesi, Patrizia Sabbatini 56, 83
Unwin, James R. 18, 43, 315, 325
Valavanis, Panos 279, 325
Vanhove, D. 275, 325
Verboven, Koenraad 273, 325
Verdelis, N. M. 161–62, 182
Vermeule, Cornelius C. 232, 268
Versnel, H. S. 94–95, 104, 228, 234, 268
Veyne, Paul 52, 83
Ville, Georges 56, 83
Vout, Caroline 248–49, 268
Wacquant, Loïs J. D. 138, 150
Waele, Ferdinand J. de 55–56, 83
Walbank, Mary E. Hoskins 10–11, 16, 18, 20–21, 23–24, 43, 54, 83, 207, 218, 225–26, 268
Wallace-Hadrill, Andrew 69, 83, 112, 131, 232, 247, 268
Walters, James C. 73, 83, 109, 111, 131, 133, 151, 280, 325
Wankel, Hermann 281, 325
Ward, Margaret M. 235, 268
Waterfield, Robin 7, 44
Waters, Kenneth L. 122, 132
Webb, William J. 240, 254, 269
Weinberg, Saul S. 1, 44, 54, 83
Weiss, Alexander 16, 44, 276, 325
Weiss, Johannes 47, 56, 69, 70, 73–75, 83
Welborn, L. L. 14, 16–17, 29, 31, 44, 73–75, 83, 133, 145, 151, 269, 273, 276, 278, 292–94, 296, 300–302, 304, 313, 325
Welch, Katherine E. 18, 44, 50, 55–56, 84
Wenham, Gordon 248, 269
Werner, Walter 162, 182
West, Allen Brown 5, 14, 44, 54, 58, 60, 63–64, 82, 84, 218, 292, 294–95, 297, 311. *See also* IKorinthWest in the primary sources index.
White, Adam G. 308, 325
White, L. Michael 310, 325
White, Peter 73, 84
Wiedemann, Thomas E. J. 56, 84
Will, Edouard 3, 44
Williams, Charles K., II 15, 49, 54, 59–60, 84, 225
Williams, Guy J. 106, 132
Williams, Hector 26, 44
Wilson, Andrew I. 172, 182
Wilson, Stephen G. 272, 326
Windisch, Hans 219, 269
Winter, Bruce W. 12, 20–21, 44, 64, 66–67, 84, 134–36, 146, 151, 225–27, 269, 277, 298–99, 308, 310, 326
Winterbottom, Michael 138–40, 151
Wire, Antoinette Clark 85, 104
Wirszubski, Chaim 239, 263, 269
Wiseman, James 8, 15, 45, 50, 54, 63–64, 84
Witherington, Ben, III 156, 183, 314, 326
Woolf, Greg 109, 132
Wright, N. T. 244, 269, 316, 326
Yoder, Joshua 21, 45
Zanker, Paul 232, 247–48, 269
Ziegler, Konrat 50, 84
Zoumbaki, Sophie 58, 61–62, 81, 199, 206, 211, 217
Zuiderhoek, Arjan 61–62, 75, 84, 307, 326

www.ingramcontent.com/pod-product-compliance
Lightning Source LLC
Chambersburg PA
CBHW021352290426
44108CB00010B/208